ENCE AND RACE

Final and Comprehensive Report to
The Commission on Race and Housing

By DAVIS McENTIRE

...een i..

...on of the au...enty-eight million Ameri-
...ts in a c.. e-sixth of the natio...—
...e stud..l to live wh...jects of
...ve b..dentia...ed in c...
...d o... ...ie ba...

with a...
...sidenc...

Residence and Race

Residence and Race

by DAVIS McENTIRE

FINAL AND COMPREHENSIVE REPORT
TO THE COMMISSION ON RACE
AND HOUSING

UNIVERSITY OF CALIFORNIA PRESS

BERKELEY AND LOS ANGELES 1960

UNIVERSITY OF CALIFORNIA PRESS

BERKELEY AND LOS ANGELES

CALIFORNIA

CAMBRIDGE UNIVERSITY PRESS

LONDON, ENGLAND

© 1960, BY

THE REGENTS OF THE UNIVERSITY OF CALIFORNIA

LIBRARY OF CONGRESS CATALOG CARD NUMBER: 60-13020

PRINTED IN THE UNITED STATES OF AMERICA

Foreword

Residence and Race is the final report of a broad study of housing problems involving minority racial and ethnic groups, conducted for the Commission on Race and Housing, under the direction of Davis McEntire.

Where the members of racial and ethnic minorities should live —whether in segregated communities or dispersed through the general housing supply—is a social problem of large and growing importance in American cities. To inquire into this problem was the purpose of the Commission on Race and Housing, formed in 1955. The Commission is an independent, private citizens' group, not a part of any other organization. Its work was made possible by a grant of $305,000 from the Fund for the Republic. The Fund's participation was limited to financial assistance, and it is not in any way otherwise responsible for the studies carried out for the Commission or for its conclusions.

The following persons served on the Commission in their individual capacities and not as representing any organizations or groups:

GORDON W. ALLPORT
  Professor of Psychology, Harvard University, Cambridge, Massachusetts.
ELLIOTT V. BELL
  Chairman of the Executive Committee and Director, McGraw-

Hill Publishing Company; Editor and Publisher, *Business Week,* New York.

LAIRD BELL
Attorney: Bell, Boyd, Marshall and Lloyd, Chicago.

REVEREND JOHN J. CAVANAUGH, C.S.C.
Director, University of Notre Dame Foundation, Notre Dame, Indiana.

HENRY DREYFUSS
Industrial Designer, South Pasadena, California, and New York.

PETER GRIMM
Chairman of the Board and Director, William A. White and Sons, New York.

COL. CAMPBELL C. JOHNSON
Assistant to the Director, Selective Service System, Washington, D. C.

CHARLES S. JOHNSON
President, Fisk University, Nashville, Tennessee. Deceased.

CHARLES KELLER, JR.
President, Keller Construction Corporation, New Orleans, Louisiana.

CLARK KERR
President, University of California, Berkeley.

PHILIP M. KLUTZNICK
Chairman of the Board, American Community Builders, Inc., Park Forest, Illinois.

HENRY R. LUCE
Editor-in-Chief, *Time, Life, Fortune, Architectural Forum, House and Home,* and *Sports Illustrated,* New York.

STANLEY MARCUS
President, Neiman-Marcus, Dallas, Texas.

HAROLD C. MCCLELLAN
President, Old Colony Paint and Chemical Company, Los Angeles. Resigned following appointment as Assistant Secretary of Commerce in 1955.

WARD MELVILLE
President, Melville Shoe Corporation, New York.

FRANCIS T. P. PLIMPTON
Attorney: Debevoise, Plimpton, and McLean, New York.

R. STEWART RAUCH, JR.
   President, The Philadelphia Saving Fund Society, Philadelphia.
ROBERT R. TAYLOR
   Secretary and Executive Director, Illinois Federal Savings and
   Loan Association, Chicago. Deceased.
JOHN H. WHEELER
   President, Mechanics and Farmers Bank, Durham, North Caro-
   lina.
EARL B. SCHWULST, CHAIRMAN
   President and Chairman of the Board, The Bowery Savings
   Bank, New York.

Professor Robert K. Merton of Columbia University, Professor
Stuart W. Cook of New York University, and Dr. Robert C.
Weaver, formerly State Rent Administrator of New York, served
as research advisors to the Commission.

The central focus of the study undertaken for the Commission
was on the problem of inequality of housing opportunity connected with racial or ethnic distinctions, with emphasis on the
situation of Negroes, Puerto Ricans, Mexican-Americans, and
Orientals. The research was national in scope and sought to com-
prehend all the more important aspects and ramifications of a
very complex problem—its causes, impacts and consequences, and
directions of change. Social scientists in a dozen universities co-
operated in various phases of the inquiry. Some thirty research
reports and memoranda were prepared for the consideration of
the Commission, culminating in the Research Director's final and
comprehensive report, which constitutes the present volume.

The Commission has previously published its own findings and
recommendations under the title, Where Shall We Live? (University of California Press, 1958). The main results of the entire
study, upon which the Commission based its own report, are
presented in the present volume by the Commission's Research
Director. In addition, the full findings of certain particular phases
of the study are published separately. Other products of the research are unpublished but available in the library of the University of California at Berkeley.

The Commission has authorized publication of the results of

research done under its auspices, desiring to share with the public the facts and analysis on the basis of which it arrived at its own conclusions. Although believing that the studies were conscientiously and competently carried out, the Commission does not assume responsibility for the accuracy of specific data nor does it necessarily endorse all the interpretations and conclusions of the authors. In particular, the Commission considers Dr. McEntire's final report to be an objective and scholarly work, but the same principle applies. The study stands on its own merits. Persons desiring to know the position of the Commission on Race and Housing are referred to its own report.

EARL B. SCHWULST, Chairman
The Commission on Race and Housing

New York City

Acknowledgments

Many persons and organizations have assisted this study. Foremost is the chairman of the Commission on Race and Housing, Earl B. Schwulst, whose constant encouragement and deep conviction of the importance of the work enabled the research director to survive the hazards and frustrations inevitable in a large and complex research project. To the members of the Commission, whose names are listed elsewhere, I am indebted for their support, their patience through a lengthy process of research, and their constructive critical judgment on the plans and the results of the study.

Members of the Commission's Research Advisory Committee—Gordon W. Allport, Stuart W. Cook, Robert K. Merton, R. Stewart Rauch, and Robert C. Weaver, in addition to Mr. Schwulst—gave invaluable advice and criticism about the scope of the study, the methods of investigation, and the analysis and interpretation of the data. The late Charles S. Johnson exercised a large influence on the initial organization of the research. IIis untimely death deprived the study of a major source of inspiration and guidance. Also among the intellectual mentors of the study is Professor Herbert Blumer. Although not formally associated with the project, the influence of his ideas will be apparent to all acquainted with his work in the field of race relations.

It is hardly necessary to say that without the generous financial support of the Fund for the Republic, this study could not have been undertaken nor carried to completion. Beyond the financial, the officers of the Fund have greatly helped by their encouragement and continuous interest in the progress of the work. In the early stages, Frank S. Loescher, Fund consultant on minority group relations, made valuable suggestions on planning the project and assisted the research director in selecting collaborators and staff.

The present volume is largely based upon a series of related studies prepared by coöperating social scientists and other experts. Philip M. Hauser and Otis Dudley Duncan (Population Research and Training Center, University of Chicago) did the basic work on population trends and outlook. Collaborating in housing market studies were Chester Rapkin and William G. Grigsby (Institute for Urban Studies, University of Pennsylvania), Luigi Laurenti (University of California, Berkeley), William Goldner (University of California, Berkeley), Fred E. Case and S. Lynn Clark (Real Estate Research Program, University of California, Los Angeles), and James H. Kirk (Loyola University of Los Angeles). Field surveys of housing industry practices were carried out by Nicholas J. Demerath (Washington University), Rose Helper (University of Chicago), Floyd K. Hunter (University of North Carolina), R. Clay Sprowls (University of California, Los Angeles), Robert H. Sollen (California newspaper editor), and William Goldner.

Local studies of minority group housing conditions in selected cities were conducted by Hylan Lewis (Atlanta University), Robert A. Thompson (Atlanta Urban League), Jack E. Dodson (University of Texas), Morris Eagle (New York University), Harry H. L. Kitano (University of California, Los Angeles), Albert J. Mayer (Wayne State University), Forrest E. LaViolette (Tulane University), Giles Hubert and Joseph T. Taylor (Dillard University), Elizabeth L. Virrick (University of Miami), and R. Clay Sprowls, Nathan Glazer (Smith College) edited a collection of these studies for publication.

Studies of interracial housing and neighborhoods were made by Eunice and George Grier (Commission staff) and Henry G. Stetler

(Connecticut State Commission on Civil Rights). Preston Valien and Jitsuichi Masuoka (Fisk University) prepared a research memorandum on social and economic consequences of residential segregation. E. Franklin Edwards and Harry J. Walker (Howard University) investigated the effects of urban renewal on Negro housing conditions. Margaret G. Reid (University of Chicago) contributed an analysis of color differentials in housing-income relationships.

Research memoranda on sociopsychological aspects of housing and minority groups, including racial attitudes, were prepared by Helen E. Amerman (Commission staff) and Stuart W. Cook and Claire Selltiz (New York University). Miss Selltiz also collaborated in the study of federal housing policies and programs affecting minority groups. Milton Nason of the Commission staff, and member of the California Bar, gave major assistance in legal analysis and the study of housing industry practices.

Several of the reports of research collaborators, in addition to being utilized in the present volume and in the Report of the Commission on Race and Housing, are published separately. Those unpublished are substantially reflected, as to their principal findings, in the present work. A complete list of the studies made for the Commission on Race and Housing, and their respective authors, is included in the bibliography at the end of this volume.

Serving on the staff of the Commission, in addition to those already mentioned, were Martin B. Loeb, consultant; Robert W. Campbell, Diana Clarkson, Bob Daniels, and Stanton Jue, research assistants; Dorothy Hassin, Lois Ness, Hanna Pitkin, and Jessie Omura Yasaki, statistical clerks; Betty Aycrigg, secretary. Maps and charts were prepared by Katherine C. Eardley, Chad W. Michel, and Rochelle Myers.

Much of the data for the present study came from governmental sources. For essential information and expert advice, I am obligated to the federal housing agencies, especially to their staff members Robert B. Pitts, George Snowden, Booker T. McGraw, Clarence R. Johnson, George B. Nesbitt, Paul F. Coe, and Flora Y. Hatcher; the U. S. Bureau of the Census, especially the chief of the Housing Division, Wayne F. Daugherty; the New York

State Commission Against Discrimination, particularly Edward Rutledge, head of the Housing Division; the New York City Commission on Intergroup Relations, especially its executive director, Frank S. Horne and assistant director, Corienne R. Morrow; the Philadelphia Commission on Human Relations, the New York City Planning Commission, and the Migration Division of the Department of Labor, Commonwealth of Puerto Rico.

Private organizations that have assisted the study in important ways are the National Association for the Advancement of Colored People, in particular its special assistant for housing, Madison S. Jones, and Constance Baker Motley, assistant counsel for the NAACP Legal Defense and Educational Fund; the National Urban League, especially its housing secretary, Reginald A. Johnson; the National Committee Against Discrimination in Housing, the National Association of Intergroup Relations Officials, the National Association of Housing and Redevelopment Officials, the American Friends Service Committee, the Southern Regional Council, the Race Relations Department of the American Missionary Association, the Anti-Defamation League of B'nai B'rith, the Hyde Park–Kenwood Community Conference, the American Council To Improve Our Neighborhoods, and the Mortgage Bankers Association.

A final word of appreciation and commendation is reserved for the Commission's able and devoted editorial assistant, June E. Harvey. To her belongs much of the credit for transforming a welter of manuscripts into an ordered series of publications. She directed the typing of manuscripts, assisted in editing them for publication, prepared the indexes, and corrected the proofs. In addition, the bibliography in the present volume is her work. These exacting and vital tasks she performed according to a high standard of excellence, with rare ability to organize masses of detail while holding in view the larger purposes.

It is evident that I have had a great deal of help in the research entering into this volume—more, undoubtedly, than I have known how to use most effectively. For all the help received, I am profoundly grateful. Responsibility, however, is not shared. The Commission on Race and Housing and the Fund for the Republic, while supporting and assisting the research to a maximum extent, have at all times accorded me as research director and my collaborators complete freedom to conduct the study and present the findings according to our own best judgment. This book, in particular, represents my judgment concerning the significant facts and conclusions that emerge from a large body of research. Consequently, for the contents of this volume, and its shortcomings, I am solely responsible.

DAVIS MCENTIRE

Berkeley, California

Contents

Part Four: The Role of Government

Tables

Appendix Tables

Figures

Maps

I

Introduction

In December, 1954, Dr. Robert M. Johnson, a young physician, moved with his wife and three children to Des Moines, Iowa, to take up a residency at the Veterans Hospital. For personal and professional reasons he wished to live within walking distance of the hospital. There were houses for sale, but no one would sell to him. He learned, in fact, that there were only a few sections in Des Moines where he could live, none considered good residential areas. In the end he settled for "adequate but not satisfactory" living quarters on the opposite side of town—a thirty-minute drive through city traffic to the hospital. Dr. Johnson is a Negro. His inability to obtain a house suiting his requirements was due solely to the fact of his race.[1]

When Major Sammy Lee of the United States Army Medical Corps sought to buy a new tract home in Garden Grove, California, a suburb of Los Angeles, the salesman said to him, "I don't have the nerve to sell it to you. Some of us could lose our jobs selling to a nonwhite person. Sorry, doctor." Major Lee is of Korean descent.[2]

In Palm Beach, Florida, Duncan MacGregor, a licensed real estate broker, was summoned to answer charges before the State Real Estate Commission, deprived of his license, and barred from

---

[1] Robert H. Spiegel, "Segregation in Des Moines," *Des Moines Tribune*, June 22, 1956.
[2] *San Francisco Chronicle*, August 19, 1955.

further practice of his profession. His offense: he had sold a house to a Jewish person, contrary to the owner's instructions restricting the sale to Christians.[3]

These are not isolated cases. Rather, they exemplify a pattern of discrimination which limits the freedom of nearly one person in every six in the United States to choose where he shall live. Most severely affected are the 19 million Americans whose racial ancestry is not white—chiefly Negroes but also persons of Japanese, Chinese, Filipino, and other racial origins. Similarly restricted, although less rigidly, are the 2.5 million or more persons of Mexican origin and upwards of a million Puerto Ricans on the mainland. Discrimination in housing is also occasionally directed against Jews, who number more than 5 million. In all, there are probably no fewer than 27 million persons in the United States whose opportunities to choose a place of residence are in varying degree restricted because of their race or ethnic descent.

Where racial and ethnic minorities should live is an old problem in American cities, enormously magnified and sharpened by the social and economic changes of the past quarter century. Before World War II nonwhites were highly restricted; their incomes were extremely low; their segregation in slums was enforced by restrictive covenants. Migration was slow compared with what was to come.

The war set in motion a huge migration of Negroes from farms to cities, from the South to the North and West, continuing to the present day. After the war came hundreds of thousands of Puerto Ricans. In the cities of the North and West, in-migrant Negroes and Puerto Ricans have replaced the immigrants of an earlier day, like them, bringing many problems of adjustment and assimilation of which the foremost is housing. To house these millions of newcomers in the existing areas open to minority groups has been manifestly impossible; yet how and, above all, where to provide the additional living space required and still preserve the traditional exclusion of nonwhites from white neighborhoods has been an aggravated problem in many communities.

Together with the redistribution of population, minority groups

---

[3] *Duncan MacGregor* v. *Florida Real Estate Commission, et al.,* 99 So. 2d 709 (1958), *Race Relations Law Reporter,* 3(2):214 (April, 1958).

have gained a new economic status. First under pressure of wartime labor needs, then in the postwar prosperity, nonwhite wage earners have seen their average income increase more than fivefold since 1939. They have benefited from fuller employment and from upgrading in the scale of occupations. Once almost wholly confined to common labor and menial service, minority workers have moved into the semiskilled ranks of industry en masse and have achieved a significant position in the skilled crafts, clerical pursuits, and the professions. Their housing needs have thus been matched by their growing ability to compete in the market for housing. Especially significant is the growth of the middle class among the minority groups, with strong motivations to acquire good homes in good neighborhoods and with the ability to pay the price.

The changing economic situation of racial and ethnic minority groups is part of a broader trend in the United States toward equality of rights and opportunity. The Supreme Court, in the past quarter century, has become increasingly insistent on the constitutional duty of government to treat citizens equally. Compulsory segregation in public schools, transportation, and other fields has been ruled unconstitutional. The Court's explicit rejection of the separate-but-equal doctrine, as applied to education, has undermined the moral and legal foundations of the whole system of segregation laws.

Several states have repealed long-standing discriminatory laws, and more than a score of state and municipal legislatures have enacted laws specifically to promote racial and religious equality. On the national level, the racially discriminatory provisions of immigration and naturalization laws have been repealed, and Congress, after a lapse of eighty years, has begun again to legislate for protection of civil rights. Presidential action has abolished segregation in the armed forces and prohibited discrimination in employment under federal contracts and in the civil service. Federal agencies have acted to promote equal treatment within their respective spheres.

Back of the proequality actions of government stands a new outlook of the American people toward racial and religious discrimination. The need to close the gap between principle and practice and to achieve full citizenship for all Americans has become widely recognized as perhaps the leading unresolved domestic problem of the nation. In the traditional American way of responding to a problem, hundreds of voluntary associations have come into existence to press for racial equality. Churches, labor unions, and community organizations have voiced their support for equality. Pledges to protect civil rights are regularly included in the platforms of the major political parties. Election to high office of members of religious minorities attests to the decline of religious prejudice as a force in politics. National public opinion polls give further evidence of diminishing racial and religious prejudice.

With the lowering of discriminatory barriers and consequent widening of opportunity, subtle but profound changes are taking place in the social outlook of the minority groups themselves. Many members of these groups are acquiring new concepts of what is desirable and possible and new images of their position in society. In becoming more like other Americans in jobs and incomes, they also tend to assimilate the goals, the status symbols, and social standards of the general community. The process is a familiar one historically in the assimilation of immigrant groups.

A parallel trend of the past quarter century has been the growth of public interest and governmental activity in housing. In programs of widening scope, government has sought to stimulate the production of housing, aid families to obtain homes, eliminate slums, and promote improvement of neighborhood conditions. "A good home in a suitable living environment for every American family" has become a goal of national policy, formally declared by Congress. This national policy and the programs to make it effective have served to focus attention on the disadvantages of nonwhites and other minorities. Indeed, President Eisenhower informed the Congress in 1954 that "Many members of minority groups, regardless of their income or their economic status, have had the least opportunity of all our citizens to acquire good homes." [4]

In the general movement toward equal rights and opportunity,

---

[4] Message from the President of the United States to the 83d Congress, 2d Session, January 25, 1954 (H. Doc. No. 306).

housing is a crucial area. One of the basic liberties of citizens in a free society is the freedom to move and to choose a place of residence. No one, of course, has complete freedom of choice in housing or any field, but to exclude persons from residence areas because of their race or ethnic attachment is to deprive them of an essential freedom enjoyed by others. This freedom is appropriately termed basic because it is essential to the enjoyment of many other rights and privileges. People who cannot freely choose where they will live are gravely hampered, not only in bettering their living conditions but also in their use of community facilities and institutions and in their participation in community life, with all that implies for opportunities and advantages.

Recent years have seen major expansion of the amount of housing available to Negroes and other minorities, and significant qualitative improvements as well. Most of this increase has come from the transition of residence areas from white to minority occupancy. In some communities, new housing developments intended for sale or rental to minorities have added substantially to the supply of good quality housing available to members of these groups. As a result, the crisis conditions of housing shortage which developed during and shortly after World War II have been in large measure ameliorated.

The fundamental problem, however, of housing for minority groups is not one of the quantity or quality of dwellings, important as these may be, but whether the minorities should continue to live concentrated in separate areas or be free to seek their housing in the general market. Racial segregation in housing is sustained by widespread popular attitudes, the practices of the housing industry, and policies of governments. Probably no aspect of racial discrimination in the United States is more institutionalized and resistant to change. Correspondingly, the elimination of racial restrictions on residence would have consequences reaching far beyond the immediate facts of housing. Just as residential segregation serves to isolate the segregated groups from the activities of the general population, so integration in housing must stimulate participation in wider areas of community life. To be a neighbor carries implications of informal friendly association, common interests, and equality of social rank. If members of minority groups should be accepted by the majority as neighbors, it would be difficult to maintain distinctions of rights or status in other respects. It seems fair to say, therefore, that the future character of majority-minority relations hinges to a great extent on the racial pattern of residence.

PART ONE

Where Minorities Live

II

Population Distribution and Trends

The population of the United States is at present in a period of rapid growth, and the nonwhite population is growing more rapidly than the white. Between the 1950 Census and mid-1958 the total population increased by an estimated 22.9 million or 15 percent, but the nonwhite population grew from 15.8 to 19.2 million, an increase of 22 percent in little more than eight years.[1] The nonwhite proportion of the total population rose from 10.4 percent to 11.1 percent.

The Negro Population

Negroes comprise more than 95 percent of the nonwhite population; in most parts of the country, Negro and nonwhite are virtually synonymous. Historically the Negro population has differed markedly from the white in distribution and routes of migration. The distribution that is emerging from recent and current migrations is still significantly distinctive.

Broad trends in the growth and distribution of the Negro population in the half century 1900-1950 are shown in table 1. In 1900 nine-tenths of all Negroes lived in the South and more than three-fourths were rural. By 1950 Negroes had become pre-

---

[1] U. S. Bureau of the Census, *Current Population Reports*, Series P-25, *Population Estimates*, no. 193 (February 11, 1959).

TABLE 1

NEGRO POPULATION, PERCENT OF TOTAL POPULATION, AND PERCENT URBAN,
BY REGIONS, UNITED STATES, 1900-1950
(in thousands)

Region	1900	1920	1940	1950
United States	8,834	10,463	12,866	15,045
Northeast	385	679	1,370	2,019
North central	496	793	1,420	2,228
South	7,924	8,912	9,905	10,226
West	30	79	171	572
	PERCENT DISTRIBUTION			
United States	100.0	100.0	100.0	100.0
Northeast	4.4	6.5	10.6	13.4
North central	5.6	7.6	11.0	14.8
South	89.7	85.2	77.0	68.0
West	0.3	0.8	1.3	3.8
	PERCENT OF TOTAL POPULATION			
United States	11.6	9.9	9.8	10.0
Northeast	1.8	2.3	3.8	5.3
North central	1.9	2.3	3.5	5.0
South	32.3	26.9	23.8	21.7
West	0.7	0.9	1.2	3.0
	PERCENT URBAN			
United States	22.7	34.0	48.6	62.4[a]
Northeast	78.3	86.7	90.1	94.0[a]
North central	64.4	83.4	88.8	93.8[a]
South	17.2	25.2	36.5	47.8[a]
West	67.4	74.0	83.1	90.1[a]

SOURCES: *U. S. Census of Population: 1950*, Vol. II, *Characteristics of the Population*, Part 1, "U. S. Summary"; Vol. IV, *Special Reports*, Part 3, chap. B, "Nonwhite Population by Race." *Sixteenth Census of the U. S.*, *1940*, *Population*, "Characteristics of the Nonwhite Population by Race." *Fifteenth Census of the U. S.*, *1930*, *Census of Agriculture*, 'The Negro Farmer in the U. S."; *Census of Population*, Vol. II, *General Report*, "Statistics by Subjects." U. S. Bureau of the Census, *Negroes in the U. S.*, *1920-1932* (1935); *Negro Population, 1790-1915* (1918).

[a] Part of the increase in percent urban from 1940 to 1950 is due to a change in the Census definition of "urban." Before 1950 the urban population was that population residing in incorporated places of 2,500 or more and areas classified as urban under special rules. In the 1950 Census the definition was broadened to include the population in all places of 2,500 or more whether incorporated or not and in the densely settled urban fringe surrounding cities of 50,000 or more. Under the old urban definition, 58.8 percent of the United States *nonwhite* population would have been classified as urban instead of the 61.6 percent reported as urban by the new definition. Data for the Negro population in 1950 are available only according to the new urban definition.

dominantly urban dwellers, and almost a third of them lived outside the South. Despite the drain of migration, the southern Negro population has continued to increase, but in consequence of the more rapid growth of the white population, the proportion of Negroes fell from one-third in 1900 to about one-fifth in 1950. In the North and West, on the other hand, the proportion of Negroes in the total population has steadily mounted.

Unlike the historic westward movement of the white population, the traditional pathway of Negro migration has been from South to North. It has been also a movement from rural areas to the large cities. Both trends have been greatly accelerated since the beginning of World War II, and in this period Negroes have also begun moving westward in large numbers. In the 1940-1950 decade, more than 3 million Negroes were added to the populations of urban areas, while the rural Negro population declined by nearly a million.[2] Regionally the number of Negroes increased 50 percent in the North and more than threefold in the West.

Available data point to sustained rapid growth of Negro population in northern and western cities since 1950, resulting both from natural increase and from migration. In Chicago, the average annual increase in nonwhite population was 23,000 in the 1940-1950 decade, but estimated at 34,000 in the period 1950-1957.[3] For New York City, the Census Bureau reported a nonwhite increase of 298,000 in the 1940-1950 period and a further gain of 206,000 during the ensuing seven years.[4] Los Angeles, which gained 143,000 in Negro population during the 1940-1950 decade, received an additional 83,000 Negroes after 1950 to February, 1956.[5]

---

[2] Part of the rural to urban shift was attributable to a new definition of urban residence adopted in the 1950 census. In the total nonwhite population (95 percent Negro) the urban gain was 3.3 million under the new definition and 2.8 million according to the definition utilized in censuses before 1950. U. S. *Census of Population: 1950*, Vol. II, *Characteristics of the Population*, Part 1, "U. S. Summary," table 34.

[3] From 1950 to 1957, the Chicago nonwhite population increased by an estimated 240,000 as compared with a gain of 227,000 in the decade 1940-1950. Chicago Community Inventory, University of Chicago, *Population Growth in the Chicago Standard Metropolitan Area, 1950-1957* (February, 1958).

[4] U. S. Bureau of the Census, *Current Population Reports*, Series P-28, *Special Censuses*, no. 1073 rev., "Population of New York City, by Age, Color, and Sex, Special Census, April 1, 1957" (March 12, 1958).

[5] *Ibid.*, no. 927, "Special Census of Los Angeles, California: February 25, 1956" (October 18, 1956).

Other Nonwhite Groups

The 1950 Census reported 711,000 nonwhites other than Negroes, including American Indians (342,000), Japanese (127,000), Chinese (117,000), Filipinos (62,000), and others (49,000). These groups are concentrated in a few sections of the country. Indians live chiefly in nine states[6] and are primarily rural. The groups of Asian origin are found mainly in Pacific coast cities with a few secondary concentrations elsewhere (table 2).

Most widely distributed geographically are the Chinese. Although the majority live in California, fully a third are in the northern states, and appreciable numbers are found in the South and elsewhere. The Chinese population of New York is second in number only to that of San Francisco, which included 30 percent of all Chinese in the United States in its metropolitan area in 1950. There are smaller but significant communities in Boston, Chicago, and Seattle. Well over 90 percent of the group are urban residents.

For many years before 1940, the Chinese population in the United States was in gradual decline, but the repeal of the Chinese Exclusion Act in 1943 and removal of other racial restrictions in immigration laws have had dramatic effects. Immigration of Chinese women as wives of American citizens permitted the uniting of long-separated families and the creation of thousands of new families.[7] The Chinese female population of the United States more than doubled between 1940 and 1950, and the sex ratio declined from 285 to 190. Partly owing directly to immigration, and partly to the upsurge in births resulting from the reuniting and creation of families, the Chinese population increased more than 50 percent during the decade. Continued immigration since 1950 and a sustained high birth rate indicate that it is continuing to increase at a rapid rate.[8]

---

[6] New Mexico, Arizona, Oklahoma, South Dakota, North Carolina, California, Montana, Wisconsin, and Minnesota. These nine states included more than three-fourths of the Indian population in 1950.

[7] Rose Hum Lee, "The Recent Immigrant Chinese Families of the San Francisco-Oakland Area."

[8] Chinese immigration in the period 1947-1956 was nearly 22,000 persons, of whom almost 16,000 were female. U. S. Department of Justice, Immigration and Naturalization Service, *Annual Report,* 1947-1956, table 10.

TABLE 2

JAPANESE, CHINESE, AND FILIPINO POPULATIONS IN THE UNITED STATES, URBAN AND RURAL, BY REGIONS AND SELECTED STANDARD METROPOLITAN AREAS, 1940 AND 1950

Area	Japanese 1940	Japanese 1950	Chinese 1940	Chinese 1950	Filipino 1940	Filipino 1950
	POPULATION IN THOUSANDS					
United States	126.9	141.4	77.5	117.1	45.6	61.6
Urban	69.7	100.4	70.2	109.0	27.6	41.0
Rural	57.3	41.0	7.3	8.1	17.9	20.6
Regions						
Northeast	3.4	7.4	19.7	28.7	4.6	6.2
North central	1.6	18.6	6.1	10.6	3.5	4.1
South	1.0	3.0	4.9	10.4	2.4	4.4
West	120.9	112.3	46.8	67.4	35.1	46.9
Standard metropolitan areas						
Boston	. . .[a]	. . .[a]	2.1[b]	2.9	. . .[a]	. . .[a]
Chicago	. . .[a]	11.2	2.3	3.7	1.7[c]	. . .[a]
Los Angeles	38.7	37.8	5.4	9.3	4.5[c]	7.1
New York	2.6	3.7	14.2	20.6	2.7[c]	4.0
San Francisco-Oakland	13.6	13.8	23.4	34.8	3.5[c]	11.8
Seattle	9.9	6.8	1.8	2.7	1.4[c]	2.7
	PERCENT DISTRIBUTION					
United States	100.0	100.0	100.0	100.0	100.0	100.0
Urban	54.9	71.0	90.6	93.1	60.6	66.4
Rural	45.1	29.0	9.4	6.9	39.4	33.6
Regions						
Northeast	2.7	5.2	25.3	24.5	10.1	10.0
North central	1.2	13.2	7.9	9.0	7.8	6.6
South	0.8	2.1	6.4	8.9	5.2	7.2
West	95.3	79.4	60.4	57.6	77.0	76.2
Standard metropolitan areas						
Boston	. . .[a]	. . .[a]	2.7	2.5	. . .[a]	. . .[a]
Chicago	. . .[a]	7.9	2.9	3.2	3.8[b]	. . .[a]
Los Angeles	30.5	26.7	7.0	7.9	9.9[b]	11.5
New York	2.0	2.6	18.4	17.5	6.0[b]	6.5
San Francisco-Oakland	10.7	9.7	30.2	29.7	7.6[b]	19.1
Seattle	7.8	4.8	2.3	2.3	3.1[b]	4.5

SOURCES: *United States Census of Population: 1950*, Vol. II, *Characteristics of the Population*, chapters for the respective states; Vol. IV, *Special Reports*, Part 3, chap. B, "Nonwhite Population by Race." *Sixteenth Census of the United States, 1940, Population*, chapters for the respective states; Series P-10, no. 1, *Racial Composition of the Population, for the United States, by States: 1940*; Series P-10, no. 20, *Racial Composition of the Urban and Rural Population of the United States, by Regions, Divisions, and States: 1940*.

[a] Data not available; population less than 1,000 in 1940 or less than 2,500 in 1950.

[b] Chinese population in five counties, only parts of which are included in the Boston Standard Metropolitan Area as defined by the 1950 Census. The 1940 figure is therefore probably somewhat larger than would have been obtained for the Standard Metropolitan Area if the latter figure were available.

[c] Data for central cities only. Not available for counties comprising the standard metropolitan areas.

The Japanese population, in contrast, experienced only a moderate increase (11 percent) during the decade but a considerable redistribution—the residue of wartime compulsory evacuation from the west coast. The area chiefly gaining Japanese population was the north central region, primarily Chicago. There is evidence, however, that the Japanese relocated in the Midwest during the war have been returning to California since 1950. One indication is the 40 percent increase in the nonwhite, non-Negro population of Los Angeles between 1950 and 1956 (see Appendix table A-3).

Wartime evacuation also heightened the urbanization of the Japanese. Before the war nearly half of them were rural, mainly farm residents, but the 1950 Census found well over two-thirds of the group living in cities. In California the Japanese are mainly concentrated in the Los Angeles metropolitan area, the residence of more than a fourth of all Japanese in the United States in 1950.

The Filipino population, although small in number, increased substantially (35 percent) during the 1940-1950 decade, largely through the formation of families and natural increase. The group is about two-thirds urban and is heavily concentrated on the Pacific coast. Elsewhere, only New York City had an appreciable Filipino population in 1950.

Spanish-name Population

The population of largely Mexican origin in the Southwest, identified in the 1950 Census by Spanish surname, is the second ethnic minority in the United States (Jews excepted). It is more than one-seventh the size of the Negro population and exceeds the latter in the five states where it is concentrated (table 3).

Nearly half of the southwestern Spanish-name population is in Texas and a third in California. The group tends to be concentrated in the southern parts of the two states, although there are many as far north as San Francisco. In this broad zone, from Texas to the Pacific coast, the Spanish-name group is rather widely distributed. More than two-thirds live in urban places. The Los Angeles metropolitan area has the largest concentration, with more than 311,000 persons in 1950. In second and third places are the San Antonio and San Francisco–Oakland metro-

TABLE 3

DISTRIBUTION OF SPANISH-NAME POPULATION 1950, BY STATES, URBAN AND RURAL,
AND SELECTED STANDARD METROPOLITAN AREAS, WITH COMPARATIVE DATA
FOR THE POPULATION OF SPANISH MOTHER TONGUE, 1940
(in thousands)

State and standard metropolitan area	Spanish-name population, 1950				Spanish mother tongue population 1940[a]	
	Number	Percent distribution	Percent of total population	Percent urban	Percent distribution	Percent urban
Total, five states	2,290	100.0	10.9	66.4	100.0	51.2
Arizona	128	5.6	17.1	61.3	6.5	42.2
California	760	33.2	7.2	75.8	26.5	68.4
Colorado	118	5.2	8.9	49.7	5.9	35.0
New Mexico	249	10.8	36.5	41.0	14.1	25.2
Texas	1,034	45.2	13.4	68.1	47.0	52.5
Standard metropolitan areas						
Los Angeles	311	13.6	7.1	92.8	...	...
San Francisco-Oakland	95	4.1	4.2	87.0	...	...
El Paso	90	3.9	45.9	80.6	...	...
San Antonio	177	7.7	35.3	93.2	...	...
All others	514	22.4	8.6	79.1	...	...

SOURCES: *U. S. Census of Population: 1950*, Vol. IV, *Special Reports*, Part 3, chap. C, "Persons of Spanish Surname"; Vol. II, *Characteristics of the Population*, Part 1, "U. S. Summary." *Sixteenth Census of the U. S., 1940, Population*, "Nativity and Parentage of the White Population: Mother Tongue."

[a] In the 1940 Census a 5 percent sample of the entire population was questioned as to the earliest language spoken in the home other than English. This made possible a tabulation of persons of Spanish mother tongue. Although not strictly comparable with the Spanish-name population enumerated in 1950, it is believed that the two populations are sufficiently comparable to justify comparison of their distribution on a percent basis.

politan areas with 177,000 and 95,000, respectively. Many foreign-descent populations in the United States are more numerous, but they have ceased to be minorities in the meaning of being regarded and regarding themselves as distinct groups.

Persons with Spanish surnames were enumerated by the Census only in the five Southwestern states of Texas, New Mexico, Colorado, Arizona, and California. The census report is, therefore, an undercount of the Mexican-American population in the whole United States. Mexican-American colonies exist in Chicago and elsewhere outside the Southwest, and there is a long-established pattern of seasonal labor migration from Texas to the Great

Lakes states involving chiefly Mexican-Americans. On the assumption that the ratio of population born in Mexico to the Spanish-name population is the same nationally as in the Southwest, the United States population of Spanish surname (not including Puerto Ricans) in 1950 may be estimated at approximately 2,600,000.

Since this population was identified by Spanish name for the first time in the 1950 Census, only limited comparisons are possible with data of previous censuses when the group was identified by different techniques.[9] Such comparisons as can be made indicate a large shift from rural to urban residence during the 1940-1950 decade, and a substantial movement to California from the other southwestern states.

Puerto Ricans

The largest movement of Puerto Ricans to the mainland has occurred since 1950, but the Census of that year reported 301,000 persons of Puerto Rican birth or parentage in the continental United States, 80 percent of whom were in New York City. Sustained migration and the high birth rate among resident Puerto Ricans brought the total Puerto Rican population on the United States mainland to an estimated 740,000 at the end of 1956, including an estimated 580,000 in New York City.[10]

The concentration of Puerto Ricans in New York City developed before 1940 with the increasing flow of migration from Puerto Rico. In recent years they have also begun to appear in noticeable numbers elsewhere than in New York. The proportion of all mainland Puerto Ricans residing in New York City may be somewhat smaller at present (1959) than in 1950, but is probably

---

[9] The 1940 Census reported statistics for persons of Spanish mother tongue, drawn from a classification of the entire population according to mother tongue, or language other than English spoken in the home in earliest childhood. The 1930 Census collected and published data on Mexicans as a racial group. See *U. S. Census of Population: 1950*, Vol. IV, *Special Reports*, Part 3, chap. C, "Persons of Spanish Surname," pp. 4-6.

[10] Estimates based on Puerto Rico Planning Board, *Puerto Rico Passenger Traffic, by Route and Method of Transport, 1950-56;* New York City Department of Health, "Selected Vital Statistics for White, Nonwhite, and Puerto Rican Populations," annual, 1950-1956 (unpublished); and opinions of experts associated with the Commonwealth of Puerto Rico, Department of Labor, Migration Division, New York City.

not less than 75 percent. Outside New York, Puerto Ricans have settled mainly along the east coast from Connecticut to New Jersey, in a few Ohio cities, and in Chicago.

METROPOLITAN AREAS: CENTRAL CITIES VERSUS SUBURBS

Negro migration since 1940 has been directed overwhelmingly toward the central cities of metropolitan areas, whereas the white population has been shifting outward from the cities into surrounding suburban territory. The result is a steadily increasing prominence of Negro and other minorities in the populations of the larger cities.

In the 1940-1950 decade, the 168 standard metropolitan areas (SMA's) as defined by the Census,[11] accounted for three-fourths of the national increase in white population but 110 percent of the total nonwhite increase, reflecting a net decline of nonwhite population in nonmetropolitan territory. The fourteen SMA's with populations of more than a million received 32 percent of the total white increase, but nearly 75 percent of the national increase in nonwhite population. Within the metropolitan areas, more than two-thirds of the added white population but less than one-fifth of the nonwhite increase found residence outside the central cities, but in the fourteen largest areas this disparity was even more pronounced.

In the years since 1950 the movements of population to metropolitan areas and from central cities to suburbs have been running even more strongly than during the 1940's. Of the increase in the civilian population of the United States between 1950 and 1956, an estimated 85 percent was accounted for by the growth of population in standard metropolitan areas, and more than 80 percent of this growth occurred outside the central cities.[12] In many cities the white population is stationary or declining while the number of nonwhites continues to mount. In New York City, for example, the nonwhite gain of 206,000 persons

---

[11] The Census defines a standard metropolitan area as a county or a group of contiguous counties socially and economically integrated with a central city of at least 50,000 inhabitants.

[12] U. S. Bureau of the Census, *Current Population Reports*, Series P-20, *Population Characteristics*, no. 71 (December 7, 1956).

in the period 1950-1957 was overbalanced by a decline of 302,000 in the white population, leaving the city with a net loss in excess of 96,000 persons. Since the Puerto Rican group, mostly white, increased by nearly half a million in the same period, the loss of white population other than the Puerto Rican must have been in the magnitude of three-quarters of a million or more.

Studies in Chicago, Philadelphia, Cleveland, Atlanta, and other large cities show similar disparate trends in population growth.[13] In Los Angeles, with much more space for growth than most large cities, the rate of white population increase accelerated after 1950 in the metropolitan area but slowed down in the city. Almost two in every five persons added to the Los Angeles population during 1950-1956 were nonwhite, as compared with one in four during 1940-1950.[14]

To see these population changes in proper perspective, it must be noted that growing metropolitan populations, of necessity, have been housed largely outside the central cities because these cities, especially the older ones, are filled up. Short of extensive rebuilding for higher densities in the central cities, there has been no alternative to building up the outlying areas.

The shift of population to the suburbs, moreover, is essentially a continuation of historic trends. American cities have always grown outward from their centers. As the metropolitan population has spread over a wide area, the political boundaries of the city have been left far behind. But, if the automobile and the super-highway have permitted enlargement of the metropolitan area, they have also served to tie the parts of the area more closely together. The functioning city of the present day is the metro-politan area and not just the territory within certain political boundaries. Hence, the outward movement of population within the metropolitan area and the expansion of the metropolitan area itself are to be seen realistically as city growth in the tradi-tional pattern, modern phase.

---

[13] Donald J. Bogue, *An Estimate of Metropolitan Chicago's Future Population: 1955 to 1965;* Chamber of Commerce of Greater Philadelphia, *Greater Philadel-phia Facts* (1956); Atlanta Metropolitan Planning Commission, *Dekalb-Fulton Metropolitan Area, Population · Housing* (1956).

[14] U. S. Bureau of the Census, *Current Population Reports,* Series P-28, *Special Censuses,* no. 927.

Movement of minority groups into the central parts of metro-politan areas is equally an historic process. In an earlier time, im-migrant groups thronging into American cities found living space in the older areas abandoned by others moving outward to newer districts. As the immigrants and their children became assimilated and improved their economic position, they in turn moved away from the areas of their first settlement in search of better living elsewhere. The in-migrant Negroes and Puerto Ricans have been housed in much the same manner as their immigrant predecessors. Given time and opportunity, these latest newcomers to the city will undoubtedly also move to more desirable residence areas. Indeed, there is evidence that this process is already underway.

THE OUTLOOK FOR POPULATION

To provide some basis for anticipating possible future develop-ments, projections of white and nonwhite populations to 1975, with urban-rural and regional distributions, have been prepared for the present study by the Population Research and Training Center of the University of Chicago. These projections are tied to the Census Bureau projections of total population, but they involve certain additional assumptions. It must be emphasized that these projections are not forecasts but rather calculations of the outcome of certain assumed future levels of fertility, mortality, migration, and urbanization for white and nonwhite populations. It is, of course, impossible to know how many children will be born or how many people will move from one part of the country to another in future years, but various plausible assumptions can be made concerning future trends. Those employed for the present projections are not necessarily the "best" among possible assumptions, but they are not unreasonable and are consistent with past trends.

If the 1950-1953 level of fertility of the general population and the 1950-1955 rate of increase in the proportion of population nonwhite should continue to 1975, the United States population in that year would exceed 221 million, of which 26 million would be nonwhite. This outcome represents increases of 46 percent in the white and 65 percent in the nonwhite over the 1950 popula-tions. About 2.2 million of the projected nonwhite increase to

1975 is predicated on the assumption that the nonwhite population will continue to increase more rapidly than the white, as has been true in recent years.

In 1950 approximately two-thirds of the nonwhite population was in the South. If the movement of nonwhites to the North and West should continue at the 1940-1950 rate (it may even have exceeded this rate during the 1950's), the proportion of the nonwhite population in the South would decline to 46 percent by 1975. The 1975 nonwhite population would be distributed regionally as shown in table 4, compared with the 1950 distribution.

TABLE 4

Nonwhite Population by Regions: Observed, 1950; Projected, 1975

Area	Nonwhite population in millions		Percent increase 1950-1975	Percent distribution	
	1975	1950		1975	1950
United States	26.1	15.7	65	100.0	100.0
North	11.0	4.4	150	42	28
South	12.0	10.3	16	46	66
West	3.1	1.0	210	12	6

Source: Population Research and Training Center and Chicago Community Inventory, University of Chicago, "Illustrative Projections of United States Population by Color, Urban-Rural Residence, and Broad Region to 1975" (Special Research Memorandum for the Commission on Race and Housing, 1956, Typewritten).

Alternatively, it would not be unreasonable to assume an unchanging proportion of nonwhites in the total population or a decrease in the rate of redistribution of the nonwhite population observed between 1940 and 1950. Under any combination of what seem to be reasonable assumptions (always assuming a total United States population of 221.5 million in 1975), the nonwhite population of the North and West will more than double by 1975. In the South, although the nonwhite population will decline relative to other regions, it will continue to increase in actual numbers if the stated assumptions are realized. A numerical decline in southern nonwhite population would mean either migration greater than that of 1940-1950 or a reduction in the rate of natural increase below the 1940-1955 level, or a combination of the two.

Urban-Rural Distribution

Future growth in urban population is projected on two alternative assumptions, namely, a moderate decline and a moderate increase in the rate of urbanization of the population, total and nonwhite, observed during the 1940-1950 period. By 1975, the proportion of the United States nonwhite population residing in urban places would be 74 percent under the low assumption and 79 percent under the high assumption, a degree of urbanization somewhat higher than that projected for the total population in both cases.

Under either assumption, all or nearly all future increase of nonwhite population will occur in the urban sector. The urban nonwhite population, if any combination of assumptions is realized, will rise from the 1950 level of 9.7 million to within a range of 17.6 to 20.6 million in 1975. These magnitudes would represent 12 to 13 percent of the total urban population of the United States.

Population Prospects in Metropolitan Areas

The shift of white population to the suburban parts of metropolitan areas and the parallel movement of nonwhites to the central cities have generated much speculation about the implications of these trends if long continued. To indicate the possible racial composition of future metropolitan and central city populations, some additional projections have been prepared, based on the preceding ones but requiring some further assumptions. Two alternative projections of total and nonwhite population in standard metropolitan areas, central cities, and outside central cities are presented in table 5.

Projection A assumes essentially that trends observed during the 1940's will continue to 1975. On this assumption the total population of central cities would rise from 49.4 million in 1950 to 58.9 million in 1975, but the suburban population would increase from 35.1 million to 88.4 million. Nonwhite population in central cities would rise from 6.4 million in 1950 to 16.2 million in 1975. Nonwhites would represent 28 percent of the total population of central cities in 1975 as compared with 13 percent in

TABLE 5

POPULATION IN THE UNITED STATES, IN STANDARD METROPOLITAN AREAS,
IN CENTRAL CITIES, AND OUTSIDE CENTRAL CITIES, BY COLOR:
OBSERVED, 1950; ESTIMATED, 1956-1957; PROJECTED, 1975

Year and color	United States	In standard metropolitan areas		
		Total	In central cities	Outside central cities
		POPULATION IN MILLIONS		
Total population				
1950	150.7	84.5	49.4	35.1
1956 (civilian)[a]	164.3	96.2	51.4	44.8
1975,[b] projected	221.5	147.3	58.9	88.4
Nonwhite population				
1950	15.7	8.2	6.4	1.8
1958[c]	19.3	. . .[d]	. . .[d]	. . .[d]
1975: projection A[e]	26.1	20.1	16.2	3.9
projection B[f]	26.1	20.1	12.6	7.5
		PERCENT DISTRIBUTIONS		
Total population				
1950	100.0	56.1	32.8	23.3
1956 (civilian)	100.0	58.6	31.3	27.3
1975, projected	100.0	66.5	26.6	39.9
Nonwhite population				
1950	100.0	52.4	40.7	11.7
1975: projection A	100.0	77.1	62.2	14.9
projection B	100.0	77.1	48.3	28.8
Nonwhite as percent of total population				
1950	10.5	9.8	13.0	5.2
1975: projection A	11.8	13.7	27.6	4.4
projection B	11.8	13.7	21.4	8.5

SOURCE: Projections for standard metropolitan areas, central cities, and outside central cities by staff of the Commission on Race and Housing, based on projections of United States population by color prepared by the Population Research and Training Center and Chicago Community Inventory, University of Chicago.

[a] U. S. Bureau of the Census, *Current Population Reports*, Series P-20, *Population Characteristics*, no. 71, December 7, 1956.

[b] United States total from Census Bureau projections. See text. Population in SMA's, in central cities, and outside central cities projected on assumption that average annual change in percent of U. S. population in each category during 1950-1956 will obtain through the projection period.

[c] U. S. Bureau of the Census, *Current Population Reports*, Series P-25, *Population Estimates*, no. 193, February 11, 1959.

[d] Data not available.

[e] United States total from table 4. Nonwhite population in SMA's, in central cities, and outside central cities projected on assumption that average annual change in percent of U. S. nonwhite population in each category during 1940-1950 period will obtain through the projection period.

[f] Assumes that the differential between the nonwhite (1940-1950) and the total (1950-1956) average annual change in percent of U. S. population in central cities is reduced by half during the projection period.

1950. In the total suburban population, nonwhites would decline to about 4 percent.

Projection A represents the outlook assuming, among other things, that nonwhites will not participate in the future suburban movement to any greater degree than in the 1940-1950 period. This assumption may well be questioned. Exclusion barriers against minorities in the suburbs seem likely to become less rigid in the future because of public pressure, legislation, and changes in federal housing policy more favorable to minority groups. As suburban housing developments age and take on more of the characteristics of older communities, opportunities for minority individuals to acquire properties will undoubtedly become more numerous than in the recent past. The preferences of the minorities themselves for urban as against suburban locations may change with the growing acculturation of these groups, and the minority homeseekers are likely to become more active in the suburban housing market. More important than any of these, perhaps, is the changing character of the suburbs. Not only homeseekers but commerce and industry are moving to suburban locations and this means, of course, that Suburbia will no longer be the preserve of middle-class commuters.[15]

Considering these factors, the alternative Projection B assumes arbitrarily that the differential between the nonwhite rate of re-distribution to central cities, 1940-1950, and that of the total population in the 1950-1956 period is reduced by half during the projection period 1950-1975. On this basis, other assumptions remaining the same, the nonwhite population in central cities would rise from 6.4 million in 1950 to 12.6 million in 1975; the nonwhite proportion of total central cities population would rise from 13 percent to 21 percent in 1975. On the same assumption, the nonwhite proportion outside the central cities, instead of declining, would rise from 5 percent to 8.5 percent.

In summary, the projections point to a nonwhite population in standard metropolitan areas in 1975 of 20.1 millions, equivalent

---

[15] See Merrill Folsom, "Outward Expansion of Industry Is Changing Face of Suburbia," *New York Times*, January 29, 1957. See also Donald L. Foley, *The Suburbanization of Administrative Offices in the San Francisco Bay Area*, Research Report 10, Real Estate Research Program, Bureau of Business and Economic Research, University of California, Berkeley, 1957.

to 13.7 percent of the total population. In the central cities of metropolitan areas the projections indicate a 1975 nonwhite population in the range of 12.6 to 16.2 millions or 21 to 28 percent of the total population.

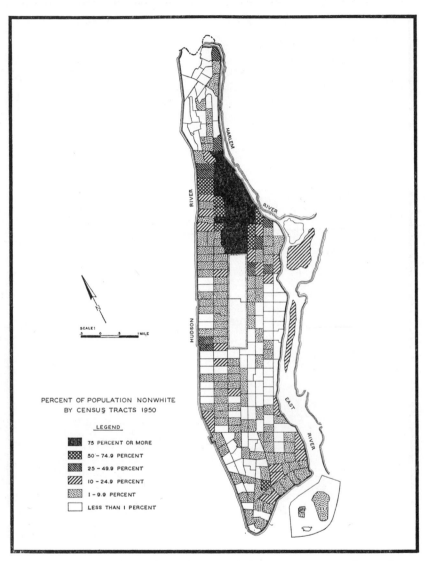

PERCENT OF POPULATION NONWHITE
BY CENSUS TRACTS 1950

LEGEND

75 PERCENT OR MORE
50 - 74.9 PERCENT
25 - 49.9 PERCENT
10 - 24.9 PERCENT
1 - 9.9 PERCENT
LESS THAN 1 PERCENT

Map 1. Borough of Manhattan, New York City, percent of population
nonwhite, by census tracts, 1950.

[25]

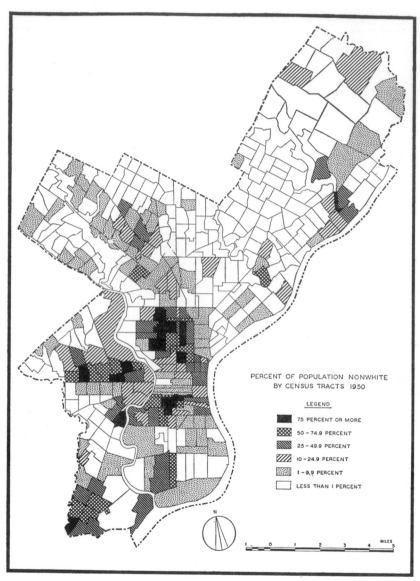

Map 2. City of Philadelphia, percent of population nonwhite, by census tracts, 1950.

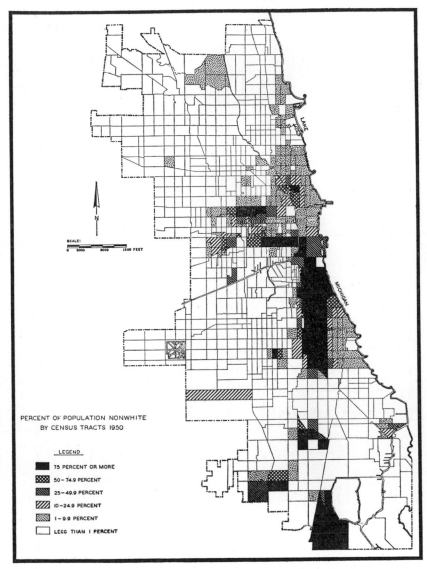

Map 3. City of Chicago, percent of population nonwhite, by census tracts, 1950.

[27]

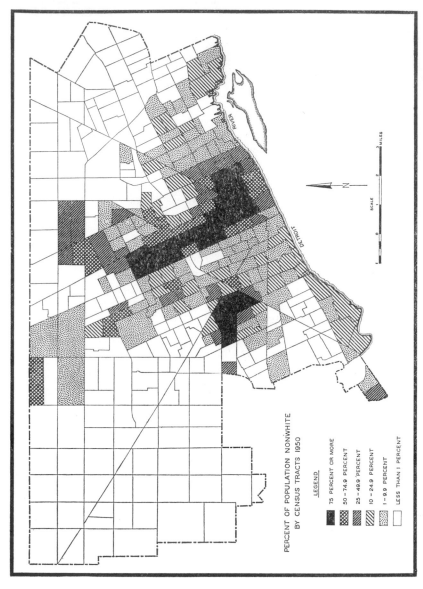

PERCENT OF POPULATION NONWHITE
BY CENSUS TRACTS 1950

LEGEND

75 PERCENT OR MORE

50 - 74.9 PERCENT

25 - 49.9 PERCENT

10 - 24.9 PERCENT

1 - 9.9 PERCENT

LESS THAN 1 PERCENT

Map. 4. City of Detroit, percent of population nonwhite, by census tracts, 1950.

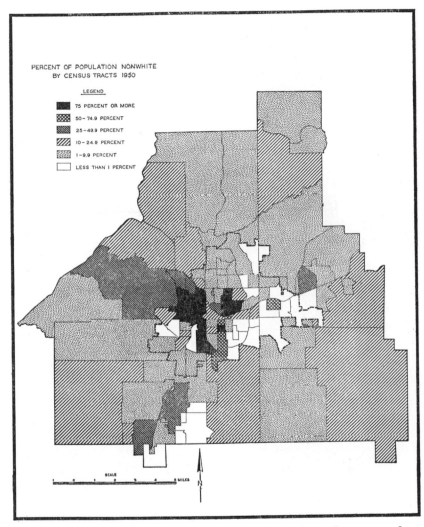

Map 5. City of Atlanta and adjacent area, percent of population nonwhite, by census tracts, 1950.

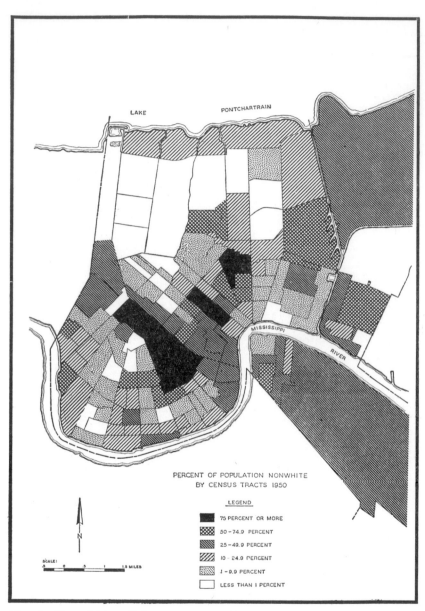

Map 6. City of New Orleans, percent of population nonwhite, by census tracts, 1950.

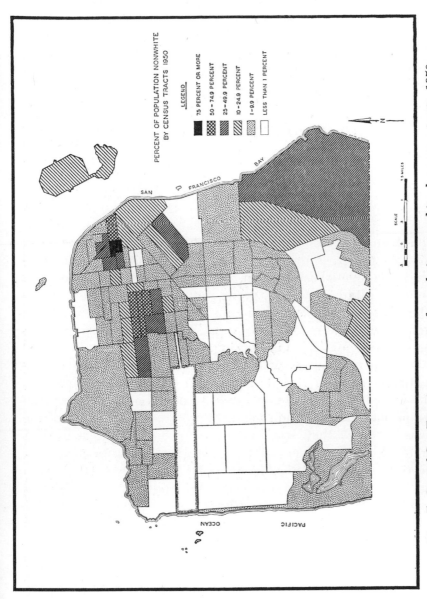

Map 7. City of San Francisco, percent of population nonwhite, by census tracts, 1950.

III

Urban Residence Patterns

The central fact in the urban housing and living situation of minority groups is their concentration in limited areas of residence. Residential segregation, whether voluntary or imposed, is a crucial feature of minority group status. Probably more than any other factor, it marks and maintains the separate identity of a group. From the enforced segregation of certain groups arises the issue of equal rights in housing.

Subsequent chapters will explore the factors sustaining residential segregation and its social and economic consequences. The present chapter attempts only to describe the existing residential patterns of certain minority groups, the character of the areas in which they live, and recent changes. The analysis is limited to twelve large cities representing the major regions of the country—New York, Philadelphia, Washington, D. C., Chicago, Detroit, St. Louis, Atlanta, Birmingham, New Orleans, Houston, Los Angeles, and San Francisco. Together these twelve cities were the residence of approximately a third of the total urban nonwhite population in 1950. During the 1940-1950 decade their combined nonwhite population increased by 1,296,000, equal to nearly half of the national nonwhite gain in the urban sector.

Lacking sanction of law, the residential segregation of minority groups in American cities is rarely, if ever, absolute. Probably the nearest approach to absolute racial segregation to be found in the United States occurs in planned housing developments where

the management, public or private, has the power and exercises
it to restrict occupants to members of a single racial group. Among
unplanned communities instances of racial exclusiveness as complete as in the great majority of new private housing developments across the country or of public housing projects in the
South would be difficult to find. In a given city, the members of
a minority group typically occupy one or more areas in which
they are almost the only residents. But not all members of the
group live in these segregated districts. Others live in variously
mixed areas, and a few are found scattered through the city. The
pattern is not the same for all groups or in all cities. In some, such
as Chicago and New York's Manhattan Borough, the great majority of nonwhites live in a single large area. In others, such as
Birmingham and New Orleans, the nonwhite minority occupies a
series of enclaves or islands scattered throughout the city. Minority residence patterns, moreover, are constantly changing under
the impact of changes in population and other social and economic
conditions.

A graphic picture of nonwhite residence patterns in 1950 in
seven cities is afforded by the accompanying maps. These show
the nonwhite proportion of the population in each census tract,
thus indicating the areas that are predominantly nonwhite occupied, those with essentially all-white populations, and others
that are racially mixed in varying degrees.[1] For convenience, the
area types shown on the maps may be designated as on page 34.
The designations, of course, are purely nominal.

Nonwhites in the "exclusion" tracts are not only few in number,
but those few are chiefly in the nonresidential status of janitors,
caretakers, and other servants. Occasional instances of nonwhite
residence in the social meaning of the term are found even in

---

[1] It should be noted that any measure or representation of the concentration
of a group is relative to the size of the units of space utilized. The smaller the
spatial unit, the more complete will the separation of racial groups appear.
Although census tracts are officially defined "small areas" for statistical purposes,
it is obvious that different racial groups may occupy separate blocks or streets
within a mixed tract. At a logical extreme, to narrow the spatial unit down to
the individual dwelling would yield a picture of all but total racial separation.
To supplement the census tract data, the present study includes a limited
analysis of nonwhite segregation by city blocks, for selected cities.

these tracts, but they are so few that these areas may be considered for practical purposes all white.

Percent of tract population nonwhite	*Designation*
75 or more....................	Segregated
50-74.......................	Concentrated
10-49.......................	Mixed
1-9........................	Dispersion
Less than 1..................	Exclusion

Characteristic of all cities studied is a principal area of non-white concentration near the business center of the city. This area consists of a "segregated" core surrounded by successive zones of "concentrated," "mixed," and "dispersion" tracts. In addition to the main area of nonwhite residence, each city contains several smaller districts where nonwhites represent a significant proportion of the population. Where secondary areas of the segregated or concentrated types occur, they tend to reproduce the structure of the major area, each one forming the center of a zone of mixed white and nonwhite residence. Thus, the map for Philadelphia (no. 2) shows nine distinct segregated areas, each bordered by census tracts of lesser nonwhite concentration. In Chicago, in 1950, there were six segregated areas detached from the major "Black Belt," each with adjacent tracts of concentrated, mixed, or dispersion types (no. 3). Similar patterns are evident in the maps of other cities. San Francisco, alone among the cities studied, contained in 1950 no Negro residence area of the segregated type. The only census tracts in San Francisco with populations 75 percent or more nonwhite were those occupied by Chinese (no. 7).

Except in San Francisco, the segregated and concentrated areas were the residence of 56 to 81 percent of the total nonwhite population of the various cities. San Francisco is unique in that in 1950 only 25 percent of its Negroes and 43 percent of the other nonwhites lived in predominantly nonwhite tracts. Los Angeles shows still a different pattern, similar to that of other cities for Negro residence, but with the large majority of other nonwhites living in mixed areas. The proportion of the white population living in all-white areas ranged from 10 percent in Birmingham,

Alabama, to more than 76 percent in Chicago. These data are summarized in table 6, with more details in Appendix table A-1.

TABLE 6

PERCENT DISTRIBUTION OF WHITE AND NONWHITE POPULATION
BY TYPES OF AREAS,[a] FOR SELECTED CITIES, 1950

City	Nonwhite population				White population			
	City total	Non-white areas	Mixed areas	White areas	City total	Non-white areas	Mixed areas	White areas
New York	100.0	68.2	29.9	1.9	100.0	1.3	32.8	65.9
Philadelphia	100.0	56.3	42.9	0.8	100.0	2.7	46.7	50.6
Washington	100.0	67.8	31.9	0.3	100.0	9.3	63.0	27.7
Chicago	100.0	81.0	18.0	1.0	100.0	1.2	22.2	76.6
Detroit	100.0	74.1	25.0	0.9	100.0	2.4	26.4	71.2
St. Louis	100.0	76.1	23.1	0.8	100.0	2.7	30.9	66.4
Atlanta	100.0	70.1	29.6	0.3	100.0	2.8	76.3	20.9
Birmingham	100.0	75.3	24.7	0.0	100.0	11.6	77.9	10.5
New Orleans	100.0	70.2	29.7	0.1	100.0	10.7	69.9	19.4
Houston	100.0	66.9	32.4	0.7	100.0	2.9	60.6	36.5
San Francisco								
Negro	100.0	25.9	73.3	0.8	100.0	1.6	61.3	37.1
Other nonwhite	100.0	42.6	55.0	2.4	...	...	...	...
Los Angeles								
Negro	100.0	62.4	36.2	1.4	100.0	1.0	35.4	63.6
Other nonwhite	100.0	14.5	75.2	10.3	...	...	...	...

SOURCE: Appendix table A-1.
[a] Areas consist of census tracts grouped and classified as follows: "nonwhite"—tracts with populations 50 to 100 percent nonwhite; "mixed"—tracts with populations 1 to 49 percent nonwhite; "white"—tracts with populations more than 99 percent white.

The distribution of a minority group within a city may be considered in terms either of where the bulk of the population is situated or throughout how much territory members of the group are spread. Both aspects are important. The northern and western cities typically contain large areas in which virtually no nonwhites live. More than two-thirds of all census tracts in the New York boroughs of Brooklyn, the Bronx, and Queens, and more than half of the tracts in Detroit, Philadelphia, St. Louis, and Los Angeles fell within the exculsion category in 1950. In Washington, D. C., on the other hand, and in Birmingham, Alabama, nonwhites were present in significant numbers (more than 1 percent of the population) in more than nine-tenths of the census tracts. In Atlanta,

New Orleans, and Houston nonwhites lived in four-fifths or more of the census tracts. In population terms, however, there is little difference between southern and northern cities in the degree of nonwhite concentration (table 6).

The wider geographic spread of nonwhites in southern as compared with northern cities means that a much higher proportion of southern than of northern whites live in census tracts where nonwhites also live. This proportion exceeds 70 percent in Atlanta, Birmingham, and New Orleans as compared with 21 percent and 25 percent of Chicago and Detroit whites. In the northern cities except Philadelphia, the large majority of whites live in all-white tracts. Washington, D. C., follows the southern pattern in this respect; also in San Francisco the majority of whites live in racially mixed census tracts.

Measures of the residential mixture or separation of racial groups are relative to the size of the spatial units employed. When city blocks are examined, rather than census tracts, a somewhat different picture of northern versus southern patterns emerges. Citywide, Birmingham and New Orleans have higher percentages of racially mixed blocks than do Chicago or Detroit and about the same as the west coast cities. Within each class of racially mixed census tracts, however, mixed blocks occur less often in the southern than in either the northern or western cities. Racially mixed residence in census tracts carries over into a high proportion of mixed blocks in the northern and western cities but not in New Orleans and Birmingham. Racial segregation in the northern cities seems to arise chiefly from the exclusion of nonwhites from large sections of each city. In southern cities, the broad areas of exclusion are lacking, but nonwhites tend to be segregated, more rigidly than in the North or West, on a block or street basis.[2]

Housing Characteristics of Nonwhite Areas

Advanced age of the buildings, a large percentage of substandard dwellings, and high frequency of crowding are virtually standard

---

[2] The census block is the smallest unit of land enclosed by streets (typically a rectangle). Although much smaller than a census tract, the block is still too large to reveal separation of residence areas by streets. Probably, in a considerable proportion of racially mixed blocks, the white and nonwhite residents live on different streets.

characteristics of the housing in areas of nonwhite residence—
North, South, and West. Summary comparisons of segregated and
exclusion areas in twelve large cities are presented in table 7, and
more complete data are given in Appendix table A-1.

TABLE 7

AGE, CONDITION, AND CROWDING OF DWELLING UNITS IN NONWHITE[a]
VERSUS WHITE AREAS,[b] FOR SELECTED CITIES, 1950
(in percent)

City	Dwelling units in structures built 1919 or earlier		Dwelling units substandard[c]		Dwelling units crowded[d]	
	Nonwhite areas	White areas	Nonwhite areas	White areas	Nonwhite areas	White areas
New York	84.6	38.2	28.8	5.2	22.6	15.2
Philadelphia	89.5	47.6	40.1	6.2	21.9	5.4
Washington	54.3	6.3	23.4	1.9	26.0	6.7
Chicago	77.3	48.1	54.4	9.6	37.0	10.1
Detroit	64.5	13.8	24.3	5.2	23.1	8.5
St. Louis	76.5	46.4	65.3	16.4	35.1	14.7
Atlanta	50.8	25.7	57.7	15.6	37.0	9.5
Birmingham	48.8	18.1	68.1	10.2	37.7	9.3
New Orleans	56.6	28.9	52.2	4.1	36.6	9.9
Houston	19.0	6.5	34.4	11.0	24.0	12.7
San Francisco	62.8	31.8	67.1	2.6	29.0	4.7
Los Angeles	34.7	10.4	18.9	5.2	20.0	7.6

SOURCE: Appendix table A-1.
[a] Census tracts with populations 75 to 100 percent nonwhite in 1950.
[b] Census tracts with populations more than 99 percent white in 1950.
[c] Units dilapidated or lacking private bath or toilet.
[d] Units with 1.01 or more persons per room.

In every city the housing is newest in the areas where nonwhites are fewest, and oldest, with rare exceptions, in the areas
where nonwhites are most numerous. Indeed, there is a wide
difference in the age of housing as between the exclusion tracts
and *all* areas where nonwhites represent as much as 1 percent of
the population. This indicates that, up to 1950 at least, nonwhites
had been able to gain access, even on a dispersion basis, only to
the older sections of each city.

From one city to another the age of the housing in nonwhite
residential areas varies, as would be expected, with the age of the
general stock of housing. In such new cities as Los Angeles,

Houston, and the Queens Borough of New York the housing stock is much newer than in such old cities as Philadelphia, St. Louis, or the Borough of Manhattan. The *relative* position of the non-white residence areas, however, is the same in the new cities as in the old, with the exception of Queens Borough. In Los Angeles, for example, although nearly 66 percent of the housing in the segregated areas was less than thirty years old, the corresponding proportion in the exclusion areas was 90 percent. Less than a fifth of the housing in Houston's segregated areas was more than thirty years old in 1950, but even this small percentage of older housing was three times greater than in the all-white sections of Houston.

Since housing quality is related to age, it is not surprising that the areas of predominantly nonwhite residence contained not only the oldest but the poorest housing in every one of the twelve cities studied. In each city the disparity in housing quality between the segregated and the exclusion areas was extremely wide. The proportion of substandard housing in the all-white areas ranged from 2 to 16 percent in the various cities, but in the segregated areas the range was from 19 to 68 percent. In six of the twelve cities, more than half of the dwellings in the segregated areas were dilapidated or otherwise substandard.

In all twelve cities the quality of housing, as measured by the percent of units substandard, improves steadily in going down the scale of areas from the segregated to the exclusion. However, when only the dwelling units actually occupied by nonwhites are considered, the striking fact appears that housing quality does not vary greatly from one area to another. Only in San Francisco are the dwellings occupied by nonwhites significantly better in the mixed areas than in the areas of concentrated nonwhite settlement. In several cities, substandard dwellings occupied by nonwhites were even more frequent in the dispersion than in the segregated areas. In all cities the quality difference between white- and nonwhite-occupied dwellings in the same districts was very wide.

From these data it is evident that the poor quality of housing occupied by nonwhites is only partly traceable to their concentration in areas of bad housing. Those residing in mixed and dispersion areas in 1950 were not sharing fully in the better housing available in such districts, but instead, usually occupied the inferior units even in areas   of comparatively good housing.

Crowding of dwelling units, in all cities except New York, was two to six times more prevalent in the segregated and concentrated nonwhite districts than in the exclusion areas. In New York the crowding rate in the predominantly nonwhite areas was one of the lowest among the cities studied, and because of the general prevalence of crowding throughout the city, differences among areas were not large. Highest rates of crowding in nonwhite areas occurred in Chicago and the southern cities except Houston, but the widest difference between segregated and exclusion areas was in San Francisco, reflecting the adverse living conditions of the Chinese population in that city.

Like the incidence of substandard housing, crowding of dwellings occupied by nonwhites occurred as frequently or nearly so in the dispersion and mixed as in the segregated areas of most cities. The evidence suggests that crowding and doubling up of families, like the prevalence of poor quality dwelling units, are related more to other factors in nonwhite housing than to concentration of nonwhites in particular areas.

Population Growth and Residence Patterns

From the vantage point of 1959, the urban residence patterns of minority groups observed in 1950 stand midway in a period of rapid urbanization of minority populations beginning during World War II and continuing unabated through the 1950's. To throw light on the manner in which growing minority populations are accommodated in American cities, it is useful to examine the changes which took place during the decade 1940-1950—the latest period for which there are relatively comprehensive data.

Under the pressure of population growth the nonwhite residence patterns in large cities changed in three principal ways. First, the areas where nonwhites were living in 1940 tended to fill up with nonwhites: white residents moved out and their places were taken by incoming nonwhites. Second, the boundaries of established nonwhite residence areas were extended, with replacement of white by nonwhite populations. And third, new "colonies" of nonwhites were created at various points more or less distant from the older settlements. In these ways, the vast majority of the increasing nonwhite population was housed. In addition, there occurred a certain amount of genuine dispersion of nonwhites among the white population in many northern and western cities. Such dispersion, however important as a possible portent of the future, was of minor consequence numerically in the 1940-1950 period.

These changes in nonwhite residence patterns are graphically shown in the accompanying maps for eight cities (Nos. 8 to 17). A basic uniformity runs through all the cities studied, although the relative magnitudes of the different types of change vary from one city to another depending upon the volume of nonwhite population growth, the capacity of existing nonwhite residence areas to absorb additional population, and decisions by public authorities on the location of housing projects. Other less tangible but undoubtedly important factors affecting the kinds of changes which took place are differences among cities in the rigidity of segregation barriers and in the extent of deliberate control over where minority groups should live.

In the southern cities, nonwhite population growth was moderate in comparison with that in many northern and western cities and hence did not create the same pressures for enlargement of living space. Instead of "pushing out" into new territory, the Negro populations in Atlanta, Birmingham, and New Orleans were apparently being "pushed in" and becoming more concentrated within a smaller space. In these cities, as the maps reveal, the areas predominantly nonwhite-occupied in 1940 received the bulk of the nonwhite population increase during the ensuing decade, whereas the tracts where nonwhites were less than 10 percent of the 1940 population tended more often to lose rather than gain nonwhite population. This trend is the more significant because of its variance from the traditional pattern of relatively widespread Negro residence in southern cities. Unlike the North and West, where racial transition seems almost always to involve replacement of white by nonwhite population, in the southern cities the process worked in both directions in different areas, with the effect of heightening the residential concentration of the Negroes.

Supplementing the maps, table 8 indicates how the growth of nonwhite population during the 1940-1950 period was distributed among the four types of settlement in eight northern and western cities. More detailed data are given in Appendix table A-2. A striking feature of these statistics is in the extreme disparity between the numbers of whites leaving and the numbers of nonwhites entering the principal areas of nonwhite settlement in several cities. In the process of becoming more heavily nonwhite, many of these areas also became much more densely populated than before. In Chicago, for example, the group of census tracts which were 10 percent or more nonwhite-occupied in 1940 lost 31,000 whites while gaining 119,000 nonwhites. In the comparable tracts of Philadelphia, 69,000 whites were replaced by 113,000 nonwhites. This increasing density of population in nonwhite residence areas was not matched by any corresponding increase in the housing supply. The result, obviously, was to aggravate conditions of crowding, contrasting sharply with the trend toward less crowding in the districts where the growing population was white.

In most of the cities studied, nonwhites became more concentrated in the areas where they made up the bulk of the population —more concentrated in the sense that these areas contained a larger proportion of the total nonwhite population of each city in 1950 than in 1940. In New York City, for example, the proportion of the nonwhite population living in segregated census tracts rose from 49 percent in 1940 to 53 percent in 1950. New York's Bronx Borough had no tracts in 1940 in which as many as three-fourths of the population were nonwhite. By 1950, there were four such tracts in the Bronx, and they were the residence of 28 percent of the borough's nonwhite population. For Los Angeles, the comparable figures were 26 percent in 1940 and 46 percent in 1950. Correspondingly, the proportions of the total nonwhite population in each city living in dispersion and exclusion areas diminished between 1940 and 1950. Comparative data for twelve cities are given in Appendix table A-2.

These tendencies are not inconsistent with the facts that the larger nonwhite populations occupied a larger total space or that somewhat greater *numbers* of nonwhites were living in dispersion

TABLE 8

Population Change, 1940-1950, by Color and Categories
of Census Tracts,[a] for Selected Cities

City and color	City total	Tracts with population 10 percent or more nonwhite in 1940	Tracts becoming 10 percent or more nonwhite in 1950		All other tracts
			Adjacent[b]	Non-adjacent	
New York City					
Manhattan					
White	−17,717	−32,849	−31,275	1,271	45,136
Nonwhite	91,433	44,596	32,919	3,383	10,535
No. of tracts	273	59	14	8	192
Bronx					
White	−18,699	−36,890	−32,440	6,868	43,763
Nonwhite	75,203	36,415	31,872	1,515	5,401
No. of tracts	397	19	13	7	358
Brooklyn					
White	−61,072	−50,057	−15,148	7,679	−3,546
Nonwhite	102,732	76,443	19,549	1,037	5,703
No. of tracts	831	63	22	4	742
Queens					
White	226,542	−12,023	−6,256	1,074	243,747
Nonwhite	26,821	14,023	7,738	156	4,904
No. of tracts	675	33	23	2	617
Philadelphia[c]					
White	16,499	−69,048	−8,626	−150	94,323
Nonwhite	131,340	112,710	11,188	3,749	3,693
No. of tracts	378	94	11	3	270
Washington					
White	43,539	10,746	−7,367	−2,334	42,494
Nonwhite	95,548	83,658	8,430	1,930	1,530
No. of tracts	96	54	8	1	33
Chicago					
White	−2,982	−31,468	−38,777	−9,011	76,274
Nonwhite	227,179	119,189	74,788	20,841	12,361
No. of tracts	908	110	60	9	729
Detroit[d]					
White	58,259	−71,068	−53,409	−6,951	189,687
Nonwhite	156,956	93,164	47,008	7,481	9,303
No. of tracts	393	65	48	9	271
St. Louis and adjacent area					
White	127,406	−5,382	−11,090	0	143,878
Nonwhite	61,754	44,681	14,115	0	2,958
No. of tracts	247	50	5	0	192
San Francisco					
White	92,367	−9,099	−1,016	26,054	76,428
Negro	38,675	10,336	10,354	13,098	4,887
Other nonwhite	11,098	1,045	4,615	1,448	3,990
No. of tracts	116	13	12	3	88

TABLE 8—Continued

City and color	City total	Tracts with population 10 percent or more nonwhite in 1940	Tracts becoming 10 percent or more nonwhite in 1950		All other tracts
			Adjacent[b]	Non-adjacent	
Los Angeles and adja-cent area					
White	1,219,158	−15,775	−1,701	2,559	1,234,075
Negro	143,156	87,126	33,202	1,844	20,984
Other nonwhite	4,982	−5,439	5,429	356	4,641
No. of tracts	764	62	41	4	657

SOURCES: *U. S. Census of Population: 1950*, Vol. III, *Census Tract Statistics*, chapters for the respective cities. *Sixteenth Census of the U. S., 1940, Population and Housing Statistics for Census Tracts*, chapters for the respective cities except New York. Welfare Council of New York City, *Census Tract Data on Population and Housing, New York City: 1940*.

[a] Tracts are those identified in the 1950 census. To secure 1940 population figures for 1950 census tracts, some tracts were combined to establish areas comparable to the 1940 tracted areas. For comparability with other tables, census tracts with less than 50 persons in 1950 were omitted from the calculations.

[b] "Adjacent" tracts are those having a common boundary with a tract whose population was 10 per cent or more nonwhite in 1940. A tract was also considered adjacent if its population became 10 percent or more nonwhite between 1940 and 1950, and it had a common boundary with an "adjacent" tract. Thus, a tract separated by several tracts from an area with a population 10 percent or more nonwhite in 1940 was considered adjacent if all the intermediate tracts had become 10 percent or more nonwhite in 1950. Tracts with only a point in common or separated by a river or a bay are not considered adjacent.

[c] Includes in addition to census tracts within Philadelphia, 24 tracts in Camden which were comparable in 1940 and 1950.

[d] Includes in addition to census tracts within Detroit, 24 tracts in Highland Park and Hamtramck.

or exclusion areas in 1950 than ten years earlier. According to this criterion, it could be said that the dispersion of nonwhites increased during the 1940-1950 decade. For the nonwhite population as a whole, however, the tendency to live in separate areas, apart from the rest of the population, was accentuated during the decade.

Evidence of increasing segregation of nonwhites is confirmed by other studies using different criteria and methods of measurement. One study, computing segregation indexes from block statistics, reached "the certain conclusion that residential segregation in these [185] American cities did in fact increase during the decade 1940-1950." [3] The trend toward sharper separation of white and nonwhite residence areas was especially marked in the southern cities. As may be seen from the accompanying maps of Atlanta and New Orleans (nos. 13 and 14), nonwhite population increases were concentrated in a few areas, while in many tracts nonwhites declined not only relatively but in actual numbers.

Among the twelve cities studied, the only ones to manifest a loosening of nonwhite segregation in the 1940-1950 period were Chicago and San Francisco. By almost any measure the nonwhites of Chicago are one of the most highly segregated racial groups in the country. More than three-fourths of them in 1950 lived in census tracts with populations 75 percent or more nonwhite—a proportion substantially higher than existed in any other of the cities examined in the present study; even so, it was lower in 1950 than in 1940. [4]

The 227,000 persons added to the nonwhite population of Chicago between 1940 and 1950 were far more than could be housed in the established areas of nonwhite residence. The entire area in which nonwhites represented 10 percent or more of the 1940 population absorbed only about half of the increase, as compared with nearly 90 percent in Philadelphia and Washington. Another third of Chicago's growth expanded into adjacent tracts, and 9 percent into new, detached colonies. The outward movement of whites from the areas of nonwhite growth was relatively slow, doubtless for lack of alternative housing. Although the segregated and concentrated areas of nonwhite residence in Chicago expanded greatly, so did the racially mixed or dispersion areas (Appendix table A-2). Most of the 114 census tracts newly entered by nonwhites [5] did not shift immediately to predominant nonwhite occupancy. As a result, the nonwhite population as a whole, although living under very crowded conditions, was less separate

---

[3] Donald O. Cowgill, "Trends in Residential Segregation of Nonwhites in American Cities, 1940-1950." The study includes all cities for which block statistics were available in 1940 and in 1950.

[4] Cowgill's study reports a small decline in Chicago's segregation index, but since most cities were tightening their segregation patterns during the decade, Chicago moved from thirteenth to forty-second place among 209 cities in relative degree of segregation. *Ibid.*, p. 45.

[5] Precisely, tracts in which the proportion of nonwhites shifted from less than 1 percent in 1940 to 1 percent or more in 1950.

from the white population in 1950 than in 1940. This may well be only a transitional phenomenon, especially considering that most of the mixed and dispersion tracts in 1950 were adjacent to areas of higher nonwhite concentration and hence may be expected to receive the principal impact of further nonwhite population growth.

Among the twelve cities studied, San Francisco alone witnessed a decline in both the actual number and the proportion of the nonwhite population living in segregated areas. This occurred while the Negro population of San Francisco was undergoing a sevenfold expansion and other nonwhite groups were increasing more than 40 percent.

The deconcentration of San Francisco's nonwhites resulted from multiple changes involving the Chinese, Japanese, and Negro populations. The segregated area was and remains occupied almost entirely by Chinese. The reduction of population in this area was the direct result of the movement of Chinese away from China-town, mainly into adjacent areas of better housing. The Japanese were forcibly evacuated as a war measure in 1942. Upon their return after the war, they did not completely reëstablish their "little Tokyo" but resettled in a more dispersed pattern. These changes are portrayed graphically in maps 15 and 17.

The large migration of Negroes into San Francisco, as shown on map 15, was accommodated in about a dozen areas in various parts of the city, plus some dispersion into two-thirds of the city's census tracts. In no tract did Negroes become as much as 75 percent of the population and in only two tracts did they reach 50 percent by 1950. The majority of San Francisco Negroes in that year lived in census tracts where they and other nonwhites constituted from 10 to 50 percent of the population (Appendix table A-2).

Shaping this result was the absence, in prewar San Francisco, of an established minority residence district capable of absorbing a large population increase. The emptied Japanese area housed about a fourth of the Negro increase; expansion from this area accounted for an additional one-fourth; the remaining half had to be accommodated elsewhere. Distinctive features of the San Francisco pattern were the high proportions of the new Negro population housed in new, colony-type settlements (one-third) or dispersed through much of the city (one-eighth). Proportionally more of the Negro growth was accommodated in these ways in San Francisco than in any other city studied. The pattern of Negro settlement in San Francisco was strongly influenced by the location of several large public housing projects for war workers in a section of the city adjacent to the shipbuilding industries but distant from the existing minority residence areas.

Minorities other than Negroes

Chinese.—Although quite widely distributed through the United States, the Chinese, in their principal cities of residence, traditionally have been highly segregated. Between 1940 and 1950 the Chinese began a remarkable exodus from their Chinatowns. In San Francisco the three census tracts which comprise Chinatown lost a fifth of their population. The change is the more remarkable in that it occurred during a period of general housing stringency and also at a time when the Chinese population was rapidly increasing.

San Francisco's Chinatown, behind its exotic façades, is a slum. More than 66 percent of the dwelling units in 1950 were substandard; nearly 30 percent were crowded—the worst housing conditions in the city. The Chinese had endured these conditions for many years, but beginning in the 1940's their search for better housing was almost like a mass movement. As shown in map 17, the major shift was from Chinatown into adjacent and near-by areas, but significant numbers moved to other sections of the city. As of 1950, only 40 percent of San Francisco Chinese were living in Chinatown. A larger number resided in adjacent areas and about 12 percent of the total were dispersed through other sections of the city (table 9). Available evidence indicates that both the spreading out movement and the dispersion trend have continued since 1950.

The Chinese in New York City made an even more decisive break from Chinatown during the 1940-1950 decade. While the Chinese population of Manhattan was increasing by nearly two-fifths, the proportion living in Chinatown fell from one-half to less than one-third (table 10). The central Chinatown tract lost 40

TABLE 9

DISTRIBUTION OF CHINESE POPULATION IN SAN FRANCISCO, 1940 AND 1950

Area	Population		Percent change 1940-1950	Percent distribution	
	1940[a]	1950		1940[a]	1950
Chinatown	12,490	9,980	−20.1	70.2	40.2
Adjacent census tracts[b]	4,300	11,947	177.8	24.2	48.2
Other areas	992	2,886	190.9	5.6	11.6
San Francisco, total	17,782	24,813	39.5	100.0	100.0

SOURCE: *U. S. Census of Population: 1950*, Vol. III, *Census Tract Statistics*, chap. 49, "San Francisco-Oakland."

[a] Distribution estimated on basis of distribution of "other nonwhites" by census tracts.

[b] "Adjacent" as defined in table 8, note b.

TABLE 10

DISTRIBUTION OF NONWHITE EXCEPT NEGRO POPULATION IN MANHATTAN, 1940 AND 1950

Area	Population[a]		Percent distribution	
	1940	1950	1940	1950
Manhattan, total	13,934	19,020	100.0	100.0
Chinatown (3 tracts)	6,999	5,890	50.2	31.0
South of mid-Central Park	3,641	7,224	26.2	37.9
North of mid-Central Park	3,294	5,906	23.6	31.1

SOURCES: *U. S. Census of Population: 1950*, Vol. III, *Census Tract Statistics*, chap. 37, "New York"; Welfare Council of New York City, *Census Tract Data on Population and Housing, New York City, 1940*.

[a] Of the nonwhite except Negro population in New York City, 1950, approximately two-thirds were Chinese.

percent of its population. Unlike San Francisco's experience, New York's Chinese did not spread out into adjacent areas to any great extent but instead moved uptown and to many locations in other boroughs.

Japanese.—The Japanese in San Francisco and Los Angeles tend to live intermingled with or in proximity to the Negro population. This relationship is not caused by any affinity between the two groups but is a result of history and restrictions on the residential opportunities of both groups. The Japanese, after their compulsory relocation during the war, returned to find their

former living areas occupied by Negroes. Many of the returning
Japanese settled in their old neighborhoods in spite of the newcomers; others sought housing elsewhere. However, the areas
where Japanese were permitted to buy or rent homes were also
open to other minorities, including Negroes. Hence the Japanese,
wherever they settled, generally found themselves not far from
Negroes. Since 1950 the expansion of Negro residence areas has
tended increasingly to overtake and encompass the residences
of the Japanese.

Mexican-Americans.—The distribution of Mexican-Americans
(Spanish-name whites) in San Francisco and Los Angeles is
shown on maps 18 and 19. Striking differences are apparent. In
San Francisco the Spanish-name population is scattered throughout the city, with only a moderate tendency toward concentration
in the lower-rent districts. In Los Angeles, on the other hand,
nearly a fourth of the group was concentrated in one area where
it represented more than 50 percent of the population; another
fourth lived in near-by census tracts with populations more than
25 percent Spanish-name. Mexican-Americans in Houston were
similarly concentrated: a fifth lived in areas of predominantly
Mexican-American population; another fourth was in census tracts
with populations 25 percent or more Spanish-name.[6]

The housing in areas of Mexican-American concentration is
similar in quality to that in nonwhite residence areas. Buildings
are old, and a high proportion of the dwelling units are dilapidated or lack sanitary facilities. Crowding of dwelling units is
even more prevalent than in nonwhite areas. In Houston, for
example, the proportion of substandard dwellings in 1950 was 20
percent for the city as a whole but 60 percent in the census tracts
where Spanish-name whites were a majority of the population.
Nearly two-thirds of the dwellings in these tracts were crowded
(1.01 or more persons per room) as compared with one-sixth of
all dwellings in the city. Similar comparisons, with lower percentages, also hold for Los Angeles and for the parts of San Francisco
in which Spanish-name whites are most numerous.

---

[6] *U. S. Census of Population: 1950,* Vol. III, *Census Tract Statistics,* chapters
for respective cities. Data available only for 1950.

Puerto Ricans.—The residence pattern of the Puerto Rican population has been investigated only in the New York City boroughs of Manhattan, Brooklyn, and the Bronx. These three boroughs were the residence of four-fifths of all Puerto Ricans in the continental United States in 1950, and they have continued to attract the bulk of Puerto Rican migrants since that date.

The distribution of Puerto Ricans is not the same in the three boroughs. In Manhattan, four areas of relative concentration accounted for about two-thirds of the borough's Puerto Rican population in 1950. The remaining third was quite widely dispersed. In Brooklyn and also the Bronx, Puerto Ricans are concentrated in two areas of each borough and few live anywhere else. Surveys indicate that the large growth of Puerto Rican population since 1950 has occurred mainly within the general areas where Puerto Ricans were previously living, with some expansion of these areas. This means, of course, that Puerto Ricans are numerically dominant in only a few areas of census-tract size, but numerous smaller areas are occupied largely and in some cases entirely by members of this group. In each census tract containing an appreciable number of Puerto Ricans, they are apt to be found in a series of clusters which may be certain streets or just certain buildings.[7] With the rapid growth of Puerto Rican population since 1950, residential clusters of Puerto Ricans have both increased in size and multiplied in number.

A census of Puerto Rican and foreign-born pupils, conducted by the New York City Board of Education in 1955 found well over 90 percent of all Puerto Rican pupils enrolled in 40 percent of the city's elementary and junior high schools. Among these schools were forty-two where 50 percent or more of all pupils were Puerto Rican, and ten with enrollments 70 percent or more Puerto Rican.[8]

Few Puerto Ricans are found in the areas of concentrated nonwhite population, but the majority live adjacent to such areas and many share the mixed districts with nonwhites. The Puerto Rican areas are similar in housing quality to the areas occupied

[7] Morris Eagle, "The Puerto Ricans in New York City."
[8] Unpublished data made available by the New York City Board of Education, Bureau of Administrative and Budgetary Research.

by nonwhites, with high proportions of old structures and sub-standard dwelling units.

The 1950's: Decongestion

The increasing concentration of Negroes during the 1940-1950 period occurred in a time of general housing scarcity. The housing shortage undoubtedly served to strengthen segregation barriers and inhibit the expansion of minority residence areas. In the years since 1950, the general housing supply situation has changed substantially. The building of millions of new dwellings, chiefly in the suburban parts of metropolitan areas, and the accelerated shift of the white population to the suburbs have made it easier for minority homeseekers to acquire existing housing within the central cities. In many cities, extensive additional areas have been opened to minority occupancy. Between April, 1950, and December, 1956, dwellings occupied by nonwhites in the North and West increased by nearly 539,000 units or 41 percent, according to estimates of the Census Bureau's *1956 National Housing Inventory*.[9] Total occupied dwellings in the same regions increased 17 percent. Thus it seems that nonwhites in the North and West were, to some extent, catching up with the white population in the number of available dwellings, although, of course, much of the increase in nonwhite housing was absorbed by the continuing flow of migrants from the South.

From all evidence, additions to the housing supply available to minority groups since 1950 have taken essentially the same form as before, that is, extension of the boundaries of minority residence areas, the replacement of white by nonwhite population, the creation of new minority colonies, and a limited amount of dispersion. The principal difference between the post-1950 and the preceding period has been apparently not in the pattern but

---

[9] U. S. Bureau of the Census, *1956 National Housing Inventory*, Vol. III, *Characteristics of the 1956 Inventory*, Part 1, "United States and Regions." The total nation-wide increase in nonwhite-occupied dwellings was estimated at 550.7 thousand units, of which all but 11.9 thousand were accounted for by the North and West. Because of the nearly static situation in the South, on a national basis the nonwhite population was still lagging behind the white in rate of growth of housing. Nationally the percent increases in occupied dwelling units were 14.6 for nonwhite and 16.6 for whites. These figures represent *net* increases.

in the extent and rapidity of change in the transition areas. Within the pattern, the housing made available by departing whites has evidently been sufficient in many cities to permit considerable decongestion of the minority group residence areas and probably an improvement in the quality of housing available to these groups, as well.

In Baltimore, an FHA analysis of the housing market in 1953 reported that the rate of shift in areas changing to nonwhite occupancy had accelerated since 1950, with a substantial part of the shift occurring in sections of high quality housing.[10] The analyst believed that "the extensive movement into these former white areas [had] undoubtedly done much to relieve the pent-up requirements of the nonwhite population for additional dwelling space."

In the District of Columbia, a 1956 study observed "an extensive and continuing dispersion of nonwhite residence. . . . Residential properties of virtually every type generally available in the District [are] available to the nonwhite bidder." [11]

In Buffalo, New York, a state survey of rental housing calculated that during the 1940-1950 period nonwhites in that city acquired an additional dwelling unit for every 5.5 persons added to the population, but from 1950 to 1955, they obtained dwelling units at the rate of one for each four added persons. The report observes, "The housing needs of the nonwhites which were building up in the 1940's are being met in the 1950's. For the most part, nonwhites have had to wait for the overcrowded housing conditions of whites to ease before they could obtain relief. . . . This process, however [expansion of the nonwhite residence area], has not made available an adequate supply of housing, qualitatively or quantitatively, to a growing nonwhite population . . ." Buffalo nonwhites enjoyed better housing conditions in 1955 than in 1950, but they still held only 7 percent

---

[10] U. S., Federal Housing Administration, "Report on the Housing Market, Baltimore, Maryland, Standard Metropolitan Area, as of September 1, 1953," by Ralph S. Weese (Washington, D. C.: typewritten [1953]). See also Maryland Commission on Interracial Problems and Relations and Baltimore Commission on Human Relations, *An American City in Transition* (Baltimore, 1955), chap. ii, "Housing and the Negro Public."

[11] George B. Nesbitt, "Non-white Residential Dispersion and Desegregation in the District of Columbia," *The Journal of Negro Education*, Winter, 1956, pp. 5, 7.

of all occupied dwelling units, although they were 9 percent of
the city population; their average household was still nearly a
person larger than the white average; they occupied substandard
rented dwellings nearly three times as frequently as white-renter
households.[12]

A special census of Los Angeles records changes in the racial
residential pattern of that city between 1950 and 1956 which are
probably in some measure typical of recent changes in many
large northern and western cities.[13] In less than six years the
nonwhite population of Los Angeles increased by almost 100,000
or nearly 50 percent. Instead of heightening the congestion of
nonwhite residence areas, this rapid growth of nonwhite population was accompanied by an expansion of minority living space
sufficient to permit considerable decongestion. Nearly all census
tracts where nonwhites were in the majority in 1950 experienced
population losses between 1950 and 1956. The group of census
tracts with 1950 populations 10 to 50 percent nonwhite lost
74,000 whites while gaining only 38,000 nonwhites. This was a
dramatic reversal of the 1940-1950 situation, when the areas
open to nonwhites were receiving four arriving Negroes for
every departing white or Japanese (table 8). Nearly two-thirds
of the Negro population increase in Los Angeles, 1950-1956,
and more than nine-tenths of the added "other nonwhites"
(mainly Japanese) went into census tracts where populations
were less than 10 percent nonwhite at the beginning of the
decade. The Los Angeles map (no. 20) gives a graphic picture
of the shift of nonwhite population from the older areas of concentration into new territory. The statistics are summarized in
Appendix table A-3.

Because the white population moved out of the nonwhite
expansion areas more rapidly than nonwhites came in, the enlargement of nonwhite living space produced little if any increase
in the interracial occupancy of housing areas. Although the
density of nonwhite population declined, the tendency for non-

[12] State of New York, Temporary State Housing Rent Commission, *People,
Housing and Rent Control in Buffalo* (New York, 1956), pp. 36-39. The survey
was conducted by the U. S. Census Bureau for the State of New York.

[13] U. S. Bureau of the Census, *Current Population Reports*, Series P-28, *Special
Censuses*, no. 927.

whites to live in separate areas increased. The percentage of
Los Angeles Negroes living in census tracts where a majority of
the population was nonwhite was greater in 1956 than in 1950.
Negroes living in census tracts where the population was 90
percent or more white were fewer in actual number in 1956 than
in 1950. The Japanese were more dispersed among the white
population than were Negroes, but they, too, became concentrated in nonwhite areas to a much greater extent in 1956 than
in 1950.

What happened in Los Angeles after 1950 was a notable expansion and decongestion of minority living space within the
traditional system of separate areas for white and nonwhite.
Where previously residence areas have commonly passed from
white to nonwhite occupancy under conditions of rising density
of population and increasing crowding of dwelling units, racial
transition in Los Angeles during the 1950's was accompanied by
declining population density in many areas.

The provision of good quality housing for minorities on a
segregated basis has been called the "polished ghetto." In the
same terms, it is permissible to name the nonwhite residence area
of Los Angeles in 1956, the "spacious ghetto." It was made
possible by a large-scale redistribution of the white population
into the metropolitan area outside the city, leaving the central
city areas available for nonwhite expansion.

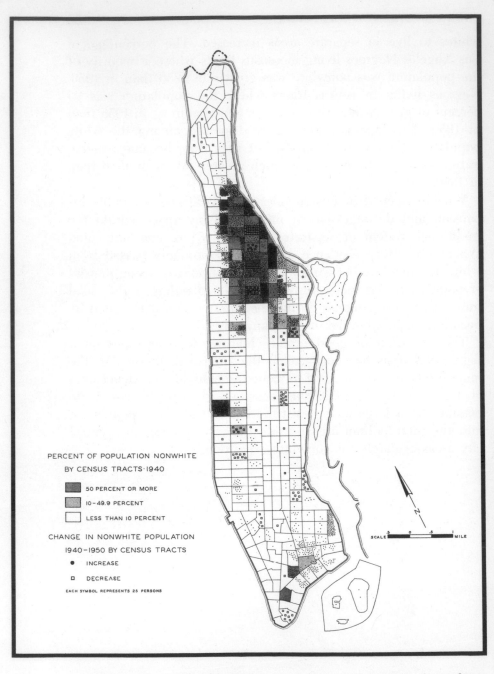

Map. 8. Borough of Manhattan, New York City, percent of population nonwhite, by census tracts, 1940, and change in nonwhite population 1940-1950, by census tracts.

[54]

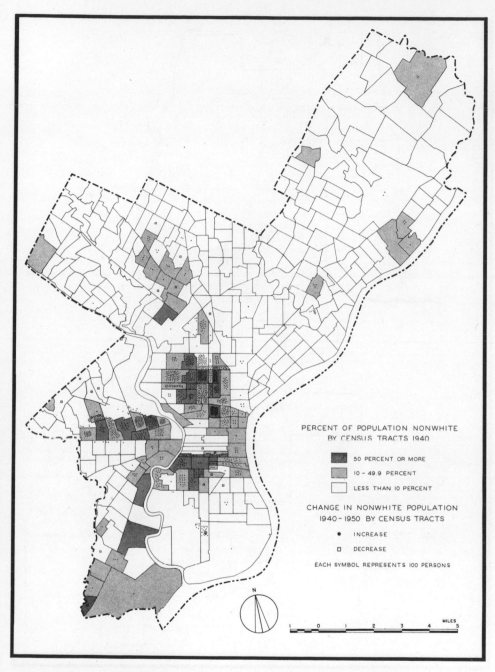

Map 9. City of Philadelphia, percent of population nonwhite, by census tracts, 1940, and change in nonwhite population 1940-1950, by census tracts.

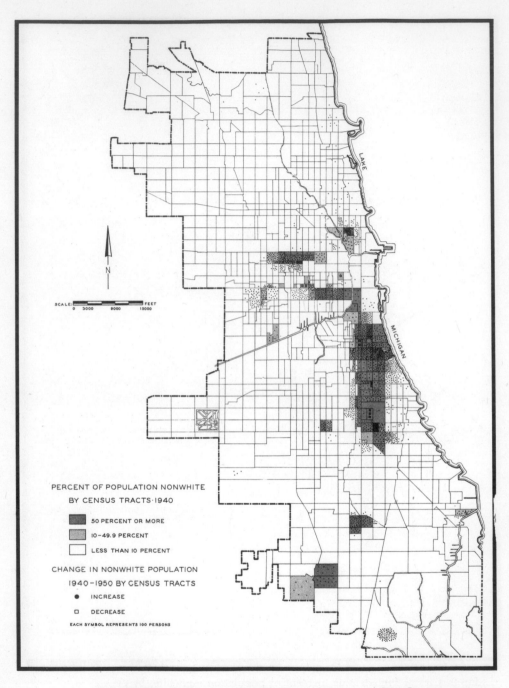

Map 10. City of Chicago, percent of population nonwhite, by census tracts, 1940, and change in nonwhite population 1940-1950, by census tracts.

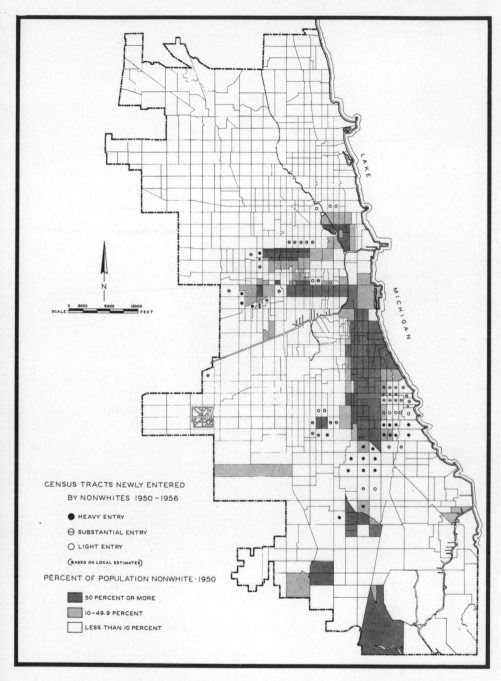

CENSUS TRACTS NEWLY ENTERED
BY NONWHITES 1950–1956

● HEAVY ENTRY

⊖ SUBSTANTIAL ENTRY

○ LIGHT ENTRY

(BASED ON LOCAL ESTIMATES)

PERCENT OF POPULATION NONWHITE · 1950

■ 50 PERCENT OR MORE

▨ 10–49.9 PERCENT

□ LESS THAN 10 PERCENT

Map 11. City of Chicago, census tracts newly entered by nonwhites, 1950-
1956, and percent of population nonwhite, 1950.

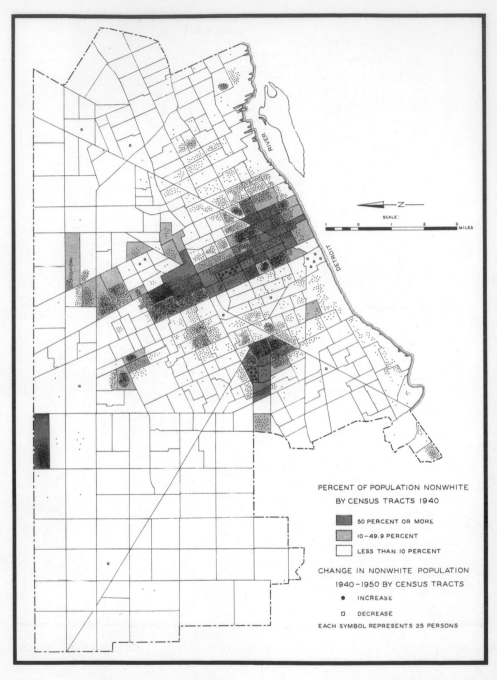

PERCENT OF POPULATION NONWHITE
BY CENSUS TRACTS 1940

■ 50 PERCENT OR MORE
▨ 10–49.9 PERCENT
□ LESS THAN 10 PERCENT

CHANGE IN NONWHITE POPULATION
1940–1950 BY CENSUS TRACTS
• INCREASE
□ DECREASE
EACH SYMBOL REPRESENTS 25 PERSONS

Map 12. City of Detroit, percent of population nonwhite, by census tracts, 1940, and change in nonwhite population 1940-1950, by census tracts.

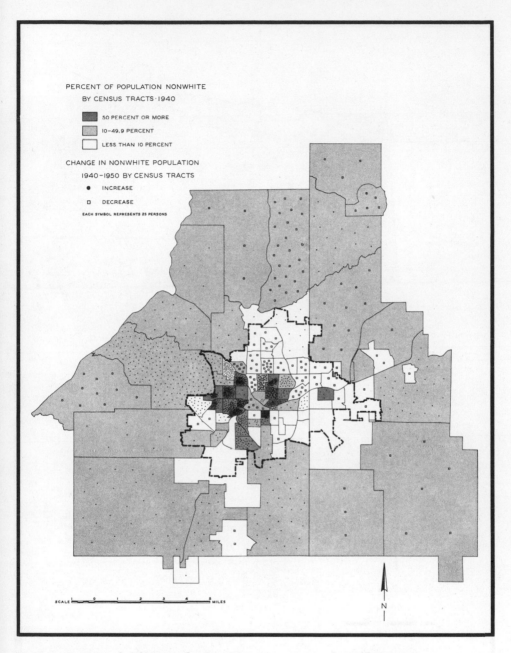

Map 13. City of Atlanta and adjacent area, percent of population non-white, by census tracts, 1940, and change in nonwhite population 1940-1950, by census tracts.

[59]

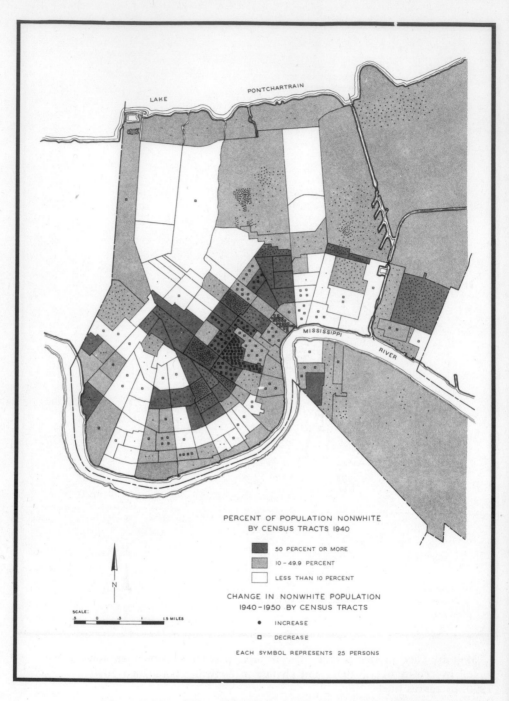

PERCENT OF POPULATION NONWHITE
BY CENSUS TRACTS 1940

■ 50 PERCENT OR MORE

▨ 10 – 49.9 PERCENT

☐ LESS THAN 10 PERCENT

CHANGE IN NONWHITE POPULATION
1940 – 1950 BY CENSUS TRACTS

● INCREASE

☐ DECREASE

EACH SYMBOL REPRESENTS 25 PERSONS

SCALE:
.5   0   .5   1   1.5 MILES

N

Map 14. City of New Orleans, percent of population nonwhite, by census tracts, 1940, and change in nonwhite population 1940-1950, by census tracts.

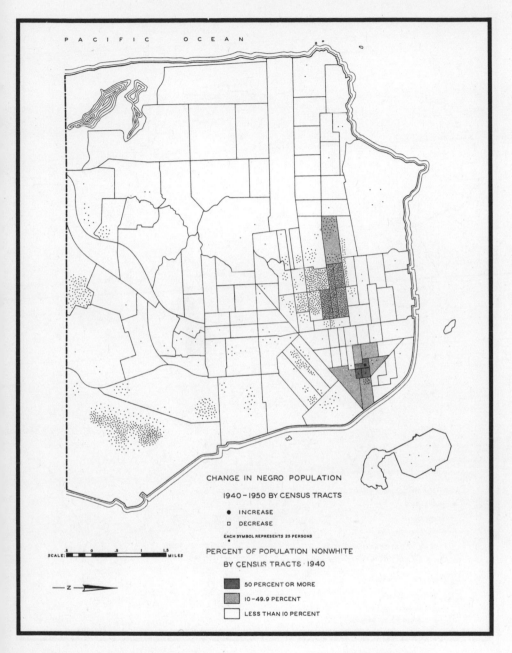

Map 15. City of San Francisco, change in Negro population 1940-1950, by census tracts, and percent of population nonwhite, by census tracts, 1940.

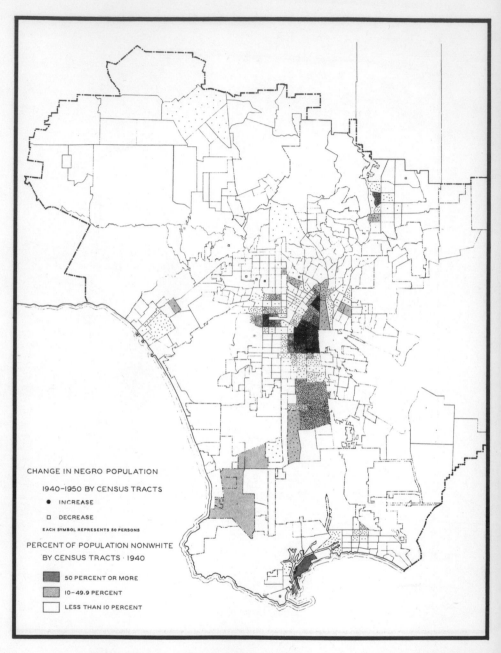

Map 16. City of Los Angeles and adjacent area, change in Negro population 1940-1950, by census tracts, and percent of population nonwhite, by census tracts, 1940.

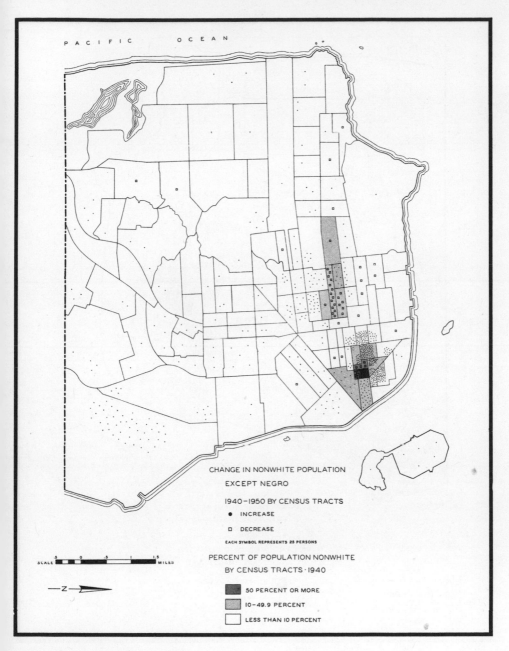

Map 17. City of San Francisco, change in nonwhite population, except Negro, 1940-1950, by census tracts, and percent of population nonwhite, by census tracts, 1940.

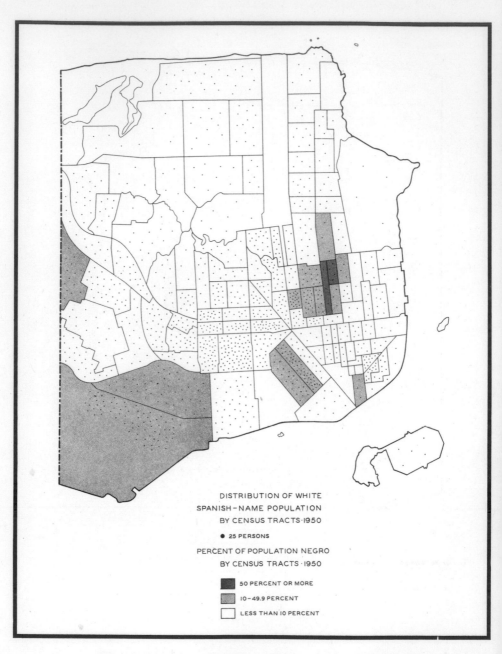

DISTRIBUTION OF WHITE
SPANISH-NAME POPULATION
BY CENSUS TRACTS·1950

● 25 PERSONS

PERCENT OF POPULATION NEGRO
BY CENSUS TRACTS·1950

■ 50 PERCENT OR MORE
▨ 10-49.9 PERCENT
□ LESS THAN 10 PERCENT

Map 18. City of San Francisco, distribution of white Spanish-name population, by census tracts, 1950, and percent of population Negro, by census tracts, 1950.

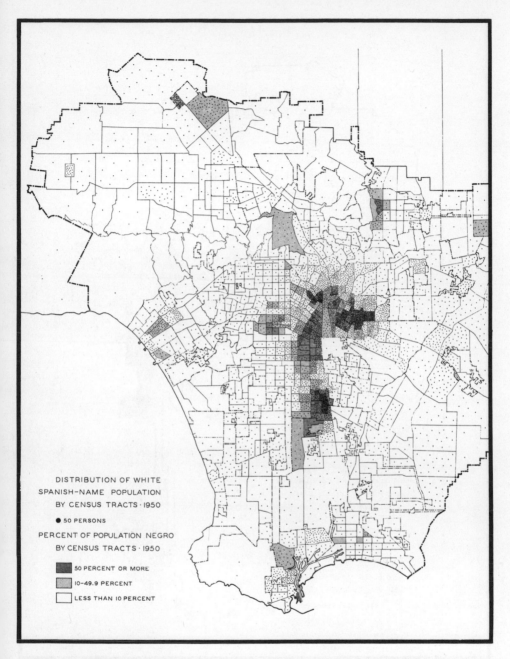

DISTRIBUTION OF WHITE
SPANISH-NAME POPULATION
BY CENSUS TRACTS · 1950

● 50 PERSONS

PERCENT OF POPULATION NEGRO
BY CENSUS TRACTS · 1950

50 PERCENT OR MORE

10-49.9 PERCENT

LESS THAN 10 PERCENT

Map 19. City of Los Angeles and adjacent area, distribution of white
Spanish-name population, by census tracts, 1950, and percent of population Negro, by census tracts, 1950.

[65]

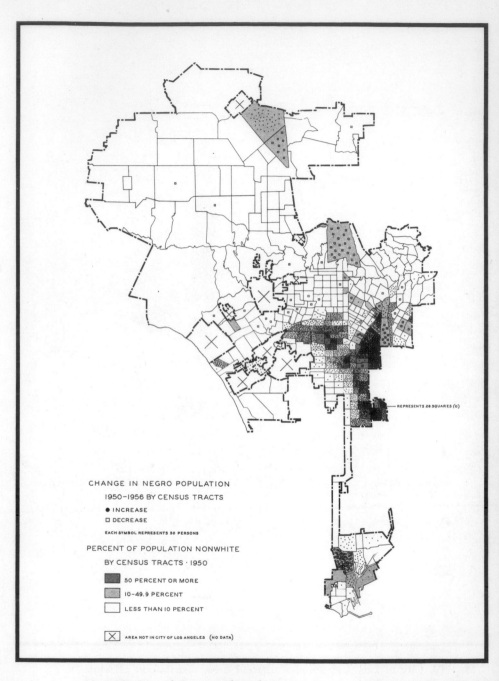

Map 20. City of Los Angeles, change in Negro population 1950-1956, by census tracts, and percent of population nonwhite, by census tracts, 1950.

IV

Determinants of Segregation

The residential segregation of racial groups is part of a larger social process in which groups differentiated according to a variety of criteria are inclined to occupy particular residence areas.[1] The wealthy, the poor, the middle classes, unattached men, various nationality groups, and others as well as racial groups all are apt to live apart from each other. Tendencies to separation by age are also apparent in such phenomena as the young-family suburb and the retirement colony.

The segregation of a group may be voluntary or imposed or it may result from economic weakness. Frequently all three factors are combined. Some groups, notably religious communities, insist on segregating themselves in order to pursue their particular way of life without interference. At the other extreme are many Negroes who would much prefer a nonracial status but are set apart by others. The desire for voluntary segregation by members of a group may be strong or weak; so also may be the forces for imposed segregation. Shared poverty may reinforce the other pressures for segregation, but a degree of economic power usually neutralizes them. Consequently, the segregation of a particular group may be relatively complete or merely a tendency.

The classic pattern of ethnic segregation and desegregation in American cities has been set by the history of many immigrant

---

[1] See Herbert Blumer, "Social Science and the Desegregation Process."

groups. On arrival, the newcomers generally settled in the slums because they could afford only the cheapest housing. But they also drew together to continue in the new environment their accustomed way of life and because they were unfamiliar with American ways. Also, being poor, ignorant, and foreign, they often were regarded by older residents with contempt and hostility. Thus, the immigrants' concentration in ethnic communities was partly economic, partly voluntary, and partly imposed upon them.

In time, the members of each immigrant group, and especially their children, improved their economic status, acquired education, learned English, and adopted American ways of behaving. In a word, they became "Americanized," and as they did so, all the forces holding the ethnic community together weakened. Individuals began moving to nonethnic neighborhoods, in the process ceasing to be identified or to identify themselves as members of an ethnic group. The immigrant colonies, no longer replenished by large-scale immigration, have declined. They still exist but only as remnants, containing, in most cities, merely a fraction of the people of their respective ethnic origins. There are, of course, many variants of this process.

Puerto Ricans.—The present settlement of Puerto Rican migrants in New York City seems essentially to fit this classic pattern.[2] Like many immigrant groups before them, the Puerto Ricans are predominantly impoverished, poorly educated, and possess a distinct language and cultural heritage. They have a tendency to congregate, but at the same time building owners and agents will ordinarily rent to them only in neighborhoods or buildings which have been turned to Puerto Rican occupancy. Puerto Ricans apparently demand, at a given rent level, less space and less building maintenance than other New Yorkers. This behavior, with the large number of Puerto Ricans seeking housing, has furnished strong incentive to many owners of marginally profitable properties to turn their buildings to Puerto Rican occupancy. In the districts where Puerto Ricans settle, moreover, other groups usually move out, leaving space for which the only

---

[2] See Morris Eagle, "The Puerto Ricans in New York City."

claimants are Puerto Ricans. The segregation pattern of Puerto Ricans in New York is thus both voluntary and imposed. Barriers against them are far less rigid than against Negroes. The process of their dispersion and assimilation is already well underway. Real estate agents assert that an educated and prosperous Puerto Rican is not expected to live in a Puerto Rican section but may live wherever he likes. Indeed, it is said, such a person is not thought of as a Puerto Rican but only as an individual with a Spanish name.

Mexican-Americans.—Poverty and cultural traits seem to be dominant factors also in the segregation of Mexican-Americans in the Southwest. Not only are the Mexican-Americans one of the most impoverished groups in the country, but their cultural tradition of rural Mexico also seems to handicap them in the competitive struggle. As a group, they have seemingly lacked drive for achievement. They have not striven for education. Many do not speak English well. Their economic and social progress has been slow and they have largely remained, even in the second generation, at the bottom of the American occupational and income hierarchy.[3]

The Mexican-Americans have suffered a great deal of discrimination, but it has been mainly based on their lower-class character rather than on their ancestry. Indeed, Spanish-Mexican ancestry actually carries prestige in the Southwest when it is associated with the region's romanticized Spanish past and not with Mexican immigrants. Generally, the Mexican-American bearing the marks of middle-class status, like his Puerto Rican counterpart in New York, has little difficulty in living where he chooses.[4] Only a small part of the group, however, has as yet achieved this level.

Oriental groups.—The Chinese and Japanese present a different picture. These groups have highly developed national cultures and are racially distinct. On the Pacific coast, they were subjected for many years to violent hostility, severe discrimination, and oppressive anti-Oriental legislation. In these circumstances they

---

[3] John H. Burma, *Spanish-Speaking Groups in the United States.* See especially chaps. iii and iv.

[4] Jack E. Dodson, "Minority Group Housing in Two Texas Cities."

formed tightly segregated communities, maintaining to a high degree a separate social and economic life.

In the rigid segregation of Oriental groups, external pressures and handicaps imposed upon them have unquestionably played the dominant role. The Oriental Exclusion Acts and denial of eligibility for naturalized citizenship represented to them an announcement from the highest authority that they were not wanted as members of the American community. During the early years of their settlement in California, the Chinese were more widely spread geographically and occupationally than later. Opposite to the universal experience of European immigrant groups, their segregation tightened as they retreated under pressure into the Chinatowns.[5]

For the Japanese, segregation reached the ultimate in their compulsory evacuation from the Pacific coast and resettlement in exclusively Japanese "relocation centers." Beyond the fact of total segregation, this action officially stigmatized all persons of Japanese ancestry as dangerous to the nation in the war with Japan.

In spite of discrimination and segregation, Oriental groups in the United States, especially the Japanese, have made substantial progress economically and socially. Their group solidarity around strongly held cultural values undoubtedly helped to sustain them against the disabling effects of discrimination. They have been remarkably free of the social pathology often characteristic of disadvantaged groups. The Japanese, particularly, have shown a strong drive for achievement, reflected in an educational level superior even to that of the white population, in a substantial economic position in certain industries, and in extensive entry into professional and technical occupations. They have been strongly motivated to homeownership and have made large expenditures for that purpose. However, comparatively few Japanese families of either the first or second generation live in good quality neighborhoods, although many have the economic ability and the desire to do so.[6]

---

[5] Mary R. Coolidge, *Chinese Immigration*, p 259; Eliot G. Mears, *Resident Orientals on the American Pacific Coast*, p. 286.

[6] Harry H. L. Kitano, "Housing of Japanese-Americans in the San Francisco Bay Area."

Anti-Oriental discrimination has been greatly reduced since the end of the war. In the situation of the Chinese, a significant factor has been the formation of many new families, resulting from the permitted immigration of Chinese women. Previously, because of the Oriental Exclusion Acts, the large majority of Chinese men had been unable to marry for lack of women, and this disability contributed to their segregation in the manner of unattached men.[7]

Jews.—Although most residence areas are open to Jews and such Jewish segregation as remains is voluntary or economic, nevertheless, this group has not yet achieved full equality with the white Christian population in choice of residence. Throughout the country there are communities and housing developments closed to Jews. Incomplete surveys have identified such *Judenrein* preserves in New York, New England, Chicago, Detroit, the District of Columbia, Miami, Houston, Denver, Seattle, and elsewhere.[8] The terms "exclusive" or "restricted," as used in real estate advertising usually mean "closed to minorities including Jews." Jewish exclusion is chiefly an upper middle-class phenomenon, and it is mainly Jews of this socioeconomic level that suffer from it.

Negroes.—The segregation of Negroes, like that of other groups, is traceable to low incomes, group cohesion, and external pressures. The crucial difference between their position and that of white ethnic groups is that actions of the dominant majority toward Negroes are based on the visible and unchangeable fact of race. Hence they cannot escape the impact of discrimination by raising their economic level or modifying their social behavior.

Moreover, the social characteristics of Negroes which encourage their segregation are primarily a long-run product of majority rejection rather than a cultural heritage. Alone among all the groups which have peopled the United States, Negroes did not import a foreign culture. Slavery cut them off completely from their homelands and gave them in return only selected elements of American culture suited to their status as slaves—the rudiments

---

[7] Rose Hum Lee, "The Recent Immigrant Chinese Families of the San Francisco–Oakland Area."

[8] Anti-Defamation League of B'nai B'rith, *Rights*, 1(8) (1957), 2(5) (1959).

of English, for example, and Christian religion, but definitely not the virtues of independence or initiative! Nor was there any place in slavery for normal family relationships. A specific legacy of slavery is an unstable family pattern which still persists in the lower class of Negroes and handicaps their efforts to obtain good housing.[9]

Since Emancipation, Negroes have continued to be restricted in many ways. Never permitted to participate fully in American life, they have lagged in acquiring the knowledge, habits, and attitudes necessary for effective social and economic functioning. Sharing a common historical experience and a common subordinate status, Negroes naturally manifest some group solidarity which is reinforced by certain institutions, notably the Negro church. For most Negroes, under existing conditions, the Negro community offers advantages comparable to the attractions of the ethnic colonies for their members. It is a place where the Negro may find cheap housing, where he may freely use such facilities as are available, participate in the social life, and escape the immediate impact of prejudice and discrimination.

Negro segregation developed differently in parts of the South than in the North. It did not exist under slavery, for the slaves ordinarily lived on the properties of their owners. In the older southern cities, a gradual separation of racial residence areas has been part of the broader southern movement for Negro segregation. Racially mixed neighborhoods are not uncommon in some southern cities, but whenever new housing areas are opened up, whether public or private, segregation is always rigidly enforced. White and Negro occupancy of the same neighborhoods does not mean that their respective dwellings are comparable. White-nonwhite differences in quality of housing are wider in the South than in the North, as shown in chapter ix below.

In the North and West and the newer southern cities where Negroes have come as migrants, they have been segregated from the start, in the manner of other newcomer groups. Their poverty, cultural backwardness, and tendency to congregate have probably been the main influences shaping their initial segregation, al-

---

[9] E. Franklin Frazier, *The Negro in the United States,* chap. xiii, "The Negro Family."

though restrictions on the amount of space available have served to overcrowd them. The continuing migration of thousands of poor and uneducated Negroes into northern and western cities strengthens segregation and will, undoubtedly, keep the Negro communities filled and growing for a long time, whether discrimination is severe or mild.

In the past twenty years, as described in detail below, Negroes have made substantial advances in income, range of occupations, and education. Discrimination against them has lessened appreciably in many respects. They have begun to participate more widely than ever before in activities of the general community—in business, professions, labor unions, government, and civic affairs. These changes are reflected in a growing diversification of the Negro population in regard to occupations, income and wealth, and cultural achievement. The differentiation of the Negro population into a variety of groups having little in common save the physical fact of color obviously weakens the disposition of Negroes to live together. A growing number become prepared to live not as members of a racial group but like other Americans of their economic and cultural level. At this point, racial discrimination emerges more and more as the dominant cause of segregation.

Mechanisms of Imposed Segregation

Exclusion.—Efforts to keep minorities out of white neighborhoods are of varying intensity and effectiveness, and there is also considerable variation in the reaction of whites to minority entry. When the pressure of growing Negro populations for more living space first became acute, about the time of World War I, several cities attempted by law to prescribe zones for the residence of white and colored persons, respectively. Although the Supreme Court in those years was sustaining segregation laws on the theory of separate-but-equal, racial zoning was held unconstitutional.[10] As a substitute for zoning, the race-restrictive covenant was developed and widely used. This was a deed restriction running with the land, providing that subject property could not be occupied by members of certain groups. Covenants enjoyed a

[10] *Buchanan* v. *Warley*, 245 U. S. 60 (1917). For fuller discussion of legal aspects of segregation, see chap. xv, "Race Discrimination and the Law."

considerable vogue during the 1920's and 1930's. They were promoted by property owner associations, real estate boards, even by the Federal Housing Administration, and drawn to exclude not only Negroes but also Orientals, Jews, Mexicans, Armenians, or, as sometimes drawn, "any race other than the Caucasian." [11] For many years the courts regarded racial covenants as a purely private matter, like real estate covenants of other kinds, but in 1948 the Supreme Court decided that their enforcement by courts, being government action, was prohibited by the Constitution.[12]

Lacking any legal foundation, the means used to exclude minorities from residence areas are entirely extralegal or illegal. One method, very widespread, is the refusal of property owners in white neighborhoods to sell or rent housing to members of minority groups. On occasion, property owners in an area will enter into a formal agreement to this effect; usually, no agreement is necessary but owners merely follow established custom backed by informal sanctions. In most all-white neighborhoods, to sell or rent to a nonwhite would be considered a serious offense to the neighborhood. An owner, consequently, who is considerate of his neighbors or who values their good opinion would not wish to introduce a nonwhite into the neighborhood.

Property owners, however, are not all equally concerned about their neighborhood or their neighbors' opinions. Moreover, an individual owner may find himself under countervailing pressures. In the Detroit neighborhood studied by Mayer, the first sale to a Negro was made by an army officer being transferred to another post and under the necessity of selling both quickly and for a good price in order to avoid a loss.[13] In this case we see both a (presumably) limited responsiveness to neighborhood opinion and financial pressure to sell. In a similar instance, a woman desperate to sell, with no white buyer in sight and a firm offer from a Negro, announced that her choice was either to lose her

---

[11] Herman H. Long and Charles S. Johnson, *People versus Property;* Robert C. Weaver, *The Negro Ghetto,* chap. xiii.

[12] *Shelley* v. *Kraemer,* 334 U. S. 1 (1948). A scholarly study of the background and litigation leading to this landmark decision on residence rights is Clement E. Vose, *Caucasians Only: The Supreme Court, the NAACP, and the Restrictive Covenant Cases.*

[13] Albert J. Mayer, "Russel Woods: Change without Conflict. A Case Study of Neighborhood Racial Transition in Detroit."

friends or her money, and she was afraid it would have to be her friends.[14] In a few cases, individual property owners have sold to nonwhites because they considered the ideal of racial justice superior to the code of the neighborhood. And sometimes sales are made to nonwhites deliberately to spite neighbors.

The policies of business groups which control the production, financing, and marketing of housing lend major support to the maintenance of segregation patterns. Segregation is nowhere more complete than in the new subdivisions where the initial occupancy of whole areas is controlled by private builders. Mortgage lenders frequently refuse housing credit to nonwhites who propose to purchase homes in white neighborhoods. Real estate brokers customarily will negotiate the sale or rental of dwellings to non-whites only in areas considered open to minority occupancy.

When a minority person finds a house to buy or rent in a white neighborhood, pressures are often exerted to discourage him from completing the transaction or to induce him to move out if he has already acquired the property. In the Detroit neighborhood mentioned above, the first Negro home buyer resold to the property owners' association and moved away, but it was only two weeks until a second Negro purchaser appeared on the scene. In a widely publicized California case, a Chinese, having contracted to buy a house, withdrew after a neighborhood vote on his acceptability went against him.[15] Persuasion shades easily into intimidation, ranging from threats to arson, bombings, and mob violence. Negro homes have been bombed in Birmingham, Atlanta, Miami, Dallas, Houston, Chicago, Cleveland, Los Angeles, and a dozen or more other cities.[16] Throughout the South, the Southern Regional Council reported more than forty bombings during a year and a half in 1951-1952.[17] Violent intimidation

---

[14] Chester Rapkin and William G. Grigsby, *The Demand for Housing in Racially Mixed Areas. A Study of the Nature of Neighborhood Change*, Appendix B, "When Negroes Came to Clearview."

[15] Bernard Taper, "South S. F. Area Votes to Exclude a Chinese Family," *San Francisco Chronicle*, February 17, 1952; Earl Raab, "Where Bigotry Won an Election," *The ADL Bulletin*, March, 1952.

[16] Robert A. Thompson, Hylan Lewis, and Davis McEntire, "Atlanta and Birmingham: A Comparative Study in Negro Housing"; Charles Abrams, *Forbidden Neighbors*, pp. 81-90 *et passim*.

[17] Southern Regional Council, "Blight, Bigotry, and Bombs," *The New South*, July, 1952.

seems to be resorted to more readily in the South than elsewhere, but it is not lacking in other parts of the country. Both Chicago and Detroit have been the scenes of spectacular racial violence around housing. Reports of the Chicago Commission on Human Relations list numerous attacks on Negro houses including window breaking, flooding, and arson.[18] The movement of a few Negro families into a public housing project on Chicago's South Side resulted in a virtually continuous riot lasting more than three years and requiring assignment of more than a thousand police to keep order.[19] In near-by Cicero, a violent mob, assembled to prevent a Negro family from moving into an apartment house, was controlled only after the Illinois governor declared martial law and called out the National Guard.[20] In Pennsylvania, when the first Negro family bought a house in all-white Levittown, crowds numbering in the hundreds gathered nightly in front of the house, shouting abuse and occasionally throwing stones. Convoys of demonstrators would drive slowly past the house late at night, blowing their horns and playing their car radios at full blast.[21] It is reported that the seller, in this case, was fired from his job shortly after his name appeared in the newspapers.[22]

In the total picture of minority movement into new areas, violent episodes like those described are comparatively infrequent. In most cities law enforcement agencies will protect minority people in the lawful occupancy of their homes. But terror, to be effective, does not need to touch every individual directly. Occasional object lessons are sufficient. A nonwhite person considering a move into territory where members of his group do not already live knows that he is apt to face unpleasantness of some kind— probably no more than cold aloofness with an occasional insult

---

[18] See, for example, Chicago Commission on Human Relations, *Six Month Report, July 1, 1956–December 31, 1956,* listing thirteen acts of vandalism against Negro property during the second half of 1956.

[19] Chicago Commission on Human Relations, *The Trumbull Park Homes Disturbances, A Chronological Report, August 4, 1953 to June 30, 1955.* (1956); *New York Times,* February 24, 1957.

[20] Abrams, *Forbidden Neighbors,* pp. 103-106.

[21] *New York Times,* August 15, 20, 21; September 19, 25, 1957.

[22] Drayton Bryant and Thomas E. Colgan, "Some Problems of the Pioneer Family in Changing Racial Patterns," *Journal of Intergroup Relations,* I, no. 2 (July, 1958), 59-67.

but, depending on the location and circumstances, possibly something worse. This expectation, unquestionably, must play an important part in leading nonwhites to limit their housing demand to the segregated areas and adjacent zones where the support of their group is close at hand. Interviews with Negroes and with Japanese concerning their attitudes toward living away from the racial community have elicited the frequent responses that they did not wish to be "pioneers" or to live "where they were not wanted."

In the past, the desperate need of Negroes for shelter has driven them to face dynamite and mobs and many lesser hazards. But the expansion of minority areas in recent years has widened the housing alternatives available to Negroes and correspondingly reduced their incentive to seek housing away from the Negro community. We see here the complex interplay of voluntary segregation and exclusion in determining the actual residence pattern of a minority group.

White withdrawal.—All the pressures and devices for exclusion have not prevented the spread of minorities into new areas. But often when nonwhites enter a white neighborhood, the whites depart, leaving the area to become an extension of the segregated minority community. The transition from white to nonwhite occupancy may be rapid or slow. Often, in the past, the anxiety of whites to get away has resembled a panic, with everyone trying to leave as quickly as possible. There are many areas, however, which have shifted gradually to minority occupancy over a period of years, and this pattern seems now to be more common than panic flight. In a significant number of cases, neighborhoods entered by nonwhites have continued to attract whites as well, thus prolonging, perhaps indefinitely, the mixed character of the area.

For a rapid change to occur, not only must whites be anxious to leave, but there must be strong demand by the minority to enter the neighborhood. Consequently, it is most apt to occur in areas of relatively inexpensive housing adjacent to minority concentrations and in periods when the supply of housing available to the minority group has lagged seriously behind the demand. During the last war the Negro areas in many cities became extremely overcrowded, but expansion was inhibited because the whites in adjacent areas had few alternatives. After the war, the combination of a building boom for whites and the pent-up housing demand of Negroes led to rapid and large-scale racial succession in areas adjacent to congested Negro districts.

In recent years, as the pent-up demand of Negroes for housing has been largely satisfied, one of the main pressures to rapid transition has been reduced. In some cities, Negroes have penetrated throughout such wide areas that there would seem to be scant possibility of complete racial turnover for many years.

The transition of neighborhoods from white to nonwhite occupancy, once the initial break has been made, is generally an uncontrolled process, with the outcome dependent on market forces. In Atlanta, however, the racial occupancy of certain disputed areas has been a subject of organized negotiation between Negro and white communities. Negro leadership in Atlanta has carried on since the war a vigorous and effective campaign to obtain better housing for Negroes, including the development of new residential areas.[23] Certain of the expansion areas desired by Negroes were violently contested. To insure peaceful transition, a biracial group was formed, unofficial, but known as the Mayor's Committee. This group, with support from both white and Negro communities, negotiated the boundaries of Negro expansion; its decisions, in the main, were respected by white and Negro populations. Areas which it designated for Negro occupancy ceased to be contested and were promptly evacuated by resident whites. In the nature of the bargaining process, not all gains were on one side. In return for peaceful possession of certain desired territory, the Negro leadership agreed not to press expansion beyond certain limits, agreements which later it had cause to regret. Intensified segregation is another price which Atlanta Negroes have had to pay for added living space.

Motivations of White Behavior

Exclusion and withdrawal, which result in imposing segregation upon minority groups, are commonly attributed to the racial

---

[23] Thompson, Lewis, and McEntire, "Atlanta and Birmingham. . . ."

prejudice held by white people.[24] That racial prejudice is very widespread in the white population and that it affects behavior are apparent to all. Yet the diversity of existing racial occupancy patterns, the varying resistance of neighborhoods to minority entry, and the differing courses of events which follow on the movement of minority families cannot be explained by any known or supposed variations in racial attitudes. However, before considering the other factors that seem to influence white behavior in interracial housing situations, we may examine the evidence concerning attitudes.

Changing racial attitudes.—During the past twenty years, there has occurred a marked change in public sentiment toward segregation in housing, according to the evidence of national opinion polls. Surveys before World War II reported white Americans overwhelmingly opposed to racially mixed neighborhoods. Recent polls, on a national basis, find people about evenly divided between those who indicate willingness to live in mixed neighborhoods and those who express opposition.

In 1939, a national poll by the Roper organization for *Fortune* found more than four-fifths of white Americans favoring segregation.[25] A change became apparent during the war. Four national surveys conducted between 1942 and 1948 found only about two-thirds of white persons interviewed voicing opposition to mixed neighborhoods.[26] In 1956, two independent nation-wide polls conducted by Ben Gaffin and Associates for the *Catholic Digest*[27]

---

[24] This section draws heavily on two unpublished research reports prepared for the Commission on Race and Housing: Clair Selltiz and Stuart W. Cook, "Studies in the Social Psychology of Race and Housing"; Helen E. Amerman, "Studies of Attitudes toward Housing and Race."

[25] Eugene L. Horowitz, " 'Race' Attitudes"; and unpublished tabulation supplied by courtesy of Elmo Roper.

[26] National Opinion Research Center, University of Chicago, unpublished tabulations covering questions from surveys conducted in 1942 and 1944, supplied by Richard D. Johnson, librarian. Results of the 1942 survey are referred to in Herbert H. Hyman and Paul B. Sheatsley, "Attitudes Toward Desegregation." Unpublished tabulation by Elmo Roper, covering results of a national survey of labor groups in 1942. Elmo Roper, "A Study of Anti-Minority Sentiment in the United States," prepared for the Anti-Defamation League of B'nai B'rith, New York, 1948 (unpublished).

[27] Ben Gaffin and Associates, Inc., "How to Solve Our Race Problem: Opinions of White and Negro, North and South." Major findings published in the *Catholic Digest*, June through December, 1956. See especially the December issue, pp.

and by the National Opinion Research Center[28] reported a further rise in stated acceptance of integration. The major findings of the two surveys were almost identical: according to one (Gaffin), 52 percent of all white respondents said they would be willing to live in the same general neighborhood with Negroes; NORC found 51 percent of its white persons interviewed saying it would make no difference to them if a Negro with the same income and education as theirs moved into their block.

The polls show the expected regional differences in attitudes but even in the South they find more acceptance of mixed neighborhoods in 1956 than appeared nationally in the prewar surveys. Both of the 1956 surveys report clear majorities of white northerners (59 percent and 58 percent) expressing willingness to live in a neighborhood where there are Negroes. Among southern whites, 32 percent said they would be willing to live in the same neighborhood with Negroes (Gaffin); 38 percent said it would make no difference to them if a Negro with the same education and experience moved into their block (NORC). Both in the North and in the South, young people were more acceptive of mixed neighborhoods than older ones, a fact which suggests probable continuance of the trend toward acceptance of integration.

The shift of opinion in the polls is consistent with other evidence of a general trend toward increasing tolerance of minority groups. In particular, it is consistent with the declining frequency of panic reactions to nonwhite penetration of white neighborhoods, as noted previously. But the poll findings raise more questions than they answer. With the definite majority of northern whites stating willingness to live in areas with Negroes, exclusion barriers should be weaker and mixed neighborhoods more stable than in fact they seem to be, if attitudes were the controlling factor. If a third of white Southerners are willing to accept Negro neighbors, as they say they are, why should the trend to segregation run so strongly in such a liberal southern city as Atlanta? Plainly, it is not attitudes alone that determine action.

13-17, "Where Shall Negroes Live?" An unpublished volume of detailed tables was made available to the present study through the courtesy of Mr. Gaffin.
    [28] Reported in Hyman and Sheatsley, *Scientific American*, 195(6):35-39.

Discussing motives to out-migration from the Russel Woods neighborhood of Detroit, Mayer writes that the departing whites, largely Jews and "intellectuals," ". . . have little prejudice themselves. They believe that Negroes and whites can live together, they are aware of the fact that the incoming Negroes are people much like themselves, they know they are well-to-do and well educated, who will be good neighbors. . . ." The racial liberals, Mayer says, have been slower to move out than other white elements, yet they move.[29] In another neighborhood, a survey showed "Evidence of a desire for interracial living, of an ability to get along, of healthy interracial attitudes," but five years after the change had begun, the population was predominantly colored.[30]

Merton has formulated the relation between prejudice and discrimination in a two-dimensional classification that is relevant to understanding behavior in mixed housing situations.[31] There are those who adhere to the creed of equal opportunity in both belief and practice. Neither prejudiced nor given to discrimination, this type Merton labels the "unprejudiced non-discriminator." There are others who, though not prejudiced, "still support or even engage in discrimination when it is the more expedient course." Probably a large part of the population falls in this category, the "unprejudiced discriminator." Similarly, reasons of expediency may often cause prejudiced people to refrain from carrying their prejudices into action, hence the type, "prejudiced non-discriminator." Finally, there is the "prejudiced discriminator . . . the bigot pure and unashamed," whose discriminatory behavior is consistent with his beliefs.

Merton's types can be found in many a racially changing neighborhood. But in addition, behavior concerning housing involves

[29] Mayer, "Russel Woods: Change without Conflict. . . ."

[30] S. Joseph Fauman, "Housing Discrimination, Changing Neighborhoods, and Public Schools."

[31] Robert K. Merton, "Discrimination and the American Creed." Other sociologists who have stressed the inadequacy of attitudes to account for interracial behavior are Herbert Blumer, *Social Problems*, Vol. 3, no. 3, (1955), 61-63; Herbert Blumer, *The Annals*, Vol. 304 (March, 1956), 137-143; Joseph D. Lohman and Dietrich C. Reitzes, *American Journal of Sociology*, LVIII (1952), 241-246; Herman H. Long, *American Journal of Sociology*, LVII (1951), 15-19; Arnold M. Rose, *Social Problems*, Vol. 4, no. 2 (October, 1956), 173-176.

considerations that are not racial at all. To explain all move-ins or move-outs from a given area in terms of reaction to the area's racial make-up would be a gross error.

From all evidence, the decisions of white people concerning residence in neighborhoods entered by minority groups are conditioned by three main sets of factors, in addition to attitudes. These are the attractiveness of the area and its housing relative to existing alternatives, the number and characteristics of the resident or incoming minority group, and social pressures.

Character of changing neighborhoods.—Many of the areas entered by nonwhites are old and deteriorated. Their residents have an obvious, strong incentive to move in search of better housing when they can afford to do so. Many other areas not blighted but containing good, substantial dwellings have nevertheless declined in desirability relative to newer districts. The Russel Woods neighborhood of Detroit is characteristic of this type. Once fashionable, it had moved well down the scale of neighborhood prestige before Negroes began moving in. The houses are of an older style of architecture, kitchens are not modern, the two- or three-story design is no longer popular. Neighborhood facilities and services had declined. The near-by shopping street had deteriorated as the better stores moved to newer shoppings centers. The quality of the school was threatened. The decline of Russel Woods was not so much absolute as relative. It was still a substantial, middle-class neighborhood, but the new suburbs offered modern styles, improvements, and social prestige highly attractive to many residents of the older area. Mayer suggests that many of the departing residents of Russel Woods were not so much "pushed out" by the incoming Negroes as "pulled out" by the superior attractions of competing new neighborhoods.[32] A similar judgment, undoubtedly, would apply to many neighborhoods not yet blighted but obsolescent.

Characteristic of many changing neighborhoods is a falling standard of institutional services and facilities. Most crucial of these, in middle-class neighborhoods, is the school. The families who are most liberal on the racial issues are also apt to place a high value on education of their children. Although they may

---

[32] Mayer, "Russel Woods: Change without Conflict. . . ."

have no reluctance to living in a mixed neighborhood or even prefer it, if an influx of deprived children lowers the quality of the school, they will be pressed to leave.[33]

If the disadvantages of a neighborhood cause residents to leave, it is equally true and demonstrated that interracial neighborhoods and housing developments offering positive advantages of housing or location can attract white residents.

Racial proportions.—It is generally recognized that as the number and proportion of nonwhites in an area increase, the proportion of white families who will consider the area as a place of residence declines. Studies have identified a significant number of neighborhoods that have absorbed one or a few minority families without provoking the resident whites to depart or noticeably discouraging others from coming in.[34] In other instances, the arrival of a few nonwhite families has signaled the beginning of an overturn in occupancy of the neighborhood. In still other circumstances, racial transition sets in only after a considerable lapse of time from the entry of the first nonwhites. The differences, so far as white reactions are concerned, seem to lie in differing expectations concerning the future racial composition of the neighborhood. When white residents or potential residents expect a neighborhood to "go Negro," they prepare to abandon it, for there are few whites, prejudiced or not, who are willing to live in a minority community. The situation envisaged by the 1956 opinion polls was one of a few Negroes in an otherwise white neighborhood. Had respondents been asked whether they would be willing to live in a predominantly Negro area, the percentage of affirmative replies would undoubtedly have been much smaller.

There has been considerable discussion in the literature of the "tip point"—the point at which a rising proportion of nonwhites will cause whites to abandon an area. Various writers have placed this critical point at nonwhite proportions ranging from 10 to 60

---

[33] *Ibid.* See also cases described by Fauman, *Journal of Social Issues.* XIII, no. 4.

[34] State of Connecticut, Commission on Civil Rights, *Private Interracial Neighborhoods in Connecticut,* by Henry G. Stetler (Hartford, 1957); Davis McEntire, "A Study of Racial Attitudes in Neighborhoods Infiltrated by Nonwhites," *Bay Area Real Estate Report,* Second Quarter, 1955; Arnold M. Rose, Frank Atelsek, and Lawrence McDonald, "Neighborhood Reactions to Isolated Negro Residents: An Alternative to Invasion and Succession."

percent.[35] The evidence indicates, however, that no one magnitude can properly be said to be the crucial one, for the meaning of any given number of nonwhites will be defined differently in different circumstances. Under certain conditions, a single nonwhite family may be enough to generate expectations of racial change. In Russel Woods, according to Mayer, residents became convinced the neighborhood was "going Negro" after the third sale of a house to Negroes within a short period. Russel Woods was squarely in the path of Negro expansion and already bordered by Negro residence on three sides.

The departure of whites from a transitional area is further stimulated when the incoming group is of lower socioeconomic status than the older residents. Even a relatively unprejudiced middle-class person is apt to find it hard to tolerate lower-class behavior, especially if his children are involved. There is one expedient by which a low-income group can compete for housing in a middle-class neighborhood, and that is by crowding (spreading the rent charge) or accepting a substandard level of services and maintenance. Not infrequently, owners of marginal buildings find their most profitable alternative in "turning" to low-income minority occupancy on the basis of reduced services and an increased number of rent payers in the same space. This has been a common feature of Puerto Rican housing in New York City and of the housing of in-migrant Negroes in Chicago. As a result, in many a middle-class although perhaps decaying neighborhood, the residents have awakened to discover that a slum had been created in their midst, almost overnight.

White exodus is often accelerated by expectations of white property owners of a fall in the value of properties. The same fear is an important psychological support of exclusion tactics. Motivated by this anticipation, whites hasten to "beat the trend" and in so doing, by glutting the market, sometimes bring about the very result which they had feared.

Expectations of racial transition have been called a "self-fulfilling prophecy." [36] People predict that a neighborhood is going to

---

[35] Robert C. Weaver, "Integration in Public and Private Housing"; Abrams, *Forbidden Neighbors*, p. 311.
[36] Eleanor P. Wolf, "The Invasion-Succession Sequence as a Self-Fulfilling

change racially, and then act in a manner to make the prediction come true. But this prediction, it must be noted, is made in certain conditions and in others is not made. When it is known that a minority group is in great need of housing, and when a neighborhood (1) is near an expanding area of minority concentration, (2) contains housing priced within the reach of a substantial part of the minority group, or (3) possesses few advantages that would make it unusually attractive to whites, it is likely to be considered a good candidate for racial change. This expectation is fortified by observation of events in similarly situated neighborhoods. On the other hand, in neighborhoods remote from centers of minority concentration, where whites aspire to live, and with relatively high-priced houses, the entry of a minority family or two may be resented by some but rarely will cause the residents to anticipate an influx of the minority group. What matters ultimately, of course, is how home buyers or renters evaluate the prospects of a neighborhood. Residents may hasten a transition process by fleeing or retard it by accepting minority neighbors as they would any other newcomers. But unless a neighborhood can attract a continuing inflow of white homeseekers, it must tend inevitably to become a minority district in the course of normal turnover.

The exodus of whites from a neighborhood which nonwhites have entered is often regarded as an unthinking reaction, driven by prejudice and fears. Two professional workers in intergroup relations write, for example: "There are no really rational reasons why this process [panic flight] takes place . . . the whites fall prey to the folklore of intolerance . . . ignorance . . . unreasonable and stereotyped thinking . . ." [37] On this assumption, intergroup relations agencies frequently strive to prevent racial transition by appealing to white residents to be calm, to think, to consider facts. Undoubtedly, the flight of whites from the presence of a minority is sometimes unreasoning, though not necessarily so. There are indeed rational reasons for wanting to avoid living in a

---

Prophecy," *Journal of Social Issues*, XIII, no. 4 (1957), 7-20. On the role of expectations in white decisions to move, see Robert K. Merton, "The Social Psychology of Housing."

[37] John McDermott and Dennis Clark, "Helping the Panic Neighborhood," *Interracial Review*, August, 1955, p. 33.

minority community—reasons that are shared by many members of the minority groups as well as by whites.

Social pressures.—The problem of housing and race is above all a social problem. The individual concerned is less free than in many other areas of life to make decisions according to whatever personal feelings he may have. His choices are shaped and limited by pressures that converge upon him from family and friends, neighbors, other associates, and the whole community.

A property owner in an all-white area, for example, knows that he must balance the good opinion of his neighbors against any advantages expected from selling to a minority buyer. However, after a neighborhood is socially defined as a changing one, the situation reverses. Pressures against sales to the minority are replaced by pressures for sales. Neighbors expect each other to sell; real estate agents who formerly played their part in keeping nonwhites out now solicit listings for sales to nonwhites. The racial attitudes of a property owner may have changed not at all, but he finds himself in a very different social situation.

Some of the strongest forces working to produce white decisions against residence in mixed neighborhoods revolve around social status. Where a person lives is an important indicator of his position in society; moreover, the residents of any neighborhood are generally presumed to stand on more or less the same social level. In any city, the various neighborhoods are quite closely graded according to social prestige; those occupied by nonwhites are almost always near the bottom of the scale, both because of their objective characteristics and the inferior social status accorded their occupants. The entry of nonwhites into a white neighborhood is, therefore, usually viewed as a threat to the status of the neighborhood and its residents. In considering whether to remain in or to enter a racially mixed area, a white person must weigh the implications for his own social standing. What will his friends and associates think of him? Will he be regarded as living in an inferior neighborhood? Will his own status be lowered by the fact of minority neighbors? If so, how much do these things matter?

People vary, of course, in the value they place on social prestige; moreover, the standards and criteria of status are not the same in all sections of the population. The social level of the nonwhite population is rising. Nevertheless, the association between nonwhite race or color and low status is profound and widespread. People who are sensitive to the opinions of others, or responsive to the dominant cultural standards, will be pressed to avoid mixed neighborhoods, whether they are racially prejudiced or not.

Conclusions

From the complex of forces and factors analyzed in this chapter emerges a picture of interrelationship, variation, and change. Many factors work together to shape the patterns of racial residence. Neither the existing segregation of any group nor the situation in any community can be adequately explained in terms of a single causative force. The factors at work are combined in a variety of ways and have differential impacts. They produce, therefore, widely varying situations and outcomes. Moreover, the determining factors of segregation are themselves changing.

At present, a major force for segregation is the diverse currents of population flow, leading to accumulation of nonwhites in the central cities and expansion of all-white communities in the suburbs, and supporting expectations of racial succession once nonwhites gain access to an urban neighborhood. Other changes in progress are weakening segregation barriers. Outstanding among these are the rising economic capacity and cultural level of the segregated groups, the shift in attitudes among the white population, and the changing role of law and government.

V

Social and Economic Consequences
of Residential Segregation

In considering the consequences of residential segregation, a fundamental distinction must be drawn between voluntary and imposed segregation. The voluntary congregation of people who seek each other's society is an exercise of freedom; if it carries disadvantages, those concerned may choose whether to pay the price of living with the group. Economic-class segregation is also a different matter because individuals may escape it by improving their economic condition. But segregation that is enforced upon a group is a deprivation of freedom—a deprivation especially onerous when its basis is the unalterable fact of race or ancestry. An eminent authority has defined personal liberty as "the power of locomotion, of changing situation, or removing one's person to whatsoever places one's own inclination may direct, without imprisonment or restraint, unless by due course of law." [1] This is the freedom abridged by compulsory residential segregation. Because it is basic to the enjoyment of many other liberties and opportunities, its restriction has far-reaching consequences which touch vir-

---

[1] Blackstone Commentaries 134, quoted in dissenting opinion of Justice Harlan, *Plessy* v. *Ferguson*, 163 U. S. 537 (1896).

tually every aspect of life of the segregated group and of the relations between them and the dominant majority.[2]

As previously described, residence restrictions are applied with varying intensity against different groups, and the subject groups vary in their response to restrictions. The Negro is everywhere the most severely limited, and also, because of his history, he has fewer cultural defenses against discrimination than the Oriental groups or Jews. Hence, the Negro suffers most from the consequences described here, which are felt in reduced measure by other groups.

Basis for Other Forms of Segregation

As Charles S. Johnson has remarked, "racial segregation in residential areas provides the basic structure for other forms of institutional segregation." [3] A group segregated in residence is necessarily segregated in schools, recreation, and other facilities organized on an area basis. Discriminatory in itself, residential segregation permits and stimulates other forms of discrimination. When a minority group is physically isolated, differential treatment follows almost as a matter of course. In the South, although legal segregation is justified as separate-but-equal, the separate facilities provided for Negroes are rarely if ever equal. The inequality of Negro schools is notorious, but as Myrdal observes, "Virtually the whole range of other publicly administered facilities—such as hospitals, libraries, parks, and similar recreational facilities—are much poorer for Negroes than they are for whites. . . . Water provision, sewage and garbage removal, street cleaning, street lighting, street paving, police protection and everything else is neglected or withheld while vice is often allowed." [4]

In the North and West, public facilities for Negro neighborhoods are more neglected than deliberately withheld. Often where Negroes have inherited the oldest districts, the school buildings and other public institutions are old and worn out. In

---

[2] In the preparation of this chapter, I have made extensive use of an unpublished research memorandum prepared for the Commission on Race and Housing by Jitsuichi Masuoka and Preston Valien of Fisk University, "Social Consequences of Racial Residential Segregation."

[3] Charles S. Johnson, *Patterns of Negro Segregation*, p. 8.

[4] Gunnar Myrdal, *An American Dilemma*, pp. 335, 643.

these heavily built-up and congested areas, parks and playgrounds are few.[5]

Mexican-Americans in the Southwest, although suffering less discrimination than Negroes, usually receive even fewer public facilities in their neighborhoods. On the West Side of San Antonio, one of the largest Mexican communities in the country, a recent study reports "many examples of what are called 'corrals,' in which up to twenty or thirty families share one pit privy and a single cold-water tap. There are great numbers of shacks on rutted, wholly unimproved streets, without inside plumbing or running water." [6] These conditions are widespread and probably more aggravated in the smaller towns and rural districts than in the larger cities. Throughout the Southwest, great numbers of poor Mexican-Americans live in all-Mexican shack towns, often called camps, that are wholly lacking in paved streets or modern sewerage facilities and are subject to flooding in wet weather. Conditions in these Mexican slums are a serious health menace.[7]

Law enforcement is usually less strict in minority neighborhoods than elsewhere. Often zoning and building laws are not enforced, leaving residents unprotected against conversions and land uses destructive of residential quality. Vice and petty crime that would not be tolerated in good neighborhoods often flourish in the Negro districts.

Against public neglect the residents of a neighborhood have ordinarily two remedies. They can move away or they can act, singly or together, to make demands upon the public authorities— demands enforceable by political process. Well-kept neighborhoods usually have some kind of defensive organization such as a property owners' association, or if not, the residents can be counted on to organize informally to repel a threat or obtain a benefit. Such organization is essential, for a high standard of public services and strict enforcement of protective laws is seldom

[5] Charles Abrams, *Forbidden Neighbors*, pp. 74-75; James Ford, *Slums and Housing*, I, p. 436; T. J. Woofter, Jr., *Negro Problems in Cities*, p. 281; Arnold and Caroline Rose, *America Divided*, pp. 160-161.

[6] Jack E. Dodson, "Minority Group Housing in Two Texas Cities."

[7] John H. Burma, *Spanish-Speaking Groups in the United States*, pp. 88-92. See also Pauline R. Kibbe, *Latin Americans in Texas*, pp. 130-132 *et passim.*

conferred upon a neighborhood by external benevolence; generally it is achieved by the watchful insistence of neighborhood
residents.

Neither remedy is fully available to the members of segregated
minority groups. They are not free to move away from undesirable
conditions. Organized action for neighborhood defense presup-
poses a degree of economic strength, cultural development, and
political experience not yet achieved by most Negroes, Puerto
Ricans, or Mexican-Americans. In much of the South, moreover,
the disfranchisement of Negroes renders them powerless to influence public officials or to protect themselves against governmental
discrimination.

Where Negroes vote and have developed leadership and some
political strength, as in Atlanta, they have been able to gain
municipal recognition of their housing needs and racially neutral
law enforcement, even under segregation.[8] In some Mexican-
American communities of California, organization and political
participation have brought paved streets and other public improvements in long-neglected neighborhoods.[9] On the whole,
however, organized effort for neighborhood defense and improvement is little developed in minority communities.

Effects on Housing

The supply of housing available to segregated groups is determined primarily not by their demand expressed in the market
but by the interplay of forces determining their segregation pattern. Minority individuals gain access to a wider range of possibilities only as the housing supply designated for the group as a
whole expands. Regulated by factors other than market demand,
additions to the minority housing supply may be too little or too

---

[8] Robert A. Thompson, Hylan Lewis, and Davis McEntire, "Atlanta and Birmingham: A Comparative Study in Negro Housing."

[9] California Federation for Civic Unity, *Get Out if You Can, the Saga of Sal si
Puedes,* an account by Fred W. Ross of an American Friends Service Committee
project among Mexican-Americans in a northern California Community (San
Francisco, 1953). Harry Lawton, "Casa Blanca—Tangible Example of Civic
Pride at Work," *Riverside Press-Enterprise,* August 18, 1956.

much in relation to the group's demand for housing at any given time. Too little means scarcity; too much raises the familiar threat of falling property values.

The housing for which minority homeseekers are permitted to compete is not only a small but on the whole a very inferior part of the total housing supply. Thus restricted, nonwhites receive poorer housing than do whites, even when they pay the same rents or purchase prices. The differential is very wide in the South, but it exists throughout the country and through the whole range of rents. There are great numbers of nonwhite families who can afford only cheap housing; yet the dwellings they receive are poorer than need be on the basis of rent alone. This problem is examined further in chapter ix below.

Disadvantage in obtaining mortgage credit is another consequence for minority home buyers of the inferior areas in which they live. In old and run-down districts, many mortgage-lending institutions will not lend at all. Mortgage credit, when available in these areas, is customarily extended in smaller amounts (relative to values) and for shorter repayment periods than loans in preferred residential areas. In these practices, mortgage lenders are discriminating against high-risk areas and not necessarily against a racial group, but the group is nonetheless disadvantaged. Direct racial discrimination occurs when lenders refuse mortgage credit to a nonwhite trying to buy a house in a white area. Where nonwhites have been able to gain access to good quality residence areas, their disadvantage in obtaining mortgage loans tends to disappear. A fuller discussion of mortgage lending practices is reserved to chapter xiii below.[10]

The most favorable terms of mortgage credit, made possible by government insurance or guarantee, have been available chiefly on new development housing in suburban locations. Because nonwhites are rarely permitted to buy into new developments (except those intended for minority occupancy), they have less than equal opportunity to share in the benefits of government mortgage insurance.

---

[10] See also Chester Rapkin and William G. Grigsby, *The Demand for Housing in Racially Mixed Areas. A Study of the Nature of Neighborhood Change.*

Minority families are often obliged to occupy housing ill-suited to their particular needs or to family use generally. Common in many areas which have passed from white to nonwhite or (in New York City) to Puerto Rican occupancy are large, old houses built for the conditions of an earlier day and for a higher-income group than the present occupants. Often they present a rather stately and graceful appearance. But even if structurally sound, these old houses were obsolescent in the white market before the minority group arrived, and many have reached the stage of heavy maintenance costs. The new occupants can make use of these old-style houses only by sharing them among several families or individuals, although they were never designed nor equipped for multifamily occupancy. Structural alterations and additional facilities needed to create livable smaller units are sometimes provided, but often the space sharing is accomplished by makeshift arrangements, placing many families in quarters without proper cooking or sanitary facilities. One type of conversion, frequent in New York and some other large cities, is the rooming house where entire families will occupy a single room without private plumbing.

Lack of space is probably the deficiency of minority-group housing most harmful in its impact on family living. Adequate space is generally recognized as an indispensable requisite of good housing, whether the buildings be new or old, well or poorly equipped. A good family life is hardly possible unless there is space for carrying on and separating different activities, and for individual privacy. To maintain cleanliness and order is extremely difficult in cramped quarters used by too many people for too many purposes. The constant association of household members, unrelieved by opportunity for privacy, is apt to generate more tension than affection. There is evidence that crowding may be damaging to mental health and to the personality formation of children.[11] Persons with concern for family life, when they are in the market for a house, try to pay particular attention to factors

---

[11] American Public Health Association, Committee on the Hygiene of Housing, *Basic Principles of Healthful Housing*, p. 16; F. Stuart Chapin, "The Psychology of Housing," quoting J. S. Plant, psychiatrist, and other authorities; Chapin, "Some Housing Factors Related to Mental Hygiene."

of design, facilities, and location which promote happy family relations.[12] But most Negro or Puerto Rican families have little opportunity for these choices.

Considerable family disorganization has long been characteristic of the lower socioeconomic class of Negroes, a legacy of slavery and the frequent inability of Negro men to discharge the economic responsibilities of husband and father. A large proportion of Negro youth, consequently, grows up deprived of the profoundly important training and personality-forming influences which only a functioning family can supply.

The housing conditions of the majority of Negroes have been an additional heavy handicap to the development of stable families. The crowded, deficient, disordered dwelling can scarcely be a home in the warm, emotional meaning of the term. As E. Franklin Frazier remarks:

Even those Negro families which are disposed to gather for meals are very often denied this opportunity because of the absence of space or facilities. . . . For a large proportion of Negro families in the city, the house is not a home but a place to cook and eat as individuals and sleep at night. When the weather permits it is generally a place from which one escapes. This is true of adults as well as children. This fact probably explains why so many Negroes congregate on the streets of Negro neighborhoods. So far as the children are concerned, the house becomes a veritable prison for them.[13]

A Stimulant to Prejudice

Compulsory segregation is a powerful stimulant to racial prejudice. In the first place, to concentrate the members of a racial group increases their visibility and causes their distinctive characteristics to stand out more prominently.[14] Persons of Irish or of Italian descent, for example, although they possess certain group characteristics, are seldom recognizable in the ordinary public

---

[12] Glenn H. Beyer, Thomas W. Mackesey, and James E. Montgomery, *Houses Are for People: A Study of Home Buyer Motivations.* See also Svend Riemer, *American Journal of Sociology,* XLVI (May, 1941), 865-872, and *American Sociological Review,* 8(3):272-278 (June, 1943) and 12(2):155-159 (April, 1947).

[13] E. Franklin Frazier, *The Negro in the United States,* pp. 635-636.

[14] Morton Deutsch and Mary Evans Collins, *Interracial Housing: A Psychological Evaluation of a Social Experiment,* p. 141.

mingling of people. But if one goes into an Irish or Italian neighborhood, he becomes immediately conscious of a distinct group. It is the same with nonwhites. An occasional dark face in the crowd will be hardly noticed, but a large number of different appearing people, all in one place, has an immediate impact. It is obvious that the tendency to think of Negroes (or Jews, or others) as all alike, disregarding individual differences (prejudice), must be enormously strengthened by segregation.

Imposed segregation connotes not merely difference but inferiority of the segregated group. When individuals or groups are excluded from a neighborhood, the inescapable implication is that they are considered not fit to live there. Since the character of neighborhoods carries corresponding implications about the the character and worth of the residents, the minority groups are further stigmatized by the obvious inferiority of their residence areas. Compulsory segregation is, therefore, an unceasing public announcement of the separateness and inferior status of the minority groups. In his famous dissent from the separate-but-equal decision of *Plessy* v. *Ferguson,* Justice Harlan asked:

What can more certainly arouse race hate, what more certainly create and perpetuate a feeling of distrust between these races, than state enactments which, in fact, proceed on the ground that colored citizens are so inferior and degraded that they cannot be allowed to sit in public coaches occupied by white citizens? . . . The thin disguise of "equal" accommodations . . . will not mislead anyone, nor atone for the wrong this day done.[15]

Segregation minimizes personal contacts which would lead members of majority and minority groups to perceive each other as individuals. Most contacts between whites and Negroes, for example, are formal or casual and marked by a wide status difference between the parties, as in employer-employee relations. Rarely do whites have opportunity to know Negroes as individual personalities or to share experiences with them, but they see them only in the mass, not as persons but as Negroes.[16] Most whites acquire their attitudes toward minority groups not from actual

---

[15] *Plessy* v. *Ferguson,* 163 U. S. 537 (1896).
[16] Deutsch and Collins, *Interracial Housing* . . . , pp. 5, 142.

contacts with members of these groups but from contact with prevailing attitudes toward them.[17] And these received attitudes tend to be self-perpetuating, since whites have few experiences which might challenge them.

Lack of communication across racial lines leads to misunderstanding and mistrust between the racial groups. A revealing instance is described in a report from Fisk University. A Negro property owner applied to the Nashville zoning board for a waiver to construct a hotel in a racially mixed residential area. Two groups of homeowners, one white and one Negro, appeared before the board. The spokesman for the white group bitterly attacked the Negro group, presuming that it had come to support the waiver request of the Negro property owner. When the spokesman for the Negro group also opposed the waiver, the whites stared in amazement. After the hearing, they surrounded the Negroes as though the latter were men from Mars. In the absence of communication, the whites had no conception of Negroes as homeowners like themselves.[18]

Under segregation, competition among individuals tends to be transformed into conflict between groups. Minority homeseekers appearing outside the segregated areas are generally regarded not as people looking for homes, who may be good, bad, or indifferent, but as invaders, to be repelled if possible or escaped if need be. The terms commonly used to describe the replacement of majority by minority group—threat, infiltration, invasion, panic, flight, and the like—are indicative of the conflict inherent in the situation.

A Barrier to Social and Economic Progress

By inhibiting the participation of the minority groups in the activities of the community, residential segregation limits their experience and their opportunities, as well as their incentives, to learn. Because of past deprivation, most Negroes, Puerto Ricans,

---

[17] Daniel M. Wilner, Rosabelle Price Walkley, and Stuart W. Cook, *Human Relations in Interracial Housing: A Study of the Contact Hypothesis,* p. 5 and authorities cited.

[18] Masuoka and Valien, "Social Consequences of Racial Residential Segregation."

and Mexican-Americans are at present poorly prepared to compete on equal terms with the white majority. In education and
occupational skills they lag far behind the general standard. They
are retarded in knowledge of the values, standards, and accepted
ways of behaving characteristic of the dominant group. In these
respects they resemble many immigrant groups of the past. The
immigrants or their children climbed the socioeconomic ladder
as they shed their foreign ways and adopted the dominant American values and behavior. If the present minority groups are to
achieve equality with the rest of the population, they, too, must
draw abreast of their fellow Americans in preparation for work
and general cultural development.

To do this is essentially a learning process. The importance of
education needs no emphasis. It has always been, in the United
States, a major avenue of social and economic advancement. In
the modern world of technology and paper work, a good basic
education plus specialized training are prerequisite to a constantly
widening range of occupations and opportunities. Formal schooling, however, is only part of education in the broad sense of
preparation for life. In the total education of a person, the family
plays a vital role, and another great part comes from associations
and experiences in the community.

The young person growing up in the isolation of a segregated
community has few contacts and few experiences that would
teach him the ways of the larger world. He is not wholly isolated,
of course, and may readily learn to desire the common goals of
money, good cars, good clothes, and the like, but he is less apt
to learn the ways of pursuing these goals and the whole complex
of values surrounding them. If he attends a segregated school, he
will miss the stimulus and broadening influence of association
with others of different backgrounds. The school itself is unable
to perform its educational function fully when all or most of the
students come from a depressed minority group. It is almost a
truism among educators that effective schooling requires the
coöperation of school, family, and community. When the community is a minority group lacking traditions of education and
many of the families are weak and disorganized, the school can

scarcely achieve a high standard. The students, coming from similar backgrounds of deprivation, cannot learn from each other, but can only reinforce each other in common ignorance. Many students fail to develop appreciation of the value of education and drop out of school. It has been calculated that if the education of Negro males were brought up to the level of white males, the number of Negro college graduates each year would be more than tripled and the number of high school graduates each year would be nearly tripled as compared with performance in 1950.[19]

In being set apart and treated as inferior, minority children may themselves develop feelings of inferiority and hopelessness.[20] The Supreme Court saw this as one of the evils of compulsory school segregation. Speaking for a unanimous Court, Chief Justice Warren said: "To separate them [Negro pupils] from others of similar age and qualification solely because of their race generates a feeling of inferiority as to their status in the community that may affect their hearts and minds in a way unlikely ever to be undone." [21]

Frazier observes that in the segregated community inferior standards of excellence are set up.[22] Lacking the stimulus of competition in the larger world, many Negro youths fail to develop aspirations or incentives to achievement. All of this, together with the objective data of education and occupations, reveal the dimensions of the cultural lag affecting Negroes and some other groups. The gap is not likely to close rapidly until Negroes are brought into more frequent contact with the white population in learning situations.

To the Negro and Oriental middle classes, segregation is an immediate and direct blockage of opportunity. These sections of the minority populations have largely overcome the cultural handicaps characteristic of their ethnic groups; they share the

[19] Eli Ginzberg, *The Negro Potential*, p. 52.

[20] Esther Milner, "Some Hypotheses Concerning the Influence of Segregation on Negro Personality Development," *Psychiatry*, Vol. 16 (1953), 291-297.

[21] *Brown* v. *Board of Education of Topeka*, 347 U. S. 483 (1954).

[22] E. Franklin Frazier, *Negro Youth at the Crossways: Their Personality Development in the Middle States*, p. 290. See also Ginzberg, *The Negro Potential*, p. 115.

behavior and values of the white middle class, but the expected rewards are in great part withheld.

Deprivation of housing opportunity is probably felt more keenly by the advanced members of minority groups than by the lower classes. The middle class, including the minority middle class, seeks not just housing but neighborhoods. For families at this level, good housing means, in addition to an adequate dwelling unit, those qualities of quiet, order, cleanliness, good facilities, and social prestige usually associated with a desirable neighborhood. Hence, for a middle-class family to be refused entry to a neighborhood of its choice is a serious deprivation not compensated for by the availability of housing elsewhere. Moreover, at higher levels of income and cost, housing requirements become increasingly individualized. The low-income homeseeker must perforce be content with little; he is fortunate to obtain a "minimum adequate" dwelling. But the family who can afford a higher-priced home and whose housing values are well developed typically brings a particular set of preferences and requirements into the market. It may want a specific location, a certain style of architecture, a certain amount of space, or a particular complement of facilities. It may place a high or low value on prestige factors. Probably not many families achieve their dream house completely. Minority families have less chance of doing so than others, and they must make more compromises because the search must be conducted in a limited part of the housing market.

The social isolation which segregation entails has direct, limiting impact on the minority middle class. In business and the professions, opportunities depend closely upon associations and participation in community groups. The person who wishes to rise in business or in a profession must know the "right" people, take part in the organized life of his business group, and live in a suitable neighborhood. This behavior is or would be appropriate to the minority middle classes. Their natural links are with others of similar business and professional interests much more than with the racial groups into which they were born. But segregation cuts them off from otherwise normal associations and in so doing obstructs the customary channels of advancement.

Consequences for Community and Nation

Enforced segregation has damaging consequences not only for the segregated groups but for the general community as well. One broad result, already touched upon, is the stimulation of racial prejudice and antagonism. In a society composed of diverse racial, ethnic, and religious groups there is an undoubted public interest in maintaining harmonious relations among the various groups. Segregation is sometimes defended on the grounds of keeping peace between potentially antagonistic groups, but it is far more likely to have the opposite effect and hence is contrary to the public interest in interracial tolerance.

Another consequence for the community, discussed at more length in chapter xix, is the hampering of slum clearance and housing improvement programs. To relocate and rehouse populations of slum dwellers is a difficult problem at best. The difficulties are vastly increased when those who must be relocated consist in great part, as they do, of groups whose housing alternatives are limited by racial discrimination. Access to a sufficient quantity and variety of housing resources is a basic condition of effective relocation. But in fact, for the large majority of displaced families, urban renewal authorities are obliged to limit their relocation efforts to that part of the housing market which is open to minority groups. Also, unless the supply of housing available to minorities in any community increases more rapidly than population, relocation will tend to increase congestion in areas that already have too many people. When this occurs, and there is evidence that it has happened, the reduction of slums in urban renewal project areas may be offset by the worsening of housing conditions in relocation areas. The ability of urban renewal programs, therefore, to achieve their purpose of housing and community betterment is dependent upon an adequate supply of housing available to minority groups.

Waste of human resources.—The largest cost of segregation to the nation is the waste of human resources which results from the retarded development of the segregated groups. The interest of the community and nation in the development of their individual members is recognized by all. It is expressed in many ways, above all in the large expenditures of public funds for education at all levels and in laws making school attendance compulsory. Any condition which prevents individuals from achieving the potential of which they are capable harms the national interest. Because racial discrimination and segregation hamper the development of many millions of people, the nation is militarily weaker, economically less productive, and culturally poorer than it would be were the disadvantaged minority groups contributing equally with the rest of the population.

Impact on foreign relations.—Still another part of the cost of racial discrimination to the nation is the damage that it does to the prestige of the United States abroad. It tends to cast doubt on the sincerity of American advocacy of freedom and equality and so impairs the moral leadership of the United States in the world. Among Asian and African peoples, almost all of whom are nonwhite, racialism is associated with the hated colonial system. It is difficult to persuade these new nations that the United States really considers them as equals when people of like racial stock are subordinated within the United States.

The racial problem in the United States is publicized throughout the world. It places in the hands of the country's enemies an easy and constantly exploited propaganda weapon. Charges of mistreatment of racial groups in the United States, however distorted, are difficult to counter because of the element of fact which they contain.

But although racial discrimination is an international liability, the fact that the United States is a racially mixed nation is potentially an important asset in its relations with Asia and Africa. The value of this asset can be realized when white and nonwhite citizens stand on an equal footing as members of the American community.

PART TWO

Minorities in the Housing Market

VI

Economic Status and Social Characteristics

of Minority Groups

The housing demand of any group of people is affected by their incomes, family structure, the place of housing in their scale of values, and their preferences. Within the limits of ability to pay, different types of housing are demanded by married couples with children, childless couples, elderly couples, and unattached persons. Consumers vary also in the part of their resources which they are prepared to spend for housing, and in their preferences for housing types, tenures, and locations. With due allowance for individual tastes, such variations are broadly patterned by groups and subject to change through time.[1]

The minority groups considered in this study, Jews excepted, have lower incomes than the majority white population and in varying degree are culturally disadvantaged as well. Each group has certain distinctive social characteristics which also seem to condition the demand of its members for housing.

---

[1] A recent study of housing trends observes a long-run decline in the size of American houses which is attributed not entirely to the increasing cost of housing but also to changing consumer tastes. The study finds "evidence of a decided shift away from shelter toward other and newer consumer durables, . . ." but "In more recent years the interest of the consumer in housing seems to have been rekindled as a result of more children and suburbanization, . . ." Louis Winnick, *American Housing and Its Use,* pp. 3, 8.

Employment and Income

The median income of nonwhite urban families in the United States in 1957 was $3,352, approximately 40 percent below the median of white urban families ($5,557).[2] Incomes of $10,000 or more were received by 9 percent of all white families, but only 1.2 percent of nonwhite families had incomes of this magnitude. At the lower extreme, 36 percent of nonwhite families received less than $2,000, but not quite 13 percent of white families were at this low income level.

The earning power of nonwhites has, nevertheless, improved greatly during the past two decades. From 1939 to 1957, the median wage or salary income of nonwhite primary families and individuals increased more than fivefold, from $489 to $2,536. The corresponding measure for whites showed somewhat less than a fourfold rise, from $1,325 to $4,831.[3] A narrowing of the racial gap therefore resulted.

In 1939, the nonwhite median family income was only 37 percent of the median for white families, but in 1957 the ratio had risen to 53 percent. For urban families, as noted, the differential was narrower, and it was less in the North than in the South. In northern cities, nonwhite families received in 1954, on the average, about two-thirds as much income as white families.[4]

Comparative income data available for specific racial and ethnic groups relate only to incomes of persons receiving income in 1949. Although the usefulness of these data is limited, they afford an index to the relative economic status of different groups. Medians are given in table 11.

The Japanese have the highest incomes of any of the minor racial groups, equal to about three-fourths of the median income of whites. The Chinese are not far behind. At bottom are the Indians with a median income little more than a third as much as

---

[2] U. S. Bureau of the Census, *Current Population Reports*, Series P-60, *Consumer Income*, no. 30 (December, 1958).

[3] *Ibid.* The smaller percent increase in the white median is due to the larger base from which the rise began. In absolute terms, the white increase was much greater than the nonwhite.

[4] *Ibid.*, no. 20 (December, 1955).

TABLE 11

MEDIAN INCOME OF PERSONS WITH INCOME
IN 1949, BY RACE AND ETHNIC GROUP

Race or ethnic group	United States	Urban	North central region
White	$2,053	$2,278	$2,144
Negro	952	1,110	1,619
Chinese	1,799	1,820	1,564
Japanese	1,839	1,945	2,147
Filipino	1,689	2,045	2,575
Indian	725	1,240	679
Spanish-name	1,223	1,385	1,628[a]
Puerto Rican	1,654	1,647[b]	...

SOURCE: *U. S. Census of Population: 1950*, Vol. II, *Characteristics of the Population*, Part 1, "U. S. Summary," tables 138, 162; Vol. IV, *Special Reports*, Part 3, chapters B, C, D.

[a] Median income of Spanish-name persons in California.
[b] New York City.

whites'. The extreme poverty of the Indians is partly attributable to their concentration in rural areas, but even in the cities, Indians earn on the average only about half as much as whites. Negroes rank just above the Indians and well below all other groups on a national basis, but their average income is lowered by their depressed condition in the South. Outside the South, the median income of Negroes rises to about three-fourths of the white level. Similarly for the Spanish-name group, median income in 1949 ranged from less than $1,000 in Texas to more than $1,600 in California.

The rising incomes of nonwhites have resulted from Negro migration from the South to the higher-income North and West, an associated shift from agriculture to industry, upgrading of all groups in the occupational scale, greater continuity of employment, and, of course, the general rise in wages. Traditionally, nonwhite workers have been heavily concentrated in southern agriculture, unskilled labor, and service occupations. Between 1940 and 1950 the proportion of Negro males employed in agriculture dropped from more than 40 to less than 25 percent. In spite of the huge migration of Negroes to industrial centers, the percent of Negro men employed at the bottom of the nonfarm occupational hierarchy increased very little. The expanded non-agricultural Negro labor force was absorbed mainly in semiskilled and skilled industrial jobs, with modest but significant gains in the white-collar and higher occupational groups. These shifts in Negro occupational distribution are graphically portrayed in figure 1.

The trends manifest during the 1940-1950 decade have continued since the latter date. By 1958 only 15 percent of Negro male workers were employed in agriculture. The proportion employed as nonfarm laborers has remained nearly stationary, but further relative increases have occurred in the higher occupational categories. The Negro population has become considerably more differentiated occupationally. Agriculture, unskilled nonfarm labor, and service accounted for more than 75 percent of all Negro male workers in 1940 but only 55 percent in 1958. Negro women workers were even more concentrated than men in these three categories, but they, too, have moved out of agriculture and upward occupationally in much the same way. Once virtually excluded from clerical and sales work, Negro women have acquired a modest foothold for the first time in this largest field of employment for white women.

Nonwhite groups other than Negro have experienced similar changes. The Chinese and Japanese have increased their representation in the professions and technical occupations to the point where they are not far behind the white population. Undoubtedly the Japanese would have made much more economic progress had it not been for the loss of their farms and other business enterprises incident to their forced wartime relocation. Significant gains were registered during the 1940-1950 decade in the clerical occupations by all the nonwhite minorities—particularly by the women workers—and also in the skilled crafts and semiskilled industrial jobs. The occupational status of the various groups in 1950 is shown in Appendix table A-4. In general, minority male workers are underrepresented in the higher-status occupations and relatively concentrated in the service and laborer jobs. A partial exception is the high proportion of Chinese who are proprietors and managers. The Chinese have not gained this status in the general world of business but mainly in the Chinatowns,

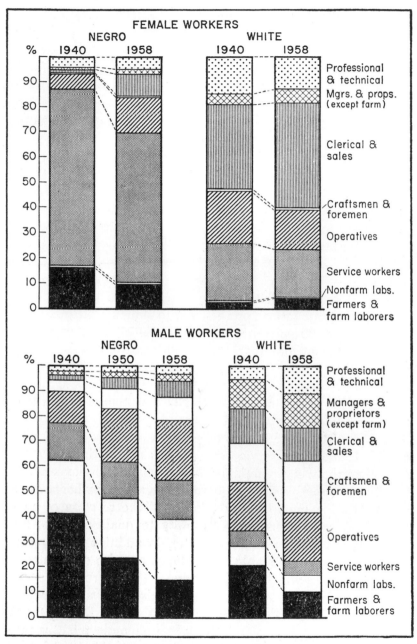

Figure 1. Occupational distribution of employed workers in the United States, by race and sex, 1940, 1950, and 1958.

purveying the products of Chinese culture (food, art, and so on) to both the ethnic group and the general population.

Of all the minorities, the most disadvantaged occupationally are the Indians, nearly two-thirds of whom were small farmers or farm and nonfarm laborers in 1950. This position, nevertheless, represented a significant advance from their occupational situation ten years before, when four-fifths of Indian male workers were engaged as small farmers or laborers.

Puerto Ricans, settled mainly in New York City, have found employment primarily in the upper part of the lower range of occupations. Not many are laborers, but almost a third of the employed men in 1950 were semiskilled operatives and another fourth were service workers. Nearly three-fourths of Puerto Rican women workers were employed as operatives.

The comparative occupational status of Negroes and Mexican-Americans merits notice. Both groups in 1950 were about equally concentrated in agriculture or nonfarm labor. The four higher occupational categories (professional to skilled craftsmen), however, included 25 percent of all male Spanish-name workers but only 16 percent of Negro males. Mexican-American women workers had nearly five times as much representation in the clerical field as Negro women. Thus it seems that a Mexican-American has a significantly better chance than a Negro of obtaining a skilled or white-collar job.

The relative concentration of minority workers in agriculture, unskilled labor, and service occupations means that they suffer more than the white population from irregular employment. This is not only a serious drag on earning power; it further adversely affects housing opportunities because of the reaction of an unstable employment pattern on ability to qualify for mortgage credit. It is probable that nonwhites, in addition to being concentrated in the less stable occupations, are also often marginal in the industries which employ them.

The incidence of unemployment tends to be about twice as great among nonwhite workers as among whites. During the first half of 1957, a period of relatively low unemployment, monthly unemployment rates of white workers varied from 3.6 to 4.4 percent, compared with a range of 7.7 to 9.3 percent for nonwhite workers. During 1958, a year of cutbacks in employment, the annual average rate of unemployment rose to 6.1 percent for white workers and 12.6 percent for nonwhites. The latter were also unemployed for longer periods, and while employed they tended to work fewer hours than whites. Considerably more than a fourth of all nonwhite workers employed during 1958 worked fewer than thirty-five hours per week, but less than a fifth of white workers were in this part-time category.[5]

Educational Attainment

Educational achievement is an index to the cultural level of a group and the ability of its members to function in a competitive society. Education is one of the criteria of social status. Traditionally, it has been a major instrument for individual and social advancement and for the assimilation of immigrant groups. The social status or cultural level of a family contributes powerfully to shaping its wants and standards for housing. Wants, of course, may run ahead or lag behind economic ability to satisfy them, but before families are willing to spend to upgrade their housing, a need must be felt for something better.

Nonwhite home buyers, and renters to a lesser extent, do not spend as large a percentage of their incomes for housing as do white families. This may represent partly an adjustment to supply conditions, but it probably also reflects a preference for competing objects of consumer expenditure as compared with housing. Similarly, the relatively high rate of room crowding in nonwhite households at all income levels suggests a lower valuation of space and privacy than is characteristic of whites. Taking expenditure and space-utilization patterns of whites as the standard, it seems warranted to conclude that housing wants of nonwhites have lagged behind the recent rise in their incomes. The lag is accentuated, of course, by the restrictions of segregation. A growing demand for better housing may be anticipated, therefore, from members of minority groups with their advancing cultural status plus their rising incomes.

The educational attainment of the minority groups, except the

[5] *Ibid.*, Series P-50, *Labor Force*, no. 85 (June, 1958) and no. 89 (June, 1959), "Annual Report on the Labor Force."

Chinese and Japanese, is far below that of the white population, but the nonwhites' deficiency is being reduced. The American Japanese are the best-educated racial group in the United States, leading the white population by a wide margin. The Chinese do not rival the Japanese in educational achievement but rank not far below the white population. Both Chinese and Japanese made much more progress educationally during the 1940-1950 decade than any other racial or ethnic group, including the white.

Substantially more than a third of all white persons twenty-five years old or more in 1950 had completed at least four years of high school. Of Negroes, Indians, Spanish-name whites, and Puerto Ricans, only about one in every eight adults was a high-school graduate. A decade earlier, however, less than one adult Negro in thirteen had completed this much schooling. Following are comparative percentages of persons twenty-five years old and more among the various racial and ethnic groups who had completed high school, in 1940 and 1950:[6]

Racial or ethnic group	1940	1950
White	26.1	36.4
Negro	7.3	13.0
Chinese	12.2	30.2
Japanese	33.2	57.7
Filipino	18.8	22.9
Indian	7.8	12.8
Spanish-name	...	11.5
Puerto Ricans	...	13.8

As in other aspects of Negro life, their educational disadvantage is most severe in the South. The proportion of high-school graduates in the Negro population in 1950 was two to three times greater in the North and West than in the South, a difference partly attributable to superior educational opportunities in the North and West, but also due in part, no doubt, to the drain of better-educated Negroes from the South by migration. Significant

[6] *Sixteenth Census of the U. S., 1940, Population*, Vol. II, *Characteristics of the Population*, Part 1, "U. S. Summary," tables 33, 34; *Characteristics of the Nonwhite Population by Race*, tables 6, 8. *U. S. Census of Population: 1950*, Vol. II, *Characteristics of the Population*, Part 1, "U. S. Summary," table 154; Vol. IV, *Special Reports*, Part 3, chaps. B, C, D.

is the fact that the North-South difference in educational level is not great for whites, but very large for Negroes.

The rising trend of educational achievement has continued since 1950. By 1957, more than 40 percent of the total population more than twenty-five years old had completed at least four years of high school and the proportion of nonwhites at this level was approaching 20 percent (fig. 2).[7] An advancing standard

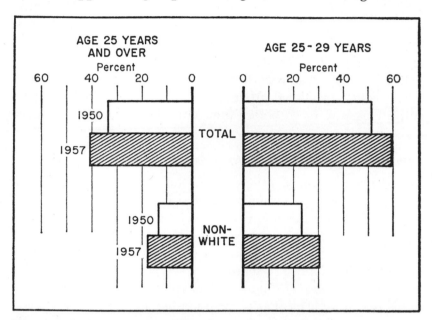

Figure 2. Percent of persons who have completed at least four years of high school, United States, 1950 and 1957.

of education is, of course, reflected mainly in the younger age groups. Thus, in the age group twenty-five to twenty-nine years, the nonwhite proportion of high-school graduates exceeded 30 percent in 1957, compared with 60 percent in the total population of that age.

Graduation from high school seems to be, at present, the limit of educational ambition of the vast majority of nonwhites (Orientals excepted). The percentage of young people attending college

---

[7] U. S. Bureau of the Census, *Current Population Reports*, Series P-20, *Population Characteristics*, no. 77, "Educational Attainment: March, 1957" (December, 1957).

has been rising less rapidly in the nonwhite than in the general population. In the age group twenty-five to twenty-nine years, more than a fifth of the general population, but only one in every eleven nonwhites, had completed one or more years of college in 1957.

The darkest side of the educational picture of nonwhites is the still significant proportion of them who are arriving at young adult ages with grossly inadequate schooling. In 1957, approximately one nonwhite in twelve, in the age group twenty to thirty years, had completed less than four years of school, that is, was virtually illiterate. A similar situation prevails among native-born Mexican-Americans.[8] Thus, in spite of the general advance in educational attainment, these minority groups have still a long way to go before their educational handicap is overcome.

Family and Household Characteristics

The demand for and utilization of housing by several of the minority groups are strongly affected by particular family and household patterns arising from the circumstances of their settlement and historical experience in the United States. The Oriental groups, on first arrival, consisted very largely of men. Subsequent restrictive legislation (Exclusion Acts) hampered what would have been the normal following immigration of women, with the result that a high proportion of male immigrants did not marry and establish families. As late as 1950, more than two-thirds of all Chinese males older than fourteen were unmarried. Obviously, the Chinese did not present a demand for housing commensurate with their population, and this was true to a lesser extent of the Japanese and Filipinos. When the lowering of immigration barriers permitted the entry of Chinese women after World War II, the Chinese formed families at a rapid rate and simultaneously began an unprecedented search for family-type housing outside the Chinatowns.

The Negro population has long been characterized by distinctive features of family and household organization significantly

---

[8] Robert H. Talbert, *Spanish-Name People in the Southwest and West*, chap. iii.

affecting its housing conditions. Compared to the white population, Negroes have a greater frequency of large families, a higher incidence of broken families, and more frequent presence of multiple families and unrelated persons in the household. A high proportion of working wives has also been traditionally characteristic of Negroes.

The average population per household in 1958 was 3.29 for whites and 3.9 for nonwhites.[9] The decline in average size of household during the past quarter century has been much greater among white than among nonwhite households. In 1930, white and nonwhite households were nearly the same size on the average, but by 1950, the households of nonwhites were substantially larger. Following are the comparative census figures:[10]

Households	Average number of persons per household			
	1930	1940	1950	1958
White...............	4.09	3.75	3.46	3.29
Nonwhite............	4.27	4.09	4.17	3.90

Large families are much more common among nonwhites than among whites. In 1957, nearly 18 percent of nonwhite families had four or more children, compared with 8 percent of white families. The average number of children less than eighteen was 1.31 for white married couples and 1.61 for nonwhites.[11]

Further salient statistics of Negro household structure are presented in table 12. The typical American household consists of husband and wife, with or without children or other persons related to them. In eight metropolitan areas, somewhat more than three-fourths of all white households were of this type in 1950, the percentage being higher for homeowning than for renter households. Of nonwhite households, however, only about half of the renters and two-thirds of the owners conformed to this pattern. In some areas, almost a third of nonwhite renter families

[9] U. S. Bureau of the Census, *Current Population Reports*, Series P-20, *Population Characteristics*, no. 88 (November, 1958).

[10] *Ibid.*, and no. 75 (June, 1957).

[11] *Ibid.*, no. 83 (August, 1958).

TABLE 12

WHITE AND NONWHITE HOUSEHOLDS BY TYPE, BY TENURE,
FOR SELECTED METROPOLITAN AREAS, 1950
(Percent of total)

Standard metropolitan area	Husband-wife families, no nonrelatives		Families with female head		Households with nonrelatives	
	White	Nonwhite	White	Nonwhite	White	Nonwhite
	OWNER-OCCUPANTS[a]					
New York	80.1	56.5	9.9	17.7	. . .[b]	. . .[b]
Chicago	81.6	61.3	9.6	17.4	6.2	22.0
Detroit	83.8	59.2	8.1	12.9	6.8	30.6
Los Angeles	77.2	65.5	13.1	16.9	6.6	19.0
St. Louis	81.0	63.9	11.0	19.6	5.1	15.7
New Orleans	80.5	67.7	12.0	19.6	4.1	9.6
Houston	85.3	70.3	8.3	19.0	5.8	9.9
Birmingham	84.6	71.2	9.5	18.5	4.3	9.2
	RENTERS					
New York	71.7	46.9	17.7	32.4	5.3	23.3
Chicago	71.7	49.6	17.1	27.8	5.8	18.8
Detroit	73.7	55.3	15.6	21.4	6.8	23.7
Los Angeles	61.3	56.1	25.2	24.5	6.0	14.8
St. Louis	73.0	52.3	17.8	29.1	5.2	15.9
New Orleans	72.0	52.4	18.3	32.8	4.7	9.5
Houston	73.6	58.3	15.4	25.0	7.5	16.2
Birmingham	80.6	61.6	13.1	24.5	3.8	11.2

SOURCE: *U. S. Census of Housing: 1950,* Vol. II, *Nonfarm Housing Characteristics,* chapters for the respective standard metropolitan areas, and unpublished special tabulations of the 1950 Census of Housing supplied by the Bureau of the Census.

[a] Restricted to single-unit properties.

[b] Data not available.

were headed by women. Moreover, although white families with a female head were generally smaller than normal families, among nonwhites they had about the same size distribution as all nonwhite families. More recent data show no diminution of this pattern.[12]

The comparative instability of Negro family life, indicated by the prevalence of broken families, is primarily characteristic of the lower socioeconomic class of Negroes. As various studies have

---

[12] *Ibid.,* no. 88.

shown, the growing middle class of Negroes places strong emphasis on conventional and "respectable" family life and social behavior generally.[13] Several factors contribute to the lower-class pattern. In the background is the tradition of slavery, when family relations existed at the convenience of the masters, and slave marital partners had neither the rights nor the responsibilities customarily attaching to the status of husband or wife. In the decades since Emancipation, the poverty of most Negroes and the inability of many Negro men to meet the economic responsibilities of husband and father have hampered the development of stable marital unions. Disorganization attendant upon migration and urban settlement under conditions of struggle for existence has been another handicap.

Broken families are at a marked disadvantage in the housing market. Those without a male breadwinner generally have much lower incomes than normal families. Less secure economically, they are less desired as tenants and unfavorably regarded by mortgage lenders. Not only in housing but in consumption generally, as Sterner observes, broken families are apt to be less able than normal families to organize their consumption efficiently, because of their smaller incomes and also because the same person often must serve both as breadwinner and as homemaker.[14]

As shown in table 12, the practice of taking in lodgers is much more widespread among Negro than among white households and is especially prevalent in northern cities. Basically a mode of adjustment to scarce housing and low income in the urban milieu, the practice seems to have become a durable custom among northern Negro families, common to homeowners and renters alike. Although helping the family budget, obviously it contributes to overcrowding.

Not infrequently the lodgers in Negro households are family groups. Doubling of families has declined significantly in recent years, but in 1956 relatively more than twice as many Negro as white married couples were sharing quarters with other families. The trend since 1940 in proportion of married couples without a

---

[13] E. Franklin Frazier, *The Negro in the United States*, pp. 279-282, 300-302, 328-333; St. Clair Drake and Horace R. Cayton, *Black Metropolis*, pp. 658-715.
[14] Richard Sterner, *The Negro's Share*, p. 47.

household of their own is represented by the following percent figures:[15]

Families	1940	1947	1950	1956
White	6.4	7.9	5.9	3.0
Nonwhite	11.3	15.1	13.8	7.1

The Negro family has traditionally depended upon the gainful employment of both husband and wife to a greater extent than white families, and this has been both a result and a cause of looser family relations among Negroes. In recent years, however, the increasing tendency of white women to continue in gainful employment after marriage has modified the distinctiveness of the Negro family in this respect. In 1958, 29 percent of white married women living with their husbands were in the labor force, compared with 42 percent of nonwhite wives.[16]

Summary

In the past, the minority groups have been handicapped in the housing market not only by segregation but also by their low incomes, retarded cultural development, and abnormal family and household organization. These disadvantages still persist in varying degrees but they are changing. Economic and cultural levels are rising more rapidly in the minority groups than in the general population, but it is apparent that many years of continued progress will be needed to overcome the severe handicaps that beset the Negro and Mexican-American populations. In certain other groups, notably the Japanese, the cultural gap has been virtually closed and economic differences largely reduced. Within each minority group, the number and proportion of individuals and families who conform to middle-class standards of income, education, and family structure are growing rapidly. As this process continues, the minorities may be expected increasingly to manifest housing and residence choices indistinguishable from those of the general population.

---

[15] U. S. Bureau of the Census, *Current Population Reports,* Series P-20, no. 75.
[16] *Ibid.,* Series P-50, *Labor Force,* no. 87 (January, 1959).

VII

Characteristics of Minority Group Housing

Population and Housing

One aspect of the rising American standard of living has been the tendency of the housing supply to expand more rapidly than population, thus providing an increasing amount of housing per capita.[1] The nonwhite population, however, has received much less than a proportionate share of the growing housing resources (table 13). In the decade 1940-1950 the percent increase in white-occupied dwellings exceeded the growth of population by a wide margin, but for nonwhites the reverse was true: population grew at a faster rate than housing units, and nonwhites had less housing per capita at the end of the decade than at its beginning. During these ten years, an additional dwelling unit was created on the average for every 2.2 persons added to the white population; nonwhites gained an additional dwelling for every 4.7 added persons.

For the white population, the favorable ratio of housing expansion to population growth has been reflected in a declining average number of persons for each occupied dwelling, but

---

[1] A qualification of this judgment is necessary if rooms rather than dwelling units are taken as the units of measurement, since the former have increased less rapidly than the latter, owing to the trend toward smaller dwelling units. Moreover, the increase in living space per capita has been largely taken up by the growing number and proportion of one- and two-person households. See Louis Winnick, *American Housing and Its Use,* p. 8 and chap. 7.

TABLE 13

PERCENT CHANGES IN POPULATION AND HOUSING, BY COLOR OF OCCUPANTS,
AND POPULATION PER OCCUPIED DWELLING UNIT,[a] UNITED STATES, 1920-1956

| Year | Percent increases by decades | | | | Population per occupied dwelling unit[b] | |
| | White | | Nonwhite | | | |
	Population	Dwelling units	Population	Dwelling units	White	Nonwhite
1920	16.0	20.2[c]	6.3	. . .	4.3	4.3
1930	16.3	23.6	14.7	15.7	4.1	4.3
1940	7.2	17.0	7.7	12.7	3.7	4.1
1950	14.1	23.6	17.1	14.9	3.5	4.2
1956[d]	10.7	16.6	15.7	14.6	3.3	4.2

SOURCES: *U. S. Census of Housing: 1950*, Vol. I, *General Characteristics*, chap. 1, "U. S. Summary." U. S. Bureau of the Census, *Current Population Reports*, Series P-25, *Population Estimates*, no. 146, "Estimates of the Population of the United States, by Age, Color, and Sex, July 1, 1950 to 1956" (November, 1956); *1956 National Housing Inventory*, Vol. III, *Characteristics of the 1956 Inventory*, Part 1, "United States and Regions."

[a] The census count is of "occupied dwelling units" for 1956, 1950, and 1940, and "families" for earlier years. The concepts are not exactly equivalent, but the census states that the differences are so small as to be negligible.

[b] These averages are based on the *total* population divided by the number of occupied dwelling units or families. They differ from the measure of persons per occupied dwelling unit which excludes the population not in private households. Total population is used in these averages to provide consistency between the statistics of the various censuses.

[c] Total families.

[d] Calculations based on census estimates of population for July 1, 1956, and housing estimates as of December, 1956. Actual population at the date of the housing estimates was, of course, somewhat greater.

among nonwhites, average population per dwelling unit has remained almost stationary for more than thirty years.

The quantitative share of nonwhites in the national supply of housing seems to have been declining since about 1920. In that year, nonwhites represented 10.3 percent of the United States population and occupied 10.4 percent of all dwelling units.[2] Each subsequent census found nonwhites occupying a smaller share of the housing supply, although by 1950 their number had increased to 10.5 percent of the national population.[3] The lagging expansion of housing for nonwhites in the 1940-1950 period existed throughout the country and was especially pronounced in

[2] Strictly "families." See table 13, note a.

[3] *U. S. Census of Housing: 1950*, Vol I, *General Characteristics*, chap. 1, "U. S. Summary," tables J and K.

many areas where nonwhite population was growing rapidly through migration. In the 106 cities of 100,000 or more inhabitants, the rate of increase in dwelling units occupied by nonwhites fell short of population growth in 89 cities, often by a wide margin. Dwelling units occupied by whites, on the other hand, increased more rapidly than white population in all but two cities.[4] The failure of nonwhites to obtain a share of housing proportionate to their numbers is the more striking in view of the substantial improvement in their employment and income during the decade.

In the years since 1950, the upsurge in housing construction has enabled minority groups to gain some relief from the desperate housing shortage which developed during the preceding decade. But they are still far short of an equitable share in the benefits of housing expansion. The Census Bureau's 1956 National Housing Inventory reported for the period April, 1950, to the end of 1956 an increase of 7,048,000 occupied dwelling units,[5] of which 551,000 were occupied by nonwhites. This figure represented an average annual increase of 81,500 units approximately, compared with a yearly average of 49,000 during the preceding decade. However, the nonwhite population was also growing more rapidly during the 1950-1956 period. As shown in table 13, nonwhite population increase continued to outrun housing growth, and the opposite remained true for whites. Average population per dwelling unit continued, for whites, its long-run decline, but for nonwhites, it remained, in 1956, at almost the same level as in 1920. In the period 1950-1956, an additional white-occupied dwelling unit was created, on the average, for each 2.2 persons added to the white population. For nonwhites, an additional dwelling was available for every 4.5 added persons.[6]

The data on a national basis tend to obscure significant improvements in the housing supply situation for nonwhites which

[4] *U. S. Census of Population: 1950*, Vol. II, *Characteristics of the Population*, Part 1, "U. S. Summary"; *U. S. Census of Housing: 1950*, Vol I, chap. 1.

[5] The reported net increase in all dwelling units, occupied and unoccupied, was in excess of 9,358,000. U. S. Bureau of the Census, *1956 National Housing Inventory*, Vol. III, *Characteristics of the 1956 Inventory*, Part 1, "United States and Regions" (1959).

[6] Both ratios are slightly too low because of being based on population in July and housing in December, 1956. See table 13, note d and sources.

occurred in various parts of the country during the 1950-1956 period. Of the total increase of 551,000 nonwhite-occupied dwelling units, nearly 539,000 units were accounted for by increases in the North and West. In these regions the expansion of nonwhite-occupied housing exceeded 40 percent, sufficient to permit substantial easing of the housing shortage for nonwhites in many localities.[7]

Housing Quality

The disadvantage of minority groups is even more pronounced in housing quality. The share of housing which they receive consists primarily of dilapidated or otherwise deficient dwellings.

The Bureau of the Census defines a standard dwelling unit as one that is not dilapidated and that is equipped with a private toilet, bath, and hot running water. This is not a very exclusive standard as witnessed by the fact that nearly two-thirds of all occupied dwellings in the United States and more than four-fifths of all urban dwelling units conformed to it in 1950. But only one-fourth of the nonwhite dwellings and one-third of those occupied by Spanish-name households came up to this modest standard.

Some statistics on the prevalence of substandard housing among whites, nonwhites, and Spanish-name whites are given in table 14 and figure 3, with more detailed data in Appendix table A-5. As might be expected, homeowners have better housing than renters, and urban dwellings are superior to rural. Even among urban nonwhite owners, however, fewer than half had standard dwellings; 30 percent lived in units which were dilapidated or without running water or both. Poorest of all were the dwellings of rural farm tenants. Of these, occupied by nonwhites, only one in a hundred could be classified as standard. More than

---

[7] The post-1950 expansion of minority residence areas is discussed in chapter iii. It should be borne in mind that the figures cited in the text relate to *net* housing inventory changes, *i.e.*, dwelling units created minus units removed by demolition or other causes. In the South, nonwhites in 1956 occupied an estimated 548,000 dwelling units created since 1950, including 331,000 units of new construction, but this inventory gain was largely balanced by losses due to structural changes, demolition, vacancies, and transfer to white occupancy. U. S. Bureau of the Census, *1956 National Housing Inventory*, Vol. I, *Components of Change, 1950 to 1956*, Part 1, "United States and Regions" (1958).

TABLE 14

Percent of Occupied Dwelling Units Substandard,[a] 1950

Area	All dwelling units occupied by		
	Whites	Nonwhites	Spanish-name whites
	UNITED STATES		
Total	31.8	73.2	65.6[b]
Urban	18.2	61.2	57.8[b]
Rural nonfarm	50.4	94.4	82.2[b]
Rural farm	72.8	98.1	85.3[b]
	STANDARD METROPOLITAN AREAS[c]		
New York	9.9	33.8	...
Philadelphia	10.0	42.8	...
Washington, D. C.	8.0	33.9	...
Chicago	17.6	59.3	...
Detroit	10.1	29.3	...
St. Louis	28.1	75.0	...
Atlanta	27.3	77.2	...
Birmingham	31.6	88.2	...
New Orleans	30.0	82.9	...
Houston	17.3	69.3	64.5
San Antonio	35.6	62.5	76.5
San Francisco–Oakland	9.1	25.6	16.1
Los Angeles	8.2	19.0	32.2
	SELECTED STATES[d]		
California	11.5	27.3	36.1
Texas	33.4	80.5	81.6

Sources: *U. S. Census of Housing: 1950*, Vol. I, *General Characteristics*, chap. 1, "U. S. Summary" and chapters for the respective states; *U. S. Census of Population: 1950*, Vol. IV, *Special Reports*, Part 3, chap. C, "Persons of Spanish Surname"; unpublished tables and special tabulations of 1950 Housing Census data supplied by the Bureau of the Census.

[a] "Substandard" defined to include all dilapidated dwellings plus others lacking private toilet, bath, or hot running water.

[b] Based on census data for the five states of Arizona, California, Colorado, New Mexico, and Texas, the only states where the Spanish-name population was enumerated in the 1950 Census.

[c] For the standard metropolitan areas of New York, Chicago, Detroit, St. Louis, Birmingham, and New Orleans, data are for nonfarm dwelling units only, based on a 20 percent sample.

[d] Nonfarm dwelling units only.

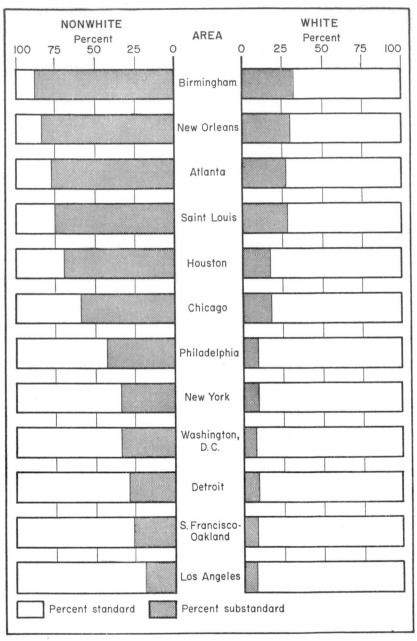

Figure 3. Percent of occupied dwelling units substandard, selected metropolitan areas, 1950.

half were dilapidated, and of those not dilapidated, almost all lacked running water.

Among thirteen standard metropolitan areas studied, the proportion of nonwhite households living in substandard dwellings varied over a wide range—from 19 percent in Los Angeles to more than 88 percent in Birmingham, Alabama. In every metropolitan area, the frequency of substandard dwellings was two to four times greater among nonwhite than among white households. Housing was poorest in the South, both for whites and nonwhites, and the racial difference was much greater in the South than in the North or West. In the northern and western metropolitan areas, except St. Louis and Chicago, about nine-tenths of the white households had standard dwellings, as did two-thirds to four-fifths of the nonwhite households. In the southern metropolitan areas, from two-thirds to three-fourths of the white households lived in standard dwellings, but less than one-fourth of the nonwhites were comparably housed, except in San Antonio and Houston where the proportion of nonwhite standard dwellings rose to about a third. Nonwhite housing is poorest in Birmingham, although this is one of the highest income areas for Negroes in the South.[8] Among northern and western metropolitan areas, St. Louis and Chicago afford the poorest housing for nonwhites, with the widest racial differences in housing quality.

The Spanish-name population, on the whole, enjoys housing of somewhat better quality than that of the nonwhites in general, but with wide variation. There is a large difference between Texas and California in the quality of housing occupied by the Spanish-name group. In Texas, more than four-fifths of Spanish-name households occupied substandard dwellings in 1950, compared with about one-third in California. Spanish-name whites and nonwhites in Texas have housing of similar quality, both far inferior to that of the general white population. The Spanish-name households of California are not only much better housed than their Texas counterparts, but the gap between them and the general population, in respect to housing quality, is also narrower. San Antonio and Los Angeles, the two largest centers of Spanish-

---

[8] Robert A. Thomson, Hylan Lewis, and Davis McEntire, "Atlanta and Birmingham: A Comparative Study in Negro Housing."

name population, afford a striking contrast in housing quality. In the former, more than three-quarters of Spanish-name-occupied dwellings are dilapidated or lack plumbing, compared to one-third in Los Angeles.

Since 1950, substantial improvement has occurred in the condition and plumbing facilities of the general housing inventory. The proportion of standard dwelling units rose from two-thirds in 1950 to more than three-fourths in 1956.[9] Much of the improvement resulted from the construction of nearly eleven million new dwelling units, the vast majority of which had all plumbing facilities. Nonwhites, undoubtedly, have shared in the general improvement of housing quality but probably not to the same extent as whites. More than 20 percent of all white-occupied dwellings in 1956 had been built in 1950 or later, as compared with 11 percent of the dwelling units occupied by nonwhites.

Dwelling Space and Crowding

In the United States in 1950 one in every eight white-occupied, nonfarm dwelling units contained fewer rooms than persons, but one-third of all nonwhite dwellings and more than half of all Spanish-name units (nonfarm) were crowded by this criterion (table 15).

In thirteen metropolitan areas for which data are available, the proportion of dwelling units crowded was two to four times greater among nonwhite than among white-occupied dwellings. As would be expected, crowding of nonwhite dwellings was most prevalent in the southern areas—about 40 percent—but Chicago and St. Louis were not far behind.

For Spanish-name dwellings the proportion crowded varied from 22 percent in San Francisco–Oakland to 56 percent in San Antonio. Even the latter figure is lower than the crowding rate of Spanish-name dwellings in the whole of Texas, which rose to more than 60 percent.

The high frequency of crowding in minority households reflects the combined influence of smaller dwelling units and larger households. In the United States in 1940, the latest year for which national data are available, the typical nonfarm dwelling

---

[9] U. S. Bureau of the Census, *1956 National Housing Inventory,* Vol. III, Part 1.

TABLE 15

MEDIAN NUMBER OF ROOMS AND PERCENT OF DWELLING UNITS CROWDED,
BY COLOR OF OCCUPANTS, AND FOR SPANISH-NAME OCCUPANTS, 1950

| | All nonfarm occupied dwelling units[a] | | | | |
| | Median number of rooms | | Percent crowded[b] | | |
Area	White	Nonwhite	White	Nonwhite	Spanish-name
United States	4.6[c]	...	13.3	32.1	50.8[d]
Selected states					
California	4.4[c]	...	12.0[c]	...	37.3
Texas	4.2	3.6	22.3	28.9	61.5
Standard metropolitan areas					
New York	4.3	4.1	12.4	24.4	...
Philadelphia[e]	5.7[c]	...	7.1	21.9	...
Washington, D. C.[e]	4.6	4.2	9.3	28.7	...
Chicago	4.6	4.4	11.7	35.9	...
Detroit	4.9	4.8	9.6	25.3	...
St. Louis	4.2	3.1	16.6	35.2	...
Atlanta[e]	4.3[c]	...	9.1	39.4	...
Birmingham	4.6	3.2	14.7	40.2	...
New Orleans	4.3	3.1	16.2	38.6	...
Houston	4.8	3.8	13.8	34.2	53.7
San Antonio[e]	4.1[c]	...	26.5	24.0	55.9
San Francisco–Oakland[e]	4.6[c]	...	7.8	29.8	21.7
Los Angeles	4.5	4.1	9.7[e]	22.7[e]	37.2[e]

SOURCES: *U. S. Census of Housing: 1950*, Vol. I, *General Characteristics*, chap. 1, "U. S. Summary," and chapters for the respective states; Vol. II, *Nonfarm Housing Character-istics*, chapters for the respective states. *U. S. Census of Population: 1950*, Vol. IV, *Special Reports*, Part 3, chap. C, "Persons of Spanish Surname." Housing and Home Finance Agency, Office of the Administrator, Division of Housing Research, *Housing of the Non-white Population, 1940 to 1950* (1952). Unpublished tables and special tabulations of 1950 Housing Census data supplied by the Bureau of the Census.
[a] Data refer to nonfarm dwelling units only, unless otherwise specified.
[b] Percent of dwelling units with 1.01 or more persons per room.
[c] All races.
[d] Data for the five states of Arizona, California, Colorado, New Mexico, and Texas.
[e] Data for total dwelling units.

unit occupied by a nonwhite family was nearly a room and a half smaller than the median white unit.

Census data for 1950 on number of rooms are available for nine standard metropolitan areas, as shown in table 15. In all these metropolitan areas, the nonwhites' dwelling units were smaller than the white occupied. The widest racial differences were in the South. In Birmingham, New Orleans, and Houston, the typical nonwhite dwelling was smaller than its white counterpart by an entire room or more. In the northern and western metropolitan areas except St. Louis, nonwhite dwelling units averaged considerably larger than in the South and approached more nearly the white standard of size.[10]

Home-owning nonwhites in the northern areas had nearly the same, and in Los Angeles did have the same, number of rooms as white homeowners. In all the southern metropolitan areas, however, and in St. Louis, nonwhite owner-occupied dwellings were considerably smaller than the houses of white owners (Appendix table A-7).

Rented units, as would be expected, were much smaller than those owner occupied in all areas for both color groups. Here again, nonwhite rented units in the South and in St. Louis were much smaller than those of whites. However, the widest racial difference was not in the South but in Chicago. In that metropolitan area, the nonwhite rented dwellings, on the average, were smaller than white units by an entire room. As might be expected, the rate of nonwhite crowding in Chicago is comparable to that of southern cities and substantially higher than in other northern areas except St. Louis (Appendix table A-6).

The failure of nonwhites to share fully in the expansion of the housing supply during the 1940-1950 decade is clearly reflected in the crowding situation at the two dates. The frequency of crowding diminished substantially among white households but changed very little among nonwhites. Nonwhite homeowners gained somewhat more space, but tenant households were more often crowded in 1950 than ten years earlier (table 16).

Further evidence of the extent of crowded conditions in nonwhite households is the high proportion of "doubled up" families in the same dwelling unit, discussed in the preceding chapter.

Housing deficiencies tend to occur not singly but in combination. The worst conditions of crowding are found not in the good quality dwellings but in the poorest ones. In each of seven metropolitan areas for which data are available, as shown in table 17,

---

[10] The measure of dwelling unit size is number of rooms. Data do not exist for measuring size by any other criterion.

TABLE 16

PERCENT OF NONFARM HOUSEHOLDS WITH 1.01 OR MORE
PERSONS PER ROOM, UNITED STATES, 1940 AND 1950

	White		Nonwhite	
Tenure	1940	1950	1940	1950
All households	16.2	13.3	33.8	32.1
Owners	11.1	9.4	25.4	22.0
Tenants	19.9	18.1	36.5	37.5

SOURCE: Housing and Home Finance Agency, Office of the Administrator, Division of Housing Research, *Housing of the Nonwhite Population, 1940 to 1950* (1952), table 6.

crowding is much more prevalent in the dilapidated and deficient units than in the standard dwellings. Significantly, the racial difference in rate of crowding narrows in going down the scale of housing quality. In the poorest class of dwellings, whites and nonwhites are about equally crowded. In standard dwellings, however, the frequency of crowding is two to three times greater for nonwhites than for whites. It is difficult to explain why this should be. It may be surmised that whites and nonwhites occupying the poorest class of housing are probably of similar economic and social status; further, that because segregation barriers are usually weak or nonexistent where poor housing is concerned, whites and nonwhites compete for such housing on relatively even terms. Where access to good housing is at stake, the nonwhites in the market have less purchasing power than the competing whites and also the social factors limiting nonwhites' choices come into play at this point. For both reasons, probably, nonwhites who purchase or rent standard housing tend to obtain smaller units than whites.

Homeownership

Traditionally, nonwhites have lived chiefly in rented dwellings, and comparatively few have owned their homes. They have participated, however, in the upsurge of homeownership which began during World War II.

From 1900 to 1940, the proportion of all American families owning their homes fluctuated narrowly around 45 percent. The

TABLE 17

PERCENT OF NONFARM DWELLING UNITS CROWDED[a] BY CONDITION AND
PLUMBING FACILITIES, BY COLOR AND TENURE OF OCCUPANTS,
FOR SELECTED STANDARD METROPOLITAN AREAS, 1950
(in percent)

Standard metropolitan area and color of occupants	Owner-occupied units[b]			Renter-occupied units		
	Total	Standard[c]	Dilapi-dated and deficient[d]	Total	Standard[c]	Dilapi-dated and deficient[d]
Chicago						
White	7.7	6.6	36.0	14.3	11.8	28.3
Nonwhite	21.5	17.5	38.6	40.4	30.4	49.3
Detroit						
White	8.3	7.1	42.9	11.7	8.9	27.5
Nonwhite	16.9	15.3	44.1	29.3	25.2	37.4
Los Angeles						
White	6.7	6.2	42.6	12.0	9.7	40.3
Nonwhite	15.6	14.7	35.9	26.6	22.8	46.9
St. Louis						
White	10.9	8.4	34.8	22.1	13.4	42.4
Nonwhite	24.9	16.4	34.9	28.0	24.6	42.3
New Orleans						
White	13.0	8.0	45.3	18.9	14.4	36.3
Nonwhite	33.0	21.4	45.1	41.2	30.1	45.4
Houston						
White	11.1	7.6	52.7[e]	19.2	12.9	49.7
Nonwhite	19.7	10.0	28.1	28.9	22.5	36.5
Birmingham						
White	9.5	5.1	46.1	21.4	10.2	30.0
Nonwhite	29.0	11.7	43.2	45.9	24.5	46.1

SOURCE: Computed from unpublished special tabulations of 1950 Housing Census data supplied by the Bureau of the Census. Data are based on a 20 percent sample.

[a] With 1.01 or more persons per room.

[b] Single-unit properties only.

[c] Not dilapidated, with private toilet, bath, and hot running water.

[d] Dilapidated and lacking hot water, private toilet, or bath.

[e] The high proportion of white-occupied dwellings crowded in the dilapidated and deficient category in Houston probably reflects the prominence of Spanish-name households in this class of dwelling units.

home-owning proportion of nonwhites was equally stable around 24 percent. This stability was abruptly broken after 1940. By 1950, 57 percent of all white nonfarm households were owners, and among Negroes owner-occupancy (nonfarm) increased from less than 23 percent to almost 35 percent of the total.

In thirteen metropolitan areas, the home-owning proportion of

Negro households varied in 1950 from 55 percent in Detroit to less than 12 percent in New York. For whites, the range of variation was much narrower: 33 percent to 66 percent, or neglecting New York, 44 to 66 percent. This difference suggests the presence of special conditions affecting Negro homeownership from one area to another. It might be expected that where the rate of white homeownership is high, homeownership among Negroes would also be relatively high, but this is not always true. Washington, D. C., and Chicago, for example, have almost identical percentages of home-owning whites. But relatively, more than twice as many Negroes own their homes in Washington than in Chicago (16 and 34 percent, respectively). Washington and Philadelphia have about the same proportion of home-owning Negroes (one-third), but white homeownership is much more widespread in Philadelphia than in Washington. Obviously, from one metropolitan area to another, the factors which affect the choice of ownership versus renting are not the same for Negroes as for whites. The differences are probably to be found in the different types of residence areas and housing available to Negroes in the various cities.

Nonwhites other than Negroes, in most metropolitan areas examined, are homeowners to a lesser extent than Negroes. The Spanish-name population, however, in both Texas and California and in all metropolitan areas except San Antonio, has a higher rate of homeownership than Negroes. In Texas and in the San Antonio metropolitan area, a majority of Spanish-name households are owners, although the homes which they own are chiefly of very poor quality.

Values and Rents

The median value in 1950 of nonfarm single-unit properties owned and occupied by nonwhites in the United States was $3,000, or about 40 percent of the median value of white-occupied properties (table 18). Spanish-name properties had a slightly higher median value. In Texas, however, and especially in the San Antonio metropolitan area, where the Spanish-name dwellings are poorest, the units were valued well below those occupied

TABLE 18

MEDIAN VALUE AND MEDIAN GROSS RENT OF NONFARM OWNER- AND TENANT-OCCUPIED
DWELLINGS, FOR WHITE, NONWHITE, AND SPANISH-NAME WHITE OCCUPANTS:
UNITED STATES, SELECTED STATES, AND STANDARD METROPOLITAN AREAS, 1950[a]

Area	Single-unit, owner-occupied dwellings: median value[b]			Tenant-occupied dwellings: median gross monthly rent		
	White	Non-white	Spanish-name	White	Non-white	Spanish-name
United States	$ 7,700	$ 3,000	$3,160	$44	$27	$26[c]
Standard metropolitan areas						
New York	12,350	8,600	...	49	42	...
Philadelphia	...	...	...	...	...	...
Washington, D. C.	14,550	10,700	...	64	49	...
Chicago	12,000	7,050	...	50	43	...
Detroit	9,050	7,000	...	50	46	...
St. Louis	9,100	3,350	...	41	29	...
Atlanta	8,700	3,800	...	44	24	...
Birmingham	6,950	2,800	...	38	19	...
New Orleans	10,100	3,700	...	34	21	...
Houston	7,900	3,850	4,419	47	39	30
San Antonio	7,100	4,050	3,211	36	25	23
San Francisco–Oakland	...	...	9,408	...	...	35
Los Angeles	10,007	8,156	6,878	45	39	32
Selected states						
California	9,564[d]	...	6,600	42[d]	...	31
Texas	6,245	2,207	1,883	39	25	20

SOURCES: *U. S. Census of Housing: 1950*, Vol. I, *General Characteristics*, chap. 1, "U. S. Summary," and chapters for the respective states; Vol. II, *Nonfarm Housing Characteristics*, chapters for the respective states. *U. S. Census of Population: 1950*, Vol. IV, *Special Reports*, Part 3, chap. C, "Persons of Spanish Surname." Housing and Home Finance Agency, Office of the Administrator, Division of Housing Research, *Housing of the Nonwhite Population, 1940 to 1950* (1952). Unpublished tables and special tabulations of 1950 Housing Census data supplied by the Bureau of the Census.

[a] Based on a 20 percent sample of nonfarm dwelling units.

[b] Medians rounded to nearest multiple of $50 except United States total and nonwhite medians, which were rounded to nearest $100 by the Census.

[c] Based on data for the five states of Arizona, California, Colorado, New Mexico, and Texas.

[d] Total occupied dwellings.

by nonwhites, as they also were in the Los Angeles metropolitan area.

Census data for eleven metropolitan areas reveal an expected, wide divergence of housing values between southern and northern or western areas. More significant, however, are the regional differences in comparative values of white and nonwhite properties. In the southern metropolitan areas and in St. Louis the typical house occupied by a nonwhite owner was valued at a third to half of the value of its white-owned counterpart. In the metropolitan areas of the North and West, on the other hand, with the exception of Chicago, nonwhite-owned homes approach much more closely the general standard of the community in values. The median values of nonwhite owner-occupied dwellings in the New York, Washington, Detroit, and Los Angeles areas were 75 to 80 percent of the medians of white-occupied properties.

For Spanish-name homeowners similar differences exist between the groups in California and in Texas. In California, properties with Spanish-name owner-occupants were valued at approximately two-thirds of the median value of total white owner-occupied dwellings, but in Texas the corresponding ratio was little more than one-third.

Gross rents paid by nonwhites followed a similar pattern. In the St. Louis and southern metropolitan areas, except Houston and San Antonio, nonwhites were paying median rents of half to two-thirds of those paid by whites. In the North and West, and in Houston, nonwhite median gross rents varied between 80 and 95 percent of the white medians. Considering the large differences in size and quality of rental units occupied by whites or nonwhites, the comparatively small differences in median rents suggest that nonwhites obtain less and poorer housing than whites for the same expenditures.

Summary

The statistical picture of minority group housing which emerges from the facts presented here can be summarized briefly. Minority groups receive less than a proportionate share of housing space in relation to their numbers. They have not shared fully in the expansion of the housing supply, neither before 1950 nor subsequently. Their lack of space is reflected in frequent crowding of dwelling units and doubling up of families.

The minority groups are even more disadvantaged in quality of housing than in quantity. The large majority of nonwhite and Spanish-name households occupy dwelling units which are either dilapidated or lacking essential sanitary facilities or both. However, the rents paid by nonwhites are, on the average, in many areas, not a great deal less than those paid by white households. This suggests that nonwhites may be paying more than whites for housing of similar amount and quality.

The minority groups have participated in the general movement from tenancy to homeownership which began during the 1940-1950 period. However, the white-nonwhite differential in extent of homeownership remained unchanged through the decade.

The housing disadvantage of nonwhites is more severe in the South than in the North and West. Not only do nonwhites receive less and poorer housing in the South, but the discrepancy between their housing conditions and those of the white population is much greater in the South than in the North and West. This contrast is also true for the Spanish-name population between Texas and California, the two states where this group is most numerous.

VIII

Housing in Relation to Income

The inferior housing conditions of the minority groups as compared with those of the majority white population must result, in some degree, from the former's lower incomes, as well as from racial discrimination and other handicaps. To shed some light on the relative weights of income versus other factors, the present chapter examines white-nonwhite differences in housing measures which remain when income differences are removed. The data consist primarily of special tabulations from the 1950 Housing Census in which selected characteristics of dwelling units are stratified by income classes of the occupants, white and nonwhite. The data are available for eight standard metropolitan areas chosen to represent different regions and diverse conditions.[1] The eight standard metropolitan areas are those of New York–Northeastern New Jersey, Chicago, Detroit, Los Angeles, Birmingham (Alabama), New Orleans, Houston, and St. Louis.

[1] The special tabulations supplied by the U. S. Bureau of the Census relate only to dwelling units occupied by nonwhites. Data for white-occupied units were obtained by subtraction from the published census statistics pertaining to total occupied dwelling units classified by income of occupants (*U. S. Census of Housing: 1950*, Vol. II, *Nonfarm Housing Characteristics*, chapters for the respective standard metropolitan areas). All calculations and comparisons have been prepared by research staff for the Commission on Race and Housing. The Census Bureau is not to be considered responsible for the use made here of the special tabulations.

Housing Quality and Income

The proportions of white and nonwhite households occupying dwellings of standard quality at selected levels of income are shown in tables 19 and 20. Parts of these data are also represented graphically in figures 4 and 5. If income were the only factor making for racial differences in housing quality, it would be expected that *within each income class*, the percentages of whites

TABLE 19

Percent of Renter-occupied Dwelling Units Standard,[a] by Income and Color of Occupants, for Selected Metropolitan Areas, 1950

Standard metropolitan area and color of occupants	Total reporting	Income of primary families and individuals: selected classes			
		Less than $2,000	$2,000- 2,999	$4,000- 4,999	$7,000 and more
New York					
White	87.4	77.8	83.8	91.4	96.6
Nonwhite	63.8	58.2	65.8	72.4	80.9
Chicago					
White	76.3	60.1	66.1	81.3	93.8
Nonwhite	35.4	26.3	35.6	48.2	66.1
Detroit					
White	85.1	74.8	77.8	90.1	96.5
Nonwhite	63.0	55.6	60.8	72.5	81.2
Los Angeles					
White	88.2	79.0	87.4	94.5	98.0
Nonwhite	73.8	65.8	75.3	85.1	87.9
St. Louis					
White	58.7	46.0	49.7	67.0	87.9
Nonwhite	17.9	14.1	20.1	35.3	37.0
New Orleans					
White	59.4	47.4	55.6	68.5	76.4
Nonwhite	13.3	12.3	13.0	24.7	41.7
Houston					
White	76.8	58.2	70.5	87.7	96.6
Nonwhite	27.6	25.1	30.0	33.3	65.2
Birmingham					
White	56.7	39.6	45.3	73.8	87.7
Nonwhite	7.0	7.7	5.2	7.9	21.4

Source: *U. S. Census of Housing: 1950*, Vol. II, *Nonfarm Housing Characteristics*, chap. 101, "New York–Northeastern New Jersey," table A-4, and unpublished special tabulations of 1950 Housing Census data supplied by the Bureau of the Census. Data are based on a 20 percent sample of dwelling units, hence are subject to sampling variability.

[a] Not dilapidated and containing private bath and toilet and hot running water.

and of nonwhites occupying standard dwelling units would be substantially identical. Instead, the data show a differential unfavorable to nonwhites persisting through all the income classes. At every level of income, in every standard metropolitan area, nonwhite households occupied a smaller percentage of standard dwellings than the comparable group of white families. This holds true for both renters and homeowners, although the latter

TABLE 20

Percent of Owner-occupied Dwelling Units Standard,[a] by Income and Color of Owner, for Selected Metropolitan Areas, 1950[b]

Standard metropolitan area and color of owner	Total reporting	Income of primary families and individuals: selected classes			
		Less than $2,000	$2,000-2,999	$4,000-4,999	$7,000 and more
New York					
White	95.4	88.8	92.4	96.6	98.7
Nonwhite	85.3	78.9	82.8	92.1	95.2
Chicago					
White	89.7	80.4	81.2	90.9	97.0
Nonwhite	67.5	55.9	62.9	74.2	81.7
Detroit					
White	92.6	84.1	86.3	94.2	98.3
Nonwhite	84.8	75.0	84.8	91.2	88.9
Los Angeles					
White	95.0	90.2	92.2	96.6	99.0
Nonwhite	92.9	88.9	92.7	96.0	98.5
St. Louis					
White	82.3	67.2	73.7	87.1	95.7
Nonwhite	42.1	30.9	43.5	54.6	75.5
New Orleans					
White	83.1	67.2	73.6	90.4	97.7
Nonwhite	29.3	21.3	26.8	61.5	84.8
Houston					
White	87.7	70.4	76.1	91.9	98.8
Nonwhite	38.8	27.2	41.3	62.4	76.5
Birmingham					
White	75.7	52.1	62.1	85.3	97.0
Nonwhite	20.9	15.2	20.9	43.3	70.4

Source: *U. S. Census of Housing: 1950*, Vol. II, *Nonfarm Housing Characteristics*, chapters for the respective standard metropolitan areas, table A-4, and unpublished special tabulations of 1950 Housing Census data supplied by the Bureau of the Census. Data are based on a 20 percent sample of dwelling units, hence are subject to sampling variability.

[a] Not dilapidated and containing private bath and toilet and hot running water.

[b] Data refer to total owner-occupied dwelling units.

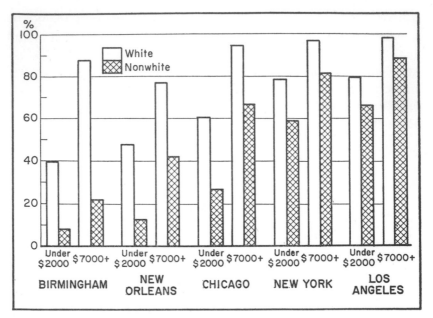

Figure 4. Rented dwellings, percent standard by income and color.

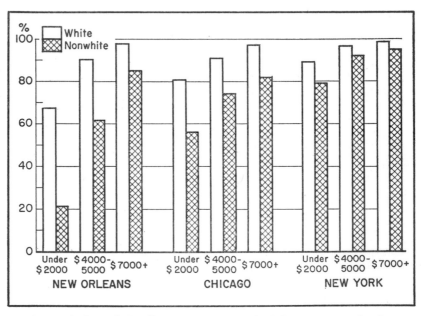

Figure 5. Owned dwellings, percent standard by income and color.

had better quality dwellings and were less disadvantaged in comparison with white owners than were the renters.

In rented dwellings for all income classes, the racial disparity was widest in the South and narrowest in the West (Los Angeles). In New Orleans, for example, the proportion of nonwhite renters with standard dwellings was only 12 percent in the lowest income group, and rose to only 42 percent in the income class of $7,000 and over. By contrast, among the lowest income group of New Orleans white renters, 47 percent had standard dwellings and this proportion rose to more than 75 percent in the top income bracket. Similar relations held in the other southern areas. In Los Angeles, on the other hand, the fraction of nonwhite renters with standard dwellings rose through the income classes from 66 percent to nearly 90 percent and was never very far below the corresponding proportion of whites. Chicago conformed more closely to the southern pattern than to that of other northern or western metropolitan areas. In the income class of $4,000 to $5,000, more than four-fifths of white Chicago renters but fewer than half of the nonwhites obtained standard dwellings.

For homeowners, the racial differential in percent of standard dwellings was fairly wide in the lower income groups in most standard metropolitan areas, but approached more closely to the white proportion at the income level of $7,000 and more. Again Los Angeles manifests the smallest racial differences and the southern standard metropolitan areas the largest.

Dwelling Space, Household Size, and Crowding

Racial differences in dwelling space (number of rooms) are strongly patterned by region and metropolitan area. In New York, Detroit, and Los Angeles, income class by income class, nonwhite renters had more rooms than whites. In Chicago, St. Louis, New Orleans, and Birmingham, nonwhite renters had fewer rooms than whites in every income class. Houston presented a mixed situation, with nonwhites having more rooms than whites in some income classes and fewer in others. The picture for owners is similar except that in Chicago, St. Louis, and the South, nonwhites had larger dwellings than whites in certain income groups. These relationships are shown in figure 6. Data are presented in Appendix tables A-6 and A-7.

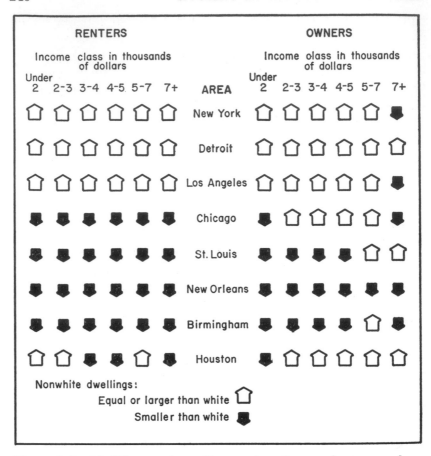

Figure 6. Racial differences in median number of rooms, by income class, 1950.

Thus it seems that in some areas but not in others, nonwhites at given levels of income are better able to obtain space than quality in their dwellings. In Chicago, St. Louis, and the South, however, regardless of income, nonwhites are disadvantaged in both quality and space. The number of rooms is significant, of course, not by itself, but only in relation to the number of people to be housed. As noted previously, nonwhite households are generally larger than white. In the eight metropolitan areas under consideration, the nonwhite households, both owner and renter, averaged larger than the white in virtually every income class in every area (Appendix tables A-8 and A-9). The slightly superior size of nonwhite dwelling units in a few areas was insufficient to balance the larger households, with the result of uniformly high rates of room crowding in all income classes.

As would be expected, the greatest frequency of nonwhite crowding and the widest racial difference in crowding rates occur in Chicago, St. Louis, and the southern metropolitan areas. Renter

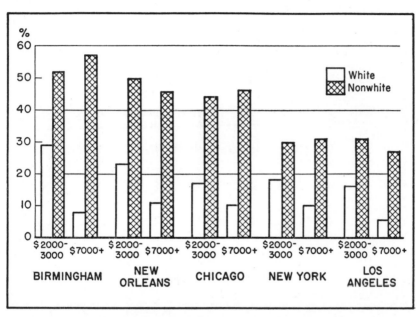

Figure 7. Rented dwellings, percent with 1.01 or more persons per room by income and color.

households are more often crowded than owners (figure 7, tables 21 and 22). The striking fact, however, that emerges from these data is the near uniformity of nonwhite crowding rates through the array of income classes. Disregarding the lowest income group, which contains many one- and two-person households, whites obtained more space per person as their incomes rose, but nonwhites generally did not. Nonwhite households with incomes in excess of $5,000 were virtually as often crowded as those in lower income groups. Plainly, the wide prevalence of crowding in nonwhite households is not associated with income.

TABLE 21

Percent of Renter-occupied Dwelling Units with 1.01 or More Persons
per Room, by Income and Color of Occupants,
for Selected Metropolitan Areas, 1950

Standard metropolitan area and color of occupants	Total report-ing	Income of primary families and individuals					
		Less than $2,000	$2,000-2,999	$3,000-3,999	$4,000-4,999	$5,000-6,999	$7,000 and more
New York							
White	17.1	12.8	18.2	20.3	19.2	17.0	9.9
Nonwhite	25.8	22.6	29.7	27.7	28.1	25.9	30.8
Chicago							
White	14.6	12.5	17.0	17.4	15.8	12.6	10.1
Nonwhite	40.6	36.6	44.0	43.3	42.7	37.5	46.0
Detroit							
White	11.8	12.3	15.5	14.4	11.0	7.8	7.0
Nonwhite	29.3	25.7	31.4	31.3	26.6	29.9	32.2
Los Angeles							
White	12.1	10.6	15.9	15.4	12.1	8.1	5.5
Nonwhite	26.3	23.4	31.1	27.1	24.5	24.8	26.9
St. Louis							
White	22.5	19.8	28.7	27.1	19.9	15.2	13.0
Nonwhite	38.0	34.7	42.1	45.8	42.9	39.6	35.7
New Orleans							
White	19.1	18.2	23.2	21.6	17.8	14.4	10.8
Nonwhite	41.2	37.9	49.7	45.4	53.9	51.5	45.8
Houston							
White	19.7	24.6	26.9	20.8	14.9	10.1	6.0
Nonwhite	29.2	25.8	33.9	32.4	40.0	38.6	20.0
Birmingham							
White	21.7	26.1	28.9	21.1	15.0	11.4	7.9
Nonwhite	45.7	40.8	51.9	61.7	64.7	63.6	57.1

Source: *U. S. Census of Housing: 1950*, Vol. II, *Nonfarm Housing Characteristics*, chapters for the respective standard metropolitan areas, tables A-7, and unpublished special tabulations of 1950 Housing Census data supplied by the Bureau of the Census. Data are based on a 20 percent sample of dwelling units, hence are subject to sampling variability.

Rents and Values Related to Income

There remains the question whether nonwhites pay as much for housing as do whites of comparable incomes. Considering the inferior quality of nonwhite dwellings contrasted with those of whites at every income level—an inferiority not compensated by additional space—we would expect, apart from racial dis-

TABLE 22

PERCENT OF OWNER-OCCUPIED DWELLING UNITS WITH 1.01 OR MORE PERSONS
PER ROOM, BY INCOME AND COLOR,[a] SELECTED METROPOLITAN AREAS, 1950

Standard metropolitan area and color of owner	Total report-ing	Income of primary families and individuals					
		Less than $2,000	$2,000-2,999	$3,000-3,999	$4,000-4,999	$5,000-6,999	$7,000 and more
New York							
White	6.5	4.4	7.3	7.6	7.4	6.5	5.8
Nonwhite	15.0	12.8	16.1	15.3	15.2	15.2	21.3
Chicago							
White	7.9	4.2	8.2	9.6	9.3	7.6	7.8
Nonwhite	20.3	16.4	22.2	20.7	20.6	23.2	22.2
Detroit							
White	8.3	5.7	9.6	10.5	9.1	7.6	6.8
Nonwhite	17.7	14.6	17.2	18.0	17.6	20.0	25.7
Los Angeles							
White	7.6	5.2	10.2	10.3	9.0	6.5	4.5
Nonwhite	16.1	13.0	17.6	17.0	14.4	17.9	25.4
St. Louis							
White	11.9	7.7	14.2	15.1	13.3	10.8	8.9
Nonwhite	25.8	22.0	28.8	30.3	28.1	23.8	29.4
New Orleans							
White	12.6	10.2	18.6	14.4	13.3	11.0	8.2
Nonwhite	30.2	26.5	36.2	33.0	34.9	37.8	18.2
Houston							
White	11.3	12.2	18.2	14.7	11.0	8.1	4.4
Nonwhite	19.2	18.4	21.5	17.4	20.4	16.3	6.3
Birmingham							
White	10.0	10.9	15.5	11.5	8.4	7.1	4.7
Nonwhite	29.2	23.9	35.9	34.1	33.8	28.4	34.6

SOURCE: *U. S. Census of Housing: 1950*, Vol. II, *Nonfarm Housing Characteristics*, chapters for the respective standard metropolitan areas, tables A-7, and unpublished special tabulations of 1950 Housing Census data supplied by the Bureau of the Census. Data are based on a 20 percent sample of dwelling units, hence are subject to sampling variability.

[a] Data refer to total owner-occupied dwelling units.

crimination, that nonwhites would pay considerably less for their housing. This seems to be true with nonwhite owners generally and with renter households in the South only. Summary measures of racial differences in gross rent and value by income class are given in tables 23 and 24, with further data in Appendix tables A-10 and A-11.

TABLE 23

RATIO OF NONWHITE TO WHITE MEDIAN GROSS RENTS BY INCOME,
FOR SELECTED METROPOLITAN AREAS, 1950

Standard metropolitan area	Total report-ing	Income of primary families and individuals					
		Less than $2,000	$2,000-2,999	$3,000-3,999	$4,000-4,999	$5,000-6,999	$7,000 and more[a]
New York	84.8	93.1	93.8	92.0	88.3	84.6	73.5
Chicago	94.2	90.0	98.5	99.0	98.3	97.3	83.3
Detroit	91.9	96.0	98.0	97.2	94.8	95.2	85.1
Los Angeles	88.1	98.8	93.9	93.3	90.3	88.6	64.1
St. Louis	71.5	85.5	85.0	81.5	85.2	81.3	62.7
New Orleans	62.7	73.1	74.4	71.7	71.2	61.1	50.4
Houston	82.2	97.9	95.9	89.5	89.1	77.6	71.1
Birmingham	50.0	66.3	66.3	58.9	48.5	49.2	35.0

SOURCE: Appendix table A-10.
[a] The sharp drop in the ratios in this open-end interval is probably due to the higher income range of whites than of nonwhites in the class. Therefore, the significant ratios are those in the preceding columns.

TABLE 24

RATIO OF NONWHITE TO WHITE MEDIAN MARKET VALUE OF OWNER-OCCUPIED,
SINGLE-UNIT PROPERTIES[a] BY INCOME, FOR
SELECTED METROPOLITAN AREAS, 1950

Standard metropolitan area	Total report-ing	Income of primary families and individuals					
		Less than $2,000	$2,000-2,999	$3,000-3,999	$4,000-4,999	$5,000-6,999	$7,000 and more
New York	66.7	69.5	75.5	79.3	75.2	73.3	76.9
Chicago	59.1	58.7	70.4	67.3	67.0	70.8	69.3
Detroit	77.8	84.6	90.6	88.3	82.6	77.8	63.5
Los Angeles	82.1	84.2	90.9	90.7	87.3	80.3	70.5
St. Louis	37.4	38.6	51.0	48.3	51.5	53.2	54.1
New Orleans	36.7	46.6	55.9	50.9	64.5	48.3	49.8
Houston	47.8	54.1	63.0	66.6	63.1	67.1	53.8
Birmingham	40.7	48.8	52.9	53.2	53.6	56.3	49.8

SOURCE: Appendix table A-11.
[a] Value data are available only for single-unit properties, hence are not strictly comparable with previous tables referring to total owner-occupied dwellings. Single-unit properties occupied by nonwhite owners tend to be of somewhat poorer quality than the two- to four-unit properties with nonwhite owner-occupants.

In the northern and western standard metropolitan areas except St. Louis, nonwhites were paying median gross rents equal to 90 percent or more of white median rents in nearly all income-area classes below the highest income group; many of the ratios exceeded 95 percent. Nonwhites were thus in a position of near equality in rent but gross inequality in the character of their dwellings. In Chicago, for example, whites and nonwhites in the income range of $2,000 to $7,000 were paying practically the same median rent, but only about 40 percent of the dwellings obtained by the nonwhites were of standard quality compared with 75 percent of the white-occupied units; moreover, the dwellings of nonwhites averaged about half a room smaller than those occupied by whites.

The housing situation of nonwhites in northern and western metropolitan areas in 1950 reflected the combined impact of restricted supply and large-scale in-migration. The pressure of a rapidly increasing population on a sluggishly expanding housing supply undoubtedly served, within the limitations of rent control, to bid up the price of shelter available to nonwhites. In addition, the fact that a great many nonwhites were newcomers placed them at a disadvantage in competing for housing in the tight wartime and postwar market.

Contrasting with the northern-western near equality of rents, New Orleans and Birmingham showed a wide gap between the median rents paid by whites and nonwhites, at the same income levels. Nonwhites in these southern metropolitan areas paid considerably lower rents than whites and received vastly inferior housing. Birmingham nonwhites, for example, with incomes of $4,000 to $7,000, paid less than half as much rent as whites in the same income groups, but their dwellings averaged about a room smaller than those of whites and fewer than 10 percent were of standard quality. Houston followed the northern pattern in the income classes under $5,000, with a marked divergence of rents appearing above that level. St. Louis fell between the northern and southern patterns.

Nonwhite homeowners occupied significantly cheaper houses than white owners at all income levels in all metropolitan areas studied, but the differences were much wider in the South than in the North and West. In the New York standard metropolitan area, the houses of nonwhite owners were valued at about three-fourths of the average value of white owner-occupied dwellings in each income class; in Chicago the ratios were about two-thirds; and in Detroit and Los Angeles, from four-fifths to nine-tenths except in the highest income class. In New Orleans and Birmingham, the homes of nonwhite owners were worth little more than half as much as those of whites in the same income classes.

As measures of housing costs or outlays, house values are, of course, not directly comparable with rents. As shown in chapter xiii, nonwhite home purchasers often receive less favorable mortgage terms than white buyers. Consequently, a house of given value or price represents a larger current outlay for a nonwhite than for a white buyer. Therefore, when annual payments of principal and interest are considered, rather than market value, the racial differential is considerably reduced.[2] This is evidenced by national statistics of residential financing in 1950. In that year, nonwhite, nonfarm mortgagors with incomes of $3,000 to $4,000 had paid a median purchase price for their properties 27 percent below the median price paid by total mortgagors in the same income group ($4,400 and $5,700 respectively). The nonwhites, however, were obligated for median annual payments only 10 percent below the median payments by total mortgagors.[3] On FHA and VA mortgages, however, where terms were substantially the same for white and nonwhite borrowers, the latter were paying only 81 percent and 86 percent respectively as much as corresponding white borrowers, approximately consistent with the differences in purchase prices.

As the data indicate, the homes owned by nonwhites are not only larger and of better quality than rented units at each income level, but the white-nonwhite differences are also much smaller.

---

[2] Payments of principal and interest on mortgages are, of course, comparable with rents only as current outlay and not in terms of economic cost. Nevertheless, for the majority of house buyers, purchasing on a low down payment basis, the housing "price" which they can afford is probably more influenced by the monthly payments than by the sales price.

[3] U. S. Census of Housing: 1950, Vol. IV, Residential Financing, Part 1, "United States," chap. 3, tables 16 and 19. The data pertain to amortized mortgages on owner-occupied, nonfarm, single-unit properties.

Moreover, the nonwhite home buyers apparently received better housing "deals" than the renters since, although their houses were less good than those of whites, they were also less expensive. It seems evident, therefore, that nonwhites who own their homes are less disadvantaged racially than are the renters.

IX

Housing Quality, Quantity, and Cost

Racial differences in housing quality and space within an income class may be due, at least partly, to differing levels of expenditure for housing. Certain groups of nonwhites—southerners and home buyers—apparently spend less for housing than whites of similar incomes. It is necessary, therefore, to supplement the analysis of income relations by examining the housing conditions of whites and nonwhites when both groups pay the same rent or buy houses of the same value. Studies of minority group housing conditions have consistently reported that nonwhites received less and poorer housing for a given expenditure than whites, or that they paid more than whites for housing of equivalent amount and quality.[1] Weaver and Robinson were the first to present systematic evidence on the subject. They analyzed data of the 1940 Housing Census, relating the incidence of substandard dwelling units to rental value by color, and concluded that "The nonwhite family receives less housing value for the same price than does the white group which has access to an open housing market . . . even when the colored person can pay an economic rent, he has less chance than a white person of getting decent shelter."[2]

A 1955 rental housing survey in Buffalo, New York, conducted

[1] See Gunnar Myrdal, *An American Dilemma*, p. 379; Richard Sterner, *The Negro's Share*, p. 197.

[2] Robert C. Weaver, *The Negro Ghetto*, pp. 261-263. The statistical analysis is attributed to Corienne K. Robinson.

by the Census Bureau for the New York State Rent Commission, found that "In general, the quality of dwelling units obtainable in the housing market improves with the payment of higher rents . . . this is true for whites but not for nonwhites." Above a fairly low level, the payment of higher rents by nonwhites brought more space but not a better quality of dwelling unit.[3]

Data from special tabulations of 1950 Housing Census statistics show the housing quality and space obtained by white and non-white households at various levels of gross rent or market value in eight metropolitan areas in 1950. Because of technical differences in census definitions and in scope, precise comparison with Weaver and Robinson's 1940 results is not possible.[4] However, the two sets of data yield the same general picture, which does not seem to have changed very much between 1940 and 1950. The broad consistency of data for different areas and dates, including the 1955 Buffalo survey, gives convincing evidence that the failure of nonwhite minorities to obtain housing of comparable quality to that of whites, even when they pay the same prices, is a basic and enduring feature of their housing situation.

Concerning nonwhite renters, table 25 shows three major facts, partly represented also in figure 8. First, substantial improvement in housing quality was gained with increasing rent in all eight metropolitan areas. Nonwhite households paying $60 or more gross rent per month obtained standard dwellings (not dilapidated, and containing private bath, toilet, and hot running water) from three to twelve times more frequently than those paying less than $20. Second, nonwhites obtained fewer standard dwellings than whites at every level of rent. The full tabulation includes nine rent classes (only five are shown in the table) and eight standard metropolitan areas, making a total of seventy-two rent-area comparisons. In all but two comparisons, the percent of standard dwellings occupied by nonwhites was smaller than

---

[3] State of New York, Temporary State Housing Rent Commission, *People, Housing, and Rent Control in Buffalo*, by Frank S. Kristof (1956), p. 40.

[4] Weaver and Robinson's analysis of 1940 census data was limited to sixteen cities in the North and West. The data here presented are the first, so far as is known, which permit comparisons among metropolitan areas in different regions of the country.

TABLE 25

Standard metropolitan area and color of occupants	Total	Gross monthly rent (selected classes)				
		Less than $15	$20-24	$30-34	$40-49	$60 or more
New York						
White	87.6	31.3	41.9	67.1	90.2	97.5
Nonwhite	63.8	19.2	27.1	51.6	68.8	80.9
Chicago						
White	76.8	11.0	24.1	48.6	79.8	94.4
Nonwhite	35.5	12.0	9.4	20.8	33.5	63.0
Detroit						
White	84.8	32.3	31.3	60.8	85.4	95.3
Nonwhite	63.0	23.5	17.4	41.7	63.5	78.4
Los Angeles						
White	88.8	17.6	58.5	85.7	94.0	98.7
Nonwhite	74.8	17.2	57.4	70.8	77.3	89.3
St. Louis						
White	59.2	5.9	10.6	45.9	78.8	87.2
Nonwhite	17.6	4.1	5.1	14.0	36.7	52.2
New Orleans						
White	71.0	26.2	39.5	73.4	90.0	96.9
Nonwhite	13.3	5.3	11.7	22.2	41.4	50.0
Houston						
White	77.8	31.0	31.3	59.6	82.3	97.0
Nonwhite	26.9	11.7	11.9	20.3	24.6	58.9
Birmingham						
White	58.8	12.5	23.0	50.5	75.4	92.8
Nonwhite	6.8	2.5	3.1	25.4	64.2[b]	15.8[b]

Source: *U. S. Census of Housing: 1950*, Vol. II, *Nonfarm Housing Characteristics*, chapters for the respective standard metropolitan areas, and unpublished special tabulations of 1950 Housing Census data supplied by the Bureau of the Census. Data are based on a 20 percent sample of dwelling units, hence are subject to sampling variability.

[a] Not dilapidated and containing private toilet and bath and hot running water.

[b] These figures are probably not reliable. They are based on a very small number of cases.

that of whites. The white-nonwhite differential was substantial in nearly all cases.

The third important fact revealed in table 25 is the much wider racial differential in the South than in the North or West, except Chicago and St. Louis. Nonwhite renters in the New York, Detroit, and Los Angeles metropolitan areas obtained standard dwellings generally from two-thirds to four-fifths as often as whites at the same rent levels. In the southern metropolitan areas, on the other

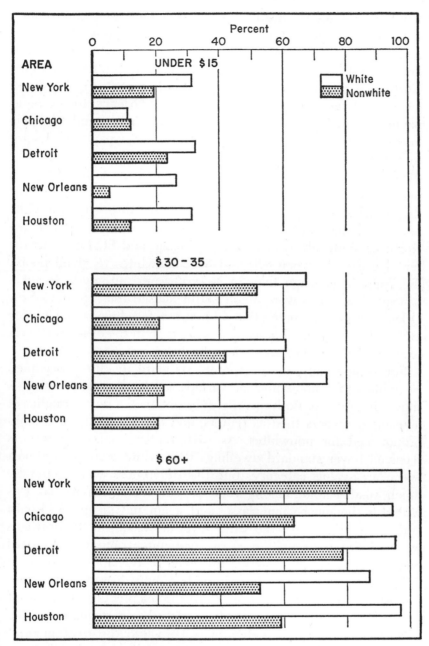

Figure 8. Rented dwellings, percent standard by gross rent and color.

hand, nonwhites received standard dwellings only a fifth to a half as frequently as did corresponding whites. Between northern and southern white renters, there is little difference in quality of housing obtained when they pay the same rent. But for nonwhites, North and South (Chicago and St. Louis excepted), the differences are large. White households in New Orleans, for example, paying $40 to $50 gross rent per month, obtained standard dwellings even more frequently than Detroit whites paying the same rent. Of Negroes in the $40 to $50 rent class, however, standard dwellings were occupied by 41 percent in New Orleans and 64 percent in Detroit. These differences support a conclusion that the nonwhite's housing dollar is not only worth less than a white person's money, but it also buys less in the South than in the North or West, always excepting Chicago and St. Louis. In the rental classes between $20 and $50, nonwhites received poorer dwellings in Chicago than in New Orleans, although, in total, Chicago nonwhites were much better housed than those of New Orleans. It must be noted that whites, too, fared worse in Chicago and St. Louis in rental housing quality than in the other northern-western metropolitan areas or in Houston.

For homeowners, the percent of standard dwellings occupied by whites and nonwhites at various levels of market value is shown in table 26. Both racial groups obtained a better quality of housing as owners than as renters, and the advantage was more pronounced for nonwhites. As with renters, nonwhite owners received fewer standard dwellings than white owners in almost every area-value category, but the differences were generally much smaller than among renters. The racial differential was widest in the lower-value classes and, again, in Chicago, St. Louis, and the South. Above the value level of $6,000, in the northern and western metropolitan areas, nonwhites obtained standard houses almost as often as whites; even in the South, the racial difference at this level was very wide only in New Orleans. It is important to note, however, that the elementary criteria of standard dwellings cease to differentiate housing quality at the higher values. Above a moderate level of value, the great majority of houses qualify as standard according to the present definition, but obviously, they still differ widely in quality.

TABLE 26

PERCENT OF OWNER-OCCUPIED SINGLE-UNIT DWELLINGS STANDARD,[a]
BY MARKET VALUE AND COLOR OF OWNER, FOR
SELECTED METROPOLITAN AREAS, 1950

Standard metropolitan area and color of owner	Total	Market value (selected classes)				
		Less than $2,000	$3,000- 3,999	$4,000- 4,999	$6,000- 7,499	$10,000 or more
New York						
White	97.3	66.4	61.8	74.4	93.0	99.4
Nonwhite	88.1	26.1	50.0	71.4	88.4	97.6
Chicago						
White	92.5	37.4	36.4	53.3	82.8	98.6
Nonwhite	68.1	16.0	28.2	41.6	76.7	94.4
Detroit						
White	93.8	44.5	48.0	72.7	94.3	99.4
Nonwhite	86.8	47.9	57.8	68.4	91.9	97.2
Los Angeles						
White	98.0	48.3	79.9	90.9	98.3	99.6
Nonwhite	94.9	51.9	81.9	85.9	96.3	99.1
St. Louis						
White	85.7	20.2	38.5	60.6	88.7	98.5
Nonwhite	40.9	5.7	28.1	55.2	82.9	90.9
New Orleans						
White	82.7	14.4	35.3	52.2	83.4	98.5
Nonwhite	26.8	2.4	17.8	37.1	47.4	73.2
Houston						
White	89.3	23.9	55.7	78.3	95.6	99.1
Nonwhite	36.8	3.3	23.1	46.3	71.9	80.2
Birmingham						
White	80.2	8.9	40.7	66.7	93.2	98.5
Nonwhite	21.8	2.4	17.1	41.8	72.3	84.6

SOURCE: *U. S. Census of Housing: 1950*, Vol. II, *Nonfarm Housing Characteristics*, chapters for the respective standard metropolitan areas, and unpublished special tabulations of 1950 Housing Census data supplied by the Bureau of the Census. Data are based on a 20 percent sample of dwelling units, hence are subject to sampling variability.

[a] Not dilapidated and containing private bath and toilet and hot running water.

Another measure of housing quality available from census statistics is the type of heating equipment. Although not valid for interregional comparisons, this characteristic throws added light on racial differences in housing quality. The racial comparisons are similar to those based on condition and plumbing facilities. In the lowest value class of single-unit dwellings (less than $2,000), those occupied by white owners were equipped with central heating about twice as frequently as the nonwhite owner-occupied, both in the North and in the South (North, including St. Louis: averages of 39 and 17 percent; South: 8 and 4 percent). Moving up the value scale, the racial differential narrowed in the North but not appreciably in the South. In the value group of $6,000 to $7,500, the average proportions of white and nonwhite owner-occupied dwellings with central heating were respectively 84 and 76 percent in the North, 30 and 18 percent in the South.[5]

The age of residential buildings is generally but not always associated with housing quality. As expected, the data (limited to owner-occupied, single-unit properties) show the dwellings of nonwhites to be usually considerably older than white-occupied dwellings regardless of value. It is striking that the highest proportions of relatively new nonwhite-owned homes (built after 1940) occurred in Chicago and New Orleans, where the quality of owner-occupied nonwhite dwellings was among the poorest in the group of metropolitan areas examined. In New Orleans, non-white-owned homes were, on the whole, newer than those of whites, but only one-fourth of them were of standard quality, compared with more than four-fifths of the latter. In Chicago there was little difference in the age of nonwhite and white owner-occupied houses, but a wide divergence in quality. In the Chicago value classes under $3,000, less than a third of the white-owned but fully half of the nonwhite-owned houses were built after 1940. At this low value level, houses of standard quality were possessed by about one-third of the white but only one-seventh of the nonwhite owner-occupants. Houston presents a similar picture in the value categories less than $3,000. In New York and Detroit, on the other hand, where practically all single-unit dwellings occupied by nonwhite owners were built before 1940, the quality of these dwellings was much better than in any of the other three standard metropolitan areas.

It seems evident from these data that in the metropolitan areas where new construction figured most prominently in the inventory of low-value nonwhite-owned homes, a great part of such construction was built below a conventional standard of minimum

---

[5] *U. S. Census of Housing: 1950*, Vol. II, *Nonfarm Housing Characteristics*, chapters for the respective standard metropolitan areas, and Special Tabulations. Data are based on a 4 percent sample of dwelling units.

quality. It follows that quality and age are probably less closely associated in nonwhite than in white ownership housing.

In view of the consistently poorer quality of housing obtained by nonwhites than by whites for the same rent or value, the question arises whether nonwhites are obtaining a larger number of rooms, in effect sacrificing quality for space to accommodate their larger households. The evidence indicates that nonwhite homeowners generally do purchase somewhat larger dwellings than whites at the same market values. In Detroit, nonwhite owners obtained, on the average, approximately one room more than whites in most value classes. Also in New York and Los Angeles, the differential favoring nonwhites was substantial at most levels of value.

Nonwhite renters, however, show no consistent tendency to obtain more space than white renters for the same rent. In some metropolitan areas, notably Detroit and Los Angeles, nonwhites tended to receive more rooms than whites, but elsewhere nonwhite rented dwellings were more often smaller than those of whites at the same rents. The nonwhite disadvantage was greatest in Chicago, where the dwellings of whites averaged fully a room or more larger than those of nonwhites through the rent range of $20 to $40. Data are presented in Appendix tables A-12 and A-13.

Although the dwellings of nonwhites, especially homeowners, were often larger than those of whites, they were not enough larger to compensate for the more numerous households of the former. In every metropolitan area, at virtually every level of rent or value, nonwhite households were more often crowded than those of whites.

Racial differences in the relation of housing quality and space to rent or value can be briefly summarized. As of 1950, nonwhite households, both renters and owners, obtained a poorer quality of housing than did whites at all levels of rent or value, in all regions of the country. Nonwhite homeowners had better quality dwellings than renters and approached more closely to the white standard, but a significant differential persisted, nevertheless, in most metropolitan areas and value classes. The racial differential in housing quality was widest in the South and in Chicago, notwithstanding the greater prominence of new construction for nonwhite owner-occupancy in these as compared with other areas.

Nonwhite homeowners obtained some offset to their quality disadvantage in the form of larger houses than those of whites. So also did nonwhite renters in a few metropolitan areas, although in most cases the rental units of nonwhites were smaller than those of whites at the same rent.

X

The Housing Market in Racially Mixed Areas

Two studies undertaken for the Commission on Race and Housing deal specifically with the impact of racial mingling in residence areas on local housing markets. One is an inquiry into the effects on residential property values of nonwhite entry into formerly all-white neighborhoods.[1] The second study is an analysis of demand for housing in racially mixed areas of one large city.[2]

Property Values and Race

According to traditional and widespread opinion, Negroes, and other minorities as well, are dangerous to property values when they seek housing, as they must, outside established minority residence areas. Underlying this belief are two basic propositions: first, that whites will not live in areas entered by nonwhites, and second, that nonwhite demand for housing is not sufficient to replace the vanished white demand and hence, prices must fall.

To many, these propositions seem self-evident, but in recent years both have been challenged. Not only have proponents of racial equality endeavored to demonstrate the error of the "property values myth," but in the real estate appraisal profession, increasing doubts have been expressed about the validity of the traditional doctrines under present-day conditions.

---

[1] Luigi Laurenti, *Property Values and Race: Studies in Seven Cities.*
[2] Chester Rapkin and William G. Grigsby, *The Demand for Housing in Racially Mixed Areas: A Study of the Nature of Neighborhood Change.*

The importance of the problem needs no emphasis. Fear of financial loss gives every property owner in white neighborhoods a direct personal stake in excluding minorities, at least up to a point. Convictions that racial mingling injures property values influence business decisions to build, finance, and sell in ways that restrict the opportunities of nonwhites to acquire housing and limit them to certain districts. In acting on the assumption that values in an area are going to fall, the housing industry and property owners may help to bring about the anticipated result. If major lenders act together to reduce their loans in an area, they may be not merely recognizing but making a shift to lower prices, by eliminating a part of the demand. Similarly, when homeowners in an affected area hasten to sell before the expected price decline occurs, the resulting oversupply of houses may push down their selling prices.[3]

The motive, moreover, of preserving capital, an eminently respectable purpose, often provides moral justification for racial discrimination. People may consider themselves not merely justified but even obligated to exclude minorities for the sake of maintaining values. The real estate board in one large city took this ground in a public statement of policy:

It is a matter of fact and experience that when a Negro or Chinese or Japanese or Filipino moves into a white district, the house values drop. . . . *We don't look at this as a social problem. For us this is an economic problem.* Looking at it this way, the Board has asked that its members not introduce into a residential district any occupancy or race which will have the effect of lowering values.[4]

In similar vein, a savings and loan association executive said in interview: "There are lots of things we would like to do personally, such as treating everybody equally, . . . but we are responsible for millions of dollars. . . . We will lend on properties up to three blocks away from colored areas but not closer. . . ."

Twenty years and more ago, real estate authorities asserted the

---

[3] This type of collective behavior, akin to panics, bank runs, and hoarding sprees, has been termed by Merton, the "self-fulfilling prophecy." Robert K. Merton, "The Self-Fulfilling Prophecy."

[4] Statement on behalf of the San Francisco Real Estate Board, reported in "The Negro in San Francisco," *San Francisco Chronicle,* November 6, 1950. Italics supplied.

adverse effect of nonwhite occupancy on values straightforwardly and with few qualifications. Fisher (1923), McMichael and Bingham (1923), Babcock (1932), Hoyt (1933, 1939), and other authors of standard texts and treatises pronounced a common judgment, accepted apparently without dissent.[5] Property appraisal standards of the Federal Housing Administration incorporated the accepted doctrine.

Since World War II, differing theories have been advanced by professional appraisers and others. According to one contemporary theory, the price depression associated with nonwhite entry is only temporary. House prices weaken in areas anticipating a racial change and may continue depressed during the early stages of transition, but after transition, prices rise again.[6] Myrdal espoused this view in the *American Dilemma* (1944).[7] More recently Charles A. Benson, chief appraiser of a leading mortgage-finance institution, reporting on a study of price changes in two Chicago areas—one all-white and one in racial transition—concludes:

. . . prices of residences are depressed from 30 percent to 55 percent when an area is threatened by transition. As soon as transition becomes a fact, prices tend to rise. . . . After transition has been accomplished, prices in the then Negro area compare favorably with prices in the city as a whole and are controlled by supply and demand.[8]

Some appraisers hold that nonwhite occupancy may actually enhance real estate values in certain conditions. According to the authorities just mentioned, active movement of nonwhites into an area is better for values than the continued threat of entry. Thurston Ross writes that "in poor and slum sections racial encroachment sometimes raises the economic standards of the neighborhood." He reports "instances where obsolescence has

---

[5] The relevant professional writings are reviewed in Laurenti, *Property Values and Race,* chap. ii.

[6] George W. Beehler, Jr., "Colored Occupancy Raises Values," *The Review of the Society of Residential Appraisers,* XI, no. 9 (September, 1945). See also Stanley L. McMichael, *McMichael's Appraising Manual,* p. 169.

[7] Gunnar Myrdal, *An American Dilemma,* p. 623.

[8] Charles A. Benson, "A Test of Transition Theories," *The Residential Appraiser,* Vol. 24, no. 8 (August, 1958), 8. Quoted with permission of the Society of Residential Appraisers.

been arrested and additional years of useful life given a neighborhood by racial encroachment, particularly when older people are displaced by younger groups of the encroaching race." [9]

The newer theories differ from the old in recognizing a variety of conditions under which nonwhite movement into an area can take place, and consequently a range of possible effects on values. Weaver especially emphasizes variation. Reviewing the evidence available in 1948, he wrote:

> The effect of Negro occupancy upon property values varies from one section of the city to another and from one time to another. . . . The arrival of a few Negroes may be the signal for a great decline in selling prices or it may lead to an appreciable increase. Much depends upon the state of the total housing market and the manner in which colored people enter an area. . . . *There is no one universal effect of Negro occupancy upon property values.*[10]

Weaver's view is reiterated by Abrams, who finds a complex of factors at work and "no fixed rules as to when minority neighbors raise or lower values." [11]

Appraisal policies of the Federal Housing Administration reflect the change in appraisal thinking. Where once the FHA flatly asserted the value-destroying tendency of mixed neighborhoods, in successive editions of the *Underwriting Manual* provisions touching race and property values have become steadily more qualified. References to "social and racial classes" have been deleted in favor of the more neutral "user groups," and the *Manual* now states,

> If a mixture of user groups is found to exist it must be determined whether the mixture will render the neighborhood less desirable to present and prospective occupants. If the occupancy of the neighborhood is changing from one user group to another, . . . any degree of risk is reflected in the rating. . . . Additional risk is not necessarily involved in such change.[12]

These judgments of real estate and housing authorities have been based mainly on professional experience and observation

---

[9] Thurston H. Ross, "Market Significance of Declining Neighborhoods."

[10] Robert G. Weaver, *The Negro Ghetto*, p. 293. Italics in original.

[11] Charles Abrams, *Forbidden Neighbors*, pp. 286, 292.

[12] Housing and Home Finance Agency, Federal Housing Administration, *Underwriting Manual*, Rev. April, 1958, sec. 1320.

rather than on research, for few factual studies have been made of what actually happens to house prices when nonwhites move into new areas. Difficult problems of method confront the study of this question. Merely to observe the course of prices in a neighborhood experiencing racial change tells little, for the movements observed might well be caused by factors other than the racial change. The measurement of racial influence on values is especially complicated by the tendency of minority groups to concentrate in slum and deteriorating sections affected by various adverse influences. To attribute the lower rents and prices in such areas solely to the presence of nonwhites would be obviously misleading.

To isolate the price effects of racial mixture, the price performance of racially mixed areas must be compared with some standard that is free of the racial influence being investigated. Laurenti's research for the Commission on Race and Housing attempts to do this. Twenty neighborhoods, recently become racially mixed, in San Francisco, Oakland, and Philadelphia were chosen for study. Each neighborhood, called a "test area," was matched with a "control" neighborhood which had remained all white. Each pair of neighborhoods was chosen according to criteria to ensure that the two would closely resemble each other in major factors affecting house prices. Criteria for matching included the age, type, and market value of houses, topography, location, land-use pattern, income and broad occupational class of residents, and the character of neighborhood development. A large number of areas were sifted in the search for matching pairs. Comparability of the paired neighborhoods was checked with local real estate brokers, appraisers, lenders, and assessors familiar with the histories of the areas. Informed local judgments were followed in fixing the area boundaries, usually marked by topographic features, arterial streets, or subdivision limits. All areas chosen were away from the central city districts and built up largely with single-unit, owner-occupied houses in the middle-value range. This collection of neighborhoods, therefore, represents the residences of the home-owning middle class in the cities studied. Within this category and subject to the limitations of matching, neighborhoods were selected to give as much diversity as possible in price class and degree of nonwhite occupancy.

The data consist of prices paid for houses in test and control neighborhoods during a period beginning before the entry of nonwhites into the test area and ending in the latter part of 1955. In most of the test areas the first nonwhite buyers arrived during the early postwar years. Sources of price data were the multiple listing services in San Francisco and Oakland, information from real estate brokers, and a real estate directory in Philadelphia, generally considered a reliable source of data for real estate transactions. Approximately ten thousand sales prices were collected, representing about half of all transactions in the San Francisco–Oakland areas and total sales in the Philadelphia areas during the periods studied.

For each neighborhood the collected prices were averaged by quarter years. In some areas with a wide range of prices, ratios of selling price to assessed valuation were computed and averaged by quarters. Using these quarterly averages, the movement of house prices in the neighborhoods entered by nonwhites was compared with price movements in matching all-white neighborhoods. Some of the twenty test areas were sufficiently similar to more than one control area to permit multiple comparisons. In all, thirty-four paired comparisons were made. Analysis yielded the following principal findings:

1. In fourteen of the thirty-four comparisons (41 percent), test prices stayed within 5 percent, plus or minus, of control prices during the observation period. This is considered to mean no significant difference in price behavior.
2. In fifteen comparisons (44 percent), test prices ended relatively higher than control prices, by margins of more than 5 to 26 percent.
3. In the remaining five comparisons (15 percent), test prices ended the observation period relatively lower than control prices, by margins of 5 to 9 percent.
4. From the date of first nonwhite entry to the end of the observation period, twenty of the thirty-four comparisons showed larger percent increases each quarter for test prices than for control prices.

At the end of the observation period (fall, 1955) the proportion of nonwhite residents in the twenty test areas varied from less than 2 percent to more than 70 percent. The data were examined to determine whether the extent of nonwhite entry affected the comparative performance of test and control area prices, with results given in table 27.

TABLE 27

PAIRED COMPARISONS OF TEST AND CONTROL AREA PRICES
BY PERCENT OF NONWHITES IN TEST AREA POPULATIONS

Test areas by percent of population nonwhite, 1955	Paired comparisons of price movements			
	Total	No significant difference[a]	Test area higher	Control area higher
30 to 75 percent 8 areas	16	10	5	1
14 to 28 percent 6 areas	9	3	4	2
6 to 7 percent 3 areas	5	...	4	1
3 percent or less 3 areas	4	1	2	1

SOURCE: Luigi Laurenti, *Property Values and Race*, Special Research Report to the Commission on Race and Housing (Berkeley and Los Angeles: University of California Press, 1960), chaps. vi, vii, and viii.
[a] Differences less than 5 percent.

As shown in the table, test areas in all ranges of nonwhite occupancy manifested both superior and inferior price performance as compared with control areas, but in every category, the majority of significant differences favored the test areas.

Distribution of test areas by percent of population nonwhite corresponds approximately to their distribution by average house value. The three neighborhoods with very limited nonwhite entry are of the exclusive type with houses considerably more expensive than any of the other areas. It is most unlikely that these neighborhoods can become all or mainly nonwhite within the foreseeable future, in contrast to the eight areas at the other end of the scale which were well on their way toward complete racial transition. It is significant, therefore, that in both classes of neighborhoods, nonwhite entry was more often associated with strengthening than with weakening house prices.

The facts of this study contradict the theory that nonwhite

entry into a neighborhood must produce a fall in property values. The findings are consistent with newer theories emphasizing a diversity of price outcomes according to circumstances; however, for the areas and time periods studied, the entry of nonwhites into previously all-white neighborhoods was more often associated with price improvement or stability than with price declines.

In assessing the significance of these findings, several factors must be borne in mind. The time period—end of the war through 1955—was one of unprecedented Negro demand for housing generated by large population movements to northern and western cities, by the new economic position of Negroes, and by the increasing availability of mortgage credit. A great backlog of Negro demand had accumulated, and the persistence of exclusion barriers through most of the better housing supply served to concentrate this pent-up demand on the areas open to Negroes.

In the neighborhoods studied, the behavior of white residents seemed to be quite different from the traditional response of whites to nonwhite entry. Although some of the areas showed considerable disturbance, there was almost complete absence of the panic flight of whites which in the past has characterized many zones of racial transition. In many of the neighborhoods, the white residents were anxious to sell but waited until they could get adequate prices from incoming buyers. Under the existing conditions, the nonwhite market offered sufficient demand to move the properties without price weakening—in fact, at prices generally somewhat higher than prevailed in comparable areas not affected by racial change.

These considerations may account for the maintenance of an orderly market and stable or rising prices in those areas heavily entered by nonwhites and evidently destined for complete racial transition. They do not explain the favorable price movements in the neighborhoods with low nonwhite proportions, for these depended upon continuing demand from whites. The conclusion must be that in these relatively expensive and desirable neighborhoods, a sparse scatter of nonwhites, almost imperceptible to most residents or prospective residents, did not noticeably affect the attractiveness of the areas in the white market.

Housing Demand in Racially Mixed Areas

The second study to be considered goes behind the facts of price movements to analyze the components of demand for housing in areas undergoing racial transition. This study analyzed all house sales recorded during 1955 in four areas of Philadelphia. Two of the areas contained relatively good housing, and in two the housing was mainly poor. Each quality pair further consisted of one area undergoing rapid racial transition and one where the Negro population was growing slowly. In all four areas, Negroes occupied 20 to 30 percent of the dwelling units.

A racial transition zone is commonly pictured as one where whites are leaving and nonwhites coming in. The Philadelphia study found the process to be considerably more complex. Among some two thousand home buyers, 443 or more than one-fifth were whites. Although outnumbered more than three to one by Negroes, the presence of white buyers in substantial numbers is, nevertheless, a significant fact from several points of view. It refutes the notion that whites will not buy in an area once entered by Negroes, and calls for inquiry into the conditions under which whites will continue to buy in such areas. As discussed previously (chap. iv), whether any area can maintain a racially mixed composition depends, of course, on its ability to attract new white residents.

Investigation of the trend of house prices in one area (good housing, rapid transition) revealed a substantial price advance from 1948 through 1955, of approximately the same magnitude as occurred in the city as a whole. The rise appeared most pronounced in the sections of heavy Negro entry and rapid departure of whites. This is further evidence that racial change is not necessarily associated with depressed prices.

Mortgage lenders often take a dubious view of racially mixed areas, but this was not true in Philadelphia. Financing was liberal and played a key role in sustaining demand and prices. Ninety percent of the white buyers and practically all the Negroes depended on mortgage financing to acquire their homes. The loans came almost entirely from established institutional sources. Negroes obtained mortgage terms more liberal than those advanced to whites. A third of the Negro buyers borrowed the entire purchase price and another third received 90 percent or more financing. Only 43 percent of the whites received 90 percent loans or better. Negro borrowers also received more favorable interest rates. Four-fifths of them paid less than $5\frac{1}{2}$ percent, as compared with three-quarters of the whites. The superior terms obtained by Negroes are explained by the higher percentage of VA and FHA loans made to this group. In addition to interest, "points" were generally charged, especially on VA loans, the typical charge being 5 percent. Point charges were usually paid by the seller but, in the judgment of informed observers, passed on to the buyer in the form of higher prices permitted by liberal VA appraisals. The role of easy financing in supporting the price rise is thus doubly apparent. Down payments of 10 percent to zero enabled large numbers of Negroes to buy who could not have met the down payment requirements of conventional loans.

The liberal policies of Philadelphia lending institutions toward these mixed-occupancy areas are a departure from the general practice of mortgage lenders. It should be noted that the loans were both safe and profitable. Nearly all were government insured or guaranteed. The willingness of sellers to pay point charges permitted lenders to combine the safety of guaranteed loans with the higher interest rates associated with conventional mortgage loans. Lenders were also influenced, undoubtedly, by the abundance of mortgage funds available in 1955. Whether they would take the same view of transition-area risks in a period of credit stringency is problematic.

Negro and white buyers paid virtually identical average prices for the homes they acquired except in the one area of poor housing and rapid transition, where Negroes paid substantially more than whites, on the average, and presumably acquired better dwellings. Negroes and whites received about the same value for their housing dollar, paying substantially the same prices for similar houses.

Analysis of the spatial distribution of Negro and white purchases reveals a marked tendency toward racial separation. Among the study areas, the ratio of Negro to white buyers was three to one in the area of good housing and rapid change, but

twenty-seven to one in the area characterized by poor housing
and fast change. In a third area, where the housing is good but
change slow, Negroes were outnumbered by white buyers two
to one.

Within the areas some blocks have become wholly Negro
occupied, others are mixed, still others have not yet received a
Negro resident. In the two areas accounting for the great majority
of white purchases, about a third of the blocks were white, but
they were the location of the large majority of all purchases by
white families.

To measure more strictly the spatial relationship of Negro and
white purchases, two calculations were made including the
proportion of white purchases made in a mixed block or adjacent
to a mixed block,[13] and the percent of white families who purchased homes on the same street front or directly across the
street from Negro residents. The second measure, obviously, is
a more critical test of residential proximity, since residents in
the same street between intersections are likely to encounter
each other frequently in the course of ordinary comings and
goings. In the study areas, moreover, the predominant row-type
single-family houses are highly homogeneous on any given street,
allowing no symbolism of status differences among the residents.

The two measures yielded a striking result. Nearly three-fourths
of the white purchases were found in a mixed block or adjacent
to a mixed block, that is, within a maximum of three linear blocks
from a Negro resident. But only 27 percent of the white buyers
acquired homes on the same street front or facing a street front
on which Negro families lived, whereas the remainder purchased
on all-white street fronts and facing street fronts. Thus, it seems
that the closer the proximity of Negroes, the smaller will be the
proportion of white purchasers in any mixed area. This result
was, of course, not unexpected. However, the significant finding
may not lie in the sharp drop-off in proportion of white purchasers,
but in the fact that 119 white families chose to buy homes on

---

[13] The unit of measurement consisted of five contiguous blocks in the shape of
a cross in which the house acquired by the white purchaser was in the central
block. If any of the five blocks was mixed in occupancy, the whole unit was
classified as mixed.

mixed streets. The other white families, moreover, by purchasing in an area of transition, exposed themselves to the likelihood of having near Negro neighbors in the not distant future.

White families who choose to buy homes in the same areas with nonwhites, because they go against a behavior norm, may be thought to have some unusual characteristics or motivations which account for their actions. The present study searched for such characteristics but was unable to find any which significantly differentiated the group from the white home-buying population at large. In many ways the white purchasers resembled the resident white population in the areas into which they bought.[14]

As in the general home-buying population, a large proportion of these purchasers were young families. Two-thirds of the family heads were less than forty-five years old. Three-fourths had children less than eighteen and half had children of school age—percentages somewhat higher than among all home purchasers in Philadelphia during 1955 and 1956.[15] About half of the purchasers had attended high school; their educational attainment was similar to that of the resident population of the study areas in 1950. Occupationally, the purchaser family heads showed no unusual concentration in professional or other groups which might be associated with special views on race. Their family incomes, from available scanty evidence, were somewhat lower than those of all recent Philadelphia home purchasers, but averaged about the same as white family incomes in the city as a whole. Two-thirds of the purchaser families were Catholic, a proportion somewhat higher than in the Philadelphia white population but similar to the composition of the study areas.

The Negro purchaser group was quite similar to the white buyers, only somewhat younger, with fewer children, slightly lower family incomes, and a smaller representation in the white-collar and skilled-craftsman occupations.

The white purchasers did not have unique or impelling motives

---

[14] Data for this phase of the study were obtained by interviews with 194 white families who purchased homes during 1955 in mixed blocks or adjacent to a mixed block, 100 white renter families in mixed blocks, and 196 Negro home purchasers in the study areas.

[15] U. S. Bureau of the Census, *1956 National Housing Inventory*, Philadelphia Supplement (unpublished).

for buying in the mixed areas. Most, in interview, gave common-place reasons for their choice, mentioning such factors as convenience to work, school, friends and relatives, suitability of the house, or simply, "I'm accustomed to the neighborhood and I like to live here." Familiarity with the neighborhood and attachment to it evidently played an important role in the housing choices of these purchasers, for more than 60 percent of them had lived in the area before buying their homes.

As to racial attitudes, the fact that this group of home purchasers decided to buy in mixed areas implies that they were at least comparatively receptive to the presence of Negroes. However, in interviews, they did not express attitudes of unusual tolerance. If any were motivated by a desire to give a personal example of racial democracy, they were few in number. More than a third of those interviewed expressed varying degrees of dissatisfaction with the presence of Negroes, but strongly negative sentiments were rare. Attitudes of acceptance or rejection were markedly correlated with the degree of hypothetical proximity. Sixty percent of the respondents expressed approval or indifference to the residence of Negroes in the neighborhood; 40 percent to residence on the same block; and 31 percent to residence in an adjacent house. Only 4 percent of the respondents voiced strong disapproval of Negro residence in the neighborhood, but 31 percent were strongly negative toward having Negro neighbors next door.

The racial attitudes expressed by these white home purchasers are fairly consistent with their observed behavior in choosing locations. All of them bought in a general area of mixed occupancy. But as the proximity of Negroes increased, in passing from area to zone to block to street, the proportion of white purchasers contracted.

Conclusions

During the time period covered by the present studies, surging Negro demand, supported by growing availability of mortgage credit and concentrated at certain points, was sufficient to maintain and to strengthen house prices in many areas of racial transition. Market stability was helped by the apparently changing attitudes of white property owners which led them generally to refrain from flooding the market with houses on the appearance of Negroes. To an appreciable extent, whites continued to buy into some racially mixed areas, and this too, of course, helped to keep prices up.

In the future, it is certain that Negroes and other minorities will continue to enter many neighborhoods that are now all-white. But some of the conditions which in the recent past generated strong Negro demand for housing in transitional areas are disappearing. Consequently, predictions from recent experience for the future must be heavily qualified. The pent-up housing demand of Negroes which accumulated during the war and early postwar years has by now been satisfied in large part. The increasing market freedom which minorities are gaining, together with the growing social differentiation of the groups, means undoubtedly that their housing demand will be more dispersed and more varied in the future than in the past. Nonwhites are apt to enter more areas than the nonwhite population can fill, and for some areas complete racial transition will be impossible. As noted, this is already true in some higher-priced neighborhoods. Hence there is likely to be an increasing number of neighborhoods where the maintenance of a sufficient market for houses will require white as well as nonwhite buyers in adequate numbers.

The Philadelphia study found white buyers in numbers which may be thought impressive yet were not sufficient to maintain for long the mixed-occupancy pattern. Where four-fifths of the purchasers in a particular area are nonwhite and only one-fifth white, the outcome is plain. The one area where only a third of the purchasers were Negro does have the prospect of a stable interracial balance, if the present ratio is maintained.

The Philadelphia white buyers did not come from any special group in the population nor were they characterized by unusually favorable attitudes toward Negroes. Their motivations for purchase were those of home buyers generally. Similar findings concerning white purchasers in new interracial housing developments are reported in chapter xii. This absence of distinctive traits coupled with the acknowledged general lessening of racial prejudice in the white population during the past twenty years suggests the existence of considerable potential demand by white families for housing in racially mixed areas.

At present, most mixed neighborhoods compare unfavorably with all-white areas in quality of housing, community facilities, or social conditions. But as minority groups gain more freedom in the housing market, an increasing number of good-quality residence areas will be brought into the mixed category. Urban renewal programs may continue to rehabilitate some of the existing deteriorated mixed areas.

The critical racial factors limiting the number of both prejudiced and unprejudiced white buyers who will purchase in mixed areas are the actual or expected number and proportion of nonwhites in the mixed community, and the spatial distribution of nonwhite residences in relation to the homes which white buyers contemplate acquiring. The two factors are related; however, the Philadelphia data show white purchasers to be more accepting of Negroes a short distance away than in the immediate vicinity. An increasing proportion of Negroes in a mixed area is reflected in a shrinkage of white demand, but the behavior of white buyers seems to be related more to the anticipated than to the actual proportion of Negroes.

The level of white demand and consequently the prospects for achieving *both* a stable racial mixture and stable or rising prices in an area depend primarily, therefore, on the expectations of white buyers. In the past, it has been the most common expectation that a neighborhood once entered by nonwhites would become wholly occupied by them, and in most cases events have justified this anticipation. The present outlook, however, is for an increasing number of neighborhoods where this expectation cannot be fulfilled. What this implies for demand and prices in those areas is problematic. If white demand for housing in a given area shrinks in anticipation of racial transition, but Negro buyers do not appear in the expected numbers, the prices of residences may well decline. But present trends may lead to a revision of expectations of white buyers, and to the extent that this occurs, race will tend to lose its importance in the housing market.

PART THREE

The Housing Industry and Minority Groups

XI

The House Building Industry

Mr. O'Hara: . . . Now in the homes that you are building, are they open to all Americans, regardless of race or religion?

Mr. Levitt: You really pick a ticklish subject now, don't you, Mr. Congressman?

Mr. O'Hara: I would regard it as a pertinent question to a congressional study of our over-all housing problem. In Philadelphia 1 out of 4 of the people who live in Philadelphia belong to a minority group. They are as much entitled to good housing as anybody else. Is private industry furnishing them these houses?

Mr. Levitt: No, private industry is not. Someday I hope they will, and I hope we will be the leaders in it.

Mr. O'Hara: Now the houses you are building, are they open to all Americans?

Mr. Levitt: Unfortunately, no.

Mr. O'Hara: They are entirely for the white people?

Mr. Levitt: Yes, and I repeat, I hope someday that will not be so, and I hope we will be the ones who make it not so.

Mr. O'Hara: We just want to get the facts. . . .

Testimony of William B. Levitt, home builder, before the Subcommittee on Housing of the Committee on Banking and Currency, U. S., Congress, House, *Hearings, Investigation of Housing, 1955*, 84th Cong., 1st Sess., 1955, p. 415.

Interest of the home-building industry in the market for housing for minority groups is essentially of post-World War II origin. In the South, small, cheap houses have long been built for rental to Negroes. A very few housing developments for Negroes built during the 1920's and 1930's were philanthropically inspired. With these exceptions, before the war, nonwhites able to afford new housing were extremely few, and they were rarely thought of as forming any part of the home builder's market. During wartime, Negroes received a small share (about 4 percent) of private war housing built under the government priorities system, although a large part of the government quota of dwellings for Negro occupancy was never built.[1]

In the postwar period, Negroes, Orientals, and Mexican-Americans in appreciable numbers have appeared in the market for new housing. The response of the vast majority of house builders has been to reject them from housing developments intended for the general market. This policy of the builders is no different from their earlier approach, but under present-day conditions its impact and effects are very different from those of the past. Because minority groups are more able to buy new housing, many more families now than formerly feel the direct impact of the builders' racial discrimination. These families, moreover, are usually the more economically and socially advanced, the more aspiring members of their racial groups—the minority middle class. Many builders, repeatedly confronted with minority would-be customers, have had to engage actively in discrimination and develop techniques for excluding unwanted groups. Few builders practice discrimination openly; but to preserve all-white developments while avoiding the embarrassments of open discrimination, or even (as in some cases) maintaining a public pose of nondiscrimination, requires considerable ingenuity.

House-building operations are carried out on a far larger scale than twenty years ago, and consequently, the decisions of builders respecting race or other matters are effective throughout wider areas than before. The modern large-scale merchant builder erecting hundreds, sometimes thousands, of houses in a single location, builds not just houses but entire communities.[2] The suburban tract has become the dominant form of new owner-occupancy housing, paralleled by mammoth rental projects in the central areas. The combination of large-scale building methods

---

[1] Robert C. Weaver, *The Negro Ghetto,* pp. 141-148.
[2] Catherine Bauer, "Housing Policy and the Educational System," citing data of the Urban Land Institute.

with racial discrimination has given rise to the phenomenon of the totally white community. In residential communities that grow by accretion, with dispersed ownership, it is rarely possible to accomplish the complete exclusion of nonwhites from any large area. There are always some owners who will sell to non-whites and, as previously shown, a substantial part, perhaps the majority of the white population, does not object to the presence of minority persons in limited numbers (see chaps. iv and x). But in a housing development, the developer has the power, and generally uses it, to exclude unwanted minority groups completely. It would be difficult to find in the United States many communities as large as the famous Levittowns without a single Negro resident. In sales developments, central control of occupancy normally ends with initial sales, but as several experiences have demonstrated, a pattern of total minority exclusion, once established, is extremely difficult to change. The multiplication of new suburban communities from which nonwhites are absolutely excluded by decision of the builders has unquestionably contributed largely to the extension and intensification of racial segregation since the end of World War II, especially of the minority middle class.

Even more important, in relation to racial segregation, is the fact that mass production of housing has been made possible by government aid. Federal insurance and guarantee of mortgages has stimulated the supply of funds for financing of housing; long-term, low interest government-insured mortgage loans requiring only small or no down payments have enlarged and sustained the market for new housing. The federal policy of giving commitments of mortgage insurance in advance of construction has enabled developers to borrow money for building scores or hundreds of houses at a time, with confidence that buyers would appear when the houses were ready for sale.[3] The benefits of government aid are apparent in the sustained high rate of housing production, the achievement of homeownership by millions of moderate-income families, and the general improvement of housing stand-

---

[3] See Paul F. Wendt, *The Role of the Federal Government in Housing;* Leo Grebler, *The Role of Federal Credit Aids in Residential Construction,* chaps. xvi and xvii.

ards. But in assisting the housing industry more effectively to satisfy the housing needs of the American people, government has incidentally strengthened the power of private builders to discriminate and segregate.

For all these reasons, new private housing is a focal point in the movement for equal opportunity in housing. Many groups have urged the federal government to condition its housing aids on nondiscrimination. State and municipal legislation for "fair housing practices" has centered on publicly assisted development housing. In litigation, the National Association for the Advancement of Colored People has argued that since government cannot lawfully discriminate on racial, ethnic, or religious grounds, those who utilize government aid in the production and marketing of housing are also obliged to refrain from discrimination. At least one lower court has accepted this reasoning.[4] It has not been tested in a higher court.

Most builders, in defending their racial policies, strongly deny any motives of prejudice or desire to injure the minority groups. They exclude members of these groups for what they consider to be reasons of good business. Racial discrimination flows from the basic assumption that the presence of nonwhites in a residential area will destroy or, at least, seriously reduce the demand of whites for housing in the area. For the merchant builder, the market is supremely important. His profit margin typically depends on a complete and reasonably rapid sell-out of the units in a given project; he has, consequently, a strong motive to avoid any condition that might depress the market for his houses. Racial discrimination has the sanction, moreover, of long-established custom in the housing industry. Individual builders may favor racial segregation as a matter of social policy, but there is no evidence nor any reason to believe that members of the housing industry are, on the whole, either more or less racially prejudiced than any other large group of Americans of comparable socioeconomic position.

The California court mentioned above, after finding that rejection of Negro applicants for tract houses was "the invariable

---

[4] *Ming* v. *Horgan,* Super. Ct., Sacramento Co., Calif., No. 97130 (1958).

practice" in the Sacramento area, assessed the motives in the following terms:

The Court further regards as established that there was no animus in this respect on the part of any of the defendants [builders and realtors]—it was simply that good business and consideration for other customers, and a proper sense of responsibility to the community, motivated defendants to continue the practice which had always been adhered to, and which they felt was the right and considerate thing to do.[5]

In spite of their discriminatory policies, builders have not been insensitive to the housing needs of the minority groups. Since racial discrimination in access to new housing became an agitated issue, home builders, both individually and collectively, have pursued two approaches toward making new housing available to minority groups. A small but growing number of commercial builders and housing coöperatives have ventured to challenge the custom of segregation and market their houses without distinction of race or color. The housing which they have produced is only a small fraction of the total volume of new housing in recent years, but this approach has the support of law in several states and seems likely to become much more extensive in the future.

Far more important numerically has been the approach of minority housing—projects intended specifically for sale or rent to minority families. This method, of course, further intensifies racial segregation although augmenting the supply and improving the quality of housing available to minority groups.

The Census Bureau's 1956 National Housing Inventory found an estimated 490,000 nonwhite households occupying dwelling units built during the period 1950-1956.[6] This number was approximately 11 percent of all nonwhite-occupied dwellings in 1956, compared with 20 percent of white households occupying new housing. The census estimate of new construction includes public as well as private housing, and the evidence indicates that a disproportionate part of the nonwhite units consisted of

[5] *Ibid.*

[6] U. S. Bureau of the Census, *1956 National Housing Inventory*, Vol. I, *Components of Change, 1950 to 1956*, Part 1, "United States and Regions."

public housing. In nine metropolitan areas for which data are available, public housing represented 53 percent of the 93,000 units of new housing occupied by nonwhites at the end of 1956.[7]

Of the recently built private units occupied by nonwhites in 1956, some unknown but certainly substantial part was not originally marketed to nonwhites but was transferred from white to nonwhite occupancy. New private dwellings initially occupied by nonwhites probably numbered in the range of one hundred to two hundred thousand units during the seven years, 1950 through 1956. Although this quantity is far short of an equal share in the products of the home-building industry, nevertheless, it is impressive. Never before has private industry provided for minority groups any similar amount of new housing. In some areas, the results have been striking. In Atlanta, for a notable example, more than one Negro household in five was living in a new, privately built house in 1956. The credit for this achievement, it must be said, belongs not to the organized building industry, but to the Atlanta Negro community and its leadership.[8] In other areas, however, such as Houston and Memphis, local builders have taken the lead in organizing production of housing for minority groups.

Several considerations in addition to ordinary business incentives have motivated builder efforts to produce minority housing. Some builders, as in Dayton, Ohio, and New Orleans, have acted from a sense of civic responsibility to assist in the solution of an important public problem, but with the hope, too, that the ventures would be profitable.[9] In Pittsburgh, Dallas, Cleveland, Houston, Savannah, and other cities, builders have formed or joined in the formation of special corporations or committees for the specific purpose of expediting building for minority groups by acquiring sites, arranging financing, obtaining governmental

[7] Federal Housing Administration, Division of Research and Statistics, "Trends in Occupied Dwelling Units and Components of Nonwhite Housing Change" (mimeographed table, March 11, 1959). The nine metropolitan areas are Boston, New York, Philadelphia, Detroit, Chicago, Los Angeles, Seattle, Dallas, and Atlanta. Similar data are not available on a national basis.

[8] Thompson, Lewis, and McEntire, "Atlanta and Birmingham. . . ."

[9] *PF—The Magazine of Prefabrication,* Reprint of series (1954); "Nonwhite Housing," *House and Home,* April, 1953; and interviews.

coöperation, and so on. In Columbus, Ohio, and also in Pittsburgh, motives of community betterment were mingled with the purpose of proving public housing unnecessary.[10]

Another consideration urged on builders by their national officers and intimated in speeches of federal housing officials has been the risk of more positive government action if the housing needs of minority groups were not met by private enterprise. Some building industry leaders, especially in the South, have also hoped to counter pressures for desegregation in housing by providing a supply of good, segregated dwellings. Both considerations were emphasized in the program of the National Association of Home Builders, adopted in 1954, to achieve the production of 150,000 dwelling units annually for minority groups. Each local builders' association throughout the country was urged to adopt a community goal and "start an aggressive campaign and effective production program to improve the housing conditions of minority groups in their own community." [11] The national association issued a "package program" containing suggestions, publicity, and promotional material.

The NAHB's ambitious program, with its emphasis on preserving segregation, was initiated in the same year that the Supreme Court declared segregation in public schools unconstitutional. The NAHB president declared:

The Supreme Court ruling concerning schools in my opinion will have a profound effect on housing. . . . The basic cause [of anti-segregation rulings and legislation] undoubtedly stems from the fact that Negroes and other minority groups have not been provided with an adequate supply of proper school facilities and proper housing. The pressures thereby engendered naturally produce an aggravated problem. . . . The home building industry must tackle this problem head-on, and we must plan and provide adequate and good housing for the minorities of this nation *in proper areas* with proper facilities or get ready for Congress and the Courts to seek their solution by decree and by statute. . . . If we meet the issue now, plan and pro-

---

[10] National Association of Home Builders, "Housing for Minority Groups: 'Package Program' " (1954); Pittsburgh Housing Association, "Housing News" (April, 1954); Dallas Chamber of Commerce, *Toward Better Understanding: Report of Joint Committee on Negro Housing* (1951); Associated Builders of Columbus, Inc., *Columbus Home Builders Meet the Challenge* (1955).

[11] National Association of Home Builders, "Housing for Minority Groups."

vide the Negro with housing on comparable financial terms, *but in planned communities,* society will be much better off.[12]

The NAHB's program came too late for national leadership. Had it been announced some years earlier, with perhaps less public emphasis on segregation, it probably would have been received with enthusiasm by those concerned with improving the living conditions of minority groups. But by 1954 the central issue was no longer one of housing supply as such, but of equal opportunity to obtain housing. A Los Angeles attorney for the NAACP also drew the parallel with education:

We have reached the same stage in housing that was attained when the first school suits were filed a decade ago. Grandiose equalization plans were announced. Maintenance of segregation was heralded as a sure prescription for the happiness of majority and minority alike. The nation is being offered the equivalent in housing of the separate but equal doctrine and in an area of our society where it will work even greater mischief than in other fields. . . .[13]

Both the NAACP and the National Urban League condemned the NAHB program in resolutions for nonsegregation in housing.[14]

The Federal Housing Administration, whose coöperation had been solicited, expressed "gratification" but withheld endorsement of the program. Instead, in a message avoiding any reference to minority housing, the FHA commissioner announced that FHA was going to "encourage the development of demonstration open-occupancy projects" and would give "every assistance to those trying to make open-occupancy housing available." He

---

[12] *Ibid.,* extracts from speech by President Hughes before the Texas Mortgage Bankers Association, San Antonio, May 21, 1954. Emphasis supplied.

[13] Loren Miller, Address to Conference of the National Committee Against Discrimination in Housing, Washington, D. C., March 14, 1955 (mimeographed).

[14] "We do not want jim-crow dwellings whether they are new or old. . . . We condemn and oppose the policy advocated by the National Association of Home Builders for planned housing developments directed toward any specific minority group on the basis of race, color, national origin, or religion." National Association for the Advancement of Colored People, *Annual Conference Resolutions,* 1954, 1955, and 1956. "While the League and its affiliates lend their support to measures designed to increase the supply of housing. . . . the National Urban League is opposed to, and unwilling to support or assist in the construction of segregated privately financed housing." *Statement and Recommendations from the Board Convention of the National Urban League,* April 15-17, 1955.

asked the home-building industry for coöperation in promoting open occupancy.[15]

The NAHB's program for rehousing the minority groups seems to have been allowed quietly to expire. No follow-up measures and no results have been announced, nor has the Association taken any position on legislative proposals for special federal assistance in the financing of housing for minority groups.[16]

Barriers to Housing Production for Minorities

The present study has attempted to examine everything that builders and their spokesmen have said in print about minority housing or open-occupancy housing during the past decade, and in addition, has consulted nearly two hundred builders throughout the country. With allowance for regional differences, the testimony of builders is remarkably consistent: building for minorities nearly always involves the builder in problems greater than he normally expects in operations directed exclusively to the white market. The extra difficulties relate to sites, financing, and the market. Typically, good building sites are scarcer; financing is more difficult to obtain and more costly; the market is "thinner" and less dependable. There are differences, of course; there are success stories and horrible examples. Generally, the obstacles have proved fewer and less stubborn in the South than in the North and West. But on the whole, it is the consensus among builders that building houses for sale or rent to minority groups is more difficult, more risky, and less profitable than building for the white market exclusively. Typical of the response of many builders to the present inquiry is the following statement from one large builder, operating in a half dozen metropolitan areas: "We feel also that the minority situation is a pressing problem and have, for years, tried independently to work out a large subdivision for these groups. However, we have invariably

---

[15] Federal Housing Administration, "Message from FHA Commissioner to be read by Insuring Office Directors at NAHB local meetings Relating to Providing Homes Available to Minorities" (Washington, D. C.: July 16, 1954).

[16] See testimony and statements on behalf of the National Association of Home Builders in *Hearings, Housing Act of 1957*, U. S., Congress, Senate, 85th Cong., 1st Sess., 1957, pp. 416-455; and House, 85th Cong., 1st Sess., 1957, pp. 163-205.

encountered such staggering problems that we have always had to drop the undertaking." [17]

The majority of builders consulted by the present study ranked financing difficulties as the major deterrent, whereas observers and students usually consider restrictions on choice of building sites as the most seriously limiting factor.[18] The difference in emphasis probably reflects a difference in the vantage point from which the problem is viewed. The builder may often not consider himself engaged in trying to produce a housing development until he has a site. Hence, land is more a general limiting factor than a limit to the particular builder whose attention is normally focused on problems arising in connection with a specific development.

Land.—The location, character, and cost of the land are, of course, crucial elements in the economic feasibility of any building venture. The prospective builder of housing for occupancy by nonwhites faces a much more restricted choice of possible sites than when building for white occupancy. In addition to all other criteria of a suitable site, land to be used for the residence of minority groups must be socially acceptable for that purpose. Pressures against minority occupancy are basically similar to those which operate to exclude nonwhites from established residence areas, plus some additional ones that apply to the creation of a new concentration of nonwhites on vacant land. Objection usually comes first from near-by property owners who fear that the value of their properties may be depreciated. A builder who persists in plans for a nonwhite development against the opposition of local property owners is apt to find that his accustomed sources of mortgage and other financing have dried up. He may find that necessary official approvals of his site, plans, and buildings are withheld or delayed, and needed public improvements

---

[17] Correspondence.

[18] Compare, for example, the following characteristic evaluations. (1) "Probably the greatest single limiting factor in all markets has been the lack of mortgage credit for nonwhite buyers." National Association of Home Builders, *Housing Almanac, 1955,* p. 40; (2) "Fundamental is the fact that good and well-located sites for housing of nonwhites are simply not available in most instances. . . . Land is by every yardstick today the hard core of the problem. . . ." George W. Snowden, Minority Group Housing Advisor, Federal Housing Administration, Statement before conference of Mortgage Bankers Association, Chicago, 1954.

are not installed. These sanctions are not often employed because their existence is well known to builders, and a threat of their employment is usually sufficient. As builders have emphasized to the present study, the individual builder is seldom in a position to stand on his legal rights. As a businessman he is not apt to have much taste for becoming embroiled in local controversy, particularly a racial one. He is dependent, moreover, on the coöperation of his bankers and of local officials. From the latter he typically needs not just minimal performance of legal duties, but active help in the provision of municipal services, prompt attention to his problems, and continuing good will. He might challenge the local authorities on a particular project and win, but he knows they would "get him" on his next subdivision. A Los Angeles builder tells how he was disciplined:

I tried to put in a subdivision in Glendale [an all-white suburb, traditionally anti-Negro] but not for Negroes. A hearing was held and I was publicly asked if I intended to sell to Negroes. The only reason I could think of why the question was asked was that I had built for Negroes in the past. The tract was turned down without any reasons given.

Although local governing bodies cannot legally regulate the racial occupancy of land, there is a multitude of ways in which controls over land use and building can be used against an unwanted development without being questioned in the courts. One easy tactic is delay, which can be serious for a builder with resources committed to a project. The typical builder operates largely with borrowed funds; if his production and sales schedule are upset, accumulating interest charges rapidly devour his profit margin. Within the discretion of officials, legal requirements can be applied with lenience or with strictness. It is a commonplace that building regulations in many cities are so complex that if they were enforced to the letter, no one could build any houses. Zoning classifications can be changed to make a proposed land use illegal, or local governments can condemn privately owned land for public use. Local officials often have wide discretion over the provision of streets, sewers, water, and other public facilities. Many suburban towns, where land is most readily available, endeavor to exclude minority groups entirely from their corporate limits. Larger cities do not necessarily oppose minority housing as such, and in a few instances have actively assisted developments, but there is general insistence on confining housing developments for minorities to certain districts.

Public housing, as described elsewhere, has encountered similar resistances to project locations. An important difference is that local housing authorities are sometimes in a position to fight for their site proposals, whereas the private builder rarely is, and his problems seldom come to public attention.

Builders and lenders who have had experience with minority or open-occupancy housing are virtually unanimous in identifying local governments as a major source of restrictions on their freedom to choose sites. Following are a few illustrative comments from interviews for the present study:

A Detroit builder: Inside the city land is short, but outside the city it is available in sufficient quantity but there are obstructions to developing it. The reason ultimately reduces to the obstructing tactics of village and township officials in preventing subdivisions being planned for Negroes. These officials have various means for this obstruction which include the issuance of building permits, hooking up sewers, building-inspection standards, and so on.

Another Detroit builder: There is no more land in the city and even land in the suburbs is getting difficult to obtain. But the Negro cannot get into this surburban environment because of the resistance of suburban officials, possibly representing the interests of their constituents.

A Los Angeles builder: Land is scarce in areas approved for minority housing; both the city and the small towns have areas "approved for minorities."

A Chicago lender: Land availability is hampered by the policies of village councils and by ward politics. If these people don't approve they can easily block any attempt to develop a subdivision through technicalities.

A Chicago suburban builder: There was a lot to be done to get this tract for Negroes. We had to approach the village council and they took persuading. . . . We were successful primarily because there were some Negroes on the other side of the project. . . . The councilmen wanted no possibility that the whites would ultimately become outnumbered. You know what that means politically!

A Norfolk, Virginia, Negro builder: There is in the first place a shortage of land; yet once Negroes get hold of some, the city and whites fight to take it away from them.

A Birmingham builder: In 1950-51 we built Honeysuckle Hills.

. . . We had a lot of trouble getting land. . . . I had intended to build more but I couldn't find the land. There was a good piece of it next to Honeysuckle Hills but there were some scattered white houses on it and I couldn't get the owners to sell nor could I get the city to make this a Negro housing area. So I stopped.[19]

House and Home, Round Table on housing policy, 1955: Land is the No. 1 problem in making better homes available to minorities. . . . The big and basic failure is the failure of local communities to make desirable land available. . . . Until the local communities recognize that this is their responsibility and do something effective about it, there is no use in denouncing the builders and lenders for not doing more for minority groups.[20]

Lest the foregoing give a misleading impression of continuous controversy over minority housing sites, it must be noted that racial restrictions on residential land use, like an iceberg, are of known presence but mostly invisible. It is only when a builder miscalculates or is prepared to fight that restrictions come into public view. Builders normally do not go looking for sites or attempt to build for nonwhites in areas known to be restricted, because they know, in the words of a Los Angeles builder, "There would be no inspections and no permits and he would be out of business."

The general rule is that developments for nonwhite occupancy must be located within or adjacent to areas where nonwhites are already living, or if elsewhere, in areas that are not wanted for white residential development. This means, obviously, that the builder's choice of sites is not only limited in general, but the available sites are usually of poor quality for residential development because of intrinsic features, presence of blighting influences, remote location, or other drawbacks.

Additional limitations on choice of sites arise from locational preferences of the minority market as builders interpret them. Notwithstanding the undesirable living conditions in minority residence areas, nonwhites will not necessarily move "anywhere" to obtain better dwellings. Experienced builders generally act on the assumption that to attract a strong demand from nonwhites, housing must be located in reasonable proximity to an

---

[19] "What Builders Are Doing about Minority Housing and What Problems They Face," *House and Home,* April, 1957.
[20] *Ibid.,* p. 140.

established nonwhite community, and evidence seems to support their belief. A major reason, undoubtedly, for the reluctance of many nonwhites to move far from their existing settlements is the lack of community facilities which the minority person may freely use outside of the minority community, and the lack of associational opportunities. The white person considering a new housing location normally takes for granted that any facilities existing (churches, stores, restaurants, parks, etc.) are available for his use, and if any are lacking, he may look forward to their being provided. The nonwhite person in a racially discriminating society, on the other hand, cannot assume that facilities will be available for his use freely and without tension, nor that his needs will be supplied. He cannot expect to find a social life other than in a minority community. Because of these factors, under existing conditions nonwhites seem less likely than whites to be attracted to housing in remote locations, although it is precisely such locations which are most likely to be available with least difficulty.

Either within the central city or in remote locations, land costs are likely to be excessive; in the first case because of initial price, and in the second because of development costs. The president of a large financial institution in Chicago remarked that "nothing is scarcer in Chicago than land for Negro building, and when you can find some, it is fantastically priced." This is especially serious, of course, for the developer trying to build low-cost houses attractive to a wide market.

Suitable sites for nonwhite housing developments have been more readily available in many parts of the South than in northern and western metropolitan areas. The reason grows out of differences in the historical patterns of Negro settlement. In the North and West, Negroes as a low-income, migrant group have settled in the central parts of the cities, entirely surrounded by white neighborhoods. In the South, on the other hand, Negroes have historically been in rural areas and hence have remained around the fringes of cities as well as in their centers. Frequently, the Negro residence pattern in southern cities takes the form of a belt or wedge extending from the center of the city outward into open country (see Atlanta map 13). Hence there is often considerably more vacant land in the Negro residential areas of southern than of northern or western cities.

Under judicial and sometimes political pressures, several southern municipal governments have moved to activate the "equal" part of the separate-but-equal theory by setting aside certain open land areas for Negro use. In Atlanta, for example, a city government responsive to the Negro vote was sympathetic toward the demands of Negro leadership for a share of the available vacant land. Even then Atlanta Negroes had to make many compromises to obtain land upon which they could build.[21] In New Orleans, city officials, on the recommendation of a group of influential citizens, earmarked for Negro use a section of the choicest vacant residential land in the city, enough for more than a thousand homes.[22]

Few southern cities have been as open toward Negro housing needs as Atlanta or New Orleans; in some, good building land available to Negroes is not less scarce than in the North or West. From Montgomery, Alabama, for example, *House and Home's* correspondent reported, "There is simply no land left for Negro homes. Negro areas within the city limits are islands surrounded by white neighborhoods or otherwise contained. On the outskirts, white subdivisions have blossomed in a virtually complete circumference of the city, blocking Negro developments in that direction." [23]

In Miami, thousands of new dwelling units have been built for rent and for sale to Negroes, but largely within existing Negro areas and under conditions of increasing population density. Much of this new housing, the *Miami Herald* declared, although modern, was "worsening and perpetuating slum conditions" by doubling or trebling the number of families in a limited space.[24]

Financing.—Problems of financing minority housing are ex-

---

[21] Thompson, Lewis, and McEntire, "Atlanta and Birmingham, . . ."
[22] Reference is to Lake Pontchartrain Homes. See Forrest E. LaViolette, "The Negro in New Orleans."
[23] *House and Home,* April, 1955, p. 206.
[24] "Is Miami Building the Nation's Most Modern Slums?" *Miami Herald,* December 18, 1955, one of a series by Lawrence Thompson, staff writer. See also Elizabeth L. Virrick, "New Housing for Negroes in Dade County."

amined here only from the viewpoint of the builder. Almost unanimously, builders consulted in the present study reported two main kinds of difficulty in obtaining mortgage commitments for their minority projects. In the first place, mortgage financing is scarcer and harder to obtain for nonwhite than for white housing developments; more sources must be investigated; more time must be spent in negotiation. Often a given mortgage source will commit only for a small part of the proposed units and several sources must be found and utilized to cover an entire project. In many cases, builders have said they were unable to find any source of financing.

Again, mortgages when offered are likely to be on less favorable terms for nonwhite than for white developments. If conventional financing is offered, larger down payments will typically be required. For FHA- and VA-loans, higher than normal rates of discount will be demanded. Larger down payments obviously reduce the builder's market. Discounts, frequently reported to run as high as 10 percent on nonwhite mortgages, also narrow the market if added to the price of houses, or narrow the builder's profit margin if absorbed by him and not reflected in higher selling prices.

Builders tell their own story in the following typical excerpts from interviews:

Norfolk, Virginia: Builders just don't know where to find mortgage money. We'd rather build for colored than for white people because we get fewer complaints. They are easier to get along with because they never had it so good. But we can't get the financing.

Norfolk real estate broker: Land is available. The big problem is still in financing. The discounts are running 10 percent for Negroes and 6 percent for whites. Money for Negroes is discounted higher because there is more risk involved.

Birmingham: Land is plentiful if we could find Negroes to qualify for loans and loan associations to accept them. FNMA is the only loan association that will take the loans of Negroes. Even if a Negro has a good credit rating . . . as soon as the mortgage association finds out he is a Negro, they don't want him.

St. Louis lender: Negroes are bumped harder in financing because of the risk. Discounts and interest rates are higher. There is not any discrimination in this; it is simply a calculated business matter.

Chicago: Money is tight in general, and the terms for Negro loans are prohibitive. Lenders want more down payments, better employment records, and higher sure earnings than from white borrowers, and even then they ask the developer to take 8 to 10 points discount on the paper. On VA loans this comes out of our profit, and on FHA it makes the down payment prohibitive, so we are caught either way.

Chicago: The problem in a nutshell is this. VA sets the sale price on a new house. They are fair, adding up the costs and adding 10 percent or 12 percent for the builder. But then you get to financing. The lending outfits know they have us over a barrel right now, so those discounts come. Since the builder has a set sale price under VA, the discount is merely a device for the financial organizations to take over most of our profit margin. For Negro housing it's even tougher because money is harder to find and the discount is higher. There is a lot of pious talk about no difference in the handling of these Negro loans, but when you get down to cases there is plenty of difference. . . . Discounts run higher on subdivisions for Negroes than on those for whites.

Los Angeles: We can get money at 8 to 10 points discount. We don't build GI or FHA anymore. We did in the past, and continually added things to the house in order to raise the price. The profit on the items we added paid the 2 or 3 extra points discount we had to pay. However, it raised the price and we lost some of our market.

San Francisco: We have to sell FNMA at about 10 points. . . . I believe this is about 3 or 4 points more than in a white development.

Detroit: Financing is a terrible story. . . . The lenders won't touch the Negro loans. They avoid them or discount them to the point where you can't go through with the transaction.

Detroit Negro real estate broker: Although financing is tight, it is not completely closed to Negroes. There are some large institutions that have a very fair policy on Negro loans although others won't touch them.

Several builders reported that the scarcity of mortgage sources for nonwhite developments had the result of exposing the builder to various demands in the nature of sharp practice. These were attributed not so much to primary lenders as to mortgage brokers who would offer to procure financing at the price of special concessions such as under-the-table payments, a share in the profits, or title to the land.

There is evidence that for a period, about 1954-1955, mortgage money for minority housing became more plentiful than before, possibly in response to pressures from government, the national trade associations of home builders and mortgage bankers, and others. However, with the onset of tight money for housing generally in 1956, mortgage funds for the nonwhite field became scarcer than ever. As noted in several of the builder statements quoted above, a great part of the mortgage money for minority housing has come not from private sources but from the federal government through the Federal National Mortgage Association.

The financing problems of minority housing builders discussed here have been those connected with obtaining financial commitments for housing developments. An additional problem emphasized by some builders (and most of the lenders interviewed) has been that of qualifying the individual home buyers for mortgage loans. A commitment by a financial institution to take the mortgages on homes in a given development is always made subject to the ability of proposed individual borrowers to meet the lender's credit standards. In this respect, builders aiming at the lower-income market have often experienced considerable difficulty. Some say they have had to sell each house several times before finding a purchaser who could qualify for a mortgage loan.

The lenders consulted agreed with the builders about the scarcity and less favorable terms of mortgage credit for nonwhite housing, although, as might be expected, they offered somewhat different explanations and generally believed that not credit but land was the principal limiting factor to housing production for minorities. It may be noted that the lenders' decisions are more likely than the builders' to reflect a judgment of the long-run economic feasibility of the housing enterprises. Although builders seem to regard the question of land availability as secondary, it seems evident that the poor quality of sites has contributed to the difficulty of financing minority housing ventures in many cases. Builders have received a good deal of advice from various sources to offer "good, well-located sites" if they wished to attract financing, but for the reasons noted, this sound advice is often very difficult for a builder to heed.

Market.—In the mid-1950's, many pronouncements issued from governmental and other sources about the "untapped minority market" and the rewards awaiting builders who would serve it. Minority housing has been termed an "open, undeveloped, market," a "$5 billion market," "the greatest opportunity for housing expansion in the immediate future of any single market

area," and so on.[25] These and many similar statements implied
that if builders would only provide the houses, a host of purchasers would come forward to buy them. Builders, however, have
found this to be not always true. Minority developments have
sometimes sold out rapidly, sometimes not. A Dayton, Ohio,
builder, for example, reports that he was three years finishing
a project for Negroes that normally would have been completed
in a year's time. The delay was ascribed partly to financing difficulties, partly to a slow rate of sales.[26] Builders of the famous
Pontchartrain Park Homes in New Orleans had to work hard
and spend money to promote sales. Their preselling campaign
has been called "a textbook of how to 'hard-sell' the nonwhite
market, too." [27] The executive vice-president of the corporation
wrote, "The minority market is here, all right, but it is not a
seller's market." [28] Many experienced builders share this judgment.

In spite of the economic progress that minority groups have
made in the past two decades, the proportion of nonwhite families
able to pay for new, private housing is still relatively small. Under
present conditions, a family income of $5,000 is virtually the
minimum needed to purchase a new house. More than four-
fifths of FHA borrowers on new family homes in 1957 had "effective" incomes at this level or higher.[29] But in the same year, total
money incomes of $5,000 or more were possessed by only one-
fifth of United States nonwhite families and slightly more than
half of all white families.[30] Moreover, owing to the frequent dependence of minority families on secondary incomes and unstable

---

[25] See Albert M. Cole, former Administrator, Housing and Home Finance
Agency, quoted in *House and Home*, April, 1955, p. 139; Joseph R. Ray, Director
of Racial Relations Service, Housing and Home Finance Agency, in "Builder
Opportunities in Minority Group Housing," pp. 4-5; "Minority Housing Can Be
Profitable," *National Real Estate and Building Journal*, 56(5) (May, 1955), 18-19;
George S. Harris, "Minorities Need Homes and Have the Money," *NAHB Cor-
relator*, 8(3) (March, 1954), 26-28.

[26] Robert L. Pine, "Financing Homes for Minority Groups," *NAHB Correlator*,
9(8) (August, 1955), 186-189.

[27] "Lesson in Merchandising," *House and Home*, April, 1955, p. 146.

[28] Morgan G. Ernst, "Selling the Minority Buyer," *NAHB Correlator*, 10(10)
(October, 1956), 100-103.

[29] Housing and Home Finance Agency, *Eleventh Annual Report, 1957*, p. 115.

[30] U. S. Bureau of the Census, *Current Population Reports*, Series P-60,
Consumer Income, no. 30 (1958). See chap. vi for further details.

income sources, the proportion with incomes sufficient to pay for new housing is considerably smaller when measured by mortgage-lending standards than appears in the census statistics. A New York State Housing Rent Commission study estimated in 1953-1954 that 18.6 percent of nonwhite families in New York City had annual incomes of $5,000 or more after federal taxes, but only 8.3 percent had effective incomes at this level according to the FHA definition.[31]

The desire for a new, owned home is evidently more widespread among minority families than the ability to pay for it. One of the most frequent complaints of builders has to do with the large number of would-be purchasers who lack funds for down payments or who cannot qualify for mortgage credit. The Pontchartrain Park officer quoted above also wrote, "The most discouraging part of selling to the minority market has been the difficulty of qualifying buyers. Despite the most careful advance screening, we have had to make five gross sales to come out with three net sales." [32] Mortgage lenders and builders alike emphasize the importance of credit screening, and though careful selection of risks makes for good repayment experience, it pares away much of the market for minority housing, especially in the lower-price ranges.

Of the minority families who have the economic capacity to buy or rent new dwellings, only a part, of course, is actually in the market for such housing at any given time. As Weaver has pointed out, not all of the higher-income nonwhite families are badly housed; some are well housed and have no immediate incentive to move.[33] Another demand-limiting factor is the width of the gap between what most nonwhites are actually paying for housing and the cost of new construction. There seems to be a well-marked tendency among nonwhites to rent or buy cheaper housing than whites on the same income levels. There is, thus, among nonwhites, a considerable potential demand for better housing, as yet unrealized.

---

[31] New York State Temporary Housing Rent Commission, *Incomes and Ability to Pay for Housing of Nonwhite Families in New York State* (1955), tables i and ii.

[32] Ernst, *NAHB Correlator*, October, 1956.

[33] Robert C. Weaver, "The Effect of Anti-Discrimination Legislation upon the FHA- and VA-Insured Housing Market in New York State."

The apparent preference of nonwhites, in a racially segregated society, for housing within or near existing minority communities further limits demand for housing remote from established minority neighborhoods.[34] This does not mean that *no* nonwhites are prepared to buy houses in remote locations, but only that the number who are able and willing to do so is usually not sufficient to satisfy the builder's economic need for reasonably rapid sellout of his development.

Finally, the housing demand of the nonwhite population is spread through a variety of types, locations, and cost levels. Hence, a particular housing development in a given location can, at best, interest only some fraction of the people actually in the market for new housing. Few, if any builders, would assert the feasibility of building for the whole range of housing demand represented in minority groups. From the standpoint of income and financial responsibility, the middle class contains the builder's and mortgage lender's best customers, among nonwhites as among whites. Yet, with few exceptions, builders of minority housing have directed their efforts to the lower-income groups because it is only at those levels that a sufficiently large population exists, in most communities, to offer prospect of filling a housing development of economic size. At higher income levels the potential market becomes too thin to justify creation of a housing development dependent upon the patronage of a particular race-income group.

Evaluation of Minority Housing

The efforts of private home builders to produce and market new development housing for minority groups may be appraised from two standpoints: the feasibility of such projects as business ven-

[34] It has also been noted that Negro demand for public housing under conditions of open occupancy tends to be concentrated on projects within or near Negro residence areas. In New York, according to Weaver, "In spite of nonwhites' widespread occupancy [in public housing] and the existence of nondiscriminatory legislation for over a decade, projects far removed from established Negro neighborhoods have only sparse nonwhite occupancy." *Ibid.* In 1956 in Seattle, where eligible applicants for public housing, regardless of race, have always been free to choose any project subject to available space, the only project fully occupied and with a waiting list, largely Negro, was one situated near the city center and the Negro district; all other projects had vacancies available for immediate occupancy. (Interviews.)

tures, and their social value in bringing good housing within reach of the disadvantaged minority groups.

The preceding analysis has described the difficulties besetting production of minority housing which have led most builders to avoid the field. Lest the picture of deterrents seem overdrawn, however, it is necessary to add that they do not operate with equal impact in all places and circumstances. In some communities, builders consider minority housing developments wholly unfeasible financially; in others, such as Miami, they have been a lucrative field for the speculative builder. In general, it may be said that housing developments for minority groups are likely to be profitable business ventures where the following conditions exist: (a) a minority population of substantial size with stable sources of employment and income, (b) suitable building sites procurable at reasonable cost within or near the existing minority residence areas, and (c) a tight segregation pattern with limited competition from existing transitional housing.

These conditions are most likely to be satisfied in the larger cities of the South. Although nonwhite incomes are higher in the North and West, the other requisites are less often found. To a limited degree they exist in some northern and western cities. Other than in the South, and perhaps there as well, it seems unlikely that private builders will find many profitable opportunities for the creation of minority housing unless substantially assisted by government.

In addition to the mortgage-insurance programs, there are two major instruments through which the federal government could assist and stimulate an expansion of private-housing production for minority groups, should it be judged sound policy to do so. One is government financing through the Federal National Mortgage Association. As described elsewhere, "Fanny May" in the past has been one of the main sources of mortgage financing for minority projects. Expansion of FNMA's role in this area has been advocated by various groups, and bills to accomplish it have been introduced in Congress (see chap. xvii).

The second instrument is urban renewal, which provides a means of making slum-cleared land available to private developers at a cost feasible for new residential construction. The slum areas involved are in most cases occupied largely by nonwhites. Whether the cleared land should be re-used for minority, white, or mixed occupancy is a question of policy.

Whether these powers of government should be used to assist and stimulate private enterprise to produce minority housing turns on the social value of housing built for occupancy by a minority group. On this question the segregationists maintain a clear and consistent position. For them, the paramount merit of housing planned for minority groups is its utility for maintaining racial segregation and neutralizing pressures for open occupancy. The southern sponsorship of bills in Congress for expanded FNMA support of minority housing suggests similar motives.

The proequality groups, on the other hand, often find it difficult to be ideologically "pure" because they desire not only racial integration, but also, usually, more and better housing available to minority groups. Thus, the NAACP and the National Urban League have both resolved against minority or "jim crow" housing. At the same time, both groups are concerned lest urban renewal operate to deprive minorities of scarce, albeit slum, living space. Even more revealing of the conflict is the support by antidiscrimination groups of proposals for FNMA support of minority housing (chap. xvii).

The difficulties of the proequality position stem from the fact that, under present conditions, the practical alternatives are usually not segregated housing versus integrated housing, but segregated housing versus none at all. Confronted with these alternatives, many men of good will, by no means advocates of segregation, have supported the building of good housing for minority groups, as worth while in itself, even though segregated. Negroes in the South often have struggled hard for the opportunity to have good homes, while leaving aside the segregation issue.

Opposition to minority developments is based on more than ideology: those who oppose the development of "planned communities" for minorities see the creation of such new areas as intensifying and perpetuating patterns of segregation. Moreover, Negroes have learned to look on any manifestation of the separate-but-equal doctrine as meaning separate but *not* equal. Historically, the Negro has rarely obtained equal facilities under the doctrine. Minority housing at best can provide only a limited choice of house types, prices, and locations. Market realities preclude it from serving the minority population at all income levels.

On the other hand, those who would not oppose minority housing fear that if the nonwhite population waits for integration, many will sacrifice immediate opportunity for good housing for a prospect that could prove ephemeral. They find it difficult to justify opposing good housing on the basis of ideological considerations. They may feel that better housing will advance the status of the disadvantaged groups, tend to change the images that the majority has of the minority and which the minority individuals have of themselves, and therefore, eventually facilitate the movement toward equality.

As a practical matter, the issue is not one which seems likely to be resolved on a uniform basis. Both minority housing and the movement for a free market have achieved considerable momentum and both will undoubtedly continue into the foreseeable future. The real issue in planning and policy is not whether one or the other approach should or will prevail to the exclusion of the other, but where the weight of emphasis should be placed.

XII

Privately Developed Interracial Housing

Although segregation is the rule in the private housebuilding industry, a number of housing developments in recent years have been open, from their beginning, to both whites and nonwhites. This chapter examines the experience of developments of this type, based mainly on a survey of some fifty projects.[1] Additional data emphasizing marketing experience are drawn from another study covering several of the same developments.[2]

First, it is necessary to clear up some uncertainties about the meaning of "interracial" or "open occupancy" as applied to housing. Both terms are often used as euphemisms to describe housing that, in fact, is intended only for Negroes. For purposes of this study, housing developments are considered "open" or "interracial" only when they actually contain both white and nonwhite residents in significant proportions. A low or high proportion of nonwhites does not have the same meaning for racial integration as the corresponding proportion of whites. For example, a project population composed 90 percent of whites

[1] Complete findings of this survey are reported in Eunice and George Grier, *Privately Developed Interracial Housing: An Analysis of Experience.*

[2] Institute for Urban Studies, University of Pennsylvania, "Market Experience and Occupancy Patterns in Interracial Housing Developments: Case Studies of Privately Financed Projects in Philadelphia and New York City" (July, 1957, mimeographed).

and 10 percent of Negroes could well be considered racially mixed, but one where these proportions were reversed would almost certainly be regarded as a Negro community. The precise limits of the mixed category are uncertain, but plainly, for a development to be considered as racially mixed, it must include a substantial proportion of whites. The present study included only projects with at least 10 percent of white residents, a minimum which could reasonably have been fixed at a higher point.

In the housing developments considered here, an interracial composition was instituted as a matter of policy. This type of racial mingling must be distinguished from the mixed occupancy which develops in residence areas undergoing racial transition. The latter is part of the processes associated with segregation, whereas the planned interracial project represents a deliberate break with the custom of segregation.

The fifty projects surveyed include all which came to our attention in the course of a systematic effort to locate developments of this type during 1955-1956. The interracial projects found were probably somewhat fewer than the number actually in existence. These fifty known developments included approximately 8,000 dwelling units, not all of which were ready for occupancy. This tiny fraction of the total volume of new, private housing would be hardly more than a curiosity were it not for the likelihood that interracial housing may become more important in the years ahead. A trend is apparent in the construction dates of the fifty known projects. Twenty-one of them began building during 1954 and 1955. Only fifteen were built before 1950 and only two before 1946. We learned of many builders who were considering opening their developments to all racial groups. Some of the obstacles to building for open occupancy, as described below, seem to be diminishing. Laws forbidding racial discrimination in the sale or rental of broad categories of housing have been enacted in a dozen states and cities and are strongly advocated elsewhere. Although it would be unrealistic to expect these laws to effect an immediate, complete reversal of segregation practices, they should, at the least, make it easier for builders interested in open occupancy to overcome obstacles that have beset them in the past.

Characteristics of Interracial Developments

Privately developed interracial housing is found in all major regions of the United States, even in the South. As might be expected, most of the known developments are in the middle Atlantic states and on the Pacific coast, with a secondary concentration in the industrial Midwest. Several developments have been sponsored by proequality organizations, notably the American Friends Service Committee, for the purpose of demonstrating that whites and Negroes could live in the same neighborhoods. Others have been built by coöperative groups organized to provide housing for their members. But more than half of all known developments were business ventures by regular builders. In many cases, builders had motives of community betterment as well as of profit seeking, but they all hoped to make money. In some cases an interracial market was cultivated because it seemed to be more profitable than segregation. Several developers of interracial housing are leading members of the home-building industry in their respective localities.

Many of the developments are small, 40 percent having fewer than 25 units. But almost the same number are 100 units or larger in size, with the largest having more than 1,600 dwelling units. Half of the known developments were built for individual ownership, approximately a third for coöperative ownership, and the balance for rental. Thirty developments consisted of detached, single units; eight were multistory apartment houses; and the rest (twelve) were other types of multiple-unit dwellings. Prices varied over a wide range. Two western projects offered low-cost housing at $5,500 and $6,250. At the opposite extreme, some of the homes in eastern suburban coöperatives cost up to $60,000 to build, including land. The bulk of dwellings, however, like most postwar construction, have been in the moderate price range: $11,000 to $15,000 for sales housing, and $70 to $100 a month for rental units.

Negroes were less than 10 percent of resident families in a fifth of the known developments and from 10 to 25 percent in another fifth. In a dozen projects Negroes and other minorities comprised 60 percent or more of the residents, ranging up to 90 percent in a few cases. Beyond this point, as noted, projects were not considered interracial.

Major Problems

Developers of interracial housing, in going against the established custom of the building industry and the white community, have generally faced special problems in acquisition of land, financing, and marketing. These problems are interrelated. To attract white residents, the open-occupancy developer must produce housing competitive with all-white developments. Yet he has, typically, far more difficulty in obtaining a good site than does the "white only" builder. His locational problems are substantially similar to those confronting the builder of minority housing (chap. xi), in both cases centering on opposition to the entry of minority groups into new areas. To avoid crippling opposition, the open-occupancy developer often resorts to sites which have disadvantages from the standpoint of attracting a broad market. Several developments, moreover, are urban renewal projects built on slum-cleared land. In a survey of eight interracial developments in the New York–Philadelphia area, the University of Pennsylvania Institute for Urban Studies judged all but two of them to be in areas of inferior residential quality.[3] Some open-occupancy projects, however, have had superior locations.

Locational disadvantages and resulting anticipated marketing handicaps react unfavorably on the judgment of mortgage lenders toward a proposed project. In addition, lending institutions sometimes use their power to withhold credit as a means of excluding minority groups from certain areas.

Some cases of land restriction.—In northern California, a large automobile assembly plant moved to a new suburban location, taking with it a racially mixed labor force. No housing was available for Negroes near the new site; they were compelled either to commute long distances or give up their jobs. To meet this community problem, the local branch of the American Friends Service Committee determined to sponsor a housing development open to families of any race. The AFSC interested a builder and

[3] Institute for Urban Studies, University of Pennsylvania, "Market Experience and Occupancy Patterns . . ."

obtained an informal promise of financing from a large life insurance company.[4]

The builder had in mind four possible sites. The one he judged best was rezoned from residential to industrial use soon after the character of the proposed development became known in the community. A second site in the same town, the builder was told, would never be approved. On a third site in another town, minimum building lot sizes were increased, making the unit land costs too high for the moderate-cost houses proposed. A fourth site was withdrawn from sale by the owner. At this point, the builder quit. He had invested a year and some thousands of dollars in frustrated attempts to obtain land. The local AFSC director explained the situation to the mortgage source:

The problem has been to get a desirable piece of land for which local government officials will approve the use we propose. Four times [the builder] has been ready to go on what we all agree were desirable locations, only to be stopped by technical objections from county or municipal agencies. At the same time, Mr. ———— has been given indications that developments would be welcome in certain other areas. These other areas, we believe, are not equally desirable. . . .

A second developer offered a suitable tract which he partly owned and partly had under option, but he ran into determined opposition from the builder of an adjacent all-white development. The latter had installed a sewer line, adequate by local regulation to drain the surrounding undeveloped territory as well. Later developers were to tie into the line, paying a fixed share of the cost according to their acreage. But while tie-in arrangements were pending, the local sanitation district board suddenly adopted a new ordinance changing the basis of payment in such a way as to increase the immediate charge to the open-occupancy project by 600 percent.

By this time, the American Friends Service Committee had been joined in sponsorship of the project by the United Automobile Workers Union. To save the enterprise, the union, under protest, paid the additional tie-in charge.

---

[4] This account is based on records made available by the American Friends Service Committee, newspaper reports, and interviews. For a more complete report, see Grier, *Privately Developed Interracial Housing*, chap. v, "Site Problems for the Interracial Developer."

The opposition next sought to prevent approval of the subdivision map by the county board of supervisors. Realizing that they were in a power struggle, the union and the AFSC mobilized their support. The public meeting of the board at which the subdivision was to be presented for approval was attended by delegations from unions, civic organizations, and church groups. Sounds of battle having reached Sacramento, the state attorney general dispatched a deputy to the scene to investigate complaints that governmental units were discriminating racially. No formal determination was made by the attorney general, but sponsors of the project believe that his intervention was persuasive to local officials. The board of supervisors approved the subdivision unanimously.

But the opposing builder was not through. He filed suit to restrain the interracial project from using a drainage ditch originally dug by him but dedicated to the county. The suit had probably little merit, but the mere fact of litigation was sufficient to halt further progress. Eventually, the union and its collaborating developer purchased the adjoining tract and so removed the last legal obstacle to their own plans. Nearly two years and many thousands of dollars had been spent in obtaining land and gaining necessary legal sanctions for Negroes and others to live on it. Success, in this instance, was achieved by the political and financial power of the project's backers. Any private builder, unaided, would have been compelled to accept defeat as, indeed, happened with the first interested builder. Subsequently, however, at least one large developer in the same area has begun to accept qualified minority families.

Sponsors of an interracial development in an upstate New York city were not so fortunate. A prominent church layman, named "Citizen of the Year" by the local council of churches, offered thirty acres of land in a near-by suburb at a low price for a housing development free of racial discrimination. A local real estate salesman and a builder undertook to plan the development with the understanding that the land would be transferred when plans were complete. The FHA approved, and one of the principal banks in the city agreed to provide mortgage financing. Both FHA and the bank understood the purpose of the project.

It soon became apparent that demand from the Negro community would be limited and the houses would have to be sold
very largely to whites. There were only about a thousand Negro
families in the city, and it was estimated that no more than 7 or
8 percent of them were financially able to buy the houses planned
to sell at $10,600 and up. A committee promoting the project in
the Negro community was able to report after six months only a
half dozen Negro families seriously interested in purchasing. The
Negro ratio in the development, assuming full occupancy, seemed
likely to be less than 10 percent.

No publicity was given to the project during the planning
stage, but neither was it kept secret. When completed plans were
presented to the town council for approval, one of the councilmen asked, "Is this the nigger project we've been hearing about?"
The council deferred approval. Opposition mobilized immediately. Reflecting the tone of the town council meeting, it was
ugly and scurrilous. The principal opposition leader, a wealthy
and respected businessman, further set the character of the campaign by declaring, in a public meeting, that he knew all people
were equal and Negroes had given their lives in the war, but that
did not give them the right to rape white men's daughters. Rumors
circulated that the promoter planned to build shacks on forty-foot
lots and that eight hundred Negro families were to be brought
out from the city slums in trucks. Violent threats were made
against the promoters and even the philanthropist who had
offered the land. A sound truck summoned residents to a mass
meeting. "Come out and protect your rights, freedom, and property," the loudspeaker said. In the end, the landowner gave in
and withdrew his offer.[5]

Comparing the New York and California experiences, attention
falls on differences in the relative strength of the groups promoting
the respective projects and in their situations. Elements of strength
in the California case were the support of a powerful labor union,
the aid of the state government, and experience in community
organization for social welfare, represented in the American
Friends Service Committee. Moreover, the California group was

---

[5] This project, since it failed before construction, is not included among the
fifty projects described elsewhere.

not dependent on a single site or a single individual, but was able to endure a succession of defeats and still continue fighting. The philanthropic and religious interests supporting the New York project, on the other hand, were comparatively powerless. All the technical elements of a successful housing project they possessed: good land at a low price, assured financing, and professional experience in the planning, promotion, and construction of housing. But they lacked strength; once the battle was joined, they were soon overpowered. Their position was intrinsically weak because the outcome hinged on a single site and a single individual. When the key man yielded to pressure, the struggle was over.

Concord Park Homes, the well-known interracial subdivision near Philadelphia, escaped opposition to its site by choosing a relatively isolated location. As it neared full occupancy, the developers attempted to buy an adjoining tract of farm land for expansion. The owner was at first interested in selling but broke off negotiations after the proposed transaction became known in the near-by small town. Informants report that pressure was brought upon the farm owner by local businessmen who are said to be resigned to the existence of Concord Park but will do everything they can to prevent it from growing.

These examples demonstrate the problem of obtaining good residential land for an open-occupancy development. Confronted with such pressures, it is clear why developers often resort to isolated or otherwise less desirable sites.

In an earlier period, the reluctance of mortgage-credit institutions to invest in racially mixed housing was one of the major obstacles to developments of this kind. The developers of Concord Park Homes approached more than two dozen mortgage lenders before finding one willing to risk their mortgages. Other builders report similar experiences. Financing, when available, was frequently offered on relatively unfavorable terms, including high discount charges (points) or low loan-to-value ratios.

The adverse attitudes of lenders seemed to rest partly on the novelty of interracial housing and lack of experience demonstrating its feasibility, and partly on the traditional concept that presence of minority groups in an area damages property values.

Some lenders indicated they would finance a sound all-Negro tract but not a mixed development. To promote a mixed community, said one rejecting lender, was "trying to force something that isn't natural." A midwestern developer reports an offer of financing conditioned on dividing the project into a white section and a Negro section. One large life insurance company with a record of financing Negro housing, committed itself to finance a California interracial project on the assumption that the tract would promptly become all-Negro. This would be a hazardous assumption in many cases. The project in question, now occupied for several years, has a minority ratio of less than 15 percent.

The Federal Housing Administration formerly considered projects of mixed racial occupancy too hazardous for government-insured mortgage loans (see chap. xvii). In the late 1940's two promising housing coöperatives, one in Michigan and one in California, with some Negroes in their membership, failed when unable to obtain FHA mortgage insurance. Both had offers of financing subject to FHA approval; they were given to understand that their racial policies were the critical factor in the withholding of FHA support, although the FHA, at the time, was also negative toward the coöperative form of organization. A third housing coöperative, in Illinois, obtained a reversal of an initial FHA rejection after the NAACP had appealed in its behalf to the White House. This coöperative, seeking FHA assistance in 1949, drew attention to the disparity between the FHA's requirement of segregation and the 1948 decision of the Supreme Court banning government enforcement of race-restrictive housing covenants. To this, FHA officials are reported to have replied they were not responsible for social policy; facts and elements of risk were the only things they could consider, and an interracial community was a bad risk which they could not insure. In a rejection letter to the coöperative the FHA explained: "If it is therefore apparent . . . that infiltration will be unacceptable to the local real estate market and desirability of properties will be reduced in the market's mind, then this Administration has no alternative but to so recognize the conditions. . . ." [6]

---

[6] Correspondence files of the coöperative and affidavit by the vice-president concerning a conference with FHA regional officials in Chicago. See Grier,

The FHA was shifting its racial policy even while some of the early interracial housing ventures were unable to obtain its support. The majority of known developments undertaken since 1950 have had the benefit of FHA- or VA-insured financing. In several cases, FHA officials have actively assisted interracial projects in obtaining land or financing, and advised them on land planning, marketing, and other problems. Present FHA policy, in effect since 1954, is "to encourage the development of demonstration open occupancy projects in suitably located key areas."

Mortgage-lending practice has also been changing in a similar direction. Several of the leading mortgage-credit institutions in the country have financed open-occupancy developments and have indicated readiness to finance further ones providing they were economically sound. This does not mean that open-occupancy housing stands on an equal footing with all-white housing in the mortgage market, for many lenders still regard racial mingling as an added risk and adjust their lending policy accordingly. But considering the availability of government mortgage insurance and the policies of leading lenders, it seems fair to say that lack of mortgage financing is no longer a major obstacle to open-occupancy housing.

The Market for Interracial Housing

From the viewpoint of builders and investors, the ultimate question about interracial (or any other type) housing is whether it will find a market, and whether the market will be sufficiently strong to enable developers to gain a competitive profit and sufficiently enduring to afford an acceptable investment for lenders. This problem is reducible to the question: what is the effect of mixed occupancy on the demand for housing in new developments?

Available data, unfortunately, do not permit a definitive answer. Each of the developments examined presented a particular constellation of features in housing type, location, price, architecture, and other factors which would affect its marketability. Market promotional methods varied widely, as did also general

---

Privately Developed Interracial Housing, chap. vii, "Financing the Interracial Development."

housing market conditions in the times and places where inter-racial developments were built. About the only common feature was the mixed racial pattern, but even this was far from being a constant factor, since the proportion of nonwhites in the popula-tions of the different projects varied from less than 5 percent to 90 percent.

Because of the variety of conditions affecting sales and rentals in the various projects, it is difficult to single out the effect of the racial factor. Conclusions which can be drawn are inevitably impressionistic and do not prove much one way or another. Some developments were outstanding market successes. Some experi-enced slow sales or excessive turnover. Concerning the successful ones, it can only be said that whatever the disadvantage of open occupancy may have been, it was not enough to prevent a grati-fying market result. For the slow-selling projects, analysis dis-closes in every case the presence of factors other than race, such as inferior sites, which probably influenced the market response adversely. A few examples will reveal the interrelationship of the racial pattern with other factors.

A Wisconsin development, offering forty prefabricated houses at $6,250 to $12,000 sold out rapidly to whites and Negroes in roughly equal proportions, even though it was in a blighted area. The city contained a substantial population of industrial workers, but virtually no new housing which they could afford, and no public housing. The scarcity of low-priced houses and the strong demand for them were evidently the significant factors in the success of the interracial project. The builder did not at first plan an interracial development. He thought he was building for Negroes, but the project became mixed because of white demand. In fact, to preserve something of his original purpose, the builder was obliged to make special efforts to cultivate the Negro market.

A rental development of some three hundred units in southern California, built as FHA defense housing during the Korean emergency, was at first a failure and then, under new manage-ment, an outstanding success. An open-occupancy project, it was primarily intended and promoted for Negroes. In its first phase, the project never achieved more than 70 percent occupancy, and the proportion of white occupants never exceeded 21 percent.

Fifteen months after opening, more than half the units were vacant, many tenants were in rent arrears, all white families except one had moved out, and the buildings and grounds were in deplorable condition. At this point, the project was sold to avert mortgage default.

The new owners kept their good tenants, dismissed the poor ones, and after renovating the buildings, undertook intensive promotion of the project in the white market. The management also instituted strict requirements of property maintenance as a condition for continued tenancy. These policies proved highly successful. Within a few months full occupancy was achieved and has been maintained, with whites making up two-thirds of the residents. White demand would probably have taken the entire project on turnover had not the management determined to maintain the two to one ratio.

This rental project enjoys an exceptionally convenient location and is a good housing value. The vital difference between the failure period and the later success was the quality of management. The new management's success in overcoming the bad reputation of the failing project and attracting white tenants was aided, probably, by the nature of the local population. The city is a military and defense-industry center with a large population of newcomers and temporary residents, who constitute the bulk of the market for rental housing. More than two-thirds of the project tenants are military personnel and defense-plant workers. Many of these, because of their recent arrival in the area, would have no memory of earlier conditions in the project. In their housing choices, moreover, factors of convenience and intrinsic attractiveness probably play a greater part and status considerations a smaller part than if they were making longer-term commitments.

Another California development of moderate-priced sales houses in a minority residence area was a market failure. Many of the local minority groups earned their livelihood from agricultural employment. The builder evidently miscalculated the effect of the lending institution's credit standards, for although many of his minority applicants had adequate incomes, the irregularity of their employment pattern led the bank to reject them for mortgage credit. At the same time, it proved difficult to interest whites in the houses because of the reputation of the area. Sales to both groups, consequently, were very slow.

The Concord Park Homes sales development near Philadelphia differs little from any number of moderate-priced suburban tracts. Its housing value is competitive but not exceptional. Negroes were anxious to buy, but sales to whites were slow. More than two years of merchandising effort were required to sell out the development on a fixed-quota basis of 55 percent whites. Competing all-white developments were selling rapidly during the same period. Concord Park could have sold faster had it been willing to accept all qualified Negro applicants, but this would have meant a higher proportion of Negroes in the project and possibly abandoning its interracial character.

In New York City, two middle-income housing coöperatives built in redevelopment areas (Queensview, 1950, and Kingsview, 1956), were almost completely sold out before construction was completed, in one case, before construction began.[7] Built under the New York Redevelopment Companies Law, they received redevelopment land from the city at cost and partial exemption from taxes. Part of the costs was paid by the sponsors, and the real estate company handling the sales charged a very low fee for marketing. As a result of these subsidies, public and private, the housing was an exceptional bargain. Monthly carrying charges, after down payments of approximately six hundred dollars per room, were 20 to 40 percent lower than rents of comparable apartments. By law, apartments were available only to middle- or low-income families.

Although the law requires open occupancy and the sponsoring organization is dedicated to nondiscrimination, Negroes showed little interest in these developments. Despite a completely open policy in both projects and, in one, special efforts to attract Negroes, the proportion of Negroes is about 3 percent in one project and 5 percent in the other. The developments have proved especially attractive to the Jewish population, drawing about three-quarters of their buyers from that group.

---

[7] Institute for Urban Studies, University of Pennsylvania, "Market Experience and Occupancy Patterns . . . ," pp. 45-59.

It was anticipated that the site of these developments in cleared sections of slum areas would be an obstacle to sales. Obviously, the attractions of the housing were enough to offset the locational disadvantage as well as any handicap connected with open occupancy.

In Philadelphia, an open-occupancy rental development of 180 units, also in a redevelopment area, achieved full occupancy in less than a year, with a minority proportion of 12 percent. Built under the Pennsylvania Housing and Redevelopment Assistance Law, the project received a state subsidy equivalent to nearly 30 percent of the total cost and an FHA-insured mortgage covering most of the balance. The comparatively low rents were evidently sufficient to offset the unattractive surroundings. A large majority of the tenants are newcomers to Philadelphia, including a high proportion of servicemen. An income limitation on eligibility and open occupancy are legal requirements. The management has promoted the project to the general market and made no special appeal to minority groups.

Controlling the Racial Proportions

It is taken for granted among most developers and observers of open-occupancy housing that the proportion of nonwhites in a given development should not rise beyond some point. Otherwise, demand from whites will be discouraged and the project will be left without a sufficient market or with only a minority market or both. Studies in racially mixed neighborhoods confirm the common observation of diminishing white demand for housing as the nonwhite proportion in the neighborhood population rises.[8]

The critical point cannot be defined with precision. The demand for housing in a particular development is affected by a variety of factors of which the nonwhite proportion is only one. A project unusually attractive to the white market because of site or price or other reasons can tolerate a higher percentage of nonwhites than one less favorably situated. Indeed, in two observed developments (Wisconsin, low-cost sales; and southern California, rental)

---

[8] See chaps. iv and x, also Chester Rapkin and William G. Grigsby, *The Demand for Housing in Racially Mixed Areas: A Study of the Nature of Neighborhood Change*, chap. iv.

white demand was so strong that managements determined to limit the proportion of whites in order to maintain an interracial pattern.

Although recognizing the necessity of maintaining an appropriate racial balance, sponsors of open-occupancy developments have been loath to enforce racial quotas because of the discrimination inherent in such devices. Quotas employed for a good purpose, that is, to promote racial integration, have been termed "benevolent."[9] Benevolent or not, application of a racial quota means that individuals will be denied the opportunity to enter a given housing community solely because of their race—because "too many" members of their race are already in residence. Many proponents of interracial housing, profoundly committed to the principle of racial equality, have been less than happy about using a discriminatory means to achieve an equalitarian end. Application of a quota may also mean a sacrifice of sales or rentals.

Open-occupancy developers, consequently, have endeavored to use other means of controlling the racial proportions, coming to quotas only as a last resort. Whether or not quotas are needed depends, of course, on the relative strength of white versus nonwhite demand for housing in a given development. Notwithstanding the general disadvantage of nonwhites in the housing market, it cannot be assumed that their demand for a particular development will necessarily exceed that of whites or that it will be strong at all. According to the experience of existing developments, three factors with significant differential effect on white-nonwhite demand are price, location, and merchandising policy. A much smaller proportion of nonwhites than of whites is able to compete for housing in the higher-price categories. Projects remote from areas of established nonwhite residence are also unlikely to attract many nonwhites. Builders of both open-occupancy and minority housing have found that to attract nonwhite prospects in any number usually requires promotion efforts directed specifically to the minority community, through minority newspapers and other special channels. Promotion is equally

---

[9] Albert Mayer, "Race and Private Housing," *Journal of Social Issues*, XIII, no. 4 (1957), 19.

essential to reach the white market, but the media differ. Advertising in newspapers seems to reach white homeseekers more effectively than nonwhite, perhaps because the latter realize that most of housing advertised in the real estate columns is not available to them. Moreover, promoters of open-occupancy developments have learned not to emphasize the interracial feature in their general advertising, in order to avoid confusion with minority housing projects. But unless the open character of a development is made known in the Negro community, many Negroes will assume, from their experience, that it is closed to them.

Of the three variables, the one most susceptible of manipulation is merchandising policy. Hillview in southern California is a striking example of a failing tract with practically no white families left, converted to full occupancy two-thirds white by skillful management with aggressive promotion to the white market. Larchwood Gardens in Philadelphia and the Queensview-Kingsview coöperatives in New York also achieved high proportions of white occupancy without quota controls. Larchwood is a rental project tenanted chiefly by families recently arrived in Philadelphia. Legally required to follow nondiscriminatory policy, the management has little interest in developing an interracial community and has advertised solely to the general market. One of the New York coöperatives made initial efforts to attract Negroes; the other did not. Negro demand, undoubtedly, was depressed by the required down payments of approximately five hundred dollars per room, although it was made possible for purchasers to borrow up to half of the down payment.

Concord Park, on the other hand, was swamped with Negro applicants in spite of promotion directed exclusively to the white market so far as possible and no cultivation of Negro interest. But the project, nevertheless, had become widely known in the Negro community; its houses were moderately priced; and it represented virtually the only new, private housing which Negroes could buy in the entire Philadelphia area. The builders hoped for a Negro proportion of about 20 percent, but of the first fifty houses sold, more than forty went to Negroes. To rescue the interracial character of the project, the management placed a limit at 45 percent on sales to Negroes.

It is evident from experience that quota controls are not always needed, and there are means available to management of influencing the racial ratio without invoking quotas. But where circumstances combine to make a development unusually attractive to a minority group, or where it lacks strong appeal to whites, a quota system may be essential to maintain an interracial pattern.

Characteristics of Interracial Housing Occupants

For the marketing of open-occupancy housing an important question is whether there are *identifiable* groups in the white population which have little or no objection or perhaps even a preference for living in racially mixed neighborhoods. Data adequate to answer this question do not exist. Available information on characteristics of white residents in existing interracial projects fail to disclose any striking or consistent peculiarities. As in the general market, high-priced developments tend to be peopled with business and professional families in the higher-income brackets. Moderate-cost suburban developments draw mainly young families with children. Low-cost developments attract working class families. Urban apartment houses contain many childless couples and many newcomers to the city.

It seems reasonable to suppose that racially liberal sections of the population, partly identifiable as members of certain organizations or readers of certain publications, should be a fruitful source of prospects for housing in racially mixed developments. On this theory, the promoters of Concord Park directed a major part of their selling campaign to groups of assumed racial liberalism. To the membership lists of selected organizations they sent out more than 25,000 pieces of direct-mail advertising. They advertised in journals noted for advocacy of racial equality and on radio programs with an assumed liberal audience. All this directed publicity yielded only a handful of sales. On the other hand, more than a third of all sales were made to people who merely happened to be passing by the project and stopped to look. Few of these had previously heard of Concord Park. A West Coast real estate broker, promoting a small open-occupancy development, also appealed for white buyers through interracial organizations, with disappointing results. No commercial developer interviewed in the course of this study reports drawing any large part of his white customers from organizations promoting racial equality. Most have relied on conventional advertising methods addressed to the general public. These findings are consistent with previously reported evidence indicating the absence of distinctive characteristics of white families buying homes in existing racially mixed areas (chap. x).

Some developments sponsored by labor unions, coöperative organizations, or religious groups were occupied largely by members of these groups. Although adhering to the principle of racial equality, these organizations were not primarily devoted to that purpose.

Several interracial rental developments (in southern California and in Philadelphia) have found a large proportion of their white tenants among people recently arrived in the area, including military personnel. This suggests that newcomers to a community or temporary residents, probably because of their relative detachment from social pressures, may be less swayed by racial considerations in their housing choices than older residents. The lesser commitment involved in renting as compared with purchase of a house is also a factor which, other things being equal, would lead renters to be less concerned than buyers with the racial pattern.

Conclusions

The experience of existing open-occupancy developments does not yield a clear picture of market response to the interracial feature apart from other factors. The most important conclusion that can be drawn from this body of experience seems to be the obvious one: that developers have found it possible to market new development housing to an interracial clientele under widely varying circumstances. Racial mixture is only one of various factors affecting demand for housing in the developments studied. Those projects able to offer exceptional housing values readily surmounted any marketing disadvantage there may have been in the mixed racial pattern.

The site of a development significantly affects the demand of both whites and nonwhites and consequently the project's racial composition. Projects in or near a Negro residence area are apt to be strongly pressed toward predominantly Negro occupancy unless the location is offset by price or other factors.

There seems to be no identifiable section of the population which can be said to constitute "the market" for interracial housing. Residents of existing open-occupancy developments manifest a wide range of socioeconomic characteristics. They are not, on the whole, crusaders for racial equality. Newcomers to a community and temporary residents, usually in the rental market, may be less resistant to interracial housing than longer-term residents.

Merchandising policy plays a vital role in attracting residents and determining the racial composition of a development. The rapidity of marketing a project and whether it attracts a high proportion of whites or of nonwhites depends in considerable measure on how it is managed and promoted.

XIII

Mortgage Financing

Discrimination and Disadvantage in
the Mortgage-Money Market

Mortgage credit is the key to acquisition of good housing via homeownership. But, of course, any person seeking a loan to buy a house must possess adequate financial status to qualify for credit according to prevailing standards, and he must also be able to offer a suitable property as security for the loan. In both respects, the minority groups are under a disadvantage. Because of their relatively low incomes and instability of income sources, fewer of the minorities than of the white majority are able to meet the customary credit standards of mortgage-lending institutions. With limited access to the housing supply, they are also less able to obtain properties mortgageable on favorable terms, or any terms. Although diminishing, these disadvantages are by no means yet overcome.

A third disadvantage arises from the economic weakness of minority housing developments, as previously described, making them poor competitors for mortgage funds. In this case, it is the builder who receives the immediate impact of the minority group disadvantage, but back of him stand the families who would buy his houses if he could finance their construction and sale.

In addition to these group disadvantages is discrimination because of race or color. Whites and nonwhites of comparable economic status and owning similar properties seem to receive, on the whole, similar treatment from most lending agencies, with one crucial exception: institutional lenders traditionally have required properties for nonwhite occupancy to be located in recognized minority residence areas, and many lenders continue to enforce this special requirement. By making mortgage credit available to minorities in certain areas and withholding it in others, lending agencies help to maintain segregation.

Mortgage Loans to Nonwhite Homeowners: Recent Trends

In the great expansion of home mortgage credit since 1950, non-whites have participated to about the same extent as the white population. In 1956, the Census Bureau's National Housing Inventory found 495,000 nonwhite families owning mortgaged properties, an increase of 85 percent over the 267,000 mortgages on nonwhite owner-occupied homes reported in the Census of 1950.[1] Total home mortgages increased by about the same relative extent—from 7,052,000 in 1950 to 12,713,000 in 1956, a percentage increase from 45 to 56. For properties of nonwhite owners, the proportion mortgaged rose from 34 percent in 1950 to 49 percent in 1956.

Almost two-thirds of white but fewer than half of all nonwhite homeowners in 1956 used mortgage financing in acquiring their homes. The nonwhites' lesser use of mortgage credit reflects their lower incomes and inferior properties. Both white and nonwhite families acquiring properties without a mortgage loan had very low median incomes: $3,568 and $2,238 respectively. Nonwhite families who purchased homes with VA or FHA mortgages[2] had

---

[1] U. S. Bureau of the Census, *1956 National Housing Inventory*, Vol. II, *Financing of Owner-Occupied Residential Properties*, p. 2. The data are restricted to one-dwelling-unit, owner-occupied, nonfarm properties. All but 12 percent of the one-to-four dwelling unit, owner-occupied, nonfarm properties in the United States, 1956, were single-unit homes. All 1956 data in this chapter are taken or calculated from this same source.

[2] A VA mortgage is one guaranteed by the Veterans Administration, often termed a "GI mortgage." FHA mortgage means one insured by the Federal Housing Administration. In both cases the loans are made by private lending institutions, the federal government only guaranteeing or insuring their repayment and prescribing uniform terms.

median incomes more than twice as large, as shown by the following comparison:[3]

Type of loan	Median family income, 1956	
	White	Nonwhite
FHA....................	$6,173	$5,319
VA.....................	5,870	4,751
Conventional............	5,750	3,835
Property acquired without mortgage credit.........	3,568	2,238

Homes acquired without a mortgage loan were much cheaper and much older than the mortgaged ones. The median market value of all mortgaged properties in 1956 was $12,416, compared with $8,447 for homes acquired without a mortgage and remaining unmortgaged. Half of all mortgaged properties were built in 1949 or later, whereas of those not mortgaged, more than half were built before 1930. Unmortgaged homes of nonwhite owners were extremely cheap. In 1950, their median market value was $2,300, compared with $4,700 for nonwhite homes with mortgages and $8,700 for total owner-occupied mortgaged properties. Obviously, many of the unmortgaged nonwhite dwellings were mere shacks.

The relation of mortgage status to house value is further revealed by the 1950 data in table 28. As indicated, with one irregularity, the proportion of properties mortgaged increased at each higher level of value. For properties worth less than $4,000 (including two-thirds of all nonwhite units), the proportion mortgaged was about the same for nonwhite as for total units. Above the $4,000 level, nonwhite properties were mortgaged more frequently than total properties.

With the rise, 1950 to 1956, in the total number of properties mortgaged, nonwhites also became more successful in obtaining government-insured loans. More than a third of all loans to nonwhite owner families in 1956 were FHA-insured or VA-guaranteed, compared with less than a fifth in 1950 (table 29).

[3] *Ibid.*

TABLE 28

Percent of Properties Mortgaged, by Value and
Color of Owner, United States, 1950[a]

	Percent mortgaged	
Market value	All owners	Nonwhite owners
All properties	45.2	34.2
Less than $2,000	14.0	12.0
$2,000-$2,999	28.0	27.0
$3,000-$3,999	36.0	35.0
$4,000-$4,999	43.0	48.0
$5,000-$5,999	39.0	42.0
$6,000-$6,999	52.0	67.0
$10,000-$14,999	57.0	47.0
$15,000 or more	48.0	69.0

Source: *U. S. Census of Housing: 1950*, Vol. IV, *Residential Financing*, Part 1, "United States," chap. 3.
[a] Owner-occupied, nonfarm, single-unit properties.

The relative disadvantage of nonwhites in access to government-insured mortgage credit, pronounced in 1950, had become much reduced by 1956. The color differential which remained is probably attributable to income difference. Even in 1950, the nonwhite disadvantage in FHA loans was confined to income groups less than $4,000. Above that income level, the percent of total mortgages insured by FHA was the same, 22 percent, for both whites and nonwhites.

TABLE 29

Percent Distribution of Mortgage Loans by Type and Color
of Owner-occupants, United States, 1950 and 1956

	Total		Nonwhite	
Type of loan	1950	1956	1950	1956
Total	100	100	100	100
FHA	17	19	9	15
VA	15	26	9	21
Conventional	68	55	82	64

Source: *U. S. Census of Housing: 1950*, Vol. IV, *Residential Financing*, Part 1, "United States," chap. 3; U. S. Bureau of the Census, *1956 National Housing Inventory*, Vol. II, *Financing of Owner-Occupied Residential Properties*.

Sources and Terms of Mortgage Credit to Nonwhites

Negroes have traditionally obtained mortgage credit from different sources than whites. Johnson, Sterner, Weaver, and other writers have noted the great dependence of Negroes upon individuals and upon savings and loan associations for mortgage money.[4] These two sources accounted in 1950 for 70 percent of all mortgage loans to nonwhites but for less than half of existing loans to white owners. Life insurance companies, on the other hand, held one in every seven mortgages on white-owned, single-family dwellings but fewer than one in twenty-five of the mortgages on nonwhite properties.

Life insurance companies and bankers consulted in the present study assert that their limited holdings of nonwhite mortgages are not due to racial discrimination but to their lending standards. In general, these institutions prefer relatively large loans on new houses in quality locations and to borrowers of higher than average income—standards which obviously rule out a great proportion of nonwhite homeowners.[5] In a San Francisco study, Wendt and Rathbun noted that Negroes were largely deprived of mortgage credit from institutional sources because "the majority of Negroes live in blighted areas . . . [and] lenders will not lend on acceptable terms (or simply refuse to lend) on properties located within these near-slum areas, regardless of the race of the applicant."[6]

The sources from which nonwhites obtain the bulk of their mortgage credit generally offer less favorable terms and charge higher interest rates than do the large institutional lenders. The median interest rate charged on first mortgages in 1950 was $4\frac{1}{2}$

---

[4] Charles S. Johnson, *Negro Housing*, p. 96; Richard Sterner, *The Negro's Share*, p. 96; Robert C. Weaver, *The Negro Ghetto*, p. 264.

[5] The median income of families who owned homes mortgaged to life insurance companies in 1950 was $4,600—the highest for any type of lender. Families with homes mortgaged to individuals had a median income of $3,300—lowest for any type of lender. *U. S. Census of Housing: 1950*, Vol. IV, Part 1, chap. 3, table 15.

[6] Paul F. Wendt and Daniel B. Rathbun, *The San Francisco Bay Area Residential Mortgage Market*, p. 43. The authors also note a requirement of Bay area lenders that property securing a loan to a Negro be located within an established Negro neighborhood.

percent by banks and life insurance companies, 5 percent by savings and loan associations, and 6 percent by individual holders. The median contract term of fully amortized mortgages varied from twenty-two years on loans held by insurance companies to ten years for those held by individuals. Interest rates, except on government-insured loans, vary with the size of the loan,[7] and nonwhites purchase cheaper properties and hence take smaller loans than whites. Consequently, on all first mortgages in effect in 1950, nonwhite owners paid a median interest rate of 6 percent compared with a median 5 percent paid by total owners. This disadvantage has been ameliorated in recent years by the shift to government-insured loans with their favorable interest rates and repayment terms.

Nonwhites generally borrow a larger part of the purchase price of their properties and rely more on second-mortgage and sales-contract financing than do white home buyers. Forty percent of nonwhite mortgagors in 1956 had borrowed 90 percent or more of their purchase prices, compared to less than 30 percent of white owners. On VA loans, 100 percent financing was received by nearly half of the nonwhite borrowers but by only one-fourth of the whites. Second mortgages were reported for 12 percent of the nonwhite mortgaged properties in 1956 and 7 percent of the white.

Of the first mortgages reported by the 1950 census on properties occupied by nonwhite owners, more than one in seven was not actually a mortgage but a contract of sale. This method of financing was used about twice as frequently by nonwhite as by white home buyers. The contract of sale leaves the title to the property in the seller, who agrees to transfer title at a future date; hence, the buyer has less control over the property than a mortgagor and fewer legal rights. Its advantage for the purchaser is that it offers a method for acquiring a property with a small down payment or none at all.

---

[7] On conventional mortgage loans of less than $2,000 existing in 1950, the median rate of interest was 6 percent, but on loans of $4,000 and more, median rates were 5 percent or less. *U. S. Census of Housing: 1950*, Vol. IV, Part 1, chap. 3, tables 7 and 7a.

Location and Discrimination

The location of a property is almost always a crucial factor in a mortgage lender's decision of whether to loan on it and on what terms. Residential properties in slum or blighted areas are normally mortgageable, if at all, only on the basis of lower appraisals, lower loan-to-value ratios, shorter repayment periods, and perhaps higher interest rates than similar properties better located. Many institutional investors will not lend at all in such areas. Hence the concentration of minority groups in blighted areas is a major disadvantage to them in obtaining mortgage credit.

In addition to property location considerations applying to all borrowers, many lenders have special location requirements for minority applicants. Wendt and Rathbun describe the policy of San Francisco lenders in this respect: "Financial institutions . . . report that they lend freely to Negroes, requiring only that applicants meet standard income, credit rating, and asset security tests used with all borrowers *and that the property securing the loan be within an established Negro neighborhood.*" [8] Since the same lenders hesitate to make loans in the near-slum areas where the majority of Negroes live, it is clear that institutions "lend freely" to Negroes only when the properties are in Negro neighborhoods *of good quality,* of which there are not many in San Francisco.

Lenders consulted in the present study agreed that the foregoing statements broadly characterized mortgage-lending practice throughout the country, although some claimed that they themselves did not discriminate in this manner, and many drew attention to variations in the rigidity of the policy and the method of its application. There is also evidence that lending practice may be moving toward fewer residence restrictions on the minority borrower.

Two reasons for the policy are advanced by lenders. One is the desire to protect property values (and hence investments) in white neighborhoods against the believed destructive effect of

---

[8] Wendt and Rathbun, *The San Francisco Bay Area Residential Mortgage Market*, p. 43. Emphasis supplied.

nonwhite entry. The other is to preserve good relations with the white people of a neighborhood and avoid being blamed for placing a nonwhite family in their midst. Part of the good relations to be preserved is with other members of the financial and real estate business community who may be devoted to keeping nonwhites out of white neighborhoods.

In an earlier period the property values motive was probably the dominant one. More recently, as the effects of mixed occupancy on property values have become debatable (see chap. x), reasons of public relations have become for many if not for most lenders the principal motive for withholding loans to nonwhites in white neighborhoods. The shift of emphasis in motive is important because factors of public relations do not exert a uniform force in all areas nor upon all lenders. Usually, too, there is room for differing judgments about the nature and extent of adverse reaction to a particular loan and consequences for the lending institution. As a result, lender policy on the issue has tended to become rather vague and variable. This is illustrated in the comment of a Cleveland banker speaking more or less for all banks in the city:

> We do not finance the *first* Negro purchaser in a white area for public relations reasons. White resentment in the area would be great, *probably* resulting in account cancellations and discontinuance of other business. However, we do not insist that neighborhoods be 50 percent colored, or insist on *any arbitrary statistical line* before lending to Negro applicants. *Depends on circumstances.*[9]

The speaker states a definite policy toward the first Negro purchaser in an indefinite area. Policy toward subsequent buyers, as he says, "depends on circumstances." From the speaker's basic premise it may be surmised that if the first Negro purchase in a given area aroused no great commotion, the banks would lend to

---

[9] *The Cleveland Press*, September 8, 1956. Emphasis supplied. The banker quoted also included preservation of property values as a secondary consideration, in the following language: "For instance, the first Negro buyer in a white area may be, and usually is, of a high-type family. But suppose some white people down the street get panicky and sell to lower-type Negroes? The neighborhood, in such an instance, is apt to deteriorate . . . *I am not saying this happens all the time or even most of the time,* but it does happen. As bankers, we have to be realistic . . ." *Ibid.* Emphasis supplied.

subsequent Negroes according to nonracial standards, but if the entry of Negroes were opposed, lenders would be chary of making loans to them.

One of the leading mortgage-credit institutions in Chicago claims to have at least 10 percent of its mortgage portfolio in loans to Negro homeowners who are "the best borrowers we have." But the president stated in an interview: "We take the position that the first two or three sales to Negroes in any block should be financed between the parties." The basis for this policy is public relations. "There are five savers in every block in Chicago." Actually, this company sets no fixed number of Negro families who must be present before it will consider Negro loans, but "we must be satisfied that the *trend* is toward racial transition."

Even large institutional investors, operating nation-wide, are in many cases unwilling to make loans to nonwhites for the purchase of property outside established nonwhite areas. Among a limited number of such investors interviewed for the present study but including several of the largest mortgage-lending institutions in the country, one-third stated they would not accept loans of this kind primarily because of their interest in maintaining property values in areas where they may have loans; another third stated the same policy but for reasons of public relations; the remainder said they had no policy on the subject but doubted that correspondents would be likely to initiate very many such loans.

Said one executive:

The infiltration of Negroes into a white section knocks h—— out of values and does it quite fast. . . . For these reasons, this company does not wish to encourage, through lending, the movement of Negroes into white neighborhoods.

Another stated:

Our company cannot make loans in these circumstances [Negroes entering white areas]. Local correspondents would not accept such loans in the first place because of the adverse effect on public relations. Besides, this [life insurance] company has policy holders in practically every section of every city in the country; if we were to finance the entry of a Negro in a new neighborhood, we would hear from the policy holders.

Where public relations is the only barrier, some lenders have been willing to accept loans of the type in question by purchase after a lapse of time from the actual movement of the nonwhite into the white neighborhood. Thus, the president of a Negro savings and loan association in Chicago informed the present study that he was frequently able to market his "block busting" loans "down town" a few months after the transactions had taken place. In a California city, a mortgage company seeking a loan for a Negro family, who had negotiated the purchase of a house in a white neighborhood, was advised by a savings and loan association to keep its name off the deed of trust because it could not afford to have any publicity, but it would pick up the mortgage in ninety days.

A very few lending institutions have made public announcement of a nondiscriminatory policy. One of these is the Bowery Savings Bank of New York whose president testified before the Civil Rights Commission:

> The Bowery never inquires regarding the race, religion, or national origin of an owner or occupant of a property on which a loan application is made. If credit checkings are satisfactory and the value of the real estate in relationship to the loan applied for meets our usual requirements, the loan is granted. . . . We make no inquiries along these lines because the information would have no influence on our decision. . . .[10]

A similar statement of policy was issued on behalf of the Bank of America in 1949:

> Our satisfactory experience extends to the so-called minority segments of the population. Bank of America has extended its lending service to these groups wherever local laws and provisions did not specifically restrict occupancy to the Caucasian race. Now that the Supreme Court has made most of such racial restrictions unenforceable our policy is to make loans to non-Caucasians to buy or build in restricted areas, provided other relationships and credit factors are

---

[10] Commission on Civil Rights, *Hearings before the United States Commission on Civil Rights, Housing*, New York City, February 2, 1959 (Washington, D. C., 1959), Statement of Earl B. Schwulst, p. 62.

favorable. . . . It is basic policy with us to provide banking service to properly qualified applicants without regard to their race or color.[11]

Development Housing

The financing of new housing developments for minority groups or for open occupancy involves broader problems than loans on individual existing dwellings. Individual nonwhites may be good credit risks, but a housing development may not be.

Most builders say that lack of financing on acceptable terms or any terms at all is the principal limitation to building for minorities (chap. xi). Lenders incline to place more emphasis on other limiting factors, such as land scarcity, and on conditions causing minority housing to be often unattractive to an investor. In any case, it is evident that mortgage credit is much scarcer for nonwhite than for white developments, and when available is usually offered on less attractive terms, especially in the form of higher discount rates.

A very substantial proportion of the mortgages on minority housing have found no other purchaser than the Federal National Mortgage Association. "Fannie May" is not a preferred lender from the builder's viewpoint because (with some exceptions) it buys mortgages only at a discount and also because the seller must purchase stock in the association with each sale of mortgages, which represents, in effect, an additional discount. Nevertheless, many builders have found no other source of financing for their minority projects.[12]

A National Urban League study reports that during a period of two months in 1953 when FNMA was authorized temporarily to serve as a primary mortgage resource for FHA-approved housing coöperatives, applications for minority housing totaled more than $24 million, of which approximately $11 million were granted. Minority applications represented well over a third of the total, but the study reports that many more applications

---

[11] E. A. Mattison, "The FHA Record of Bank of America," *Insured Mortgage Portfolio*, vol. 14, Fourth Quarter, 1949 (Washington, D. C.: Federal Housing Administration). The author wrote as Executive Vice-President of the Bank of America.

[12] See U. S., Congress, House, Committee on Banking and Currency, *Hearings, Housing Act of 1956,* 84th Cong., 2d Sess., 1956, pp. 553-554, Statement of P. S. Knox, Jr., on behalf of the Prefabricated Home Manufacturers' Institute.

would have been made had builders known of the opportunity in time to change over to a coöperative form in order to qualify.[13]

Extensive interviews for the present study with builders and lenders in Los Angeles showed that probably two-thirds or more of the development housing built for nonwhites in that area between 1950 and 1956 (about 7,000 units) had been financed through FNMA.

The financing problem for development housing is obtaining a commitment from investors, before the houses are built, to accept the eventual mortgages subject to qualification of the individual mortgagors according to usual credit standards. The attitude of lenders toward minority housing, therefore, reflects their judgment of it as a class risk, independent of the merits of specific loans to individual borrowers. Interviews and available documentary evidence suggest three main bases for the lenders' adverse judgment. These are (1) the frequent shortcomings in site, design, and construction of minority projects, (2) doubts about the market, and (3) an unfavorable evaluation of nonwhites as credit risks.

There are minority housing developments which are well located and of excellent design and construction, but they are exceptional. As previously described, builders of minority housing typically operate under a highly restricted choice of sites. They usually aim, moreover, to produce an inexpensive house in order to attract the largest sector of the nonwhite market. The result is often a product unattractive to the investor who has the alternative of investing his funds in higher-priced, better-built, and better-located housing. An executive of one large life insurance company which holds the mortgages on several minority housing developments and has expressed willingness to take more told the present study, "We don't often have the opportunity of considering a minority tract that meets our standards."

Lenders emphasize also a concern with the salability of mortgaged houses for a period of years as contrasted with the builder's interest in selling once and counting his profits (or losses). For

---

[13] National Urban League, *Mortgage Financing for Properties Available to Negro Occupancy* (New York, 1954), pp. 9-10. For further discussion of FNMA's role in financing minority housing, and the policy issues involved, see chap. xvii.

this reason, weaknesses and uncertainties in the market for minority housing (chap. xi) are likely to be viewed even more seriously by lenders than by builders. In the present organization of the housing industry, the decisions of lenders are more likely than those of builders to reflect a judgment of the long-run economic feasibility of housing ventures. The literature on minority housing is replete with appeals to builders and lenders to treat it in the same way as other housing, but such appeals seem to overlook the market implications of building houses to be sold and resold only to the members of a distinct, small part of the total population. The implications are not overlooked by lenders, however. If it is difficult for builders and market analysts to predict with confidence that a sufficient number of nonwhites will be interested in purchasing houses of a certain type in a certain place in the immediate future, it is vastly more difficult for lenders to predict the distant resale market for the same houses.

In addition to risks connected with minority housing as a business enterprise, many lenders seem to consider nonwhite borrowers as a class risk from the standpoint of loan repayment and property maintenance. It is not immediately apparent why this should be, since lenders do not make loans to populations but only to individual borrowers who, supposedly at least, have been selected according to certain nonracial standards. Nevertheless, unsatisfactory repayment experience or expectations of unsatisfactory experience are among the main reasons cited by lenders for avoiding nonwhite developments.

In the early postwar period, open-occupancy housing developments were even harder to finance than projects for minority occupancy. Weaver wrote in 1948 that whereas Negro projects had to "shop around" for capital, "a proposal for private housing open to all racial groups seldom finds any source of finance. . . . "[14] Weaver's judgment is exemplified by the struggles of some of the pioneer builders for open occupancy.

Accumulating experience and other influences, however, have apparently brought many lenders to the view that open occupancy is at least no worse from an investment viewpoint than minority

---

[14] Weaver, *The Negro Ghetto*, p. 227.

housing. As noted previously, many interracial developments undertaken in recent years have had no great difficulty in finding financial backing. The enactment of legislation in several states prohibiting racial discrimination in certain types of housing has largely removed the competitive disadvantage of open-occupancy projects in those states. Fears that antidiscrimination laws would drive investment capital out of housing have proved not justified.

The Nonwhite Borrower as a Credit Risk

Lenders report a variety of experience with Negro borrowers. There are reports that Negroes are excellent credit risks and that they are poor credit risks; that they are prompt in making payments and that they are frequently delinquent; that they take a responsible attitude toward property and that they are irresponsible. *House and Home* reports some results of its inquiries:

People's Bond and Mortgage Company, Philadelphia, has said there is no difference between Negroes and whites on the 12,000 loans [it] services. But an influential southern mortgage banker has called Negro delinquencies in his 56,000 portfolio "more than twice the over-all average." Midland Mortgage Co. in Oklahoma City says Negro delinquencies on its FNMA portfolio run to a whopping 4% [*sic*]; whites are under 1%. An official of T. J. Bettes started to keep track of this differential in his loans, but gave up after screening 1,000 cases because he couldn't find any.[15]

The New York Life Insurance Company, with a known investment in 1954 of at least $8.5 million in individual mortgages in developments built for minority groups, reports, "No problem has come to our attention. . . . [Therefore] we assume . . . that there is no distinction in this respect [repayment] between single-family loans to whites and those to nonwhites." [16] In addition to single-family mortgages, New York Life had thirty loans totaling $17 million on Section 608 rental projects for nonwhite occupancy. It reports "no distinction in performance record between buildings for white and for nonwhite occupancy."

[15] "Minority Housing," *House and Home*, April, 1955, p. 142.
[16] Charles R. Van Anden, "New York Life and the Housing of Minority Groups," *Insured Mortgage Portfolio*, 18(2) (Winter 1953-54), 5-8. The author wrote as Vice-President in charge of Real Estate and Mortgage Loans.

Experience of the Bank of America with loans on minority tract housing is described by its executive vice-president:

In southern California alone we have financed 1,302 units . . . we are committed on another 309 units. . . . Our experience here, too, has been excellent. Our delinquency experience with minorities has been no higher than with the majorities, and as a matter of fact their homes appear to be getting better maintenance than those in similar tracts which were developed about the same time for Caucasians.[17]

A large savings and loan association in Chicago which loans extensively to Negro homeowners described its experience in an interview as excellent and says, "We have never had a 'problem borrower' among our nonwhite mortgagors." The president of Illinois Federal Savings and Loan Association in the same city reports that in twenty-five years of lending to Negroes, extending through the depressed 1930's, losses on bad debts have amounted to less than half of 1 percent of loans made.[18] Orientals in the San Francisco Bay area are reported also as generally having "excellent credit standing" with banks and other lenders.[19]

Similar favorable evaluations by lenders could be multiplied.[20] Almost all *public* statements by lenders are favorable, and among the lenders interviewed confidentially for the present study, more than two-thirds described their experience with repayment by nonwhite borrowers as good or comparable to experience with white borrowers. However, a substantial minority of lending institutions reports poor experience with Negro borrowers. A San Francisco lender stated in interview: "My experience has been pretty bad. Negroes have more foreclosures which almost always goes back to marital troubles." In a Negro housing project on which his firm had lent, 80 percent of the loans were delinquent, he said. "The cost of servicing them is high. Foreclosures run 10 or 15 percent. . . . All the loan applicants were carefully

---

[17] Mattison, *Insured Mortgage Portfolio*, Fourth Quarter, 1949.

[18] Robert R. Taylor, "Making Loans to Minority Groups," *Savings and Loan News*, January, 1953, pp. 46-47.

[19] Wendt and Rathbun, *The San Francisco Bay Area Residential Mortgage Market*, p. 27.

[20] A compilation by the Minority Group Housing Advisor of the Federal Housing Administration lists about twenty favorable statements by lenders. "Mortgage Banking Experience with Negroes: They Say –––––" (Washington, D. C.: Federal Housing Administration, September, 1954).

screened. They all had good jobs and made FHA down payments. No purchaser had inadequate earnings or an adverse past credit record. The point is, none had *any* credit record. . . ."

A Birmingham loan correspondent reported, "I made them [Negro loans] in the past, but not any more. From 1949 through 1951, I made a thousand loans to Negroes. Out of these, we now have only three hundred still active. The others were foreclosed."

An executive of a large institutional investor interviewed in New York City brought forth from his files reports on nine Negro tracts, all built between 1946 and 1954, which his company had financed. The houses were all inexpensive, ranging in price from $6,000 to about $12,000. Usual standards of credit rating were followed in making loans. In seven of the nine tracts, delinquency rates were significantly higher than in the total portfolios of the servicing agency reporting, ranging up to 20 percent, and in one case, to 50 percent. Inadequate maintenance of properties and lack of pride of ownership were also reported for several of the projects. The executive emphasized that the higher-than-average delinquency rates in most of the Negro tracts were very serious from the standpoint of an investor. Although delinquencies might be reduced by an aggressive collection policy, this is not a satisfactory answer because it means higher servicing costs which reduce the attractiveness of the investment. The delinquency experience was especially disturbing, the executive said, because all loans in question had been made on the basis of usual standards of credit and income (implying that the Negro borrower does not pay his obligations as faithfully as the white borrower in similar financial circumstances).

These varied experiences and reports seem to point to the conclusion that generalizations cannot be safely made about the Negro borrower. Not only do Negroes vary in their behavior toward housing and debt, but their variation is patterned by groups; otherwise, lenders would not encounter such varying conditions among different groups of Negro home buyers.

Some light on the nature of the patterning is shed by delinquency statistics published in connection with the residential financing section of the 1950 Housing Census. The data are from a sample of all mortgages on nonfarm, owner-occupied, single-

TABLE 30

DELINQUENCY RATES ON FIRST MORTGAGES[a] BY COLOR OF OWNER, INCOME,
AND TYPE OF MORTGAGE, UNITED STATES, 1950

Income and color: primary families and individuals in 1949	Percent delinquent[b] in August, 1950			
	All first mortgages	Conventional	FHA-insured	VA-guaranteed
All owners	5.9	6.6	4.0	5.3
Nonwhite owners	13.5	14.2	5.1	16.8
Less than $2,000				
Total	13.3	13.8	4.5	16.1
Nonwhite	23.5	22.1	20.2	39.6
$2,000-2,999				
Total	6.9	7.2	3.2	7.6
Nonwhite	8.7	10.4	.4	1.8
$3,000-3,999				
Total	5.7	6.2	4.9	4.8
Nonwhite	10.7	11.5	5.2	14.1
$4,000 or more				
Total	4.1	4.4	3.7	3.5
Nonwhite	4.6	4.6	3.7	7.5

SOURCE: *U. S. Census of Housing: 1950*, Vol. IV, *Residential Financing*, Part 1, "United States," chap. 3, tables 16 and 19.

[a] On owner-occupied, nonfarm, single-unit mortgaged properties with owner who is head of household or related to head. Excludes properties for which income or relationship of owner to head of household was not reported.

[b] One or more payments past due by thirty days or more. Mortgages with no scheduled payments required are excluded from the calculations.

unit properties. As shown in table 30, the highest delinquency rates, for both nonwhite and total borrowers, occur in the groups with family incomes less than $2,000, whereas the lowest rates are in the income groups of $4,000 or more. Equally significant, the racial differential in delinquency rates is wide in the lowest income group but practically disappears at the income level of $4,000 or more.

Looking at delinquency rates according to type of loan as well as income, the data show the highest delinquency and widest racial difference in the category of VA-guaranteed loans to borrowers with incomes less than $2,000. Lowest delinquency rates and absence of any racial difference are in FHA loans to borrowers in the $4,000 and more income class. In 1950, a VA loan to a nonwhite family earning less than $2,000 a year stood a 40 percent chance of being delinquent, whereas among FHA borrowers, white and nonwhite, at the $4,000 level and higher, fewer than 4 percent were delinquent.

That the least favorable repayment experience should be connected with low down payment or no down payment loans to low-income borrowers is not surprising.[21] It is not immediately obvious, however, why there should be a marked difference between white and nonwhite delinquency rates in the lower-income groups but not in the higher ones. Any explanation of this phenomenon must necessarily be somewhat speculative. Low-income Negroes, as compared with whites in the same statistical category, are probably poorer and less securely employed; their family relationships may be less stable; and probably they are newer to the urban scene, newer to the ideals and responsibilities of homeownership, and newer to the workings of an installment-buying, debt-paying society. However, delinquency rates are not uniform among low-cost housing developments for minorities but vary widely from one project to another. This variance suggests that the character of the housing sold to low-income Negroes may also be a factor in repayment experience. In one low-cost minority tract in the San Francisco area, for example, where delinquencies and foreclosures became excessive, the mortgage-servicing agency complained of the buyers' attitudes toward their obligations, their marital instability, and their over-commitments to installment buying. A government race-relations specialist, however, pointed out that house values in the tract had not shared in the general rise of real estate values, and because of poor construction, maintenance costs had risen faster than equities were being built up. It is difficult, of course, to assess the relative roles of these two factors, but it seems not unlikely that the restrictions which make minority housing ventures difficult for builders and unattractive to lenders also make them often "poor deals" for the purchasers.

[21] Lenders generally regard the buyer's equity as the most important single factor in motivating him to maintain payments. Evaluation of a borrower's personal character has become important with the development of low down payment loans, as a substitute for the "normal" motive of an equity. See Henry E. Hoagland, *Real Estate Finance* (Homewood, Ill., Richard D. Irwin, 1954), pp. 301-303; Robert H. Pease and Homer V. Cherrington (eds.), *Mortgage Banking* (New York: McGraw-Hill Book Company, 1953), pp. 145-146, 149.

The most significant fact in the delinquency statistics is that the unfavorable showing of nonwhite borrowers, whatever its explanation, is confined to the lower-income groups, except on VA loans. The impoverished, unadjusted Negro, although his housing need is very great, is evidently not a promising candidate for homeownership. But the evidence of both statistics and lender reports leave no doubt that the middle-income Negro who has saved a modest down payment, and whose employment is sufficiently secure to meet FHA standards, is fully as good a credit risk as the white person in comparable circumstances. As the report of a committee of the Mortgage Bankers Association points out, many lenders apparently do not fully realize this basic fact, but tend to classify all Negroes together as a group risk.[22]

Conclusions

The striking improvement during the past decade in the ability of nonwhites to obtain home-mortgage financing reflects their increasing economic strength, expansion of the supply of mortgageable properties available to them, and governmental measures to stimulate and equalize the provision of mortgage credit. The growing availability of mortgage credit to nonwhites on liberal terms has sustained their strong demand for housing in the areas of racial transition (see chap. x). At the same time, it has enabled substantial improvement in the quality of dwellings purchased by nonwhites, as measured by the value difference between mortgaged and nonmortgaged properties. Mortgage-lender policies tend to discourage minority homeseekers from competing in the general market while encouraging them to concentrate their purchases in the areas of good-quality housing that have become open to minority residence. One effect of this policy is to facilitate and accelerate the occupation of transition areas by nonwhites, thus preserving a pattern of segregation. Once the racial transition of an area has been largely accomplished, the continued liberal extension of house-purchase credit to nonwhites makes no additional housing available to them and may only enable them to bid up the price of a limited housing supply. The fact,

---

[22] Mortgage Bankers Association of America, Committee on Financing Minority Housing, *Report to the Board of Directors* (October 29, 1955), p. 11.

however, that nonwhites pay more for housing of equivalent quality (chap. ix) suggests that a great deal of intraracial bidding up of house prices has taken place in the large cities. Liberal credit to buy segregated housing is not an unmixed blessing.

The evidence indicates, however, that mortgage-lending institutions, in their relations with members of minority groups, are less attached to the racial-areas principle than they once were. Some of the leading institutions have publicly announced policies of nondiscrimination. Others have no uniform policy but may or may not discriminate depending on the circumstances of particular transactions. In new housing developments, racial mixture seems to be no longer a serious barrier to financing.

XIV

Real Estate Brokers

Racial Discrimination in Real Estate Practice

One of the strongest, most pervasive barriers to the equal participation of minority groups in the housing market is the withholding
of real estate broker services, except under special conditions.
With occasional exceptions, real estate brokers offer their services
to minority homeseekers only in certain areas, usually districts
where minority persons are already living. Since many real estate
men do not do business in such areas, their services are withheld
entirely from persons who are not of the white majority.

Racial discrimination in real estate is much more than a practice
of individual brokers and salesmen. It is one of the standards of the
real estate business to which individual businessmen are expected
to conform and are liable to sanctions if they do not. The attitudes
of individuals are not relevant, for whether prejudiced or unprejudiced, members of the real estate associations or boards are
expected to observe the racial as well as other standards of the
business group. Sanctions are both formal and informal. A non-
conforming member may be expelled from the real estate board
with attendant loss of business opportunities. Such drastic puni-
tive action, however, is seldom used. The informal sanctions of
loss of reputation and loss of business coöperation are usually
sufficient to hold individuals in line. There are those, of course,
who defy the rules of the organization, but aside from nonwhite

real estate men, who are excluded from the boards, they are few in number and may be considered not reputable dealers. The pressures for conformity exercised by the real estate boards undoubtedly account for the highly uniform racial practices observed among real estate brokers in all sections of the country. A few samplings of the available data on the subject may be presented briefly.

In a Los Angeles study, 1955, a white couple, representing themselves as possible house buyers, called on twelve real estate brokers doing business in a new residential area of 12,000 homes, chiefly FHA- and VA-financed. The couple was followed after a brief interval by a Negro, also purporting to be looking for a house to buy.[1] To the white couple, all the brokers offered listings and information that many houses were available with down payments as low as $1,000. None of the realtors offered any listings to the Negro "prospect," some saying that no houses were available, others that down payments were prohibitively high—from $3,000 up. In two cases, the brokers were frank. One said, "There is nothing available in this area for colored people. It is a shame and I have run into the same thing, being a Jew. I would recommend your looking in the Smithville area." One youthful salesman was courteous and coöperative but said he would have to check with the reality association. He gave the Negro his card and invited him to return. When the Negro returned, the young salesman evidently had learned for he said, "I am in sympathy with the colored people, but selling to a Negro would be tantamount to putting myself out of business as well as ostracizing me from other brokers and residents in this area." After further frank discussion: "Eventually there will be integration, but . . . I don't have the courage to sell to a Negro."

A survey in New York City employed a similar procedure. Twenty-seven real estate firms were approached by a Negro applicant representing an income of $6,000. The Negro was followed half an hour later by a white applicant with similar income qualifications. Previous telephone inquiry had established

---

[1] James H. Kirk and Lane D. Spane, "Private Housing Boom—For Whites Only" (1955, mimeographed).

that all firms had available apartments meeting certain specifica-
tions. Of the twenty-seven brokers contacted, twenty-two turned
down the Negro but offered one or more apartments to the white
applicant.[2]

In San Francisco, interviews with representatives of sixty-four
real estate firms handling residential properties in most sections of
the city led to the conclusion that four out of five brokers offered
their services to prospective Negro home buyers either not at all
or on a restrictive basis.[3] Similar treatment of Orientals and
Mexican-Americans was reported by three out of five of the
brokers interviewed. Studies in a score of other cities, including
Chicago, Denver, Des Moines, Minneapolis, Seattle, Pittsburgh,
and others, have yielded substantially identical conclusions.

Discrimination by real estate agents against Jews is reported
in many cities throughout the country. A survey of practices of
real estate brokers in various Detroit suburbs found that more
than half discriminated against persons of the Jewish faith. Some
agents attempted to guide prospective Jewish clients to certain
residence areas, suggesting they would be happier there than
elsewhere.[4] In a case investigated by the Connecticut Civil Rights
Commission, a real estate agent asked the complainant, who had
telephoned about a house advertised for sale in a Hartford suburb,
if she were Jewish. When the complainant said she was, the
agent replied he was sorry but the house was in a Christian
community, the neighbors wished to keep it that way, and therefore he could not show her the house.[5]

It is often asserted that brokers do not initiate discrimination
but only follow the wishes of their principals, the sellers, and that if
the latter were willing to accept minority buyers, the brokers

---

[2] Committee on Civil Rights in East Manhattan, Inc., "Summary of Procedures
and Findings in Housing Surveys" (1955, mimeographed). Also reported in the
New York Times, February 12, 1956. This experimental study was planned and
supervised by a group of social scientists associated with the sponsoring Committee.
[3] Council for Civic Unity of San Francisco, "Civil Rights Inventory: Real
Estate Brokers and Lending Institutions."
[4] Anti-Defamation League of B'nai B'rith, *Rights*, 2(2) (April-May, 1958).
[5] Connecticut Committee to Combat Discrimination in Housing, "Is There
Housing Discrimination in Connecticut?" (New Haven, 1955, mimeographed),
cases from files of Connecticut Civil Rights Commission.

would be equally willing. Although sellers frequently do give
discriminatory instructions to their agents, there is abundant evidence that brokers and their boards take an independent view
of their responsibilities and will refuse to participate in transactions violating their racial mores, regardless of the wishes of
individual buyers and sellers. In a recent San Francisco case, a
famous Negro, member of the Giants baseball club, arranged
directly with the builder-owner for purchase of a home in a
prestige neighborhood. A real estate firm held an agency contract
with the owner entitling it to receive a commission on the sale
no matter who made it. The firm, however, canceled its contract
and sacrificed its commission rather than be a party to the sale
to a Negro.[6]

There is no recorded instance of any real estate board's an-
nouncing that introduction of a minority buyer into a white
neighborhood was permissible if the seller were willing. On the
contrary, real estate boards commonly prohibit their members
from having anything to do with a transaction involving the
movement of a nonwhite person into an all-white neighborhood.
The role of the St. Louis Real Estate Board is illustrative although
more specific than most:

> No member of our board may, directly or indirectly, sell to Negroes
> or be a party to a sale to Negroes, or finance property for sale to or
> purchase by Negroes, in any block, unless there are three separate
> and distinct buildings in such block already occupied by Negroes.[7]

In Los Angeles County in 1955, a local board expelled two of
its members for participating in selling homes to families whom
the board's directors considered "a clear detriment to property
values." One of the purchaser families was of mixed Italian-Span-
ish descent; the other was Mexican-American. Contesting a suit
for reinstatement, the board argued that the expelled brokers
were bound as members to observe the board's bylaws to "make
every honest and honorable attempt to place families in a

---

[6] Council for Civic Unity of San Francisco, "Housing a Giant: Memorandum
on the Willie Mays Incident," by Edward Howden (1957).

[7] St. Louis County Real Estate Board, *Bulletin to All Active Members,* June 1,
1955.

neighborhood where such families will and do fit in with the neighbors and general character of the neighborhood. . . ." [8]

Real estate broker practice with minority groups embraces on the one hand exclusion from white residence areas and on the other hand positive guidance toward districts where minorities are already living. Many brokers do not handle properties in the latter areas, but others, both white and nonwhite, specialize in such districts. Neighborhoods undergoing racial transition frequently offer lucrative opportunities to real estate salesmen. In many cases, real estate agents strive to accelerate the transition by playing upon the racial fears and prejudices of the white residents to induce them to sell. Repeated calls will be made on white property owners, using such appeals as, "You are living in a fringe area; sell now while you can get a good price," or, "This neighborhood is going Negro; let us sell your house before the bottom drops out of the market." Such tactics are considered unethical by many real estate boards and by the National Association of Real Estate Brokers (Negro), but the opportunities for profit in the racial turnover of neighborhoods are not easily foregone by many agents.

Real estate men explain their reasons for not selling to minorities in white neighborhoods largely in terms of social pressures. Harm to their business is the motive most often stated. Reprisals are anticipated from neighborhood residents, other brokers, and mortgage financiers. In Chicago, where violence has been a traditional part of race relations, brokers also express fears for their personal safety. Following are illustrative examples:[9]

In business the main thing is to stay out of trouble in the first place, and one sure way of getting into trouble is to put one Negro in a white building. It's a matter of being realistic about it. There would be no limit to the trouble you could get. I could get killed . . .

---

[8] *Wing* v. *Southeast Realty Board* and *Beddoe* v. *Southeast Realty Board*, Superior Court of California, County of Los Angeles, Department A, SG C-1125 and SG C-1050 (1956).

[9] From interviews by Rose Helper in "The Racial Practices of Real Estate Institutions in Selected Areas of Chicago." Miss Helper's dissertation is the most searching inquiry available into the race relations of the real estate business.

When you assume that responsibility [being the first to sell to Negroes in a neighborhood] someone can be hurt . . .

I wouldn't want my plate glass window broken. If I moved colored in they'd do it.

In an area where it is all white, I would not put a colored family. First, because of the safety of my own skin . . .

As a secondary motive, many real estate men believe they are doing a service to the community by helping to keep minority groups out of white neighborhoods. Believing, as they usually do, that nonwhite entry causes property values to fall and the neighborhood to deteriorate, real estate brokers see themselves as acting in defense of home and neighborhoods, and hence justify their discrimination against nonwhite groups.[10] Although these beliefs are not without some apparent basis in experience (chap. x), they seem to be held by many real estate men with more fervor and tenacity than the facts warrant. The value of these beliefs in providing moral justification for racial discrimination is probably one of the reasons for their popularity among real estate brokers.

Another basic assumption in the real estate business is that majority and minority groups will not willingly share the same residence areas, and consequently a neighborhood once entered by nonwhites must tend inevitably to become all nonwhite. Guided by this assumption, brokers who work to promote white to nonwhite property transfers in mixed neighborhoods can regard their activities as only a business adjustment to the inevitable. It seems to escape the notice of most real estate men that their own racial practices contribute heavily to making their predictions come true. When a neighborhood is entered by a few nonwhites, real estate brokers generally write it off so far as the white market is concerned. Taking for granted that whites will not purchase or rent housing in such a neighborhood, brokers cease to offer or show properties in it to white clients, and some agents may actively try to persuade the remaining white residents to sell out.

---

[10] *Ibid.* Among ninety real estate brokers interviewed in Chicago, three-fourths believed that entry of nonwhites into a neighborhood damaged property values. Evidence from a variety of sources indicates that this proportion is approximately the same among real estate men in other cities.

Policies of Real Estate Boards

Real estate boards not only make rules to guide the practice of their members; in the arena of public policy, the organized real estate business has often cast its influence on the side of segregation. Efforts of real estate boards to restrict Negroes and other minority groups to certain areas have a history extending back at least to World War I, when the migration of Negroes to northern cities created a crisis in housing. In 1917 a committee of the Real Estate Board of Chicago proposed a plan. Recognizing the need of the growing Negro population for more space, the committee declared:

> The old districts are overflowing and new territory must be furnished. . . . It is desired in the interest of all, that each block shall be filled solidly and that further expansion shall be confined to contiguous blocks, and that the present method of obtaining a single building in scattered blocks be discontinued. Promiscuous sales and leases here and there mean an unwarranted and unjustifiable destruction of values. . . . In the face of existing conditions the Committee has in an unprejudiced spirit reached the above conclusion and hopes for active coöperation from all civic bodies.[11]

In St. Louis in 1923, the restriction of Negroes to certain districts was approved by a realtors' referendum. Adoption of the plan meant that the St. Louis Real Estate Exchange would recommend that none of its members sell or rent property to Negroes outside the specified districts.[12]

The *Milwaukee Journal* reported in 1924 that:

> Milwaukee will have a "black belt" if the Real Estate Board can find ways and means to make it practicable. At the weekly luncheon of the board Tuesday noon, the advisability of restricting the Negro population in a certain area on the West side was discussed. The members say that the Negro population of the city is growing so rapidly that something will have to be done. . . .[13]

In the same year, the New York Realtors Association sought to learn from the Birmingham Real Estate Board how southerners

---

[11] Everett C. Hughes, "A Study of a Secular Institution: The Chicago Real Estate Board," pp. 303-305.

[12] "Segregation of Negro Districts Approved by Realtors' Referendum," *St. Louis Real Estate Bulletin*, September 1, 1923.

[13] *Milwaukee Journal*, September 16, 1924.

"prevent negro encroachment on white residential territory."
The reply stated that

. . . Things like this simply don't happen down here. If one of our
white men sells a fine lot in white territory to a negro, he usually meets
with serious embarrassment of one sort or another.[14]

By 1925, real estate boards in various parts of the country
had taken measures to restrict Negroes and other minority groups
to certain districts. In some communities, with the hope of excluding nonwhites altogether, real estate boards pledged their
members against any dealings with persons not of the white race.[15]

The widespread concern of real estate boards with the racial
problem during the 1920's found expression nationally in the
Code of Ethics of the National Association of Real Estate Boards.
Article 34 of the Code, adopted in 1924, provided:

A Realtor should never be instrumental in introducing into a neighborhood a character of property or occupancy, members of any race
or nationality, or any individuals whose presence will clearly be detrimental to property values in that neighborhood.[16]

This article, copied and enlarged upon in the codes of ethics of
local boards across the country, became the national standard of
real estate practice in relation to minority groups. It was variously
implemented and supplemented by designation of areas open to
minorities, by board reviews of sales to nonwhite buyers,[17] and
most of all by encouragment of race-restrictive covenants in
property deeds.

The Supreme Court's 1948 decision making race-restrictive

---

[14] "New York Has Color Line Idea," *Birmingham Age-Herald*, January 19,
1924.

[15] For example, the following resolution of the Eagle Rock (California) Realty
Board: "Therefore be it resolved . . . that we as a board and as individuals
pledge ourselves against the selling, leasing, or renting of property, or being a
party to any negotiation affecting anyone other than of the Caucasian race. Be it
further resolved that we discourage and hold it highly unethical to sell or lease
any property either by the owner or agent, to such a person or to any person of
undesirable or questionable character." *Glendale News*, February 8, 1924.

[16] National Association of Real Estate Boards, *Code of Ethics*, Part III, "Relations
to Customers and the Public," Article 34 (1924).

[17] In Spokane, Washington, no realtor could sell property to a Japanese unless
the sale was approved by a special committee of the realty board. Sales to Negroes
required similar approval if outside designated areas. Tolbert Hall Kennedy,
"Racial Survey of the Intermountain Northwest," p. 174.

covenants judicially unenforceable provoked dismayed outcry from some real estate boards. The Los Angeles Board appealed to the National Association to sponsor a constitutional amendment to reverse the Court's decision. This board took occasion to remind its members that the decision did not protect them from ouster if they violated the code of ethics concerning the sale of property to undesirables.[18] The San Gabriel Valley (California) Realty Board declared in a resolution to the Los Angeles County Board of Supervisors that the Supreme Court's decision had "created chaos, with persons buying in restricted districts." [19]

The NAREB's Article 34 stood for more than a quarter of a century. In 1950, to align its official position on race with changing public policy, the association revised the article, omitting references to race, nationality, and "individuals." The revised Article 34 (now Article 5) provides: "A Realtor should not be instrumental in introducing into a neighborhood a character of property or use which will clearly be detrimental to property values in that neighborhood."

Notwithstanding the altered wording of the article, some local boards continued to interpret it as forbidding sales or leases to Negroes in white neighborhoods. The St. Louis Real Estate Board, for example, observing that realtors from outside the city were offering property to Negroes in white blocks within the city, in 1955 called upon the St. Louis County Real Estate Board to respect the city board's rule against such sales. As basis for requesting coöperation, the St. Louis Board cited Article 34 of the National Code, in the following terms:

This rule [restricting sales to Negroes] is of long standing and has our interpretation to be directly associated with Article 34 of the Code of Ethics of the National Association of Real Estate Boards. . . . It is our further interpretation that our rule and Article 34 of the Code of Ethics is also enforceable against all members of any Real Estate Board affiliated with the National Association of Real Estate Boards when dealing in property located in our jurisdiction which is the corporate city of St. Louis.[20]

---

[18] Milton A. Senn, "Report on Efforts in the Los Angeles Area to Circumvent the United States Supreme Court Decisions on Restrictive Covenants," p. 1.

[19] *Ibid.*, p. 3.

[20] St. Louis County Real Estate Board, *Bulletin to All Active Members,* quoting letter from the St. Louis Real Estate Board, June 1, 1955.

In 1958, the National Association of Real Estate Boards published a presumably authoritative interpretation of the controversial article.[21] The interpretation, by the association's executive vice-president, is literal. The article is said to refer only to the characteristics of property and its employment or utilization, and not to occupancy. "Character or use does not include 'occupancy.' The word was stricken from this Article. . . . While the qualities of the property and its utilization are subject to the provisions of this Article, any question as to its habitation is subject only to local determination in accordance with local practice." [22]

On occasion the National Association of Real Estate Boards has endeavored to promote better housing for Negroes and to overcome unfavorable attitudes toward Negroes as home buyers. In 1944 the association created a special committee on Negro housing and announced that it was recommending to local real estate boards throughout the country that they undertake programs to provide better housing for Negro families.[23] It listed as problems to be solved "adequate financing," "construction of Negro housing," and "management of Negro rental properties . . . on a parity with that given to other types of property."

A significant feature of this announcement was an apparent effort by the association to take a position of neutrality toward the segregation issue. The association would not establish ". . . any national formula or suggestion as to location of Negro housing, exclusiveness of use of such housing, or similar matters. These are problems which must be solved by each community. . . . It would take no part in the social, political, or racial issues which are often injected into the discussion of housing for Negroes." Article 34 in its original form was in force at the time of this declaration.

Following the announcement of its Negro housing program, the National Association publicized the results of a study which, it said, "exploded a number of long accepted generalities that

---

[21] National Association of Real Estate Boards, "Protecting Neighborhoods," by Eugene P. Conser, Realtor's Headlines.

[22] Ibid.

[23] National Association of Real Estate Boards, News Service, no. 65, for release June 14, 1944.

have tended to discourage entry into the Negro housing field." [24]
Experience indicated that

> . . . As a class, the Negro home buyer meets his payments faithfully
> —often more faithfully than other race groups in the same economic
> level—and that if his property is in good repair when he obtains it, he
> takes care of it after he buys it. As a tenant, he takes as good care of
> such premises as other tenants of his economic class.

In a formal policy statement adopted in 1945, the association's
board of directors emphasized two themes. First, "We believe it
is our duty to seek the ways and means by which housing of
Negroes and other minority groups shall be provided . . . ," and
second, "Where such housing shall be placed in any community
is a local problem to which there can be no national solution." [25]
This statement, reiterated in the 1958 interpretation of Article 5,
cited above, remains the policy of the National Association of
Real Estate Boards.

Local boards, too, have generally adopted a position of neutrality in regard to public utterances about housing and race.
Rarely, indeed, will real estate boards now publicly advocate
segregation, as many did in an earlier period. When real estate
spokesmen oppose measures for equal rights in housing, they do
so on grounds other than the merits of segregation, as such. Thus,
the Real Estate Boards of New York City, declaring themselves
opposed to prejudice and in favor of laws against discrimination
in public housing, attacked the proposed antidiscrimination law
for private housing as a "wanton invasion of basic property
rights." [26] The Pittsburgh Board of Realtors opposed the fair
housing law in that city on similar grounds. [27]

Exclusion of Nonwhite Brokers from Real Estate Boards

With few exceptions, real estate boards throughout the country
restrict their membership to white persons. Up to 1945, according

[24] *Ibid.*, no. 78, for release November 15, 1944.
[25] National Association of Real Estate Boards, *Headlines,* Vol. 12, no. 6 (February 5, 1945), Part II, "Statement of Policies."
[26] *New York Times,* June 14, 1957.
[27] *Pittsburgh Sun-Telegraph,* November 26, 1958.

to the National Association, no local board in the continental United States had elected any colored persons to membership.[28] In recent years, eight real estate boards are reported to have allowed a small number of nonwhite brokers to join.[29] There may be a few additional boards with nonwhite members, but not enough to change the general picture of exclusion.

Local real estate boards determine their own membership policies. The National Association has not taken any position with respect to racial discrimination in memberships, but its officials have recommended that Negroes should organize separate boards.[30] Negroes have done so, forming the National Association of Real Estate Brokers. Thus, there are two NAREB's, separate but far from equal.[31]

The exclusion of real estate brokers who are not white from the trade associations testifies to the racial attitudes of the real estate fraternity and symbolizes the separate housing market for minority groups. To those excluded, their rejection is felt as an arbitrary denial of opportunities for wider business and professional contacts and facilities which the trade associations provide for their members. The real estate boards, in their own estimate, constitute "the organized real estate industry." They guard its interests and strive to influence public policy in housing and real estate. Exclusion of nonwhites from membership signifies, therefore, that they are not considered part of the organized real estate business nor entitled to a voice in forming its policies.

For the real estate boards, a "lily white" membership policy is plainly an essential support for racial discrimination in the real estate business. If minority brokers were admitted to membership on the same basis as whites, the boards would, at least, have to

---

[28] Letter dated July 12, 1945, in the Vertical Files of the Library, National Association of Real Estate Boards, Chicago.

[29] Pittsburgh, Gary (Indiana), South Bend (Indiana), San Diego, Seattle, Pasadena, Manhattan, and Brooklyn Real Estate Boards.

[30] Letter described in note 28 above.

[31] "The National Association of Real Estate Brokers, Inc., was formed out of necessity. . . . The real estate profession is one of the few that has trade organizations wherein Negro Americans are not generally allowed to join as full-fledged members. Therefore, . . ." *Your Future and the N.A.R.E.B.*, brochure of the National Association of Real Estate Brokers.

listen to the minority viewpoint, and their maintenance of a double standard in business would be seriously embarrassed if not destroyed. This, undoubtedly, is the basic reason for the tenacity with which almost all real estate boards have clung to the color bar in membership.

PART FOUR

The Role of Government

XV

Race Discrimination and the Law

The most serious forms of discrimination are those embodied in laws and regulations, legally establishing or permitting acts of discrimination; those practised by authorities and public officials in enforcing the law, and the arbitrary discriminatory measures taken by such authorities and public officials.

United Nations, Commission on Human Rights, *The Main Types and Causes of Discrimination* (1949).

Relations among racial groups, and particularly the status of nonwhite minorities, have long been a subject of government regulation. Since the Civil War, three constitutional amendments, a half dozen federal statutes, at least a score of presidential executive orders, and a huge volume of state and municipal legislation have been adopted to govern the status of minority groups. Much of the state and local legislation has been enacted to segregate and subordinate the Negro and other nonwhite groups, but there is a growing body of state law that aims to promote equal rights and opportunities. The Supreme Court, through the varying latitude which it has allowed for federal and state legislation on race relations, has always exercised a decisive influence on the legal status of minority groups.[1]

The modern movement for equal rights and opportunity relies heavily on government and law. Marking the progress of this movement have been a series of favorable judicial decisions, ad-

---

[1] The law of race relations, including court cases, legislation, orders, and regulations has become sufficiently voluminous to justify a specialized legal journal in the field. See *Race Relations Law Reporter*.

ministrative actions for equality at all levels of government, the passage of a federal civil rights law, and antidiscrimination legislation in states and cities of the North and West. Despite the long history of government intervention in race relations, the feasibility of achieving racial equality by legal means and the wisdom of attempting to do so are controversial. Many who favor the objective of racial equality are skeptical that social customs and private attitudes which underlie discrimination can be changed by law. Others, to the contrary, regard the power of government as a principal instrument for advancing equal rights. It is worth noting, in passing, that the problem apparently has not troubled the advocates of racial discrimination. They seem always to have taken for granted that law was an effective means to segregate a minority group and impose upon it a subordinate status.

Following the Civil War, to raise the former slaves to the status of citizens, Congress proposed and the states ratified three amendments to the Constitution. The Thirteenth Amendment abolished slavery. The Fourteenth withdrew from the states the power to abridge the "privileges and immunities" of United States citizens or to deny any person the "equal protection of the laws" or "due process of law." The Fifteenth Amendment protected the right to vote regardless of "race, color, or previous condition of servitude." Implementing these amendments, Congress enacted a series of civil rights laws providing for equal treatment of citizens of every race and color in regard to property rights, voting, jury service, public accommodations, transportation, and other areas.

The protection of Negro rights intended by these laws was frustrated partly by decisions of the Supreme Court, partly by the political failure of the whole policy of Reconstruction. The laws were actively enforced for less than a decade after the Civil War. Federal courts in the South handled around a thousand criminal cases under the federal civil rights laws in each of the years 1872 to 1874, but the number of southern cases fell to 221 in 1875 and to 25 in 1878, the year following withdrawal of federal troops from the South.[2] As Berger writes, "the powerful

---

[2] W. W. Davis, "The Federal Enforcement Acts," cited in Morroe Berger, *Equality by Statute*, p. 9.

and constant opposition of the substantial white minority in the South won out over the shifting and less adamant majority throughout the nation." [3] For the white South, continued sub-jugation of the Negro was *the* issue, but the rest of the country had other issues and other problems, notably economic expansion, which deflected attention from the Negro question. Outside the South, the status of the Negro receded from public attention and did not return to national prominence until World War II. After 1875 Congress enacted no further laws on civil rights until 1957.

The federal civil rights laws of 1866-1875 not only lacked solid political support, but also ran afoul of the Supreme Court's de-limitation of federal and state powers under the new constitu-tional amendments. In the first case arising under the Fourteenth Amendment, the Court distinguished two kinds of citizenship, federal and state, and held that the amendment placed under federal protection only the "privileges and immunities" of federal but not state citizenship. Nearly all civil rights, the Court decided, belonged to state citizenship and therefore were not under federal protection.[4]

In another case, where defendants had been indicted under the Civil Rights Act of 1870 for conspiring to prevent citizens from exercising their rights under the Constitution and laws of the United States, the Supreme Court ruled that the crimes charged were not federal violations but offenses against the State of Louisiana, where the acts took place.[5] Previously, the Court had invalidated Sections 3 and 4 of the 1870 Act prohibiting interference with Negro voting rights, on the ground that these provisions were too broad and exceeded the powers of Congress under the Fifteenth Amendment.[6]

In 1883 the Supreme Court completed the wreckage of the federal civil rights program by invalidating the Civil Rights Act of 1875.[7] In so doing, the Court announced a fundamental inter-

---

[3] Berger, *Equality by Statute*, p. 12.
[4] *Slaughter-House Cases*, 83 U. S. 36 (1873).
[5] *United States* v. *Cruikshank*, 92 U. S. 542 (1876).
[6] *United States* v. *Reese*, 92 U. S. 214 (1876).
[7] *Civil Rights Cases*, 109 U. S. 3 (1883).

pretation of the Fourteenth Amendment which it has followed ever since. The restraints imposed by the amendment, the Court held, apply only to state action and not to the acts of private persons. But Congress, relying on the clause giving it authority to enforce the provisions of the amendment "by appropriate legislation," had attempted to restrain individuals from violating the civil rights of others. This, said the Supreme Court, the federal government could not constitutionally do. This decision placed a sweeping limitation on the power of the federal government to act in protection of civil rights. Justice Harlan, dissenting, declared that "the substance and the spirit of the recent amendments of the Constitution have been sacrificed by a subtle and ingenious verbal criticism." [8]

Having determined that not private persons but only states were limited by the Fourteenth Amendment, the Supreme Court was next called upon to specify how far the states could go in discriminating against a racial group. It determined that they could go far. In the famous case of Plessy versus Ferguson (1896),[9] the Court embraced the doctrine of "separate but equal," the overruling of which nearly sixty years later was to cause such consternation. A state law requiring Negroes to ride in separate railway coaches, the Court held, did not violate either the Thirteenth or the Fourteenth Amendments, providing that the facilities available to each racial group were equal. Justice Harlan again dissented. Anticipating the consequences that were to follow from this judicial sanction of compulsory racial segregation, he wrote, "In my opinion the judgment this day rendered will, in time, prove to be quite as pernicious as the decision made by this tribunal in the Dred Scott case." [10]

Separate-but-equal swung open a wide door to compulsory, legal segregation which was just gathering headway at the time the doctrine was announced. The "Jim Crow" legislation in the South is of more recent origin than is often supposed. As Woodward and others have shown, enforced segregation of the Negro

---

[8] *Ibid.*, at p. 26.
[9] *Plessy* v. *Ferguson*, 163 U. S. 537 (1896).
[10] *Ibid.*, at p. 559.

and his disfranchisement did not develop immediately after Reconstruction but only much later and after considerable controversy.[11] Churches and schools had become racially separate during Reconstruction, but afterward, for a decade or two, Negroes and whites generally continued to use the same facilities for eating and drinking, transportation, and recreation. Negroes also continued to vote and hold minor public offices. Thoroughgoing racial segregation as a "way of life" was a product neither of slavery nor of Reconstruction nor of Redemption, but of twentieth-century racism. Laws requiring racial separation of passengers on trains began to be enacted during the 1880's, but up to 1900 this was the only segregation law (aside from separate schools) adopted by the majority of southern states. Even this type of law was not adopted in South Carolina until 1898, North Carolina in 1899, and Virginia in 1900.[12]

By 1900, racism had triumphed in the South and the legal status of Negroes thereafter underwent a rapid and extreme change. Southern legislatures adopted hundreds of Jim Crow laws and ordinances, extending compulsory segregation into every area of life, seemingly, which the lawmakers could think of. In transportation, not only separate cars but separate waiting rooms in the stations were required. Interracial use of eating and drinking facilities was prohibited. Segregation became the rule in virtually all types of public institutions. Where separate establishments were not feasible, laws required separate entrances, exits, lavatories, drinking fountains, ticket windows, and so on. New Orleans required white and Negro prostitutes to ply their trade in separate districts. An Oklahoma statute specified separate telephone booths for white and colored patrons.

The Jim Crow codes continued to expand until recent years. An

---

[11] C. Vann Woodward, *The Strange Career of Jim Crow*, pp. 13-47. See also Franklin Johnson, *The Development of State Legislation Concerning the Free Negro*, Part II, "Chronological Record of the Laws." Immediately following the Civil War, the former slave states adopted "Black Codes" regulating the behavior and duties of Negroes. These laws, soon repealed, are sometimes thought of as forerunners of Jim Crow, but in fact they were very dissimilar in character and purpose from the subsequent segregation laws. Johnson, p. 4.

[12] Woodward, *The Strange Career of Jim Crow*, pp. 81-82.

Atlanta ordinance segregated taxicabs in 1940, ordaining "white drivers for carrying white passengers and colored drivers for carrying colored passengers." A Virginia law of 1944 called for separate waiting rooms and separate other facilities in airports.[13]

This great mass of racist legislation was judicially reconciled with the Constitution by the legal fiction of separate-but-equal. The Supreme Court did not regard this doctrine as fictional but endeavored to uphold the rights of the segregated group to "equal" facilities whenever inequality could be specifically demonstrated apart from the fact of separation.[14] Moreover, where the asserted "equality" became too patently spurious, the Court declined to follow the doctrine. Notably, separate-but-equal was rejected as a defense for residential segregation. Beginning with Baltimore in 1910, many southern and border cities passed ordinances specifying the districts in which Negroes and whites respectively would be allowed to live. Defending this legislation before the Supreme Court, it was argued that members of both racial groups were treated equally because residence areas were allotted in proportion to respective populations and no prohibition was imposed on one racial group that was not also imposed on the other. Rejecting these arguments, the Court held that the constitutional right to equal protection of the laws was a personal one and could not be satisfied by according privileges or rights to a group; moreover, the deprivation of a personal right could not be rectified by imposing a similar deprivation on someone else.[15]

In this legal reasoning the Supreme Court was actually recognizing that segregation of residence is "inherently unequal." The same reasoning which led the Court to invalidate the residential segregation laws could have been applied with equal logic and effect to virtually all other forms of statutory segregation. If equal rights for housing are not satisfied by provision of

---

[13] *Ibid.*, pp. 103-104.

[14] As in *McCabe* v. *Atchison, Topeka, and Santa Fe Railway*, 235 U. S. 151 (1914); *Missouri ex rel Gaines* v. *Canada*, 305 U. S. 337 (1938); *Sweatt* v. *Painter*, 339 U. S. 629 (1950); *McLaurin* v. *Oklahoma State Regents*, 339 U. S. 637 (1950).

[15] *Buchanan* v. *Warley*, 245 U. S. 60 (1917).

particular houses, it would seem not less true that the right to quench one's thirst or to enter a building equally with other citizens is not realized by provision of fountains or entrances "for colored." However, apart from housing, the Supreme Court continued to endorse separate-but-equal. Nearly four decades were to pass before the Court would term any form of segregation "inherently unequal."

Separate-but-equal was a lawyer's doctrine which flourished only in the court room. In reality, the driving force for Jim Crow laws was white-supremacy politics and their undisguised purpose was the opposite of equality. Segregation was one edge of a double-edged sword against the Negro. The other edge was disfranchisement. Negroes voted in the South during Reconstruction and continued to vote in large numbers for a score of years thereafter. But simultaneously with the drive for segregation, southern states adopted a variety of laws to deprive the Negro of voting rights, such as the "grandfather clause," the "good character clause," the poll tax, and the white primary. Under the impact of these and other devices, the number of registered Negro voters in the state of Louisiana fell from more than 130,000 in 1896 to scarcely 1,300 in 1904.[16]

The southern campaign to segregate and disfranchise the Negro was not an isolated phenomenon but a particularly virulent manifestation of a general upsurge of racist ideology throughout the country. The early twentieth century was the heyday of the Nordic cult of "the white man's burden" and the "yellow peril." It was a period of anti-Oriental agitation dating from the 1870's. Originating on the Pacific coast, the campaign against Orientals was carried onto a national basis because its main objective was congressional action to stop Oriental immigration. For more than half a century the national public listened to a barrage of propaganda on the alleged misbehavior and undesirable character of Orientals. Charges against the Orientals had much in common with southern race theories. Both laid stress on "race purity"; both asserted the superiority of the white race; and where the

---

[16] Woodward, *The Strange Career of Jim Crow*, p. 68.

southern racists appealed for "white supremacy," those of the West demanded that the United States be kept "a white man's country."

In the period of anti-Chinese agitation, largely ended before 1900, California cities adopted numerous discriminatory laws against the Chinese, subjecting them to special taxation, restricting their employment and business activities, and harassing them in a variety of ways. No formula was invented to save the constitutionality of these laws, and most of them were promptly invalidated by the courts. The earliest law, so far as is known, for compulsory residential segregation, was a California statute of 1880 empowering and directing local authorities to compel the removal of Chinese to prescribed areas.[17]

Legal discrimination against the Japanese was tempered by federal intercession motivated by protests from Tokyo. The Chinese had submitted to school segregation, but when San Francisco in 1905 ordered Japanese children to attend an Oriental school it provoked an international incident and the personal intervention of the president.[18] The principal state action against the Japanese was the enactment of the Alien Land Laws in which California and other western states seized upon the racially discriminatory provisions of federal naturalization laws to prohibit "aliens ineligible to citizenship" from owning land.[19]

Through slavery and Reconstruction there had been always a substantial body of opinion in the North concerned with the South's treatment of the Negro. But the early twentieth-century suppression of Negro rights provoked no opposition from the North. The northern temper of those times was expressed in a *New York Times* editorial of May 10, 1900, which observed that "Northern men . . . no longer denounce the suppression of the Negro vote as it used to be denounced in the reconstruction days. The necessity of it under the supreme law of self-preservation is candidly recognized." [20] Nor did the Negroes themselves offer resistance to the new status being imposed upon them. Instead,

---

[17] Eliot G. Mears, *Resident Orientals on the American Pacific Coast*, pp. 84-85, 90, 347. See also *Yick Wo* v. *Hopkins*, 118 U. S. 356 (1886).

[18] Mears, *Resident Orientals* . . . , p. 51.

[19] *Ibid.*, pp. 166-167, 179-180.

[20] Cited in Woodward, *The Strange Career of Jim Crow*, p. 55.

the most prominent leader of the race at the time, Booker T. Washington, preached a philosophy of accommodation and acceptance of segregation.[21]

For lack of opposition, the racists were given a free hand to subordinate the Negro in the South and erase much of his social and economic progress achieved since Emancipation. The Supreme Court, as noted, interposed few barriers to this process although it drew the line at residential segregation. Antiminority sentiment continued dominant through the 1920's as reflected by a wave of race riots after World War I, the national popularity of the Ku Klux Klan, and the achievement of Japanese exclusion in 1924.

The present revival of concern for minority rights dates from the late 1930's. Since the end of World War II, both public sentiment and Supreme Court decisions have shifted in favor of equal rights as decisively as they moved in the contrary direction half a century earlier. Negroes have fought the Jim Crow laws in the courts and have won a series of legal victories. One of the first cases indicating the Supreme Court's new concern for minority rights was decided in 1935 when the Court ruled that the absence of Negroes from jury lists and juries over a long period of years, when there were Negroes qualified for jury service, was sufficient to establish the fact of racial discrimination in jury selection.[22] Previously, although discriminatory exclusion of Negroes from jury service had been prohibited since 1879, the courts had required proof of discrimination in the form of direct evidence that exclusion was on grounds of race or color—a proof obviously very difficult to supply. By permitting the existence of discrimination to be *inferred* from observable facts, the Supreme Court gave genuine substance to the constitutional protection. The same principle was applied in a series of subsequent decisions.[23]

---

[21] As in his famous "Atlanta Compromise" speech of 1895: "In all things that are purely social we [the races] can be as separate as the fingers, yet one as the hand in all things essential to mutual progress." Booker T. Washington, *Up From Slavery: An Autobiography* (New York, 1915; first ed. 1900), p. 221. Quoted in Gunnar Myrdal, *An American Dilemma*, p. 65.

[22] *Norris* v. *Alabama*, 294 U. S. 587 (1935).

[23] *Pierre* v. *Louisiana*, 306 U. S. 354 (1939); *Smith* v. *Texas*, 311 U. S. 128 (1940); *Hill* v. *Texas*, 316 U. S. 400 (1942); *Patton* v. *Mississippi*, 332 U. S. 463 (1947); *Hernandez* v. *Texas*, 347 U. S. 475 (1954).

In another line of cases beginning in 1941, the Court revived the authority of the federal government to protect the rights of suffrage in both primary and general elections for federal office,[24] and invalidated the white primary and other devices for disfranchising Negroes.[25] In transportation and education, the Supreme Court manifested an increasing insistence on the "equal" part of the separate-but-equal principle.[26] Equal accommodations on railway trains, the Court ruled in 1941, must be provided even though there might be little demand from Negroes for accommodations of a given (luxury) type. A personal right, said the Court, could not be made dependent upon the number of people wanting to exercise it.[27] Later, the Court ruled that reservation of a single table in a railway dining car for use by Negroes was not enough to satisfy the equal facilities requirement.[28] By extending the same insistence on equality to professional and graduate education in state-supported universities where equal facilities were, in fact, impossible to provide, the Court in effect invalidated segregation in higher education, while continuing technically to maintain the separate-but-equal doctrine.[29] Finally, in 1954, the Supreme Court met the issue squarely and ruled that in education, segregation could not be justified by equal facilities but was "inherently unequal" and hence contrary to constitutional limits on federal or state powers.[30]

Subsequent to the school cases the Supreme Court has invalidated segregation in certain types of public recreation facilities and local transportation.[31] Lower courts have ruled against segre-

---

[24] United States v. Classic, 313 U. S. 299 (1941).

[25] Smith v. Allwright, 321 U. S. 649 (1944); Terry v. Adams, 345 U. S. 461 (1953).

[26] The Supreme Court has also invalidated state laws requiring segregation of passengers on interstate common carriers on the grounds that such regulations were a burden on interstate commerce contrary to the commerce clause of Article I of the Constitution. Morgan v. Virginia, 328 U. S. 373 (1946). This decision was a milestone in the judicial history of minority rights because it was the first to declare a state segregation law unconstitutional.

[27] Mitchell v. United States, 313 U. S. 80 (1941).

[28] Henderson v. United States, 339 U. S. 816 (1950).

[29] Berger, Equality by Statute, pp. 94-97, and cases cited in footnote 14 above.

[30] Brown v. Board of Education of Topeka, 347 U. S. 483 (1954); Bolling v. Sharpe, 347 U. S. 497 (1954).

[31] Holmes v. City of Atlanta, 350 U. S. 879 (1955); Gayle v. Browder, 352 U. S. 903 (1956).

gation in public housing. If the new concept of "inherently un-equal" should be applied generally, as the present Supreme Court seems inclined to do, the whole system of Jim Crow laws must fall.

While becoming increasingly critical of segregation, the Court has also widened its definition of state action to which constitutional restraints apply. This has had particular significance for housing. After the Supreme Court in 1917 held racial zoning invalid, the chief legal instrument for excluding minorities from residential areas became the race-restrictive covenant. Such covenants were private and applied to specific properties, but when their use became widespread, they accomplished much the same purpose as racial zoning. In 1926 the Supreme Court upheld race-restrictive covenants as private agreements not violating any provision of the Constitution.[32] Twenty-two years later, the Court ruled that whereas such covenants were not in themselves public acts, state courts could not enforce them because judicial enforcement was state action incompatible with the Fourteenth Amendment.[33]

The broad principle enunciated by this decision would seem to be that though the Constitution does not prohibit private discrimination, the power of government may not be used to give effect to the discriminatory acts of individuals. A related issue is whether private activities that are assisted by government may discriminate among persons according to race or color. This question is also very important for housing, because federal housing aids, particularly mortgage insurance, are distributed to a great extent through private builders and lenders. The latter, within wide limits, are allowed to determine who shall be eligible to buy or rent housing which they build or finance with government aid. As elsewhere described, private builders and lenders, with few exceptions, insist on racial segregation except in those states where discrimination in publicly assisted housing has been made unlawful.

---

[32] *Corrigan* v. *Buckley*, 271 U. S. 323 (1926).
[33] *Shelley* v. *Kraemer*, 334 U. S. 1 (1948). Racial covenants in the District of Columbia were declared contrary to public policy and the Civil Rights Act of 1866. *Hurd* v. *Hodge*, 334 U. S. 24 (1948).

The question remains unsettled. In the only case to reach the Supreme Court where the issue involving housing was squarely presented, the Court refused to review a New York decision which upheld the refusal of the Metropolitan Life Insurance Company to rent apartments to Negroes in Stuyvesant Town in Manhattan.[34] This is a housing development built on land obtained by eminent domain and assisted financially by a tax subsidy and a municipal grant of a part of the land. Although the refusal to review allowed the New York decision to stand, it left the way open for the issue to come up again. Decisions in the lower courts are conflicting. An action to compel the builders of Levittown to cease discrimination against Negroes in the sale of houses financed with federal mortgage insurance was decided against the plaintiffs in a federal district court.[35] But in a similar case, a California state superior court ruled that private builders and real estate agents operating under federal housing laws and seeking to gain the advantages thereof, were as much bound as the administrative agencies of government by the constitutional rule against racial or religious discrimination.[36]

Without any doubt, the most drastic action ever taken by the federal government against a racial group was the compulsory evacuation of all persons of Japanese ancestry from the Pacific coast during World War II and their detention in "relocation centers." This action was an executive war measure based on grounds of military necessity. The Supreme Court sustained the evacuation orders but with evident reluctance and recognition of a major break with constitutional tradition. Opinions in the first case on the issue contain dicta such as Justice Stone's "distinctions between citizens solely because of their ancestry are by their very nature odious . . ." and Justice Murphy's ". . . this goes to the very brink of constitutional power." [37]

---

[34] *Dorsey* v. *Stuyvesant Town Corporation*, 339 U. S. 981 (1950). Earlier, the Supreme Court had ruled that a labor union, authorized by the federal Railway Labor Act to represent an entire craft, could not discriminate in its representation of workers on the basis of race or color. *Steele* v. *Louisville and Nashville R. R.*, 323 U. S. 192 (1944).

[35] *Johnson* v. *Levitt and Sons*, 131 F. Supp. 114 (1955).

[36] *Ming* v. *Horgan*, Super. Ct., Sacramento Co., Calif., No. 97130 (1958).

[37] *Hirabayashi* v. *United States*, 320 U. S. 81 (1943).

In a second case more directly involving the evacuation program, a majority of the Court upheld the government while declaring that ". . . all legal restrictions which curtail the rights of a single racial group are immediately suspect. . . . Pressing public necessity may sometimes justify the existence of such restrictions; racial antagonisms never can." [38] Three justices dissented vigorously. Justice Murphy wrote that the majority decision "falls into the ugly abyss of racism." [39] Justice Jackson implied that the defendant's only crime was that he was born of Japanese racial stock.[40]

In another case testing only the detention feature of the evacuation-relocation programs, separate from the exclusion orders, the Supreme Court had no difficulty in unanimously deciding that the federal government could not legally detain an evacuee whose loyalty was not in question.[41]

The foregoing brief historical review illuminates the great extent to which discrimination against certain minority groups, notably Negroes and Orientals, has been created and sustained by law. It has been the role of the Supreme Court to set limits upon the power of legislatures and government executives to discriminate among people according to race, color, ancestry, or creed. Over a long period, as seen, the limits were broad and allowed wide latitude for discriminatory legislation. More recently, the Court has progressively narrowed the scope for legal discrimination and at present seems inclined to deny completely this power to public authorities.

The many legal victories won by Negroes in recent years have been successes against discrimination practiced by public authorities. More than any other group, the Negroes have suffered from governmental discrimination, and this explains the emphasis of the NAACP on litigation of constitutional issues. In contrast, Jews have made little use of litigation because discrimination against them is practiced mainly by private groups not subject to the restraints of the Fifth or Fourteenth Amendments.[42]

---

[38] *Korematsu* v. *United States*, 323 U. S. 214 (1944).
[39] *Ibid.*, at p. 233.
[40] *Ibid.*, at p. 243.
[41] *Ex parte Mitsuye Endo*, 323 U. S. 283 (1944).
[42] Will Maslow, "The Uses of Law in the Struggle for Equality."

From the standpoint of promoting equality, the most that courts can do, in their function of judicial review, is to restrain legislatures and public officials from unconstitutional discrimination. From the record it is clear that this is a function of the greatest importance. However, if government is to be a positive force for equality, not merely the courts but legislatures and executives must act. In the recent past, while the Supreme Court has been destroying the discriminatory race laws of the states, a considerable body of legislation and executive policy has developed aimed at sustaining equal rights. Much of this legislation is not new. Some fragments of the post-Civil War federal legislation for civil rights still survive. After the Supreme Court invalidated the Federal Civil Rights statute in 1883, northern and western states began to enact laws prohibiting various types of discrimination. The most frequent object of statutory protection was the right to equal accommodations in public places, but some states also prohibited discrimination in jury service, transportation, life insurance, and segregation in schools.[43]

The major development of recent years has been the extension of equal rights legislation into new areas, notably to employment and housing. A compilation of state laws on race and color in 1949 reported ten states with "fair employment" legislation, twice as many prohibiting discrimination in public employment, and eleven states with some form of antidiscrimination law in the housing field.[44] By 1959, seventeen states and fifteen cities had legislated for equal rights in some aspect of housing. These states and cities and the subjects of the respective laws are shown in table 31.

Much of this legislation is limited in scope, but there has been a definite trend toward laws of wider coverage. Early laws applied only to publicly subsidized housing. Beginning with New York state, the definition of "publicly assisted" housing was widened to include housing developments financed with government-insured or -guaranteed mortgages; by the end of 1957, six states

---

[43] Johnson, *The Development of State Legislation* . . . , pp. 53, 62-207. Johnson lists twenty-two states (including five southern ones) with public accommodation laws in 1900 and fourteen states which prohibited segregation in the schools.

[44] Pauli Murray, *States' Laws on Race and Color* and *Supplement.*

TABLE 31

STATES AND CITIES WITH STATUTES, ORDINANCES, OR RESOLUTIONS
FOR NONDISCRIMINATION IN HOUSING, JULY, 1959

State or city[a]	Provisions applying to				
	All housing with exceptions	Urban renewal	Other publicly assisted housing[b]	Public housing	Other
STATES					
Colorado	x	x	x	x	...
Connecticut	x	x	x	x	...
Massachusetts	x	x	x	x	...
Oregon	x	x	x	x	...
Michigan	...	...	...	x	...
Minnesota	...	x	...	x	x
New Jersey	...	x	x	x	x
New York	...	x	x	x	...
Rhode Island	...	...	...	x	...
Wisconsin	...	x	...	x	...
Washington	...	x	x	x	x[c]
California	...	x	x	x	...
Indiana	...	x[d]	...	...	...
Pennsylvania	...	x	...	x	x[e]
Illinois	...	x[f]	...	...	...
Kansas	...	...	...	...	x[g]
Alabama	...	...	...	...	x[g]
CITIES					
New York	x	x	x	x	...
Pittsburgh	x	x	x	x	...
San Francisco	...	x	...	x	...
Hartford	...	x	x	x	...
Pontiac	...	...	...	x	...
St. Louis	...	...	...	x	...
Cleveland	...	x	...	x	...
Toledo	...	...	...	x	...
Providence	...	...	...	x	...
Boston	...	...	...	x	...
Chicago	...	...	...	x	...
Philadelphia	...	...	...	x	...
Los Angeles	...	x	...	...	...
Cincinnati	...	x	...	...	...
Sacramento	...	x	...	...	...

SOURCE: Housing and Home Finance Agency, Racial Relations Service and Office of the General Counsel, *Nondiscrimination Clauses in Regard to Public Housing, Private Housing, and Urban Redevelopment Undertakings* (Washington, D. C.: Revised, October, 1958); Pauli Murray, *States' Laws on Race and Color* (Cincinnati: Woman's Division of Christian Service of the Board of Missions of The Methodist Church, 1950 and 1955); inquiries to selected states and cities.

[a] Includes only acts of state legislatures and city legislative bodies. In seventeen additional cities, the public authorities or urban renewal agencies have adopted resolutions for nondiscrimination.

[b] Subsidized housing not included under the urban redevelopment programs. Includes housing assisted by money grant, tax exemption, public loans, and in New York, New Jersey, Washington, and California, development housing financed with FHA or VA mortgage loans.

[c] Washington law prohibits discriminatory questions on applications for loans, including housing loans.

[d] Prohibits exclusion of racial, ethnic, or religious minorities from redevelopment areas.

[e] Pennsylvania prohibits discrimination in veterans' housing.

[f] Illinois prohibits racial covenants on urban redevelopment land.

[g] Kansas and Alabama prohibit racial zoning.

prohibited discrimination in essentially all types of publicly assisted housing. New York City was the first jurisdiction to legislate against racial or religious discrimination in the housing market generally, with certain exceptions. The New York City Fair Housing Practices Law, adopted in December, 1957, was followed a year later by a similar ordinance for the City of Pittsburgh, Pennsylvania.[45] During 1959, four states (Colorado, Connecticut, Massachusetts, and Oregon) enacted fair housing practices laws of broad scope. Colorado's law applies to all housing except owner-occupied dwellings. The Connecticut and Massachusetts laws apply to multiple dwellings and housing developments. Oregon's law prohibits discrimination in the sale or rental of any real property by a person who sells or leases real property "as a business enterprise."[46] Thus, although the individual homeowner is allowed to discriminate, brokers may not do so.

As indicated by the Oregon provisions just cited, there has been a trend in state and municipal legislation not only toward encompassing broader categories of housing, but also toward regulation of housing market institutions. The Pittsburgh ordinance, like the Oregon statute, specifically declares unlawful certain practices of real estate agents and salesmen. A 1959 Washington law and the Pittsburgh ordinance as well enjoin lending institutions from discriminating in the extension of housing credit.[47]

In Congress, the balance of political forces prevented for more than three-quarters of a century any legislation on minority rights, either for or against equality, with exception only of provisions in immigration and naturalization laws. Not until 1957 were the proponents of equality able to overcome southern opposition in the enactment of a law to protect voting rights—the first federal legislation on civil rights since 1875.[48]

---

[45] New York City, Local Law No. 80, "Discrimination and Segregation in Private Dwellings," approved December 30, 1957, effective April 1, 1958. City of Pittsburgh, Ordinance No. 523, "An Ordinance against Discrimination in Housing," approved December 15, 1958, effective June 1, 1959.

[46] Colorado, House Bill No. 259, *Colorado Fair Housing Act of 1959,* approved April 10, 1959. Connecticut, Public Act No. 113, approved May 12, 1959. Massachusetts, Gen. L. Mass. L. 1959, ch. 239, approved April 22, 1959. Oregon, Ore. Rev. Stat. L. 1959, ch. 585, approved May 25, 1959.

[47] Rev. Code Wash. L. 1959, ch. 68, effective June 11, 1959.

[48] *Civil Rights Act of 1957,* approved September 9, 1957. Text in *Race Relations Law Reporter,* II, no. 5 (October, 1957), 1011.

Immigration and naturalization laws have traditionally contained racist features. From 1790 to 1870, the privilege of acquiring United States citizenship by naturalization was limited to "free, white persons." In the latter year the privilege was extended to persons of African origin or descent, but all other races, notably the Oriental groups, continued to be ineligible for citizenship. Beginning with the Chinese in 1882, Orientals were also excluded from immigration. The immigration quotas adopted in 1924 were fixed to favor "Nordics" as against southern and eastern European nationalities. The first breach in this discriminatory system (after 1870) came during World War II when Chinese, Indians, and Filipinos were assigned token immigration quotas and permitted to become naturalized. Immigration and citizenship bans against other Asians were repealed in 1952, but in the context of a general immigration law which on the whole strengthened and extended the racist provisions of existing law.[49]

The executive branch of the federal government has taken a number of administrative actions for equality having some force of law. The most important of these, unquestionably, has been the elimination of racial segregation in the armed forces. The significance of this measure goes far beyond its immediate effect, for it continuously exposes large sections of the population to interracial experience on a basis of equality and to acquaintance with members of minority groups in roles of equal status. Moreover, wherever American troops are stationed abroad, their unsegregated composition symbolizes American racial equality.

Without congressional sanction, the federal executive branch has also acted to promote equal employment opportunity. During the 1930's, nondiscrimination was the rule in employment on federal public works, public housing construction, and work-relief projects. In 1941, a few months before Pearl Harbor, the president, by executive order, required all defense contracts to

---

[49] This was the McCarran-Walter Immigration and Nationality Act of 1952, passed over President Truman's veto and termed discriminatory both by him and later by President Eisenhower. The American Jewish Congress and the National Association for the Advancement of Colored People denounced the law as "one of the strongest manifestations of hostility toward minorities that we have seen in a generation." American Jewish Congress and NAACP, *Civil Rights in the United States, 1952: A Balance Sheet of Group Relations* (New York), pp. 13-15, and *Ibid.*, 1953, pp. 14-15.

include "a provision obligating the contractor not to discriminate against any worker because of race, creed, color, or national origin." A committee on fair employment practices (FEPC) was established with some powers to implement the order.[50] First strengthened, then weakened by subsequent executive orders,[51] the committee endured five years of controversy until Congress killed it by refusal to renew its appropriation.[52] The rule of non-discrimination in employment on federal contracts continued technically in effect, but lacking enforcement procedures, it was widely ignored. In 1951, the nondiscrimination policy was re-affirmed in a series of executive orders directed to various departments and agencies, and a President's Committee on Government Contract Compliance was created to study and report on compliance procedures.[53] Under the subsequent administration, this committee was reconstituted and authorized to receive complaints of violation of the nondiscrimination clause and transmit them to the contracting agencies, which in turn were required to report back to the committee concerning action taken on complaints. Although the committee has no enforcement powers of its own, it reports that "heartening progress has been made." [54]

Corollary to requiring nondiscrimination by government contractors, in recent years two presidents have issued executive orders to establish equal opportunity for employment in the federal civil service with procedure for handling complaints.[55]

In housing, the federal agencies, under pressure, have taken various steps to encourage greater participation of minority groups in the government benefits, but have stopped short of requiring

---

[50] U. S., the President (Roosevelt), Executive Order 8802, June 25, 1941. The federal FEPC was established only after extreme pressure by Negro organizations, including a planned "March on Washington" which would have been embarrassing to the national administration in the defense emergency. Louis Ruchames, *Race, Jobs, and Politics: The Story of FEPC*, pp. 12-21.

[51] U. S., the President (Roosevelt), Executive Orders 9346 (May 27, 1943) and (Truman) 9664 (December 20, 1945).

[52] Ruchames, *Race, Jobs, and Politics*, pp. 132-136.

[53] The President's Committee on Government Contracts, *Equal Job Opportunity Program*, p. 2.

[54] *Ibid.*, p. iii.

[55] U. S., the President (Truman), Executive Orders 9980 (July, 1948) and (Eisenhower) 10590 (January, 1955).

nondiscrimination in the distribution of benefits. Federal housing policy toward minorities is discussed further in following chapters.

The Efficacy of Law in Intergroup Relations

Controversy over the possibility of promoting racial equality by law turns on two related basic questions: can social customs be changed by law, and can law change attitudes and sentiments?

The Supreme Court gave a negative answer to both questions in its famous prosegregation decision of 1896.[56] Distinguishing between legal and social equality, the Court declared the Fourteenth Amendment could not have been intended to establish social equality because "Legislation is powerless to eradicate social instincts or to abolish distinctions based on physical differences. . . . If one race be inferior to the other socially, the Constitution of the United States cannot put them upon the same plane."

The doctrine of the futility of legal efforts to change social customs is particularly associated with the name of William Graham Sumner. Viewing the racial scene in the South in 1906, Sumner wrote that the two races had not yet learned how to live together under nonslavery relations:

Vain attempts have been made to control the new order by legislation. The only result is the proof that legislation cannot make mores. . . . The two races are separating more than ever before. . . . It is evidently impossible for anyone to interfere. We are like spectators at a great natural convulsion. The results will be such as the facts and forces call for.[57]

The ideas of *Plessy* v. *Ferguson* and of Sumner were in the tradition of *laissez-faire* social philosophy. In the past quarter-century, however, the vast expansion of government activity has been accompanied by new concepts of the role of government. In this context, the use of law to promote racial equality appears as part of the larger movement to utilize the power of government for all sorts of welfare purposes such as the promotion of full

---

[56] *Plessy* v. *Ferguson*, 163 U. S. 537 (1896).

[57] William Graham Sumner, *Folkways* (Boston: Ginn and Company, 1906), pp. 77-78.

employment, good housing, economic security, and many others.

Nevertheless, the older ideas still persist. The failure of Prohibition is often cited as evidence of the futility of law to change social habits and attitudes. In relation to the controversy over desegregation in the public schools, President Eisenhower has been quoted as saying, "I have been trying to convey the idea that you cannot legislate morality. It must come from within." [58] In similar vein, a member of the New York City council, explaining his opposition to a bill prohibiting discrimination in private housing, emphasized that he opposed housing segregation, but he believed the proposed law would "never open one piece of property to any individual or any minority group." "As much as you would like to," he said, "you cannot change people's moral principles by legislation. We won't have any more success with this bill than we had with Prohibition." [59]

Modern social scientists, however, maintain that, in some circumstances, law can be a significant force for changing social customs; also that law can contribute indirectly but importantly to the formation of new social attitudes and sentiments. To be effective in a free society, a law must have the support of a substantial body of public opinion. Notwithstanding the widespread practice of racial discrimination, there can be no doubt that most Americans believe in the principle of equal rights and equal opportunity for all. Observers of the American scene, from de Tocqueville to Myrdal and later, have remarked on the equalitarian outlook of the American people and their attachment to the principles embodied in the Constitution and Declaration of Independence. Equality of opportunity has been traditionally a touchstone of American politics and reform movements. The conflict between racial discrimination and American ideals is the essence of the race problem in the United States, what Myrdal aptly termed "an American dilemma."

A law against racial discrimination, therefore, though running counter to customary practice, is consistent with the moral principles held by most Americans. Proposals to prohibit discrimina-

---

[58] *New York Times*, September 16, 1957.

[59] Councilman Maurice J. McCarthy, Jr., quoted in the *New York Times*, December 6, 1957.

tion by law are often vigorously attacked for various reasons but scarcely ever on the ground of an undesirable objective. Even in the South, racial inequality is usually concealed behind the formula of "separate but equal." It may be said, therefore, that the "morality" of which President Eisenhower spoke is already in existence, and the present problem is to bring practices into line with accepted moral standards.

Moreover, customs and practices involving minority groups are far from uniform.[60] Members of the dominant majority are by no means of one mind concerning the proper status of minority groups, and the treatment accorded the latter varies widely from one group to another, from place to place, and in different aspects of life. Nor are practices static. They have undergone many changes in the past, and in recent years have been undergoing rapid change in the direction of equality.

The disparity between ideals and practice and the variety of existing customs and attitudes mean that lawmakers, including legislatures and courts, have a choice, within wide limits, of the moral codes or customs which they will uphold. Historically, as shown in preceding discussion, lawmakers have exercised this choice. For many years, law was used mainly to support inequality; of late years, judicial, legislative, and executive powers have been employed more and more to favor equal rights.

The controversy over the effectiveness of law in race relations is one-sided. The power of legislation to accomplish the subordination of minority racial groups has rarely, if ever, been questioned, but the theories of legal futility in race relations usually neglect this aspect of the matter. William Graham Sumner's observation in 1906 that the races were "separating more than ever before," and his likening of this movement to "a great natural convulsion" took no notice of the hundreds of laws being enacted at that very time in the southern states to compel segregation. The Supreme Court's interpretation of the Fourteenth Amendment as not intended "to enforce . . . a commingling of the two races" was spoken in the context of upholding a state

---

[60] On the diversity of racial practices in the South see Charles S. Johnson, *Patterns of Negro Segregation.* See also Myrdal, *An American Dilemma*, pp. 1048-1055, *et passim*.

law *prohibiting* racial "commingling" in transportation.[61] Twenty years earlier, however, the Supreme Court had announced a quite different view of the effect of law in race relations, more consistent with the Court's recent thinking. Legal exclusion of Negroes from juries, the Court then declared, "is practically a brand upon them, affixed by law, an assertion of their inferiority, and *a stimulant to that race prejudice* which is an impediment to . . . equal justice. . . ."[62]

On the possibility of changing attitudes by legal means, social and psychological research draws attention to the dependence of attitudes upon environmental conditions, and in particular to the social conditions which support attitudes of race prejudice. The visibly bad living conditions generally characteristic of minority groups, their equally obvious inferior occupations, and the fact of their segregation from the general population cannot fail to have a profoundly negative effect on the manner in which these groups are perceived by others. The segregation of a minority group, powerfully strengthens the psychological tendency to think of members of the group as being all alike and different from other human beings (see chap. v). Although law may not touch attitudes directly, it can be a force for change in the social conditions which nourish certain attitudes and thus, indirectly, react upon the attitudes themselves. "Any step that will remove these environmental supports," say the authors of a standard work in social psychology, "will contribute to the control of race prejudice. . . . The use of legal force in changing beliefs and attitudes is frequently a psychologically sound procedure."[63]

Allport observes that discriminatory laws *increase* prejudice and asks, "Why, then, should not legislation of the reverse type *diminish* prejudice?"[64] From the evidence of attitude changes following the ending of discrimination in cases of employment, housing, and the armed forces, he finds that "when discrimination is eliminated, prejudice . . . tends to lessen. . . . But it often takes a law, or a strong executive order, to start the process

---

[61] *Plessy* v. *Ferguson,* 163 U. S. 537 (1896).

[62] *Strauder* v. *West Virginia,* 100 U. S. 303, 308 (1880). Italics supplied.

[63] David Krech and Richard S. Crutchfield, *Theory and Problems of Social Psychology,* pp. 506, 512.

[64] Gordon W. Allport, *The Nature of Prejudice,* p. 469.

moving." This authoritative study of prejudice concludes that although law can control only the outward expression of intolerance (*i.e.*, discrimination), "outward action, psychology knows, has an eventual effect upon inner habits of thought and feeling. And for this reason, we list legislative action as one of the major methods of reducing, not only public discrimination, but private prejudice as well." [65]

The United Nations Commission on Human Rights, observing that legal action was not "omnipotent" and could not alone eradicate discrimination, declared nevertheless that "many forms of discriminatory conduct may be suppressed or greatly lessened by legal measures." Law, said the Commission, "fosters the conviction that discrimination is wrong. . . . People who have little respect for the law are nevertheless afraid of the consequences of unlawful conduct. . . . Whatever the motive, the resulting daily behaviour tends to create social customs which are in harmony with the law." [66]

President Truman's Committee on Civil Rights (1947) took a similar view of the role of law in overcoming race prejudice. In the opinion of the Committee, "The achievement of full civil rights in law may do as much to end prejudice as the end of prejudice may do to achieve full civil rights. The fewer the opportunities there are to use inequality in the law as a reinforcement of prejudice, the sooner prejudice will vanish." [67]

Studies of interracial housing projects have shown how the members of different racial groups tend to develop more favorable attitudes toward each other through the experience of living in the same immediate vicinity, getting to know each other as individuals, and sharing some common interests. In the two racially integrated projects studied by Deutsch and Collins, about 60 percent of the white housewives reported their attitudes toward Negroes had become more favorable since coming to live in the project. In contrast, less than a fourth of the whites interviewed in two segregated biracial projects used as controls reported a

---

[65] *Ibid.*, pp. 471-472.

[66] United Nations, Commission on Human Rights, *Main Types and Causes of Discrimination*, p. 43.

[67] *To Secure These Rights*, The Report of the President's Committee on Civil Rights, p. 134.

favorable change in their racial attitudes.[68] For the Columbia-Lavanburg researches, Merton reports that "many fair-weather illiberals *will* live in interracial housing projects in order to enjoy the rewards of superior housing at a given rental. And some of the illiberals thus brought into personal contact with various ethnic groups . . . come to modify their prejudices." [69] The significance of these findings, in present context, lies in the fact that all the projects studied were public housing and their integrated or segregated character was determined by public administrative policy.

Social scientists who have studied the problem of controlling group prejudice generally agree in rejecting as unsound the either-or dichotomy of action (including law) versus education. This judgment does not discount the value of soundly conceived educational measures, but holds that examples and demonstrations of equal opportunity in practice are often more effective educational devices than direct appeals to reason or sentiment. Efforts to obtain legislation often afford an exceptional opportunity for community education. As Louis Wirth has said:

> Participation and experience in the making of decisions is worth more than any amount of preaching. . . . The attempt to enact laws in our society is one of the greatest educational experiences. It is in the discussion and airing of the issues that occur whenever a law is being considered that people get a vital part of their education.[70]

The various federal and state commissions which have been set up to enforce antidiscrimination laws have uniformly considered education a major part of their task, essential to securing compliance. The existence of enforceable laws is viewed as equally essential to effective education.

The Enforcement of Laws against Racial Discrimination

Turning now from the theory of law in intergroup relations to the facts of its application, it is to be noted first that laws against racial discrimination have rarely, if ever, been strictly enforced.

---

[68] Morton Deutsch and Mary Evans Collins, *Interracial Housing: A Psychological Evaluation of a Social Experiment*, pp. 97-102.

[69] Robert K. Merton, "Discrimination and the American Creed," in R. M. MacIver, *Discrimination and National Welfare*, p. 119. Italics in original.

[70] Louis Wirth, *Community Life and Social Policy*, p. 402.

Before World War II, state legislation in this field, pertaining mostly to public accommodations, provided no administrative machinery for enforcement. Depending on statute provisions, an aggrieved person could sue for damages or file a criminal complaint. In either case, the burden of initiating proceedings and proving the case was on the complainant. Penalties for violation were small. Even when an instance of discrimination could be proved in court, it settled only that particular case and did not necessarily affect the discriminator's policy. The laws were seldom invoked and had little effect on discriminatory practices.[71]

Wartime federal executive orders on fair employment practices introduced a new pattern which, in essential features, has been followed in much of the postwar state and municipal legislation. For the first time since Reconstruction, a special agency of government—the Fair Employment Practices Commission—was created to enforce an antidiscrimination law. A second major innovation was the method of enforcement developed by the Federal FEPC, relying primarily on inducing voluntary compliance with the executive order rather than on formal legal procedures.[72] The Commission's choice of methods was partly governed by circumstances, since its enforcement powers were limited and vague. It was not empowered to seek enforcement of its orders. The most that it could do formally was to report cases of noncompliance to the president. In these circumstances, the Commission placed major emphasis on informal negotiation and adjustment of discrimination complaints. When these procedures failed, the Commission could hold a public hearing to air the facts and issues and bring the pressure of public opinion to bear on a resistant employer or labor union. Public hearings, however, were held only in exceptional cases, partly because of the Commission's limited funds. More than 95 percent of the complaints made to the Commission were handled on an informal basis.[73] Very important, nevertheless, was the fact of sanctions in the background. Although no one knew exactly what the FEPC could do, the possibility of some action by the procure-

---

[71] Berger, *Equality by Statute*, pp. 13, 108.
[72] Ruchames, *Race, Jobs, and Politics*, pp. 138-155, *et passim.*
[73] *Ibid.*, p. 151.

ment agencies of government or the president was always present. In developing this combination of persuasion and conciliation with latent sanctions, the FEPC made a fundamental contribution to the theory and methods of law in intergroup relations.

When the New York legislature in 1945 enacted the first state law prohibiting discrimination in employment because of race, color, creed, or national origin, it followed the federal precedent in creating a State Commission Against Discrimination to enforce the new law. Other states have modeled their recent civil rights legislation after that of New York. At the end of 1958, thirteen states had established commissions to enforce racial equality legislation applying to employment, housing, and other fields.[74] The scope, powers, and resources of the several commissions vary, but their methods of operation are substantially similar. All have operated with great circumspection, making minimal use of formal legal procedures, and relying chiefly on conference and conciliation to secure voluntary compliance with the laws. Education of the public through publicizing facts and problems has also been a major activity of most state commissions.

This is something new in law enforcement. Although unenforced laws are no novelty, the deliberate enforcement of a law through persuasion is relatively new. The commissions do not, of course, accept the Sumnerian doctrine of the futility of law to alter customs, but they seem to have proceeded on the basis that their purposes could best be accomplished by methods other than application of legal penalties to violators in the traditional manner of the law. At the same time, the "persuasion" emphasized by the commissions is not pure persuasion, because in the background is their power to invoke penalties if voluntary compliance is not forthcoming.

The basic administrative activity of the state commissions is the handling of complaints from individuals that they have been

---

[74] The states are Colorado, Connecticut, Massachusetts, Michigan, Minnesota, New Jersey, New Mexico, New York, Oregon, Pennsylvania, Rhode Island, Washington, Wisconsin. In some of these states, including New Jersey and Wisconsin, responsibility for enforcement of civil rights laws is assigned to a special division within an existing agency of the state government. In addition to the states, most of the cities with modern civil rights ordinances have created enforcement agencies.

subjected to unlawful discrimination. Typically, the laws specify four procedural stages for handling a complaint. The first is an investigation to determine the facts. If the investigation shows probable cause to believe the complaint justified, agents of the commission then attempt to eliminate the unlawful discrimination by conference, conciliation, and persuasion. These proceedings are conducted informally and without publicity. If they fail, formal procedures begin. The commission may order a public hearing on the complaint, followed by an official finding of facts, and if the evidence warrants, the issuance of an order to cease the discriminatory practice. If the order is not obeyed, the commission may seek enforcement through the courts.

In the first ten years and a half of its operation, the New York State Commission Against Discrimination disposed of 3,150 complaints, only four of which reached a public hearing.[75] More than half of all complaints were dismissed after investigation or withdrawn by the complainants; the remainder, except a very few, were adjusted by conference and conciliation. The record in other states has been similar though on a smaller scale. Experience has demonstrated the importance of the investigation procedure to establish the facts of alleged discrimination. It is frequently not easy to determine in a specific case whether an individual has suffered discrimination because of his race, religion, or national origin, and charges of discrimination are often made without justification. Individuals may honestly believe themselves discriminated against when, in fact, they are not. Thus, it is extremely important to determine the factual merits of a complaint before instituting further proceedings. In this way, the commissions serve not only to provide a remedy for victims of discrimination, but also to shield employers and others from unwarranted charges. Investigation, moreover, frequently brings to light and permits correction of discriminatory practices beyond the allegations of the particular complaint. Thus the New York State Commission verified the specific allegations in only 26 percent of the complaints filed during its first ten years and a half, but

[75] Actually, twenty-one separate complaints reached the hearing stage, but they involved only four respondents and four hearings were held. New York State Commission Against Discrimination, *1955 Report of Progress,* p. 10.

in an additional 19 percent of the cases, other discriminatory practices were found and eliminated.[76]

Conciliation, as developed by the New York Commission, is comparable to a consent decree since it takes the form of a written agreement specifying the manner of ending the particular discrimination. Such an agreement has an importance beyond the immediate case because it commits the party concerned to a future course of action. A single complaint, therefore, when adjusted by a conciliation agreement, may lead to a new and lasting pattern of conduct. The New York Commission polices its conciliation agreements by reviewing compliance approximately six months after closing a case and subsequently if necessary.

Another important feature of the legislation in some states (Connecticut, Massachusetts, Rhode Island, Washington) is the authority given the commission to initiate proceedings on its own motion without waiting for a complaint. Other states, including New York, New Jersey, New Mexico, and Oregon, authorize the attorney general or the state labor bureau to file complaints with the commission. Given the basic purpose of the laws to eliminate the practice of discrimination and not just to settle individual cases, the ability of the commissions to operate against discrimination is substantially enhanced when they can act on problem situations irrespective of specific complaints.

Parallel with law enforcement, all the commissions conduct, within their resources, state-wide programs of information and education authorized by the legislation. One device in New York and elsewhere is the creation of community councils in principal cities with the functions of studying problems of discrimination, fostering good will and coöperation among the various groups in the population, and advising the state commission concerning policies and programs. In addition, the commissions sponsor research and prepare and distribute informational material to schools, colleges, community group, and the general public.

Most of the state commissions were originally established to enforce fair employment laws. As new laws have been adopted against discrimination in other areas, including housing, their

---

[76] *Ibid.*

enforcement has been entrusted to the commissions. Also, in several states (New York, Connecticut, Rhode Island, Massachusetts, Washington), the older public accommodation statutes have been revitalized by giving the commission authority to enforce them. The Massachusetts Commission, among other duties, enforces a statutory prohibition of employment discrimination because of age. As jurisdictions of the commissions have widened, their new functions have been handled according to the already established philosophy and procedures. In the brief period during which laws against discrimination in housing have been in force, commissions have handled complaints in the manner previously described, but the greater part of their housing activities have been of an educational and "helping" character, endeavoring to encourage acceptance of the law and to remove obstacles to compliance.[77]

Enforcement procedure became a major issue in connection with the New York City Council's debate on a measure to prohibit discrimination in all multiple-unit housing and not just in the publicly assisted category. The bill as drawn provided for direct penal enforcement with violations punishable by fines up to five hundred dollars. The proposed law was combatted by real estate and property owner groups, but the enforcement provision drew the opposition also of civil rights proponents who supported the objectives of the bill. A United States senator from New York, known for his strong support of civil rights legislation, and the chairman of the State Commission Against Discrimination both urged modification of the enforcement procedure to place greater reliance on conciliation, with court orders a last rather than first resort.[78] The bill was finally adopted after deletion of the penal provisions and substitution of a conciliation and hearings procedure with court enforcement. A novel provision was the division of administrative responsibility between the city Commission on Intergroup Relations, assigned the conciliation function, and a

---

[77] See New York State Commission Against Discrimination, *Summary Progress Report on Housing for the Year of 1956* (mimeographed) and *Progress Report on Integration in Publicly-Assisted Housing* (March, 1957, mimeographed).

[78] "Javits and Abrams Bid City Soften Bill on Bias in Housing," *New York Times*, July 8, 1957.

special Fair Housing Practices Board, given the authority to hold hearings and initiate court action.[79]

Effects of Legislation for Racial Equality

Probably not even the staunchest advocate of the legal prohibition of racial discrimination anticipates that discrimination of any major kind can be substantially ended with the passage of a law, even a law with "teeth." Proponents of laws against discrimination generally regard them as one of several tools to be employed simultaneously. Social scientists now recognize the possibility of induced social change, but they hold that to alter an established custom requires a many-sided attack.

During the period that modern antidiscrimination laws have been in force in several states, it is generally agreed that a significant lessening of discrimination has taken place. Various factors other than the laws have contributed to this result, and it is difficult to identify the particular contribution which the laws have made. A few judgments may be ventured.

In the general movement toward equalization of rights and opportunities, the commissions enforcing nondiscrimination laws can be credited with a number of strategic break-throughs. Several of the commissions, both federal (FEPC) and state, have been directly influential in bringing about the cessation of discrimination by certain large employers and labor unions, and they have been able to open opportunities to minorities in certain types of employment previously closed to them. This break-through function will be particularly important in housing because the introduction of a single minority family into a neighborhood or housing project is often sufficient, almost by definition, to change the exclusive character of the area.

The laws and commissions have afforded opportunities, which otherwise would not have existed, for community education. Both the campaigns to enact legislation and the public-information activities of the commissions have served to broaden public knowledge of the discrimination problem.

Some value must be attached to the laws as official, public expressions of equalitarian ideals. The prohibition of racial dis-

[79] New York City, Local Law No. 80.

crimination by law, even if not strictly enforced, places the moral authority of the state on the side of equality. Racial prejudice and discrimination thus lose the support of legal respectability. This, of course, is not an argument either for "toothless" laws or for nonenforcement of legislation.

On the whole, it seems beyond doubt that nondiscrimination laws and executive orders have played a significant, if not measurable, part in the widening of opportunities for minority groups during the past two decades. Other studies confirm this judgment. The wartime FEPC, according to the most thorough study of its history, enjoyed considerable success in the North but relatively little in the South.[80] Southern members of Congress, nevertheless, thought well enough of FEPC's potentialities to strive hard and successfully for its abolition. Berger concludes that the New York fair employment law has reduced job discrimination in that state.[81]

Antidiscrimination laws are often compared with the Prohibition Amendment and statutes which also sought to suppress a widespread custom not previously defined as illegal. There are major differences, however, which throw further light on the possible effects of laws against discrimination. Unlike the antidiscrimination statutes, the Prohibition laws did not attempt to seek voluntary compliance but operated on a straightforward repressive-penal basis. They were, thus, far more stringent and controlling than racial equality laws have attempted to be. At the same time, the moral authority back of Prohibition was certainly much weaker than the equalitarian ideals which underlie the antidiscrimination laws. Even so, the public revulsion against Prohibition which led to its repeal was connected not only, perhaps not primarily, with its inroads on personal liberty, but also with its undesirable consequences, such as the growth of criminal gangs and the corruption of public officials which arose because of the profitability of violating the law.

Opponents of racial equality laws have predicted that the latter, too, would have undesirable consequences such as reduction of employment, decline of demand for housing, discourage-

---

[80] Ruchames, *Race, Jobs, and Politics*, p. 149.
[81] Berger, *Equality by Statute*, p. 116.

ment of mortgage funds from housing construction, and increased racial antagonisms. There is no evidence, however, that these harmful effects have actually been realized under the laws thus far enacted. No claims have been made of unemployment or other economic loss resulting from fair employment practices legislation. Instead, after an initial period of testing, the laws appear to have been generally accepted by employers and unions. The housing laws are still too new to permit definitive appraisal of their effects; but in the states where they have been adopted, there have been no claims of damage to the housing market or the building industry. Although individual employers or builders may fear economic loss from compliance with nondiscrimination law, there seems scant possibility for any substantial economic interest to gather around violation of these laws. As to racial tensions, experience indicates that intensified antagonism is not a necessary consequence of racial change and usually can be avoided with proper planning and preparation. An abrupt change in the racial *status quo* may provoke hostility and resistance as in the prolonged racial disturbance which followed the Chicago Housing Authority's introduction of Negroes into the previously all-white Trumbull Park area.[82] On the other hand, experience with racial integration in industry, the armed forces, public housing, and public schools in such cities as Washington, Louisville, and St. Louis demonstrates beyond question that racial discrimination and segregation can be terminated "by fiat" peaceably and with improvement rather than worsening of interracial relations.[83] The immediate effects on race relations of a shift from segregation to integration, it seems clear, cannot be categorically predicted, but depend on factors in the situation and the manner of accomplishing the change. Recognition of this principle is apparently

---

[82] City of Chicago, Commission on Human Relations, *The Trumbull Park Homes Disturbances, A Chronological Report* (1956).

[83] The following studies, among others, support this conclusion: Deutsch and Collins, *Interracial Housing*; A. M. Rose, "Studies in the Reduction of Prejudice"; S. A. Stouffer *et al.*, *Studies in Social Psychology in World War II*, Vol. I, *The American Soldier: Adjustment during Army Life*, chap. 10 (Princeton: Princeton University Press, 1949); Bonita H. Valien, *The St. Louis Story: A Study of Desegregation* (New York: Anti-Defamation League of B'nai B'rith, 1956); R. M. Williams, Jr., *The Reduction of Intergroup Tensions: A Survey of Research on Problems of Ethnic, Racial, and Religious Group Relations.*

one of the bases for the flexible and conciliatory enforcement procedures characteristic of the various commissions. Apart from the uncertainties of change, measures that stimulate dispersion of minority groups and lessen their segregation may be expected to promote harmonious racial relations (see chap. v).

Fears that nondiscrimination laws will disrupt the housing market reflect the belief that entry of nonwhites into a housing development or neighborhood will discourage demand from whites for housing in the area. This belief, as shown elsewhere, is warranted by events in those circumstances where whites expect a given neighborhood to become occupied by nonwhites. The movement of a few nonwhites into a neighborhood, however, depending on circumstances, may or may not generate this expectation (chap. x).

It seems at least very doubtful that housing demand patterns in a racially discriminating housing market (and expectations based upon them) will be also characteristic of markets wherein discrimination is prohibited. In the first, and traditional, situation, the housing demand of nonwhites is concentrated on the few areas open to them, and whites have a choice between racially mixed or all-white neighborhoods. In these conditions, neighborhoods where nonwhites have been allowed to live have often tended to become increasingly nonwhite in composition, and beyond a certain point, no longer attractive to whites. Under conditions of nondiscrimination, however, nonwhite demand may be dispersed over a larger part of the housing market while whites, no longer having the same alternatives of mixed or racially exclusive neighborhoods, may be less inclined to flee from the presence of nonwhite neighbors.

The residential concentrations of minority groups, as previously described, are supported not only by exclusion from other areas but also by the limited purchasing power of the minorities and other factors, including associational opportunities, churches and other social institutions, economic advantages for the business and professional classes, and reluctance to encounter the prejudices of neighbors in white areas. It is, therefore, not to be expected that nonwhites will immediately disperse themselves in response to nondiscrimination laws, but most, undoubtedly, will continue for some time to seek housing within or near the existing minority residence areas.[84]

All factors considered, nondiscrimination laws in housing seem unlikely to have any immediate effects of a dramatic nature, either on existing residence patterns or on the housing market. Their immediate importance must be judged in terms of the value of removing a stigma from the minority groups and of allowing to the individuals who desire to leave the racial ghetto the opportunity for doing so. Over a longer period, the effects may be felt in a gradual decline of the segregated communities and the assumption by the minorities of the housing patterns common to other Americans.

Discrimination by Abuse of Legal Powers

An important aspect of government intervention in race relations, especially significant for housing, is the use of discretionary powers under nonracial legislation in a racially discriminatory manner. Local government bodies exercise extensive controls over land use and building through planning and zoning, subdivision regulation, building regulation, control of water supply and sewage disposal, provision of public parks and playgrounds, and other ways. The administration of these laws typically place wide discretionary powers in the hands of administrative boards or officials. Local government agencies cannot, of course, legally segregate or discriminate among persons by reason of race or color, but there is evidence that not infrequently they use their discretionary power to do just that.

Local governments in the South have traditionally considered it their duty to uphold white supremacy by all necessary means, legal, illegal, and extralegal. A tradition of illegality has been part of the general inequality of southern justice in regard to Negroes.[85] In the North and West, formal equality of justice has been the general rule, with inequality in the application of housing laws a conspicuous exception. Local government actions to main-

---

[84] See chap. iv. For another analysis leading to similar conclusions, see Robert C. Weaver, "The Effect of Anti-Discrimination Legislation upon the FHA- and VA-Insured Housing Market in New York State."

[85] Myrdal, *An American Dilemma*, pp. 448-451.

tain segregation, being an abuse of power, are usually covered up and the motive can only be inferred from circumstances. It is not possible, therefore, to know exactly how extensive are the practices in question nor even to supply legal proof that they exist at all. Certainly there are many local officials and governments which administer the law equally and with fairness to all concerned. There is evidence, however, of a great deal of abuse of governmental powers to restrict the housing opportunities of nonwhite minorities. Charles Abrams, noted authority on housing and former chairman of the New York State Commission Against Discrimination, considers that "The greatest dangers to minority rights lie in ever-widening areas which can no longer be effectively reached by the judicial process. Public officials today are often effecting discriminations through subtle administrative determinations and through official acts in which the discrimination cannot be identified and subjected to judicial scrutiny." [86]

An inquiry into privately developed interracial housing throughout the United States found opposition of local government units to be one of the principal barriers which developers of open-occupancy projects have had to contend with. Several promising developments have been defeated by zoning changes or refusal of local officials to grant needed approvals which, apparently, would have been granted routinely except for the interracial character of the projects proposed.[87] Builders consulted in the present study have consistently described the policies of local governments as one of the major factors restricting the use of land for minority or interracial housing (see chap. xi).

A well-documented instance of municipal action to contain Negroes within existing Negro residence areas is Meyerson and Banfield's study of public-housing sites in Chicago.[88] As these authors bring out, the Chicago City Council viewed the problem of approving public-housing sites mainly in terms of the effect of proposed sites (which would be open to Negroes) on the existing pattern of segregation. Sites which would result in admit-

---

[86] Charles Abrams, *Forbidden Neighbors*, p. 304.

[87] Eunice and George Grier, *Privately Developed Interracial Housing: An Analysis of Experience.*

[88] Martin Meyerson and Edward C. Banfield, *Politics, Planning, and the Public Interest: The Case of Public Housing in Chicago.*

ting Negroes into new areas were not politically feasible unless the councilman whose district contained a proposed controversial site was at odds with the machine and a candidate for punishment. The Chicago case is unique only in its political particulars. Persons familiar with the selection of sites for public housing in many cities know that local official approval of a site available to nonwhites ordinarily turns on the acceptability of the area for minority residence.[89]

Near St. Louis, the all-white character of suburban Creve Coeur was preserved when the local board of aldermen condemned for a public park a two-acre homesite previously acquired by a Negro surgeon.[90] In the San Francisco area, developers of an open-occupancy subdivision were confronted suddenly by a new regulation of the local sanitation district, adopted after the interracial project had become controversial, increasing six-fold the cost of a sewerage connection.[91] These examples illustrate two points common to this type of governmental discrimination. First is the obscurity of motives. In both cases the local government bodies were acting well within their legal authority and both insisted their actions were not racially motivated. The effect, in both cases, was to burden the efforts of minority individuals to obtain housing, and the minority interests were convinced that such was the purpose of the actions taken.[92] In the second place, the incidents exemplify the wide range of devices which local government agencies can use to restrict the residence of minority groups if they wish to do so.

On occasion, racial motives in application of zoning and build-

---

[89] Interviews with Public Housing Administration officials. See also "Site Selection Bumps up against Race Segregation," *House and Home*, August, 1956.

[90] *St. Louis Post-Dispatch* and *St. Louis Globe-Democrat*, October 28, 1956.

[91] Memorandum Report, May 9, 1955, and Minutes of Meeting, April 28, 1955, Santa Clara County Community Relations Committee, American Friends Service Committee.

[92] The Creve Coeur condemnation of the Negro surgeon's property was voted after his $55,000 house was half completed and after the city had denied him a plumbing permit. Articles in the local press reported the city had no plans or revenues for financing purchase of the condemned land, but a group of property owners had pledged $25,000 toward the cost. A city official declared charges of racial discrimination were "ridiculous" but the Negro doctor took a different view as did also, apparently, the mayor who vetoed the condemnation but was overridden, the Negro press, the Catholic Interracial Council and the Archbishop, and fourteen Creve Coeur residents who published a statement in support of the doctor. *St. Louis Globe-Democrat*, November 3 and 6, 1956.

ing laws come out into the open. In Detroit, opponents of an interracial housing coöperative petitioned the city council to change the zoning classification of the coöperative's land from multiple- to single-unit dwellings. The coöperative had planned and arranged financing for multiple-unit structures and was not in position to reorganize on a single-unit basis. When opponents were unable to obtain sufficient votes in the council to effect the zoning change, they persuaded the mayor to veto the plan commission's approval of the coöperative's site plan.[93]

Many suburban communities, including some cities of substantial size, endeavor to exclude Negroes altogether from residing within their limits. The discretionary land use and housing powers of local government are employed to implement the exclusion. In Dearborn, Michigan, for example, Negroes are reported to be "barred, completely and semiofficially," although thousands of Negroes work there. The Mayor was quoted in 1956 as saying, "Every time we hear of a Negro moving in we respond quicker than you do to a fire. That's generally known. It's known among our own people, and it's known among Negroes here." [94] According to the same report, a Negro who moved into Dearborn in defiance of the exclusion policy "found his gas turned off, his garbage uncollected. Finally he moved out."

Glendale, California, adjacent to Los Angeles, has excluded Negroes even more effectively than Dearborn, without any public announcement. Although the Los Angeles area has been the main western goal of Negro migration for many years, the 1950 Census counted only twenty-six Negroes in Glendale's population of 96,000. None of the thousands of houses built for sale to nonwhites in the Los Angeles vicinity has been located in Glendale. Builders know, if they should venture to sell houses to Negroes in Glendale, "there would be no inspections and no permits and they would be out of business" (builder interview).

Related to interest in excluding minority groups is the acknowledged desire by many suburban governing bodies to limit their population to families of above average economic status and

---

[93] From a diary kept by the developer, and *Detroit Free Press*, March 15, 1950.
[94] "A Northern City 'Sitting on Lid' of Racial Trouble," *U. S. News & World Report*, May 11, 1956, p. 40. The 1950 Census counted fewer than a hundred nonwhites in Dearborn's population of 95,000.

prevent the entry of lower-income groups. A variety of regulations touching minimum-lot area and house size can be adapted to this purpose. Subterfuge is also involved here because economic status classification must be masked behind traditional bases of the police power such as public health, safety, and morals.[95] The resemblance between economic and racial discrimination ceases at this point, however, because the former is accomplished by legislation subject to judicial review, whereas racial purposes are served, apart from southern Jim Crow laws, by abusive application of valid law.

Against this type of concealed, legal discrimination, minority individuals are virtually helpless. They may prosecute and win an occasional law suit, but in most cases discriminatory intent cannot be proved in court. Even when a suit can be won, since the law itself is not challenged, the court decision settles only the particular case. Nor can public opinion be relied upon to supply a corrective, again largely because of the difficulty of producing firm evidence of discriminatory purpose.

The only remedy would seem to be some form of administrative check on local officials by federal or state authority. Such a check, to be effective, would probably not need to involve supervision or control of local agencies. Since the abuses in question live in the dark, concealed behind pretexts, a simple fact-finding procedure carrying the threat of exposure to public view would probably eliminate many of them. If fact finding were coupled with informal conciliation, on the model of the existing state commissions, its effectiveness would be enhanced. Demonstrating such a possible remedy, when controversy over a proposed interracial housing development was at its height in a California community, the state attorney general ordered an investigation to determine whether any state laws were being violated. The investigation resulted in no charges; it was not even clear what formal proceedings, if any, could have been contemplated; but the presence of a deputy attorney general on the scene, inquiring into the facts and talking with the various parties involved, was reported to have had a salutary influence (see chap. xii).

---

[95] Corwin W. Johnson, "Constitutional Law and Community Planning," *Law and Contemporary Problems,* Vol. 20, no. 2.

XVI

Federal Housing Programs: A General View

Over the past quarter century, the federal government has come to exercise a major influence on housing. Although it has been a cardinal policy not to replace but to support private enterprise, nevertheless, the amount of housing produced, the types and locations of new dwelling units, the terms of their sale or rental, and the volume of consumer demand for housing depend in large measure upon decisions taken by the federal government.[1] Unavoidably, the status of minority groups and the problem of racial discrimination in housing are involved at many points in these decisions.

The scope and goals of federal housing policy have vastly widened since the 1930's when the federal government first entered the housing field on a large scale. Housing programs of the New Deal were conceived primarily as measures to alleviate the depression. Stimulation of employment was the first of two objectives described by President Franklin D. Roosevelt in proposing to Congress a system of federal home-mortgage insurance in

---

[1] The far-reaching consequences of federal policy for the housing industry, the mortgage-money market, communities, and the housing consumer have been the subject of several studies. See Leo Grebler, David M. Blank, and Louis Winnick, *Capital Formation in Residential Real Estate*, chaps. x, xvi, *et passim;* Grebler, *The Role of Federal Credit Aids in Residential Construction;* Paul F. Wendt, *The Role of the Federal Government in Housing;* Miles Colean, *The Impact of Government on Real Estate Finance in the United States.*

1934.[2] Also in the Housing Act of 1937, establishing a program of low-rent public housing, the first stated objective was "to alleviate present and recurring unemployment." [3] During wartime, federal control of housing rents and production was, of course, oriented to the needs of the war economy. Early postwar measures aimed at remedying the housing shortage and assisting certain groups, notably veterans, to acquire homes.[4] In the Housing Act of 1949, Congress enacted a broad program with a sweeping declaration of objectives. The goal of national housing policy, states the Preamble to the 1949 Act, is "a decent home and a suitable living environment for every American family." [5] Again, in the Housing Act of 1954, Congress stated its policy "to seek the constant improvement of the living conditions of all the people under a strong, free, competitive economy, and . . . the operation of that economy to provide adequate housing for all the people." [6]

Notable in these policy statements is the repeated emphasis on good housing for everybody and the absence of ulterior purposes. Adequate housing for the entire population has become an objective of national policy, justified on its own merits and not as a means to some other purpose.

To accomplish this objective, the federal government has developed three basic programs including housing-credit aids, subsidized low-rent public housing, and loans and grants to local communities for slum clearance and renewal of blighted areas. The credit aids are designed to encourage private investment in housing on terms calculated to stimulate consumer demand. Mortgage insurance and mortgage guarantees, administered by the Federal Housing Administration and the Veterans Administration, have been the major programs in this field. In addition, the Veterans Administration and the Federal National Mortgage Association have provided, on a limited scale, direct government loans to certain groups of home buyers.

---

[2] U. S., *Congressional Record,* 73d Cong., 1934, p. 8739.
[3] Public Law 412, 75th Cong., 1937.
[4] Public Law 346, 78th Cong., Public Laws 87, 269, 292, 336, 341, 388, 79th Cong.
[5] Public Law 171, 81st Cong.
[6] Public Law 560, 83d Cong.

The nonwhite population has been slow to achieve equal participation in the mortgage-insurance and -guarantee systems, but its relative access to these benefits has largely improved in recent years. Federal policy toward minority participation has evolved from official advocacy of segregation, through neutrality," to endorsement of equal opportunity in principle, but stopping short of *requiring* equal access to federal housing benefits. Federal agencies have sought to ameliorate the disadvantaged status of minorities by various special aids, such as the appointment of Racial Relations Officers to give special attention to the needs of minority groups, the purchase of mortgages on minority housing developments by the Federal National Mortgage Association, and assistance in mortgage placement through the Voluntary Home Mortgage Credit Program. In public housing, federal policy has focused on attempting to assure the minority groups an equitable share of the units built in the various communities, but leaving to local communities the manner of providing the share, whether in segregated projects or by access to the general supply of public housing.

The evolution of federal policy toward housing and race has been marked by growing recognition that provision of housing specifically for minority groups is not equivalent to nor a substitute for equal access to housing resources. Formerly, to the extent that problems of housing for minority groups were considered at all, they were usually perceived in terms of a need to build or otherwise provide housing for occupancy by minority families. Public housing's concern with equitable shares, the wartime programming of housing production separately for white and nonwhite workers, and special assistance measures all reflect the older point of view. In recent years the problem has been redefined as one of reducing barriers to the equal participation of all citizens in government housing benefits. Official statements now are studded with references to "racial exclusion," a "free market," "free choice," and the like, and "housing *for* . . . " has been superseded by "housing available to. . . ."

The responsibility of government for assuring equal opportunity in housing was asserted by President Eisenhower in a 1954 message to Congress:

It must be frankly and honestly acknowledged that many members of minority groups, regardless of their income or economic status, have had the least opportunity of all of our citizens to acquire good homes. . . . The administrative policies governing the operation of the several housing agencies must be, and they will be, materially strengthened and augmented in order to assure equal opportunity for all of our citizens to acquire, within their means, good and well-located homes. We shall take steps to insure that families of minority groups displaced by urban redevelopment operations have an opportunity to acquire adequate housing; we shall prevent the dislocation of such families through the misuse of slum clearance programs; and we shall encourage adequate market financing and the construction of new housing for such families on good, well-located sites.[7]

The Administrator of the Housing and Home Finance Agency in the same year declared that

. . . we need . . . more homes in good, sound neighborhoods that minority families . . . are free to rent or buy without opposition. . . . The only answer . . . that really counts in solving the minority housing problem is . . . to ensure greater availability of more and better homes for minority families to live in.[8]

Similar pronouncements by federal officials have been numerous. The federal housing agencies, nevertheless, have moved slowly and with caution toward implementing a policy of equal access to housing benefits. The agencies' reluctance to act decisively toward a problem of acknowledged gravity has to be understood in terms of the various forces that impinge on the federal agencies around this issue, some pushing toward equality, others toward discrimination.

A fundamental factor is the manner in which the federal housing programs operate, coupled with the ruling philosophy of the federal authorities concerning their proper relations with private business and local communities. With few exceptions, the federal government does not confer its housing benefits directly on the ultimate recipients, but operates instead in a helping role to private business and, in public housing and urban renewal, to local public authorities. It is basic policy, repeatedly

---

[7] U. S., President (Eisenhower), Message to Congress, January 25, 1954, *Congressional Record,* 83d Cong., 2d Sess., 1954, C, Part 13, p. 712.

[8] Albert M. Cole, Address to the National Urban League, Pittsburgh, Pennsylvania, September 8, 1954.

affirmed by Congress, that federal aid to housing should take the form, primarily, of encouragement and assistance to the housing industry with as few restrictions as possible. As stated by the HHFA Administrator:

All of the programs administered by this Agency rely basically upon private and local initiative and place heavy reliance upon local responsibility in meeting housing needs. The role of the Federal Government in the housing programs is to assist, to stimulate, to lead, and sometimes to prod, but never to dictate or coerce, and never to stifle the proper exercise of private and local responsibility.[9]

Under this definition of the federal government's role, the housing agencies have left to the businessmen and local authorities most of the critical decisions concerning the participation of minority groups in federal housing programs. Although the federal agencies have the duty to set standards, they have generally been loath to make requirements at variance with accepted principles of good business or local community customs. To require that the benefits of government housing programs be made available to all citizens on an equal basis would bring the agencies into collision with the practice of racial discrimination in the building and real estate industries. It would also involve upsetting racial customs in many local communities where the claims of minority groups characteristically receive far less consideration than at the national level.

Another deterrent to action by the housing agencies is the absence of direction from higher levels of government with respect to racial matters. The lack of legislative guidance reflects the divided opinion within Congress which for decades prevented it from enacting any legislation on the subject of race, apart from immigration and naturalization laws. It can be argued, of course, that statutory references to housing for "every American family" and for "all the people" imply that governmental housing benefits should be equally available to all persons. It can also be argued, with logic, that Congress, being bound by the Constitution, could not intend otherwise than equal treatment of all citizens under

---

[9] Letter from Albert M. Cole, Administrator, Housing and Home Finance Agency, to Senator Prescott Bush, May 3, 1956, *Congressional Record*, 84th Cong., 2d Sess., 1956, Vol. 102, no. 103, p. 9673.

any legislation. Nevertheless, although Congress has prohibited discrimination in public housing against families with children[10] or against families receiving public assistance,[11] it has been silent on racial discrimination.

The president, from whom directions on major policy issues might also come, has not been silent, but under no administration has there issued any executive order on racial discrimination in housing. Nor has the responsibility of the federal agencies in this area been specified by any judicial decision.

In these circumstances, the housing agencies are not only left to formulate any racial policies on their own initiative and responsibility, but should they act too firmly for equality, they risk reprisals by prosegregation members of Congress. This practical consideration may well restrain government officials more effectively than the debatable existence of legal authority to act. Some insist on segregation as the price of their continued support of housing legislation; some have even threatened to oppose public housing because of judicial decision against segregated projects. During the Senate debate on the Housing Act of 1954, for example, the senior senator from South Carolina, who had been strongly supporting an expanded program of public housing, shifted to opposition after the Supreme Court let stand a lower federal court decision upsetting racial segregation in San Francisco public housing.[12] This episode, obviously, must have been an object lesson to any federal administrator contemplating action against segregation.

On the other hand, the housing agencies confront strong pressures for racial equality in the distribution of government housing benefits. Most important of these are decisions of the Supreme Court outlawing racial segregation in education, transportation, some aspects of housing, and other fields. Although not directly affecting the federal housing agencies, yet as definitions of con-

---

[10] *National Housing Act,* 1951, Title IV, Sec. 903(a).

[11] *Housing Act of 1949,* Title III, Sec. 301(8)(c).

[12] *New York Times,* May 26, 27, 1954. The following headlines in the *New York Times* reveal the sequence of events: May 16: "Maybank [Senator from South Carolina] to Help Push Housing Bill"; May 19: "Senate Unit Aids Housing Program"; May 26: "Maybank Now to Fight All New Public Housing"; May 27: "Anti-Bias Ruling Hits Housing Bill; Southern Senators Change to Opposition Because of Supreme Court Stand."

stitutional principle from the most authoritative source, the Court's decisions set a standard beyond the immediate scope of the rulings. It was scarcely possible, for example, for the Federal Housing Administration to continue endorsing race-restrictive covenants after the Supreme Court determined that neither federal nor state courts could enforce such devices.

Other forces for equality have been the generally favorable disposition of recent national political administrations toward equal rights, the spread of state and local legislation against housing discrimination in the North and West, and the growing strength of voluntary citizens' groups devoted to the cause of equal rights. Some two dozen national organizations are joined in the National Committee Against Discrimination in Housing, which serves as a spearhead of the movement for equal rights in the housing field. This committee keeps a close watch on federal and state activities touching housing and minority groups, makes representations to government agencies, appears before committees of Congress, and publishes information on pertinent events and conditions.[13] National organizations which have pushed for federal action against discrimination in housing include the National Association for the Advancement of Colored People, the National Urban League, the National Association of Intergroup Relations Officials, the Anti-Defamation League of B'nai B'rith, The American Friends Service Committee (Quaker), and others.

---

[13] Organizations forming the National Committee Against Discrimination in Housing are the following: Amalgamated Clothing Workers of America, AFL-CIO; American Civil Liberties Union; American Council on Human Rights; American Ethical Union; American Friends Service Committee; American Jewish Committee; American Jewish Congress; American Newspaper Guild, AFL-CIO; American Veterans Committee; Americans for Democratic Action; Anti-Defamation League of B'nai B'rith; Congregational Christian Churches, Council for Social Action and Race Relations Department, Board of Home Missions; Coöperative League of the USA; Friendship House; International Ladies' Garment Workers' Union, AFL-CIO; Jewish Labor Committee; League for Industrial Democracy; The Methodist Church, Woman's Division of Christian Service; Migration Division, Puerto Rican Department of Labor; National Association for the Advancement of Colored People; National Association of Intergroup Relations Officials; National Council of Negro Women; National Council of Churches of Christ, Race Relations Department; National Urban League; Presbyterian Church, USA, Department of Social Education and Action; United Auto Workers of America, AFL-CIO; United Steelworkers of America, AFL-CIO.

These conflicting powers and pressures seem to have resulted in a kind of ambivalence on the equal rights issue in housing. The federal agencies officially disavow discrimination and on occasion speak out strongly for equality. At the same time, they refrain from imposing restraints on the racial practices of their business and local community partners. In consequence, discrimination continues to be the rule in most of the housing produced with the assistance of government.

XVII

Housing Credit Aid Programs

The Federal Housing Administration

The changing federal outlook toward housing and race is nowhere
more clearly exemplified than in the evolution of Federal Housing
Administration policy. The FHA administers a system of mortgage insurance designed to make credit available to home
purchasers with longer terms, lower down payments, and lower
interest rates than the market otherwise provides, by insuring
lenders against loss. For veterans, the Veterans Administration
administers a similar program of mortgage guarantees. From its
beginning in 1934 to the middle of 1959, FHA insured the
mortgages on nearly 3.7 million new nonfarm dwelling units,
equal to more than one-fifth of all new, private nonfarm residential construction. An additional 2.5 million FHA-insured mortgage
loans were issued on existing dwellings.[1] At the end of 1956,
more than 40 percent of all mortgages in force on owner-occupied,
single-unit, nonfarm properties were either FHA-insured or VA-
guaranteed.[2] In the field of large-scale residential developments
by merchant builders, the vast majority of mortgages are covered
by FHA and VA programs.

[1] Housing and Home Finance Agency, *Housing Statistics*, September, 1958, p. 1
and August, 1959, p. 1; *FHA Monthly Report of Operations*, July, 1959. U. S.
Department of Labor and Department of Commerce, *Construction Volume and
Costs, 1915-1954* (December, 1954), p. 43.

[2] The FHA proportion was 17.2 percent; that of the VA, 23.4 percent. U. S.
Bureau of the Census, *1956 National Housing Inventory*, Vol. II, *Financing of
Owner-Occupied Residential Properties*.

Participation by nonwhites in the FHA program increased substantially during the period 1950 to 1956. The proportion of first mortgages on nonfarm, single-unit, owner-occupied properties insured by FHA remained at approximately 17 percent for white owners, but for nonwhite owners, the FHA proportion rose from 9 percent to more than 12 percent.[3] The increased use of FHA financing by nonwhite home buyers is associated with policy changes by the FHA aimed at eliminating the racial discrimination formerly embedded in its underwriting standards and making insured mortgages more accessible to minority groups.

The smaller participation of nonwhites than of whites in the FHA program is traceable, in part, to the former's lesser ability to meet the down payment and credit requirements for an FHA loan. Another contributing cause of broader significance is the character and location of the properties which nonwhites are able to offer as security for loans. FHA sets minimum property and neighborhood standards for the loans which it will insure. The blighted areas, to which most nonwhites are restricted, generally do not conform to FHA standards, and many of the properties acquired by nonwhites are also unacceptable because of poor quality or age. As shown elsewhere, the nonwhite owner-occupied properties with FHA loans in 1950 averaged much higher in value than conventionally mortgaged properties (chap. xiii).

The Housing Act of 1954 authorized FHA to set aside its usual location standards and insure mortgages in blighted areas for which an approved urban-renewal plan is in effect (Section 220). Terms of insured mortgages under this section are more liberal than under other FHA programs. Section 220 has large potential significance for minority groups, but it has been slow in moving into operation. No significant amount of mortgage insurance was written under the program until the latter part of 1957. Up to 1959, mortgages had been insured on only 1,200 owner-occupied homes and 15,000 units of rental housing.[4]

The larger problem back of the unacceptability of much non-

---

[3] See chap. xiii. Data from U. S. Bureau of the Census, *1956 National Housing Inventory*, Vol. II.

[4] Housing and Home Finance Agency, *Housing Statistics, Historical Supplement*, December, 1958, pp. 177-190; *FHA Monthly Report of Operations*, July, 1959.

white property for FHA loan purposes relates to restrictions on the ability of minority persons to purchase property in locations which would meet FHA standards. The FHA started its career by accepting the prevalent real estate doctrine that nonwhites should be kept out of white neighborhoods in order to protect property values. FHA appraisers were instructed that "if a neighborhood is to retain stability, it is necessary that properties shall continue to be occupied by the same social and racial classes." Appraisers were to predict "the probability of the location being invaded by . . . incompatible racial and social groups." [5] The "surest protection" against such an eventuality was said to be restrictive covenants including "prohibition of the occupancy of properties except for the race for which they are intended." [6] Such restrictions were recommended for "all land in the immediate environment of the subject location," particularly in undeveloped or partly developed areas.

FHA did not invent the race-restrictive covenant nor the ideology behind it, but in adopting both, it gave them official sanction and stimulus which they had not had before. It is the judgment of observers that FHA's influence contributed largely to the spread of racial restrictions, particularly in newly developed areas, with consequent narrowing of the residence area potentially open to minority groups. [7]

When FHA became sensitive to criticism of the racial discrimination implied in its valuation procedures, it omitted references to race from its *Underwriting Manual,* substituting terms such as "user groups" and "incompatible groups." Race-restrictive covenants ceased to be recommended to developers. This was in 1947. Statements on the relation of user group changes to property values were couched in more cautious and qualified language than before. Valuators were advised to study the significance of "a mixture of user groups" or a change in occupancy of the neighborhood from one user group to another, but the revised

---

[5] Federal Housing Administration, *Underwriting Manual,* 1938, Sec. 937.

[6] *Ibid.,* 1939, Sec. 980.

[7] Writers sharing this judgment include Gunnar Myrdal, *An American Dilemma,* p. 349; Oscar Stern, "The End of the Restrictive Covenant"; Richard Sterner, *The Negro's Share,* p. 316; Norman Williams, "Planning Law and Democratic Living."

Manual added that "additional risk is not necessarily involved in such change."[8]

Other changes followed. After the Supreme Court had ruled race-restrictive covenants judicially unenforceable,[9] a 1949 revision of the FHA *Manual* declared that the rating of a property "takes no cognizance of the effect of the subject property upon the neighborhood."[10] A supplementary letter elaborated:

. . . No application for mortgage insurance shall be rejected solely on the grounds that the subject property or the type of occupancy might affect the market attitude toward other properties in the immediate neighborhood. . . . Mortgage insurance shall not be precluded because of a different type of occupancy . . . nor . . . on the ground that the introduction of a different occupancy type may affect the values of other properties in the area.[11]

Evidently this meant that a minority homeowner should not be denied mortgage insurance because he had moved into an all-white neighborhood.

In December, 1949, references to race again appeared in the *Manual,* but now with an equalitarian character. A new section (No. 242) announced the attachment of FHA to the principle of equal opportunity:

Underwriting considerations shall recognize the right to equality of opportunity to receive the benefits of the mortgage insurance system in obtaining adequate housing accommodations irrespective of race, color, creed or national origin. Underwriting considerations and conclusions are never based on discriminatory attitudes or prejudice. Determinations which adversely affect the eligibility for mortgage insurance, the degree of mortgage risk, or the valuation of the property to be insured shall be supported by observable conditions, precedent or experience directly applicable to the subject case.

Another section of the new *Manual* seemed to discard the racial theories of previous appraisal procedure:

Requirements and standards applying to real estate pertain to characteristics of the property . . . and are technical in character.

---

[8] Federal Housing Administration, *Underwriting Manual,* 1947, Sec. 1320(2).

[9] *Shelley* v. *Kraemer,* 334 U. S. 1 (1948).

[10] Federal Housing Administration, *Underwriting Manual,* Rev. February, 1949, secs. 1116(4) and 1306(2).

[11] Letter from the FHA Commissioner to Directors and Chief Underwriters of all Field Offices, February 18, 1949.

They do not pertain to the user groups, because homogeneity or heterogeneity of neighborhoods as to race, creed, color or nationality is not a consideration in establishing eligibility.[12]

A section on the nature of mortgage risk directed appraisers to take account of "local real estate market reactions and the attitudes of borrowers," but it added ". . . risk is never attributed solely to the fact that there is a mixture of user groups due to differences in race, color, creed, or nationality." These revisions, all adopted in 1949, have remained unchanged in subsequent editions of the *Underwriting Manual.*

The FHA had ceased to advocate or require race-restrictive housing covenants before the Supreme Court declared them unenforceable, but it did not oppose their voluntary adoption by private builders using mortgage insurance. The agency took the position that it was not "authorized" to withhold its benefits from persons who had executed but did not seek judicial enforcement of racial covenants.[13] This was *after* the Supreme Court decision on covenants, the basis of which was that no agency of government could lend its authority to the support of racially discriminatory agreements. Not until nearly two years after the decision did the FHA move to align itself formally with the Court's ruling. In December, 1949, together with the changes in property valuation standards, the agency ordered that for properties submitted for mortgage insurance, no restrictions upon sale or occupancy by reason of race, color, or creed should be recorded after a certain date.[14] With this regulation, a procedure once virtually mandatory was now prohibited.

Since the disapproved restrictions were not judicially enforceable in any case, FHA's action was of small practical consequence. By some, however, it was interpreted as a major change in policy.

---

[12] Federal Housing Administration, *Underwriting Manual,* Rev. December, 1949, Secs. 203(2) and 303. Italics supplied.

[13] Letter from FHA Commissioner Franklin Richards to Thurgood Marshall, National Association for the Advancement of Colored People, replying to the latter's protest against FHA's insurance of mortgages for the Levittown housing development on Long Island, New York, where purchasers were asked to sign race-restrictive agreements. Quoted in NAACP "Memorandum to the President of the United States Concerning Racial Discrimination by the Federal Housing Administration," February 1, 1949.

[14] Federal Housing Administration, Form No. 2004c.

The solicitor general announced that FHA would "refuse to aid the financing of any properties the occupancy or use of which is restricted on the basis of race or creed or color." [15] A *New York Times* columnist wrote, "The origin of the new rules makes it obvious that complaints lodged and sustained that applicants for FHA loans have a policy of discrimination as to tenants and possible purchasers will exclude such applicants from these loans, . . ." [16] But these interpretations were plainly wrong. FHA's action did not affect discriminatory practices as such but only the use of a certain type of instrument no longer of any legal standing. The *Architectural Forum* observed that ". . . When everyone had read the fine print, however, the breathing was easier. . . . [FHA] would not attempt to control any owner in determining what tenants he shall have or to whom he shall sell his property." [17]

The evolution of FHA policy toward race and housing appears also in its attitude toward open-occupancy or racially mixed housing developments. During the period of its attachment to segregation, the agency looked with extreme reserve upon proposals for housing projects open to both whites and nonwhites. Two instances of substantial housing coöperatives which failed because of FHA objections to their interracial membership are described elsewhere.[18] From the standpoint of FHA policy before 1950, these coöperatives had at least two grave shortcomings: they proposed to introduce nonwhites into areas where nonwhites were not then living, and the memberships represented a mixing of the "inharmonious groups" warned against in the *Underwriting Manual*. Their unsuccessful struggles to obtain mortgage insurance occurred during a particular stage in the evolution of FHA policy, when the agency had removed explicit references to race from its written procedures, but had not yet moved to change the substance of its older policy. In a communication to one of the coöperatives, the FHA stated its position as follows:

[15] Solicitor-General Philip B. Perlman, Address to conference of the New York State Committee on Discrimination in Housing, December 2, 1949.

[16] Arthur Krock in the *New York Times*, December 6, 1949.

[17] "FHA Bans Discrimination," *Architectural Forum*, January, 1950, pp. 9-10.

[18] See chap. xii and Eunice and George Grier, *Privately Developed Interracial Housing: An Analysis of Experience*, chap. viii.

This administration does not use the mortgage insurance system either to promote or to discourage any proposal on the ground that it involves interracial characteristics. Such aspects . . . are given the same consideration as all other characteristics, such as transportation, taxes, community facilities, livability and design of structure. If the study on any of these points indicates probable adverse effect upon continued market acceptance to a degree significantly increasing the risk, we are not warranted in accepting the risk, regardless of the nature of the cause producing the effect.[19]

This was in July, 1947, two years and a half before FHA decided that "requirements and standards applying to real estate . . . do not pertain to the user groups," and the racial composition of a neighborhood "is not a consideration in establishing eligibility." [20]

For some time after the 1949 changes in underwriting policy, FHA's official attitude toward interracial housing was described as neutral; it was willing to insure mortgages on such developments, but it took no steps to stimulate them.[21] In 1952, however, in connection with the programming of housing for nonwhite defense workers during the Korean War, the FHA directed its field offices to give "some preference" to proposals for open-occupancy developments as against all-minority projects.[22] Two years later the FHA commissioner announced the intention of taking "active steps to encourage the development of demonstration open-occupancy projects in suitable key areas." [23]

In the seven years, 1947 to 1954, FHA policy toward minority groups moved from requiring segregation to expressing encouragement of open occupancy. The agency's efforts to encourage a "free housing market" have taken several forms. Officials have

---

[19] Letter from Raymond M. Foley, FHA Commissioner, to Community Homes, Inc., July 3, 1947, quoted in NAACP, "Memorandum to the President of the United States . . . ," February 1, 1949.

[20] Federal Housing Administration, Underwriting Manual, Rev. December, 1949, sec. 303.

[21] Donald M. Alstrup, Assistant to the Commissioner, Federal Housing Administration, Statement at the Second Annual Conference of the National Committee Against Discrimination in Housing, New York, June 6, 1951. This was similar to the agency's earlier "neutral" policy toward race-restrictive covenants.

[22] Federal Housing Administration, Assistant Commissioner's Letter to Directors of All Field Offices, Programmed Housing No. 7. December 10, 1952, and Commissioner's Clearance No. 2732, DHP-17, August 14, 1952.

[23] Federal Housing Administration, "Message from FHA Commissioner to be read by Insuring Office Directors at NAHB local meetings Relating to Providing Homes Available to Minorities," July 16, 1954.

delivered addresses before housing industry groups and other audiences to publicize the problem and FHA's official attitude.[24] An open-occupancy policy on repossessed housing has been announced. The agency's Race Relations Officers (now Intergroup Relations Officers), first appointed in 1947, have been permitted to explore ways of stimulating provision of housing available to minorities and to assist particular projects. Housing market surveys with emphasis on minority needs and demand have been conducted in major metropolitan areas. Within the agency, steps have been taken to orient the staff to new concepts and policies.

However, it remains the basic policy of FHA that private builders and lenders should be left free to make their own decisions about who shall be permitted to buy or rent the houses built with federal mortgage assistance. Given this dominant policy, there is obviously not a great deal that the agency can do to overcome discrimination in the distribution of its benefits. Neither the FHA nor other housing agencies of the federal government have been prepared to require nondiscrimination on the part of builders and others using the facilities of federal programs.[25] FHA has taken one limited step in this direction. It announced in 1957 that builders operating in New York were expected to conduct their operations in conformity with state laws which prohibit racial discrimination in publicly assisted housing. "Failure to do so could impair their ability to qualify for future FHA mortgage insurance pending satisfactory correction of the non-compliance." [26] Although an agency of the federal government cannot be responsible for enforcing a state law, the FHA commissioner said, "Such an agency as the FHA

[24] Charles E. Sigety, Deputy Commissioner, FHA, "The Negro Family in the Housing Market," *Real Estate News* (Greater New York Taxpayers Association), March, 1957.

[25] It may be noted that in the earlier period when FHA was advocating segregation, it did not leave the decisions concerning minority participation up to the businessmen. Racial restrictions were virtually mandatory on those who desired FHA financing. Builders who did not discriminate were unable to obtain FHA approval of their plans. It is, of course, much more difficult to require nondiscrimination, since that would involve conflict with established practice of the housing industry as well as with prosegregation members of Congress.

[26] Housing and Home Finance Agency, Office of the Administrator, Press Release No. 1192, February 9, 1957. See also Charles Grutzner, "U. S. Backs State on Housing Bias," *New York Times*, February 15, 1957.

has an obligation to see that its facilities are available to those builders who do business ethically, which naturally means conducting their operations in conformity with valid state and local laws." He added that FHA's "primary emphasis" in connection with this policy was "toward the objective of assuring to all Americans the right of free choice in seeking to satisfy their housing needs." [27]

Government-guaranteed Loans to Veterans

Government-guaranteed mortgage loans are available to veterans under terms generally more liberal than those of FHA loans, including, at one time, the privilege of buying homes with no down payment. In volume of individual home loans guaranteed, the Veterans Administration program has exceeded that of FHA. In 1956, almost a fourth of all existing first mortgages on nonfarm, owner-occupied, single dwelling units in the United States were VA-guaranteed.[28] Like FHA, the VA makes advance commitments on development housing, thus making possible large-scale building operations.

Because of its more liberal underwriting policies, the VA program reaches further down in the income hierarchy than the FHA, and for this reason it has been of more direct help to members of minority groups. Nearly 18 percent of all first mortgages on nonwhite, owner-occupied, nonfarm properties in 1956 were guaranteed by VA as compared with 12 percent insured by FHA.[29] The differential, however, between the proportions of white and nonwhite homeowners, respectively, who have benefited from the program is about the same for VA as for FHA.

VA does not differ from current FHA policy in its formal position of equal treatment of all veterans without distinction by race, color, or creed. Also, like FHA, it does not place any requirement of nondiscrimination upon builders, other than the purely formal one of refraining from use of race-restrictive covenants in property deeds. But whereas FHA has always been concerned with the racial occupancy pattern, at first favoring

---

[27] Housing and Home Finance Agency, Press Release No. 1192.
[28] U. S. Bureau of the Census, *1956 National Housing Inventory*, Vol. II.
[29] *Ibid.*

segregation, then by degrees shifting to support of open occupancy, the VA has never taken a position on this question.
Several racially mixed housing projects have enjoyed VA financing
without objection from the agency. At the same time, there is no
record of any VA encouragement of open-occupancy developments. VA employs no advisors on race relations, issues no policies
or orders with respect to race, and its officials make no speeches on
the subject. The agency's official position seems to be that it will
approve any veteran's application which meets its technical
standards, but it does not concern itself with the actual extent
or character of minority-group participation in the program.

The official VA attitude toward questions involving minority
groups is well exemplified in the following testimony by the chief
of the Loan Guarantee Program before a committee of Congress:

Mr. Edmondson: I also wonder if you feel that we have an adequate
home-loan program for our minority groups in the country. Do you
feel that your minority groups are getting housing under this farm-
loan program?

Mr. Sweeney [VA]: Mr. Chairman, we keep no records of whether
we are making a loan to any nationality or any color.

Mr. Edmondson: I am aware of that. [But] are you receiving no
complaints . . . ?

Mr. Sweeney: Well, Mr. Chairman, we have some indication that
there is not available housing for minority groups. That would include
Negroes, Mexicans, and Puerto Ricans.

Now, as to the extent that the demand is being satisfied, I would not
know. I would only know that there are certain representatives of the
minority groups that are indicating that the housing is not sufficient. . . .

. . . The voluntary home-mortgage credit committee has a plan
to take care of the minority groups. . . . Just how far they have
advanced in that, I do not know. . . .

Mr. Ayres: Do you think it would be feasible to expand the direct-
loan program to minority groups . . . ?

Mr. Sweeney: Mr. Ayres, I think that is a matter for determination
by the Congress. . . . In our direct-loan program, we do not allocate
any money for minority groups per se.[30]

---

[30] U. S., Congress, House, Subcommittee on Housing of the Committee on
Veterans' affairs, *Hearings, Operations of Loan Guaranty Program and Placing
Farm Home Loans on Parity with City Loans,* 84th Cong., 1st Sess., 1955, pp.
323-324.

Federal National Mortgage Association

Designed to strengthen the secondary market for FHA and VA mortgages, the Federal National Mortgage Association in the postwar period has mainly served to support the VA home-loan program by providing a source of mortgage funds at VA's fixed interest rate of 4 percent.[31] It has purchased loans which private investors were unwilling to acquire. At times, under congressional authorization, "Fannie May" has engaged in essentially direct lending by giving advance commitments to purchase mortgages, enabling lenders to originate loans for immediate sale to FNMA. Its purchases are restricted by law to loans of not more than $15,000 original principal amount, thus serving further to channel government aid to the lower housing price classes.

Although statistics are few, it is evident that Fannie May has been an important source of mortgage money for housing available to minority groups. A substantial part of VA and FHA mortgages on properties occupied by nonwhites has been purchased by the FNMA. For the year 1955, the FNMA reported that 13 percent of the mortgages purchased under its secondary market operations were on housing for minority groups.[32]

Some of FNMA's advance commitments have been specifically for minority housing. In 1953, for example, when the agency was authorized to issue commitments up to $30 million on coöperative housing eligible for FHA insurance, more than half of the resulting dwelling units were in coöperatives intended for minority-group occupancy. The actual number of dwelling units involved was less than 1,600 because of the limited funds available. Fewer than half of the applications received could be accepted; many of those rejected for lack of funds were also for minority-group housing.[33]

Special assistance functions.—In addition to secondary-market operations, the FNMA also provides mortgage funds under several

---

[31] Leo Grebler, *The Role of Federal Credit Aids in Residential Construction*, pp. 45-48; Paul F. Wendt, *The Role of the Federal Government in Housing*, p. 15.
[32] Housing and Home Finance Agency, *9th Annual Report, 1955*, p. 355.
[33] Housing and Home Finance Agency, *7th Annual Report, 1953*, p. 37.

categories of "special assistance." [34] This involves the use of government funds for the purchase of certain types and classes of home mortgages under special housing programs for "segments of the national population which are unable to obtain adequate housing under established home-financing programs." [35] This amounts to direct government lending. Categories for which special assistance has been authorized by Congress or the president include housing for victims of major disasters, housing in Guam and Alaska, urban renewal housing, defense and military housing, coöperative housing, and housing for the elderly.

Considerable controversy has revolved around this part of Fannie May's activity. One of the issues has been the desirability of recognizing housing available to minority groups as a category for special assistance. This program obviously contains the machinery whereby the federal government could readily channel mortgage funds into the production of housing open to minorities. Proposals to do so, however, raise the question of whether the solution of the housing needs of minorities should be sought via special assistance or through integration in other programs.

Bills to authorize a special assistance program through the FNMA for members of minority groups were introduced in Congress during 1957. [36] The measures were strongly supported by various organizations and individuals but, significantly, *not* by the recognized spokesmen for the minority groups. [37] Two state-

[34] A third class of FNMA activities, titled "Management and Liquidating Functions," relates to its mortgage portfolio and purchase contracts antedating the *Housing Act of 1954,* which gave FNMA a new charter. Housing and Home Finance Agency, *9th Annual Report, 1955,* p. 357.

[35] Public Law 560, Title III, Sec. 301(b), 83d Cong., 2d Sess., 1954.

[36] S. 1633 and H. R. 1060, U. S., 85th Cong., 1st Sess., 1957. The proposals for special aid to minority groups were part of a larger movement to expand the FNMA special-assistance programs for the benefit of moderate-income families, elderly persons, large families, and minorities, in addition to the previous special-assistance categories. The HHFA Administrator advised the Senate that the proposed legislation "would make eligible for special FHA terms and for FNMA special assistance a tremendous segment of the population now served through regular channels." U. S., Congress, Senate, Subcommittee on Housing of the Committee on Banking and Currency, *Hearings, Housing Act of 1957,* 85th Cong., 1st Sess., 1957, p. 63. Of the new groups proposed for special assistance, only the elderly survived in the law as finally enacted. *Housing Act of 1957,* Public Law 85-104, 85th Cong., 1st Sess., Sec. 205.

[37] Among the organizations and individuals advocating use of special-assistance funds for minority housing or housing "available" to minorities were the A.F.

ments will serve to typify the thesis of the advocates. The mayor of Philadelphia, representing the American Municipal Association declared:

Finally the minority groups. We believe that the present programs, while they sound fine while somebody is listening to them, have been completely ineffective. We do believe that the only way we are going to be able to take care of the minority groups . . . is by direct loans from the Government. We just do not think that any of these other things work.[38]

Congressman Charles E. Bennett of Florida rejected the suggestion that the needs of minorities could be met under a general provision for low-income groups:

I regret to say I think nothing but a head-on meeting of this problem will be very much of a solution, because just wishfully saying it is going to be a small-income situation is not an answer. . . . There is no assurance that any of these small-house loans will go to Negroes. The main problem is the fact that mortgage money just doesn't run to colored people.[39]

Members of the Senate and House committees vainly inquired of witnesses concerning the attitude of the NAACP and the National Urban League toward the special-assistance proposals. Neither organization appeared at the hearings nor communicated any views on the subject to Congress. From the silence of these leading spokesmen for Negroes on this important issue, it seems a logical inference that they did not wish to confuse their campaign for integration by asking special assistance for members of their group. They probably realized, too, that the bulk of any special-assistance funds for minorities would undoubtedly go for the building of minority housing projects, which they had previously condemned.

---

of L. and C.I.O., the National Housing Conference, the National Committee Against Discrimination in Housing, the American Municipal Association, and Americans for Democratic Action. Not all of the support came from liberal or antidiscrimination groups. The Senate and House bills to provide special FNMA assistance to members of minority groups were introduced respectively by Senator John J. Sparkman of Alabama and Congressman Charles E. Bennett of Florida. Senate, *Hearings, Housing Act of 1957;* U. S., Congress, House, Subcommittee on Housing of the Committee on Banking and Currency, *Hearings, Housing Act of 1957,* 85th Cong., 1st Sess., March 4-5, 1957.

[38] Senate, *Hearings, Housing Act of 1957,* p. 595.
[39] House, *Hearings, Housing Act of 1957,* p. 536.

The Housing and Home Finance Agency opposed the special-assistance proposals on the ground, among others, that the housing needs of minority families could be better met through general programs and other special-assistance functions, than by placing minority families in a special category.[40]

Voluntary Home Mortgage Credit Program

Another phase of the credit-aid system is the Voluntary Home Mortgage Credit Program (VHMCP), authorized in the Housing Act of 1954, at the instance of the life insurance companies, as an alternative to direct government lending. Its purpose is to obtain FHA or VA loans from private lenders for two categories of disadvantaged borrowers: those residing in small towns and remote areas where mortgage funds are scarce, and members of minority groups regardless of location. Only the former was specified in the legislation.[41] As indicated by its title, the program contemplates voluntary action by lenders. It operates through national and regional committees composed of builders, lenders, and brokers. Government participation is limited to advice and provision of facilities and staff. When a loan applicant can produce evidence of having been refused credit by at least two mortgage lenders, and if he seems qualified for a mortgage loan, his application is referred to a lending institution participating in the program. The lender acts on the application according to its usual credit standards.

During 1956, the VHMCP placed nearly 13,000 loans, but thereafter its loan volume declined sharply. Only about 6,000 loans were placed during 1958 and 3,300 during the first half of 1959.[42] Among the first 27,000 loans placed (through February, 1957), somewhat fewer than 5,000, or 18 percent, were made to minority home buyers, representing more than half of the applications.[43] By both proponents and critics, this performance is considered small in relation to assumed need. Applications from

[40] Senate, *Hearings, Housing Act of 1957*, pp. 62-64; House, *Hearings, Housing Act of 1957*, pp. 759-760.
[41] Public Law 560, Title VI, 83d Cong., 2d Sess., 1954. See also Housing and Home Finance Agency, *9th Annual Report, 1955*, pp. 35-37.
[42] Housing and Home Finance Agency, *Housing Statistics*, August, 1959, p. 75.
[43] Senate, *Hearings, Housing Act of 1957*, p. 96.

the minority groups have fallen below expectations of sponsors of the program. Before a committee of Congress in 1957, the executive secretary of the VHMCP testified that the volume of applications from minority borrowers "has been frankly surprising to us. We thought that it would be higher." After noting what had been done to make the minority groups aware of the program, the secretary concluded, "I can only imagine that either there is not sufficient demand or they are satisfying it some other way. . . . There apparently is not a large number of cases that actually are in need of mortgage financing, because if there were . . . we would get a higher proportion of them, a greater number." [44]

In another communication to the same committee, the HHFA seemed to attribute the small performance of VHMCP to the scarcity of investment funds: "The VHMCP could undoubtedly provide for more insured and guaranteed loans for minority group members from private fund sources if general market conditions were such as to induce a greater flow of investment funds into insured and guaranteed loans." [45]

The life insurance companies which sponsored the program blamed its shortcomings on VA's "frozen interest rate" and "competition from government lending programs [VA and FNMA] on unfair terms." If these difficulties were removed, "VHMCP . . . can solve completely the problem of making Government-insured and guaranteed mortgage credit generally available in remote areas, small communities, and for minority groups." [46]

The small response from the minority groups to the VHMCP, in terms of applications, is difficult to explain with confidence, but it is consistent with other evidence that lack of credit per se is ceasing to be a critical limiting factor on minority housing opportunities. Elsewhere it has been shown that mortgage loans on existing houses seem to be generally available to nonwhites who can meet customary credit standards and whose properties are situated in areas that are not blighted, and are considered open to minority groups. Demand for VHMCP assistance, therefore,

[44] House, *Hearings, Housing Act of 1957*, p. 778.
[45] *Ibid.*, p. 760. Letter from Albert M. Cole, Administrator, HHFA.
[46] Senate, *Hearings, Housing Act of 1957*, p. 405. Statement of the American Life Convention and the Life Insurance Association of America.

would be expected to come mainly from nonwhites desiring to purchase homes in white neighborhoods and from builders of minority housing projects. In the first category there are few houses which minority individuals can buy, with or without mortgages. Although builders frequently assert lack of financing as the chief barrier to their efforts for minorities, it seems clear that building for minorities is more seriously hampered by other factors, including locational restrictions and market uncertainties (chap. xi).

With the scarcity of existing houses available to nonwhites in areas where credit might be difficult, it would be expected that volume demand for VHMCP assistance would come not from individual home purchasers but from builders seeking financing commitments for minority developments. There have been few of these, however. Builders accounted for only 15 percent of all loans placed by the program up to the middle of 1959.[47] Whatever the reasons, it is plain that the mortgage assistance provided by VHMCP has not given any significant stimulus to builders to undertake new housing construction for the minority market.[48]

---

[47] Housing and Home Finance Agency, *Housing Statistics,* August, 1959, p. 75.

[48] It is worth noting that the National Association of Home Builders, in the course of extensive testimony and statements before congressional committees in 1957, made no representations concerning either the proposals for special credit assistance to minority groups, or the VHMCP except to say that the latter had become "unrealistic" because of the low discount rate permitted on VA loans. Senate, *Hearings, Housing Act of 1957,* pp. 416-455; House, *Hearings, Housing Act of 1957,* pp. 163-205.

XVIII

Low-Rent Public Housing

The minority groups have shared much more in public housing than in the housing aids distributed through the private market. From the beginning, more than a third of all public housing units were occupied by Negroes; in recent years this proportion has risen to about 44 percent.[1] The Negro share in public housing has thus been much greater than the percentage of Negroes in the population, although probably not greater than their percentage among low-income slum dwellers, whom public housing is designed to serve.

Compared with the credit-aid programs, public housing has been of small magnitude.[2] At the end of June, 1959, the total stock of public housing in the United States amounted to approximately 484,000 units, or less than 3 percent of all nonfarm dwellings constructed in the period 1937-1958.[3] The low-rent program was suspended during the war, but in the Housing Act of 1949 Congress authorized 810,000 units to be built during a six-year

---

[1] Housing and Home Finance Agency, Public Housing Administration, *Trends Toward Open Occupancy, 1956,* and unpublished data for 1957 supplied by Public Housing Administration, Statistics Branch.

[2] Public housing carried a major role in national housing policy only during World War II, when more than 600,000 units were produced, not for low-income groups but for war workers. Housing and Home Finance Agency, *8th Annual Report, 1954,* p. 384, and unpublished data supplied by Public Housing Administration, Statistics Branch.

[3] Housing and Home Finance Agency, *Housing Statistics,* August, 1959, p. 85.

period.[4] In each subsequent year, however, Congress or the president placed a lower limit on the rate of building, but even the reduced authorizations were not wholly taken up, with the result that fewer than 230,000 units were actually built from 1949 to the end of June, 1959.[5]

Public housing has never been a popular program. Nearly a quarter century after its beginning in the Housing Act of 1937, it remains as controversial as ever.[6] Opposition from building and real estate interests has been unflagging; the rising trend of income and large volume of housing production have given room for much argument about the need for publicly subsidized housing; and among those who affirm the need for public aid to rehouse low-income groups, many have voiced dismay over some of the social consequences of public housing in its present form.[7] Particularly, the tendency for public housing projects to become a type of low-income, minority ghetto under public management is unfavorably regarded alike by friends and foes of the program.[8]

Publicly subsidized, low-rent housing serves the twin purposes of helping to eliminate slums and providing shelter of standard quality for families who are unable to afford adequate housing on the private market. The problem of relocating families displaced by urban-renewal operations has led to an emphasis on the first objective, although the extent of need for public housing in urban renewal is debated.[9]

Rents in public housing are required by law to be set at least

---

[4] Public Law 171, 81st Cong., 1st Sess., 1949.

[5] Housing and Home Finance Agency, *Housing Statistics*, August, 1959, p. 84.

[6] Subsidized public housing actually began in the Public Works Administration in 1933, but was placed on a statutory, permanent basis by the *United States Housing Act of 1937*, Public Law 412, 75th Cong., 1st Sess.

[7] Catherine Bauer, "The Dreary Deadlock of Public Housing"; Paul F. Wendt, *The Role of the Federal Government in Housing*, pp. 21-29; Elizabeth Wood, *Public Housing and Mrs. McGee.*

[8] *Chicago Daily Tribune*, Editorial, October 24, 1956; *Pittsburgh Courier*, August 4, 1956; and sources cited in footnote 7 above.

[9] Expansion of public housing has been strongly urged as essential to make urban renewal work, by providing an outlet for displaced low-income families. The former HHFA Administrator, however, opposing a bill in Congress for increased public housing, implied that there were better alternatives. The bill, he said, ". . . ignores the need for an overall approach to the slum problem, and lacks the incentive to communities to do more than build more public housing." *New York Times*, June 30, 1956.

20 percent below rents for "decent, safe, and sanitary" units in the private market. The difference between a local housing authority's revenues and the amount required for meeting its financial obligations is made up by an annual federal contribution.

Tenants are selected according to need with statutory priority for families displaced by slum clearance and families of veterans or deceased veterans. Tenant families must not have more than a certain income; if their incomes rise above the limit, they must leave the housing project.

Public housing is built, owned, and managed by local housing authorities. In theory the federal role is limited to providing financial assistance subject to statutory conditions. In practice, the federal government works closely with local authorities in the planning of projects and exercises extensive supervisory authority.

In relation to minority groups, public housing has several notable achievements. It has distributed its benefits on the whole equitably among racial groups; it has pioneered demonstrations of unsegregated housing; and it has been open to the participation of Negroes as members of local housing authorities and as employees in administrative positions throughout the country.

In none of the legislation on public housing is there any reference to race or minority groups. The legislative situation in this respect is the same as for other parts of the federal housing program. However, in striking contrast to the FHA, which for years seemed to think of minorities only as a threat to real estate investments, the administration of public housing has always operated on the principle that the minority groups were entitled to share in the benefits of the program. As Robert Weaver has said, public housing from its inception had "a positive racial policy" directed to equitable participation of minorities as tenants, in management, and in construction employment.[10]

A Racial Relations Service was early established in the United States Housing Authority (created under the 1937 law) and given responsibility for reviewing local programs and projects from the standpoint of racial equity. The administration did not issue any specific rules or procedures concerning minority participation,

---

[10] Robert C. Weaver, *The Negro Ghetto*, p. 158.

but supported its racial relations officers in working for a maximum degree of equity for minority groups, community by community. The results were somewhat uneven; there were many reported cases of conspicuous inequity, including some communities where Negroes were not accepted in the program at all, but on the whole, nonwhites received about a third of the public housing units before the war.

Explicit regulations and directives on minority participation came during World War II, when low-rent housing had yielded place to war housing. In 1942 the National Housing Agency ordered that "in determining the need for war housing . . . no discrimination shall be made on account of race, creed, color, or national origin." [11] This was not an antisegregation order as subsequent practice made clear. Federal authorities did not require war-housing projects to house war workers of whatever race. Instead, war housing was programmed separately for whites and nonwhites; federal policy directives were aimed at assuring equitable shares. Under this policy, Negroes ultimately received about 15 percent of all public war-housing units.[12] Without attempting to judge whether this share was in fact equitable, it is worth noting that it represented almost six times as many units as were provided for Negro occupancy under the larger program of private (FHA) war housing—84,000 as compared with 15,000 units.[13] In access to the total war-housing supply, Negroes were seriously disadvantaged, as evidenced by the crisis conditions of housing affecting Negroes in many centers of war production.[14]

In planning for postwar resumption of low-rent housing, the administration built upon precedents of wartime and developed standard procedures for estimating the housing needs of racial groups in a community and hence of judging the racial equity of proposed programs. These procedures became known as the

[11] National Housing Agency, Administrator's Order No. 9, August 10, 1942 (revised).

[12] National Housing Agency, Federal Public Housing Authority, Report S-602 (1945).

[13] Ibid.

[14] Weaver, The Negro Ghetto, p. 163. Compare also the racial differentials in housing changes during the 1940-1950 decade as shown in chap. iii of this volume.

"racial equity formula." A formal requirement of "racial equity" was written into the *Low-Rent Housing Manual* in 1951:

Programs for the development of low-rent housing, in order to be eligible for PHA assistance, must reflect equitable provision for eligible families of all races, determined on the approximate volume and urgency of their respective needs for such housing.

While the selection of tenants and the assigning of dwelling units are primarily matters for local determination, urgency of need and the preferences prescribed in the Housing Act of 1949 are the basic statutory standards for the selection of tenants.[15]

Racial Segregation versus Open Occupancy in Public Housing

Although the apportioning of dwelling units by race has undoubtedly been less than equitable in some localities, on a national basis the record of public housing has never been seriously questioned. Equity as between racial populations, however, is not the same as equal opportunity or equal rights of individuals, as the Supreme Court held many years ago in restraining cities from zoning residence areas by race.[16] In public housing, problems of minority participation have increasingly centered more on the issue of segregation than on the fairness of racial group shares. There is irony in the fact that the federal administration of public housing first issued an explicit requirement of "equitable provision" in 1951, when not equity but segregation had become the major racial issue in housing and other fields, and the whole concept of separate-but-equal was under attack.

The federal administrations of public housing have left the question of segregation to the decision of local authorities, and most of those, until recent years, have chosen to segregate their minority tenants in separate projects or parts of projects. The major basis, undoubtedly, for the federal policy, or lack of policy, is the absence of statutory guidance from higher levels of policy making, combined with the practical necessity of deference to the political power of segregationists in Congress and elsewhere. As the least popular and politically most vulnerable of the federal

---

[15] Housing and Home Finance Agency, Public Housing Administration, *Low-Rent Housing Manual*, Sec. 102.1, February, 1951.

[16] *Buchanan* v. *Warley*, 245 U. S. 60 (1917).

housing programs, public housing has particularly needed to hold the support of southern representatives in Congress. "Racial equity" is politically defensible within the separate-but-equal ideology, but many southern congressmen have made plain their opposition to public housing on any but a segregated basis. In commenting on the implications for housing of the Supreme Court decision against segregation in public schools, the economist for the National Association of Home Builders observed:

There is little doubt that the support given public housing by many southern politicians was due to the opportunity that it offered to provide additional housing for Negroes and to clear up some of the most nauseous slum conditions without expanding the area of colored occupancy. Since it will not be possible to use public housing in this way any longer, an important source of support has been removed.[17]

In the prewar period of public housing, a few local authorities, as in Seattle and New York City, adopted policies of integration.[18] In more instances, however, public housing established or strengthened segregation in communities where enforced racial separation had not previously existed. In San Francisco, for example, where, except for the Chinese, racial residence patterns had been traditionally flexible, the local housing authority insisted on strict segregation of Negroes until forced to change by a court order which the authority contested up to the Supreme Court.[19] In San Diego, where Negroes had not been segregated, the wartime Federal Public Housing Authority adopted a segregated pattern for its federally managed projects, there being no local housing authority in the city.[20]

In most cities, although nonwhites are concentrated, there are few areas of any size that are totally occupied by nonwhites. The creation of a housing project tenanted 100 percent by nonwhites,

---

[17] National Association of Home Builders, "Effect of U. S. Supreme Court Decision," *Housing for Minority Groups*, "*Package Program.*"

[18] Housing Authority of the City of Seattle, *Housing the People* (1946); Weaver, *The Negro Ghetto*, pp. 186-188.

[19] *Banks* v. *Housing Authority of San Francisco*, 120 Cal. App. 2d 1 (1953); Cert. denied, 347 U. S. 974 (1954).

[20] Weaver, *The Negro Ghetto*, p. 166, and interviews with Public Housing Administration officials. A federally managed project at Berkeley, California, however, was racially integrated. Seemingly, the federal PHA allowed its own employees, managing federal projects, much the same freedom as local housing authorities to determine the racial pattern.

represents, therefore, an extreme of racial segregation seldom equaled even in Negro neighborhoods. Considering the repetition of this process in scores of projects, Weaver has termed public housing, "an instrument for the spread of segregation." [21] An earlier inquiry, part of the monumental Carnegie-Myrdal study of the Negro in America, concluded that public housing projects had "on the whole, strengthened rather than weakened housing segregation." [22] This judgment was even more accurate in 1957 than when it was made in 1942, notwithstanding the adoption of nonsegregation policies by a considerable number of local housing authorities.

Beginning during the war, a significant shift from segregation to open occupancy has appeared in public housing. Wartime pressures to house workers needed in the war industries led in many areas to some relaxation of the custom of separate projects for whites and nonwhites respectively. More than fifty war-housing projects, including some directly owned and managed by the federal government, were reported in 1945 to be operating without racial restrictions.[23] At the same date, 21 of the existing 363 low-rent projects were reported integrated. The number of racially integrated projects rose to 76 by 1952, and to 385 in March, 1957.[24] At the latter date, 20 percent of all low-rent projects in the country were operated on an open-occupancy basis. Nearly 300 communities, or more than a third of all localities with low-rent public housing programs, had adopted open-occupancy policies, although in some communities the policy had not yet been made effective. Localities with integrated projects were not confined to the North and West but included such border cities as Washington, Baltimore, Wilmington, and St. Louis. One inter-racial project was reported in Texas and one in Louisiana.

One of the important factors stimulating the movement to open occupancy has been the changing pattern of need and

---

[21] *Ibid.*, p. 164.

[22] Richard Sterner, *The Negro's Share*, p. 320.

[23] HHFA, PHA, "Participation by Negroes in Projects Where the Pattern of Occupancy Is Uncontrolled" (as of July 31, 1945). Racial Relations Service, unpublished report.

[24] HHFA, PHA, *Trends Toward Open Occupancy*, no. 5, March, 1956; Letter from Ruth Voris, Director, PHA Statistics Branch, July 2, 1957.

demand for public housing accommodations. In many areas, Negroes have formed a rapidly increasing proportion of the population eligible for and wanting public housing. This has occurred mainly because of the continuing migration of Negroes to northern and western cities, the limited access of nonwhites to the private housing market, and the displacement of population, largely Negro, by slum-clearance programs. With fixed quantities of public housing units reserved for white and nonwhite occupants respectively, even though the allocations may have been fair initially, this shift in need and demand has meant that the individual Negro applicant had less chance of obtaining a unit than his white counterpart. Detroit affords a clear illustration. In May, 1950, approximately 30 percent of all Detroit public housing units were reserved for Negroes, but the latter comprised more than two-thirds of all eligible applicants. During the year 1949, two out of every five eligible white applicants were admitted to public housing projects, but only one in ten eligible Negro families could be admitted.[25] The Detroit situation was by no means exceptional.

Segregation produced its most inequitable and discriminatory results in the frequent instances where vacancies appeared in housing projects reserved for white tenants, while projects for nonwhites had growing waiting lists. This meant that eligible Negro applicants were not merely passed over in preference for whites, but were refused housing while dwellings provided at public expense stood vacant. In these circumstances, the housing authority found itself not only practicing a highly obvious form of racial discrimination, but also violating the statutory mandate to select tenants according to need.[26]

A second important motive force behind the movement to open

[25] *Detroit Housing Commission v. Lewis,* 226 F. 2d 180 (1955); *Race Relations Law Reporter,* 1(1) (February, 1956), 159, Stipulation of Facts; and additional unpublished data compiled by the National Association for the Advancement of Colored People, Housing Division.

[26] For examples of this situation see Weaver, *The Negro Ghetto,* pp. 174-176. The pressure of vacancies has caused even one or two southern housing authorities to abandon segregation. Thus, the executive director of the Housing Authority of Crystal City, Texas, explains: "We had not thought of this [shift to integration] as being anything unusual. We had . . . housing units for rent . . . and there were families who needed and wanted them." HHFA, PHA, *Trends Toward Open Occupancy,* no. 5, 1956, p. 48.

occupancy has been the enactment of state and local laws prohibiting discrimination in publicly assisted housing. Court decisions have been a third force. Unlike the private business concerns through which the housing credit agencies work, the local housing authorities are public agencies and hence subject to the constitutional restraints on state action. The landmark judicial decision in the public housing field came in 1952 when a California state court held the Housing Authority of San Francisco in violation of the equal protection clause of the Fourteenth Amendment for assigning Negroes, Chinese, and whites to separate projects, although housing units were allocated to the three racial groups in proportion to applications from each group. On appeal, the U. S. Supreme Court refused to review the decision.[27] Similar decisions have been handed down in subsequent cases involving the housing authorities of Detroit, St. Louis, Columbus, Toledo, and other cities.[28] Although none of these cases has been reviewed by the Supreme Court, the overruling of the separate-but-equal doctrine in the school desegregation cases[29] seems to have established definitely that agencies of state government (including local housing authorities) may not provide their services on a racially segregated basis.

The Location of Public Housing

Another major issue in public housing, of which the race problem is an inseparable part, is the question of where projects should be located—whether in slum areas or on vacant land, and whether projects should be large or smaller and scattered. Although a principal aim of public housing is to rebuild slums, it is important to locate a substantial part of the new housing on vacant land. Slum districts are typically overcrowded. If their rebuilding is to be guided by sound standards of residential density, some part of the population must be relocated elsewhere. Moreover, there

[27] *Banks* v. *Housing Authority of San Francisco.*

[28] *Detroit Housing Commission* v. *Lewis; Davis* v. *St. Louis Housing Authority,* U. S., D. C., E. D. Mo., No. 8637 (December 27, 1955); *Ward* v. *Columbus Metropolitan Housing Authority,* U. S., D. C., S. D. Ohio (November 4, 1955); *Vann* v. *Toledo Metropolitan Housing Authority,* U. S., D. C., N. D. Ohio, 113 F. Supp. 210 (1953).

[29] *Brown* v. *Board of Education of Topeka,* 347 U. S. 483 (1954) and *Bolling* v. *Sharpe,* 347 U. S. 497 (1954).

must be housing into which the slum dwellers can move while the slums are being cleared and rebuilt; otherwise, the demolition of slum housing works great hardship on the displaced families. Relocation is, of course, especially difficult when those to be rehoused are Negro or Puerto Rican or other minority.

Federal housing legislation permits public housing to be built on either slum or vacant land sites. The Public Housing Administration, in policy statements and directives since 1949, has repeatedly called attention to the relocation problems inherent in use of slum sites, stressed the necessity of providing for displaced families, and urged construction of initial low-rent housing projects on open land.[30]

Many observers have questioned the social desirability of concentrating low-income families in publicly owned and managed projects, and isolating them from the general community. Concentration and isolation become most pronounced in the large project where not only size but architectural distinctiveness and institution-like appearance tend to set the project and its residents apart from surrounding neighborhoods. To minimize these tendencies, it has been often proposed that public housing should be built in relatively small, scattered projects which would blend into their surroundings.

For the minority groups a crucial need is not only for better dwelling units but for more places to live. Public housing on vacant land adds to the living space available to minorities, whereas building in slums tends to stabilize, even intensify existing patterns of segregation. Housing projects built in or adjacent to areas of minority concentration seem virtually certain to attract a preponderance of minority occupants regardless of official policy toward racial occupancy.

The choice of sites thus exerts a large effect on the nature and outcome of the public-housing program in any community, particularly on the racial pattern. Housing authorities, however, are seldom at liberty to choose the most appropriate locations accord-

---

[30] Housing and Home Finance Agency, "Joint Statement on Relationship of Slum Clearance and Low Rent Housing Programs," June 29, 1950; Public Housing Administration, *Low-Rent Housing Manual*, Sec. 213.2 (1951), Sec. 208.8 (1952), Sec. 209.1 (1956). For further discussion of relocation problems in urban renewal, see chap. xix.

ing to technical criteria. Proposals to locate public housing in nonslum areas frequently meet vehement resistance from the neighborhoods affected, motivated by desire to keep out low-income groups and, above all, minorities. In a number of cities, the selection of public-housing sites has been a major political issue.

A case in point is Chicago, where a proposal of the housing authority to build forty thousand units of public housing pursuant to the Housing Act of 1949 precipitated a furious political controversy in the city council, which had to approve the authority's program.[31] There was never much doubt that a majority of the council wanted and would approve a public-housing program. The issue was that of sites, and this was an issue because it contained the question of where Negroes were to live in Chicago. As Meyerson and Banfield defined the situation, ". . . the leaders of the Council wanted some public housing. On the other hand they did not want to do anything which would encourage the spread of Negroes into the outlying white neighborhoods."[32]

The housing authority's proposal called for building two-fifths of the new housing on vacant land. Most of the feasible sites were in outlying areas of Chicago's South Side, where entry of Negroes had been resisted by neighborhood improvement associations for many years. These associations and their allied groups were able to generate much political power around local issues.

The housing authority chose its sites by such technical standards as the respective functions of slum and vacant land sites, avoidance of large-scale economic class segregation, economy, proximity to employment sources, availability of community facilities, and the like. In the ensuing battle in the city council, however, the considerations became purely political. Although it was good politics to favor slum clearance, it was very poor politics for an individual councilman to permit the relocation of slum dwellers in his own district. A sure way to embarrass any councilman with a nonslum constituency was to locate a public-

---

[31] The controversy is reported and analyzed in detail in Martin Meyerson and Edward C. Banfield, *Politics, Planning, and the Public Interest: The Case of Public Housing in Chicago.*

[32] *Ibid.*, p. 253.

housing project in his district. An equally good way to embarrass
the housing authority and its supporters was to give them slum
sites without the sites needed for relocation purposes. Consequently, proposed sites were treated as political hot potatoes and
judged less on their merits for housing purposes than on their
value for punishing opponents and rewarding friends.

Eventually, the city council approved about a third of the
total units proposed by the housing authority. Only one-sixth of
the approved units could be built on vacant land instead of the
two-fifths proposed by the housing authority. The authority estimated that land clearance for the approved projects in slum
areas would displace approximately twelve thousand families,
mostly Negro, whereas relocation housing (vacant sites) was
provided for only two thousand families. The heavy Negro displacement meant that practically all new housing would have
to be occupied by Negroes, regardless of the authority's nonsegregation policy. Population density in the congested slum
areas was left unchanged. The program contained most of the
shortcomings which housing authority planners had hoped to
avoid, but politically it was attractive because "it seemed to
keep the Negroes in the Negro area while making it possible for
the politicians to claim that they had increased the total number
of dwelling units."

The Public Housing Administration delayed its approval of the
Chicago program for more than a year, but in the end, overruled
its race relations advisors and accepted the program as the best
that could be obtained in Chicago, and better than none at all.
A few years later the same drama was repeated. The housing
authority sought approval of eleven additional sites, and the city
council rejected six of them. All but one of the rejects were
located in outlying predominantly white areas of Chicago.[33]

A similar conflict between local neighborhood interests and
city-wide housing policy developed in Philadelphia in 1956. The
housing authority of this city, in a deliberate attempt to overcome
the evils of large-scale public housing in the slums, proposed
twenty-one small projects, mostly of less than a hundred units

---

[33] *House and Home,* March, 1957.

each, on vacant plots scattered throughout the city.[34] Architecturally, the buildings were planned to be similar to the two- and three-story row houses prevalent in Philadelphia. Because of their small size, the projects would not significantly alter the composition of the larger surrounding neighborhoods, nor burden their schools, playgrounds, or other facilities.

In race relations, Philadelphia has enjoyed the reputation of a liberal city. Compared with Chicago, it lacks the latter's tradition of racial violence; nonwhites are less tightly segregated; and the city government is more than just formally committed to policies of nondiscrimination and nonsegregation. The housing authority's program had strong leadership and support from the mayor. Nevertheless, from most of the neighborhoods in which the new, small projects were proposed to be located came strenuous opposition. In a series of neighborhood meetings the mayor and housing authority representatives tried to defend the program and relieve the residents' fears, but they found the opposition in no mood to be reasoned with. The character of the meetings is suggested by newspaper headlines such as "Mayor, Audience Shout It Out on S. Phila. Public Housing," and "500 Boo Talks on Northeast Housing Sites." [35] At one meeting, when a speaker began to talk about the need for public housing, the chairman reminded him that "this meeting was to protest the housing, not to debate it." Following are parts of a newspaper account of one meeting:

"We're faced with a difficult choice," he [city official] went on. "Should we say we don't want public housing?"
"Yes," chorused the audience. . . .
"Give them Fairmount Park," suggested someone. "Put them near the Navy Yard—or near your house," someone else called. . . . Someone in the gathering asked Councilman-at-Large John F. Byrne, Rhawnhurst real estate man, to state his position. The residents have "a legitimate gripe," Byrne said, "and public housing will never go through on the Hartel site."

[34] Philadelphia Housing Authority, *Facts Regarding Philadelphia's City Housing Program* (1956).
[35] *Philadelphia Bulletin*, April 20 and 27, 1956. For other reports on the controversy see the *Philadelphia Inquirer*, April 22, 1956, and the *Bulletin* for April 4, 5, 9, 12, 15, 17, 19, 21, and 29.

As chairman of City Council's streets and services committee, Byrne promised that "they'll wait three and a half years until I'm no longer in office before they'll get streets and sewers there." This was acknowledged with wild cheering.[36]

In the end, the Philadelphia City Council approved a public-housing program on fourteen sites instead of twenty-one; all of the sites which had generated controversy were eliminated, and some alternative locations, not in the original program, were substituted.[37]

Status and Prospects of Public Housing

Public housing has been a major source of new, good-quality dwellings available to minority families, and it has provided successful demonstrations of unsegregated housing in many northern and western cities. The magnitude of these contributions has been always limited by the relatively small role of public housing in the total housing picture. Recent developments have further and seriously reduced the importance of public housing, both as a source of dwellings and as a force for residential desegregation.

Annual congressional authorizations for additional public housing have been reduced to less than a fourth of the yearly volume authorized in 1949—but even this modest quota has exceeded the applications from local authorities. New construction of public housing, in recent years, has fluctuated between ten and twenty thousand units.[38] Even the existing stock of public-housing units has not been fully utilized. Notwithstanding the persistence of a great deal of slum housing, extensive vacancies have appeared in the low-rent projects in many communities. Of the eligible families who apply for dwellings in public-housing projects, an increasing proportion are members of minority groups. In several major cities, including Chicago and Los Angeles, more than three-fourths of public-housing dwelling units were occupied by Negroes in 1957. Nationally, the proportion of units Negro-occu-

---

[36] *Ibid.*, April 5, 1956.
[37] *House and Home*, August, 1956.
[38] Housing and Home Finance Agency, *Housing Statistics*, December, 1958, p. 228; August, 1959, pp. 84-85.

pied had reached 44 percent.[39] Obviously, this trend is fast obliterating the effects of nondiscriminatory policy so far as interracial patterns of occupancy are concerned. As the mayor of Philadelphia has said,

> We all accept the idea that public housing should be nondiscrimina-
> tory . . . but arithmetic is against us. There are two Negro families
> eligible by income for public housing for every eligible white family.
> . . . The whole scheme of things makes for more segregation, not
> less. . . . New housing developments outside the city limits are an
> essential part of the problem.[40]

Because of differences in income and quality of housing occupied, the Negro population contains a higher percentage of families eligible for public housing than does the white population. Racial restrictions in the private-housing market also tend to make Negroes more dependent than whites on public housing. These factors alone, however, are scarcely sufficient to explain the growing concentration of Negroes in public housing. Additional important factors are the manner in which the program operates and the limitations placed upon it by Congress and the local communities. To a great extent, public housing no longer serves the general population of low-income and poorly housed families, but is tied to urban-renewal operations. Statutory preference in tenant selection must be given to families displaced by urban renewal, and these families are largely Negro because of the character of urban-renewal areas. A second policy factor previously described is the emphasis in many communities on locating public housing in or adjacent to minority slums. Projects so located have small prospect of attracting many white families. Income limits for continued tenancy are a third factor which tends to push out more whites, relatively, than Negroes. Finally, a trend toward all-colored occupancy, beyond a certain point, becomes self-propelling. As shown in chapters iv and x, interracial

---

[39] Public Housing Administration, Statistics Branch, unpublished data, and *House and Home*, March, 1957. In Detroit in 1954 Negroes represented more than 90 percent of eligible applicants for public housing. *Detroit Housing Commission* v. *Lewis*, Stipulation of Facts in *Race Relation Law Reporter*, February, 1956.

[40] Joseph S. Clark, Jr., quoted in *Journal of Housing*, 11(7) (July, 1954), 237.

occupancy can be stable and acceptable to the white majority, if the minority group does not become or seem likely to become too numerous. But whites become unwilling to remain in or enter a community when the minority proportion goes beyond some undefined but critical point.

Another tendency which has plagued public housing in recent years is the increasing number of problem families among the tenants. These are families of low social and housekeeping standards, chronically involved in various kinds of antisocial conduct. Although forming not more than a small percentage of public-housing tenants, according to available evidence, the presence of even a small number of maladjusted, ill-behaving families can have destructive effects on community life in a housing project and on the reputation of public housing among prospective tenants. A New York City study reported that many families eligible for public housing were avoiding it because problem families had given it a bad name.[41]

Problem families, if they existed in prewar public housing, did not attract notice. Their appearance in troublesome numbers during the 1950's probably reflects a change in the character of the low-income population. During the depression decade, a great many families were poor because of the malfunctioning of the economy. But in the economic conditions which have generally prevailed since the war, low income is more likely to be connected with personal disabilities such as illness, physical incapacity, or psychological disorders. During the earlier period, moreover, public-housing managements enjoyed some freedom of judgment in the selection of tenants. At present, the statutory preferences prescribed by Congress leave little room for selection on an individual basis.

The impact of problem families is compounded by the enforced exodus of the more capable families because of too-high income. Some type of criteria is obviously necessary to insure that the housing subsidy will go to the low-income group as intended. Nevertheless, to compel families to leave their homes solely because their income has increased beyond some point, as

---

[41] Elizabeth Wood, Study for the Citizens' Housing and Planning Council of New York, reported in *New York Times,* May 6, 1957.

the law requires, amounts to a penalty on initiative. It tends also to create an abnormal community situation adverse to the basic purposes of public housing. As one analyst and former administrator of public housing has remarked, "so long as public housing is the *temporary* home of the capable, the honest, the ambitious . . . but it is the *permanent* home for the damaged, the non-normal, the deceitful, [it] will not produce good neighborhoods." [42]

Other features of public housing probably contributing to consumer resistance are the large size and semi-institutional appearance of many projects, the bureaucratic management, and the charity stigma attaching to it. Catherine Bauer sums up the multiple disadvantages of public housing from the tenant's standpoint in the judgment that "Life in the usual public housing project just is not the way most American families want to live. Nor does it reflect our accepted values as to the way people should live." [43]

In the present moribund condition of public housing, those who have always fought it demand it be given a *coup de grâce*. Many of its proponents urge basic changes.[44] In general, the changes proposed are directed to removing the features of public housing which give it a "special" character and tend toward economic class or racial segregation. It is often proposed that future projects be small and architecturally integrated with surrounding neighborhoods. Some would eliminate projects entirely and instead have the public-housing authorities build new or acquire existing individual, scattered dwellings or buildings for rental to low-income tenants. Another reform proposal would eliminate the income limit on continued residence in public housing, allowing the over-income tenant to retain his dwelling on payment of an

---

[42] Wood, *Public Housing and Mrs. McGee*, p. 13.

[43] Bauer, *Architectural Forum*, May, 1957, p. 141.

[44] A symposium of public housing reform proposals by eleven recognized authorities on urban problems is "The Dreary Deadlock of Public Housing—How to Break It," *Architectural Forum*, June, 1957, a sequel to Miss Bauer's article in the May, 1957, issue of the same journal. See also statements presented to the Subcommittee on Housing of the Committee on Banking and Currency, U. S., Congress, Senate, *Hearings, Housing Act of 1957*, 85th Cong., 1st Sess., 1957, pp. 756-757 (National Association of Housing and Redevelopment Officials), pp. 599-601 (American Municipal Association), and pp. 798-800 (National Housing Conference, William L. C. Wheaton).

economic rent. Extending this principle, some advocate no income limits at all, so far as admission to the housing is concerned, but subsidies to families below a certain income level. Essentially, this proposal would attach the subsidy to the family rather than to the dwelling unit.

An evaluation of these and other proposals is beyond the scope of the present study. It seems evident, however, that the whole concept of public housing, its purposes and its methods, is in need of revision.

XIX

Urban Renewal

Of all the housing activities of government, none has potentially a greater impact upon the housing conditions of minority groups and racial residence patterns than urban renewal—the federal-local program for clearing slums and conserving areas threatened with becoming slums. Not only do nonwhites, Puerto Ricans, and Mexican-Americans live mainly in deteriorated areas, but under existing conditions they are fast becoming the principal occupants of the slums (see chap. ii). In addition, the processes of housing the growing numbers of low-income minorities in the larger cities tend strongly toward the creation of new areas of blight. Efforts, therefore, to eliminate or prevent slums squarely confront the issue of where and under what conditions the minority groups are to live.

The public-housing program, initiated during the 1930's, had slum clearance as one of its objectives, incidental to the rehousing of slum families. In the Housing Act of 1949, Congress authorized a more ambitious, direct attack on slums. Under Title I of this act, local governments could purchase properties in designated slum areas, remove the buildings, and resell the cleared land for new development according to an approved plan. Federal grants were provided to cover up to two-thirds of the cost including a "write down" of land costs to make redevelopment attractive to private investors. Unlike the public-housing approach, in this program the rehousing of the slum residents was subordinate to the primary goal of clearance and redevelopment.

The Housing Act of 1954 created a broader program. In addition to slum clearance, provision was made for projects aimed at rehabilitating and conserving areas still sound but threatened with blight. Federal aid was conditioned upon the development, by each local community, of a workable program for preventing the growth of slums. Elements of the workable program include the enactment and enforcement of housing codes, a master city plan, a plan for rehousing displaced families, and plans for financing, administrative organization, and citizen participation. Special terms of FHA mortgage insurance were authorized to stimulate new housing construction in project areas and for displaced families within or outside such areas. Consistent with the broadened scope of the program, its official name was changed from "Community Development and Redevelopment" to "Urban Renewal."

In theory, the minority groups—the principal victims of slums —should have the most to gain from their elimination. But there is another side to the picture—the possibility that projects of urban renewal, by displacing people without adequate provision of alternative housing, may actually worsen slum conditions and aggravate the housing scarcity for minorities. Urban renewal on any substantial scale necessarily involves displacement of people. Slum clearance has visible and dramatic impact. Buildings are torn down and the entire population of an area must seek new homes. Theoretically, the displacement may be only temporary during the time that the area is being rebuilt,[1] but in practice, the displaced residents are seldom able to return to their old neighborhood. The demolished housing, in most cases, is replaced at a much higher price level, beyond the means of the former residents, or the new units are of different types and sizes than the old, not adapted to the needs of erstwhile resident families. Frequently, too, the slum-cleared area is redeveloped wholly or in part for nonresidential purposes such as hospitals, parking

---

[1] Federal law requires local communities receiving federal aid to provide only for "the temporary relocation of families displaced . . . ," *Housing Act of 1949*, Sec. 105(c), as amended, Public Law 171, 81st Cong.

lots, or cultural facilities.[2] Although occasionally some public or other low-cost housing is built in slum-clearance areas for occupancy by the former residents, in the main, redevelopment plans contemplate re-use of the land by different economic or racial groups.

Other forms of urban renewal also force people to leave their homes. The enforcement of health and housing codes results in condemnation of some dilapidated and unsafe buildings. In other cases, slum property owners may choose to take their units off the market rather than incur the expense of complying with legal requirements. Some families will be evicted for violation of housing space standards. As part of their urban-renewal programs, several cities have adopted legal standards for housing, which, if suddenly and strictly enforced, would cause an enormous upheaval. Slums are characteristically crowded beyond the limits of health or decency. Hence, the imposition of sound density and occupancy standards, whether by redevelopment or other means, must usually result in some reduction of population.

As would be expected from the concentration of minorities in slums, displacement by urban renewal falls heavily upon these groups. Official statistics for 231 urban-renewal projects, approved for advanced planning or execution at the end of 1957 and reporting color of population, show a total of 112,000 resident families of whom 56 percent were nonwhites. From 115 projects reporting (77 cities), 43,000 families had been relocated by the end of 1957, of whom more than 30,000 were nonwhite.[3] Of those classified as white, an unreported but certainly substantial number were Puerto Rican.

Urban renewal thus generates two kinds of housing need which, in the whole field of housing policy, have proved most difficult to supply, namely housing economically accessible to low-income families, and housing available to minority groups. It is generally recognized that adequate alternative housing is an indispensable prerequisite to urban renewal; but whether the

---

[2] See "Redevelopment Today," *Architectural Forum*, April, 1958, a review of seventeen redevelopment projects completed by 1958.

[3] Housing and Home Finance Agency, Urban Renewal Administration, *Relocation from Urban Renewal Project Areas through December, 1957* (Washington, D. C., 1958).

housing supply was in fact adequate has been continuously controversial, on the national level and in virtually every city that
has undertaken a sizable program.

Redevelopment under the 1949 Housing Act was launched in
the midst of the postwar housing shortage. The act authorized
810,000 units of low-rent public housing, but, as previously noted,
only a small part of this program was actually built. Otherwise,
no special provision was made for rehousing the people to be
displaced other than the general requirement that "decent, safe,
and sanitary dwellings" should either exist or be provided for
the displaced families at rents and prices within their financial
means.[4] How to do this was for the local communities to determine.

To relocate the entire populations of slum-clearance areas under
conditions of general housing shortage, proved to be extremely
difficult, often requiring years to complete. The displaced residents were rehoused partly in public housing but primarily in the
existing stock of private housing. Evidence accumulated that
many of the families involved were moving from clearance sites
into near-by areas already overcrowded and indeed, in some cases,
marked for later redevelopment. Although the relocated families
usually obtained standard dwellings and probably improved their
housing in many cases,[5] their movement often tended to heighten
congestion in areas of destination. The minority groups saw a
part of their living space being taken away by slum clearance
without the opening of other areas where they could live.

Viewing these tendencies led many observers to conclude that
slum clearance, as operating under the 1949 Housing Act, was
defeating its own, larger purposes. Catherine Bauer, long a leading advocate of rehousing the slum dwellers, termed redevelopment "A Misfit in the 'Fifties." [6] The Federal Housing
Administrator warned that "No program of housing or urban
improvement . . . can hope to make more than indifferent progress until we open up adequate opportunities to minority families

---

[4] *Housing Act of 1949,* Sec. 105(c).

[5] From the beginning of the program to the end of 1957, of 52,400 families
relocated, more than 70 percent were reported to be rehoused in standard
housing. HHFA, URA, *Relocation . . . through December, 1957.*

[6] Catherine Bauer, "Redevelopment—A Misfit in the 'Fifties."

for decent housing." [7] A Presidential Advisory Committee declared in 1953 that "A piecemeal attack on slums [i.e., the program then existing] simply will not work—occasional thrusts at slum pockets in one section of a city will only push slums to other sections unless an effective program exists for attacking the entire problem of urban decay." [8]

The revised and rechristened program adopted in 1954 contained some measures aiming to stimulate private housing production in conjunction with urban renewal. For families displaced by urban renewal or related government action, Section 221 of the Housing Act authorized FHA-insured mortgages up to 100 percent of appraised value with down payments of two hundred dollars and repayment periods of up to forty years. Similar terms were provided for rental housing where the owner-mortgagor was a nonprofit corporation. Mortgage insurance on these liberal terms is available only in cities which have requested it and which have approved workable programs of urban renewal. Mortgages may not exceed $9,000 or, in high cost areas, $10,000. A companion section of the law, no. 220, provided similar but somewhat less liberal terms of mortgage insurance for housing constructed within urban-renewal areas.

Local communities have been slow to make use of these provisions. More than two years passed before any mortgages were insured under Section 221; and not until 1958 did the FHA begin insuring relocation-housing mortgages in any appreciable volume. [9]

Responsibility for relocation, under the National Housing Act, belongs to the local urban-renewal agencies, but the federal authorities have the duty to see that requirements of federal law are carried out, as well as to assist and guide the local agencies. As with other housing programs, the federal agency has avoided any requirements or controls which might interfere with local practices of racial segregation. Although the large majority of families displaced by urban renewal are nonwhite, the nearest approach to a federal regulation on racial aspects of the program

---

[7] Albert M. Cole, "What is the Federal Government's Role in Housing?"

[8] President's Advisory Committee on Government Housing Policies and Programs, *Report to the President of the United States*, p. 1.

[9] Housing and Home Finance Agency, *Housing Statistics, Historical Supplement*, December, 1958; *Housing Statistics*, August, 1959.

has been the issuance of a communication to local agencies warning against diminishing the living space of minority groups. Slum clearance, this document states, "could result in a worsening, instead of the desired improvement, of the housing conditions of Negro and other racial minority families if the administration of these programs resulted in decreasing the living space presently available in any community to such groups." [10] Without indicating that local agencies should take any action in the matter, the letter described three alternative procedures for preventing a loss of minority living space. Redevelopment housing could be made available to all racial groups, or minorities could be allotted a reasonable share of new housing in a given redevelopment area, or housing could be made available to minority families in other areas not generally less desirable and "not theretofore available for occupancy by Negro or other racial minority families." The two latter alternatives obviously assume segregation, whereas the third one gives federal approval to the complete exclusion of minority families from a redevelopment area formerly occupied by them, providing comparable space is made available elsewhere.

Public housing has been used much more for the rehousing of displaced nonwhite than of white families. Well over a fourth of all nonwhite families relocated up to the end of 1957 were placed in public housing, as compared with 10 percent of white families.[11] Public housing built within urban-renewal projects and occupied at the end of 1957 was tenanted almost exclusively (97 percent) by nonwhites.[12] In absolute figures, during the period under consideration, urban-renewal programs utilized a total of slightly more than 11,000 units of public housing, of which nearly 9,700 units, or 88 percent, were occupied by nonwhites. Urban renewal has thus given a major impetus to the trend, previously described, toward filling up public housing with minority groups.

---

[10] Housing and Home Finance Agency, Local Public Agency Letter No. 16, "Living Space Available to Racial Minority Families," February 2, 1953.

[11] Housing and Home Finance Agency, Urban Renewal Administration, *Relocation . . . through December, 1957*, p. 7.

[12] Unpublished data supplied by courtesy of the Urban Renewal Administration.

Rehabilitation and Conservation

Urban renewal embraces both the clearance and rebuilding of slums and the rehabilitation of blighted areas. Up to the present, local programs have emphasized clearance and redevelopment, but there has been growing interest in the possibilities of rehabilitation. Projects of slum prevention and rehabilitation seem likely to play a larger role in the future than in the past, if for no other reason than the probable lack of funds to clear more than a part of the slums.

Rehabilitation requires broader action by local governments and makes more demand upon the initiative of citizens in the affected areas than does slum clearance. The latter can be, and usually is, imposed upon an area from the outside; but a program of neighborhood rehabilitation necessarily consists in large part of helping the local people to help themselves. Theoretically, municipal governments can do many things to combat slum conditions. They can enforce legal minimum housing standards, zone out various blighting influences, provide parks, control traffic, maintain sanitation, and give police protection against antisocial elements. But such governmental controls and services are not likely to yield much result unless the local residents appreciate their value, know how to use them, and coöperate actively in house and neighborhood improvement.

A certain amount of experience has accumulated from the efforts of some cities and voluntary groups to salvage deteriorating neighborhoods.[13] One of the best known experiments of this kind was developed in Baltimore and is known as "The Baltimore Plan." It consists in systematic, complete enforcement of the housing laws in selected areas, combined with efforts to "rehabilitate the people as well as the houses."[14] Operating at first

---

[13] A penetrating study of experiences in slum rehabilitation and prevention is Martin Millspaugh and Gurney Breckenfeld, *The Human Side of Urban Renewal.*

[14] *Ibid.,* p. 3 ff. See also Citizens Planning and Housing Association, *Something Is Happening in Baltimore* (Baltimore, 1952); American Council To Improve Our Neighborhoods, Inc., *Housing Court: Baltimore,* Report from ACTION No. 2, and *Fight-Blight Fund, Inc.: Baltimore,* Report from ACTION No. 3; "Baltimore Plan Stops Blight with a Housing Code," *Architectural Forum,* October, 1950.

on a block-by-block basis, the city authorities determined in 1951 to attempt the rehabilitation of an entire neighborhood, hoping to create a rehabilitated area large enough and with sufficient identity to maintain itself after being once brought up to standard. Experience with the block system had indicated that improvements, although initially significant, were transitory. The individual block was unable to resist the depressing influence of the surrounding slum.

The first neighborhood chosen was a fourteen-block area in a late stage of racial transition. Most of the houses were sound but badly run down, unsanitary, and vermin-infested. The residents were mainly industrial workers and their families, not in extreme poverty but with incomes well below the city average. Many were recent migrants from the South. The educational level was low. About half of the families owned their homes.

Inspectors from the city agencies enforcing the health, building, electrical, zoning, and fire prevention codes examined each of the seven hundred fifty houses in the area, listing all violations of law. The homeowner or landlord was then given a notice of repairs required to bring his property into conformity with law. Failure to comply was punishable by fine or vacating of the property. A housing court had been created previously to handle housing cases.

Concurrently with the law enforcement campaign, steps were taken to assist the residents in compliance, win their coöperation, and stimulate them to do more than the law required. A hearing board considered the cases of property owners who were financially or for other reasons unable to make the required repairs and helped them find solutions. Committees of residents were set up on law enforcement, social services, education, health, recreation, and for liaison with City Hall. Several churches lent their support to the program. A group of Baltimore businessmen organized a nonprofit fund to lend money for home improvements to impoverished homeowners who could not borrow from regular credit institutions.

The program brought dramatic results. The neighborhood was cleared of accumulated trash and filth, and with the cleanup, the rats disappeared. Nearly 90 percent of the housing law violations found by inspectors were corrected within two years. Some homeowners improved their properties beyond the legal minimums. There was evidence of increase in residents' pride in their neighborhood and a new appreciation of cleanliness and order.

Unfortunately, these beneficial results were not lasting. After the intensive law enforcement ceased, the violations, the filth, and the rats began to return. In searching for the reasons why more lasting results were not achieved, Millspaugh and Breckenfeld emphasize the blighting influences at work in the neighborhood which the program was powerless to control.[15] The area was overcrowded at the beginning of the program and became even more congested. Housing law enforcement could affect only the houses: the city did not use its powers to create any open space, reduce the heavy traffic through residential streets, or reduce the numbers of taverns and blighting commercial uses. Indeed, although the area already possessed more than one tavern for every block on the average, additional liquor licenses as well as zoning exceptions were granted by city authorities while the rehabilitation program was going on. Law enforcement, moreover, was more effective with homeowners than with the slum landlords. The latter, controlling half of the housing, resisted the enforcement of standards and conformed only to the least possible extent. They were fertile in evasion and subterfuge, and some preferred to pay the moderate fines imposed rather than incur the expense of repairing their buildings.

The architects of the Baltimore Plan hoped to generate a "civic force" among the neighborhood residents which would be capable of protecting the neighborhood after the intensive program ceased, but in this they were disappointed. A protective and improvement association was formed, but it never took root. The people of this area, poorly educated, of deprived backgrounds, and with limited experience, apparently lacked a concept of what they might do for themselves by organized action. Hence, although the residents, on the whole, responded to help proffered from outside, they were unable to mobilize any significant force on their own behalf.

In the second neighborhood to which the Baltimore Plan was applied, capacity for organization and leadership were present to

---

[15] Millspaugh and Breckenfeld, *The Human Side of Urban Renewal*, pp. 20-21.

a high degree. This was the Mount Royal district of Baltimore, a downtown, middle-class neighborhood threatened with blight by the conversion of its large, old houses to tenements, and recently entered by Negroes.[16] The homeowners in this area were not poor and semiliterate workingmen but substantial business and professional men. During the law-enforcement campaign, the existing neighborhood property owners' association was revitalized with new leadership, intelligent, aggressive, and sophisticated in dealings with public authorities. This leadership proved able to grapple with problems before which the previous slum neighborhood was helpless. It insisted on having the neighborhood officially designated as an urban-renewal area, backing up its demands with an urban-renewal rally attended by hundreds of local property owners. It persuaded the district police commander to put extra patrols of plain-clothes men in the neighborhood. It formed a real estate corporation to buy up houses threatened with deterioration, renovate, and resell them to acceptable families. It effectively opposed additional tavern licenses and zoning exceptions. When the Liquor Board decided against the neighborhood in a critical instance, the association took the case to court and won.

The Mount Royal leaders undertook to stabilize the racial composition of the neighborhood. First, they persuaded their association to agree that Negro homeowners would be accepted in the neighborhood and welcomed to membership in the improvement association. With this policy established, they sought and obtained the coöperation of the Urban League in a plan for informally limiting the percentage of Negroes in the area and also endeavoring to keep out families of either race who would not meet the social standards of the neighborhood.

This demonstration that the neighborhood could act effectively toward solution of its problems did much to restore confidence in its future. Membership in the improvement association climbed steeply; the exodus of white homeowners subsided; middle-class families again began moving into the neighborhood. With urban

---

[16] *Ibid.*, pp. 67-89. See also Frances H. Morton, executive secretary, Citizens Planning and Housing Association of Baltimore, "Law Enforcement, Rehabilitation and Urban Renewal in Baltimore," Address to the Montclair (N. J.) League of Women Voters, May 23, 1955.

renewal and the promise of governmental action on a wider scale there were grounds for hope that the neighborhood would remain a preferred place for family living—with Negroes.[17]

One of the most notable attempts of a neighborhood to save itself from sinking into a slum is the case of Hyde Park and Kenwood in Chicago.[18] These districts, adjacent to the University of Chicago, were once one of the city's best neighborhoods, the residence of wealthy families and a prosperous upper-middle class. But for years they have been prey to virtually the whole gamut of slum-producing influences: conversion of large homes to rooming houses and small apartments, neglected building maintenance, unsavory commercial development, inadequate public services, negligent law enforcement, and the steady increase of lower-class Negroes, desperate for shelter, unadjusted to urban life, and with ways of living repellent to the older residents.

Blight in Hyde Park–Kenwood was well advanced when two organizations were formed in the early 1950's to try to salvage the neighborhood. These were the Hyde Park–Kenwood Community Conference—a wholly voluntary citizens' group—and the South East Chicago Commission, supported by the University of Chicago and several business and civic groups. Although differing in methods, the two organizations had essentially the same objectives: to stop illegal conversions, obtain more law enforcement, obtain more public services and facilities, and stimulate the residents to maintain better standards of housing and cleanliness. Both organizations assumed the area would continue to be biracial, but they hoped to stabilize the racial proportions at some point acceptable to the white population.

Both organizations were reasonably well financed, ably led, and enlisted widespread citizen participation. The numerous academic and professional people in the area provided abundant resources of expert assistance. With an organized subunit in nearly every

---

[17] Millspaugh and Breckenfeld, *The Human Side of Urban Renewal*, pp. 88-90.
[18] *Ibid.*, pp. 91-117. See also American Council To Improve Our Neighborhoods, *Organization of Block Groups for Neighborhood Improvement: The Hyde Park–Kenwood Community Conference*, Report from ACTION No. 14 (New York, September, 1956); Hyde Park–Kenwood Community Conference, *Original Policy Statement*, December 12, 1949, *Addendum to Policy*, December, 1954 (Chicago, 1955, mimeographed).

block, headed by a block captain, the Community Conference has been held up as a model of citizens' organization to fight slum conditions.[19] Millspaugh and Breckenfeld consider it "probably the most comprehensive citizens' organization ever formed to help do a job which the city government had defaulted" (*i.e.*, keep watch on housing and zoning law violations).[20] The South East Commission, for its part, was expert on law enforcement; it was tough in the best Chicago tradition, and it was adept in pursuing its aims through the maze of Chicago politics.

The Community Conference and the SECC have substantial achievements to their credit. Illegal conversions have been largely halted, new schools built, street cleaning and maintenance brought up to a reasonable standard, the crime rate reduced. The two organizations were influential in obtaining an urban-renewal project which will clear and rebuild pockets of irredeemable slums. The American Council To Improve Our Neighborhoods declares: "The record of the Hyde Park–Kenwood Community Conference shows that a neighborhood, well on the way to becoming a slum, can reverse the process." [21]

In its effort to stabilize the racial balance, however, the Community Conference has faced seemingly insuperable contrary pressures. In Chicago powerful forces are arrayed to contain the Negro population within the areas where it is already present. Negro housing demand, in consequence, is channeled disproportionately into areas such as Hyde Park and Kenwood. A stable interracial neighborhood is hardly possible if white residents and potential residents anticipate a predominance of Negroes and under existing circumstances this expectation seems not unreasonable for Hyde Park–Kenwood. The instability is aggravated by the wide disparity in economic and cultural levels between the white residents and the incoming Negroes.

From these and other experiences in neighborhood rehabilitation, some conclusions may be ventured concerning the prospects for rehabilitation of deteriorated minority or interracial neighborhoods. It is evident in the first place that to hold promise of

---

[19] ACTION, *Organization of Block Groups for Neighborhood Improvement.*
[20] Millspaugh and Breckenfeld, *The Human Side of Urban Renewal,* p. 96.
[21] ACTION, *Organization of Block Groups for Neighborhood Improvement,* p. 15.

success, a rehabilitation program must be broad, coping with all the important factors that produce blight in a given area. To deal only with certain aspects of the problem, leaving others aside, is unlikely to yield lasting results. It is further apparent that participation, initiative, and leadership from within the affected population is a vital ingredient of effective rehabilitation.

Citizen initiative and leadership for neighborhood betterment presuppose a level of cultural development and economic competence not yet achieved by most Negroes, Mexican-Americans, or Puerto Ricans. Consequently, neighborhoods occupied mainly by these groups, aside from the occasional Negro middle-class neighborhood, have meager capacity, by themselves, to initiate or sustain a rehabilitation effort. Programs of home and neighborhood improvement have been carried to Negro communities by government, as in Baltimore, or by philanthropic groups; the residents themselves have seemingly lacked the attitudes, knowledge, and social habits needed to take the initiative or carry responsibility for a community program. Educated, socially sophisticated persons in such neighborhoods are usually too few to set the standard for the total group. Moreover, even the middle class of Negroes, never before allowed to participate fully in the larger society, has lagged in acquiring the skills of effective participation (see chap. v).

Implications for urban renewal in minority neighborhoods are fairly obvious. Much more responsibility must be carried by government and community agencies, more must be done "for" rather than "with" the people in these areas than for those in white middle-class neighborhoods. Moreover, as experience in the initial area of the Baltimore Plan amply demonstrated, an effective program must deal with much more than just housing, for the housing problems of slum families are often inseparable from family and community disorganization, low standards, and ignorance. Hence, a program to improve the housing and neighborhood must be prepared to assist families in finding solutions to other unresolved problems; it must inculcate new concepts of what is desirable and possible, and educate the people in how to achieve a better life.

For racially mixed areas, especially those where the racial

groups differ widely in cultural level, a fundamental objective must be to stabilize the racial proportions at a point acceptable to white residents and potential residents. Attitudes favorable to neighborhood conservation, especially readiness to invest money and effort in neighborhood improvement, obviously cannot flourish if white residents are expecting to abandon the area. To make racial stabilization generally feasible, however, requires the opening of housing opportunities for minority groups in a variety of locations, so that their housing demand will not have to be concentrated on a few areas.

XX

Conditions and Prospects for Housing Desegregation

In these times, the vital importance of good housing for individual and social well-being is generally recognized, and there is also consensus that government should act on a broad scale to eliminate slums and assist families to acquire homes. "A decent home and a suitable living environment for every American family" has been for more than a decade a goal of national policy.

Racial and ethnic minority groups, especially Negroes, other nonwhite groups, Puerto Ricans, and Mexican-Americans have been traditionally ill-housed. In spite of recent improvements, their housing remains far inferior to the general standard. To a much greater extent than other citizens, they suffer from dilapidated and deficient dwellings, overcrowding, and all the evils of slum environments. To achieve the aims of national housing policy, therefore, it is necessary to give particular attention to the needs of these groups who total nearly one-sixth of the United States population.

But housing for minority groups involves larger issues than the amount or quality of their dwelling units, important as these are. Housing has become a major arena in the movement to achieve full citizenship and equal rights for all Americans. The paramount issue is segregation—whether the minorities shall continue to be confined to certain areas or, like other citizens, have the freedom to compete for housing in the general market.

In large measure, the housing disadvantage of minority groups, especially of Negroes, is traceable directly to restrictions on their competitive freedom. Because of low income, most minority families can afford only the cheaper dwellings. But their housing is poorer than it need be on the basis of price alone. Segregation tends to create a special scarcity of housing for the segregated groups, enabling higher prices to be charged than in the general market for similar dwellings. Nonwhite families, on the average, obtain less space and a poorer quality of dwellings than do white families, even when they pay the same rents or purchase prices.

It is unlikely that the housing of minority groups can be brought up to the general standard of quality while segregation persists. Indeed, certain important components of good housing, such as variety to suit individual wants and purses, and prestige locations, are obviously impossible to provide within any limited area to the same degree as in the housing market as a whole. Recognition of this truth was the basis of the Supreme Court's refusal ever to apply the separate-but-equal doctrine to matters of residence.

Desegregation of residence further implies a significant equalization of social status, and broadened opportunity to participate in community activities. Where a family lives is a mark of its social position, and people living in similar houses in the same neighborhood ordinarily are judged to be on the same social level. Many business and civic activities are associated directly or indirectly with place of residence and are not readily accessible to the segregated minorities.

Ultimately, it is no exaggeration to say that the separate existence of minority groups is bound up with their segregation. A certain concentration of numbers seems to be, almost always, an essential condition of group life. As the history of many immigrant groups in the United States has demonstrated, when the members of an ethnic group cease to live together, their ties to the group become weakened and the group itself tends to dissolve. Although nonwhites will continue to be identified by others as a distinct group, so long as race conciousness persists, nevertheless, the degree of awareness of a minority group is closely dependent upon its numbers and concentration. A few people of darker complexions in a crowd may attract little notice, whereas a compact group of nonwhites, especially if numerous, has an inescapable psychological impact.

In the past quarter century, and especially since the end of World War II, a variety of forces has impinged upon the residence situation of the minority groups, some tending to sustain, others to weaken segregation. Foremost among the sustaining factors have been the massive and diverse currents of migration—the movement of millions of Negroes and smaller though large numbers of Puerto Ricans into the larger cities, and the parallel exodus of the white population from the cities to the surrounding metropolitan territory. The minority newcomers have been for the most part poor and culturally retarded. To incorporate them immediately into the existing social fabric has been a manifest impossibility. In the traditional manner of low-status immigrant groups, they have clustered together, while the older residents have drawn apart from them. The divergent movements of population have resulted in simultaneous expansion of minority residence areas in the central cities and of all-white communities on the periphery.

Another important stimulus to segregation has been the shift to large-scale methods of housing production, giving greater scope to the racially discriminatory decisions of private builders, lenders, and real estate brokers. Most new private housing developments, except those specifically intended for minority occupancy, exclude minority groups completely, as a matter of policy. The housing industry has changed its building and financing methods but not its traditional racial policies. Thus there has emerged, in the postwar years, the phenomenon of huge, new communities, as well as many smaller ones, without a single Negro resident. Large-scale building methods have been made possible by government-assisted financing and other public aids. Hence, government housing policy has indirectly served to promote segregation. In an earlier period, the influence of the FHA was directly exerted to encourage segregation.

Factors tending toward integration are the rising incomes of the minority groups, enabling them to compete more strongly in the housing market; the growth of minority middle classes, culturally as well as economically prepared to associate with the white population on equal terms; favorable judicial decisions; the decline of racist ideology and the increase of racially tolerant attitudes among the white population; the growing body of legislation for equal rights in housing and other areas; organized pressure by many groups against discriminatory practices; and the impact of world opinion toward racial discrimination in the United States.

Balanced between these opposing forces, segregation at present can be judged to be either increasing or decreasing depending on the criteria employed. Considering the total nonwhite population of any city and how it is distributed geographically in relation to the white population, the data show, for most cities, a heightening of segregation between 1940 and 1950; that is, the tendency for nonwhites to live in areas of predominantly nonwhite population was more pronounced in the latter year than in the former. This trend has continued since 1950 according to all available evidence. At the same time, however, a growing *number* of nonwhites are living in desegregated situations; and an increasing number and proportion of the neighborhoods in most northern and western large cities are becoming racially mixed in some degree. It seems evident that southern cities are moving toward stricter segregation according to both standards, but in the North and West, fewer and fewer neighborhoods remain totally white. Nor is new housing as segregated as it once was. A small yet significant number of new private housing developments have deliberately attracted a mixed racial population, and there appears to be a trend toward such open developments.

Future of Mixed Areas

Whether areas which have become racially mixed can remain so indefinitely is a crucial question for future residential patterns. In the past, the tendency of neighborhoods once entered by nonwhites to fill up with them has been so much a part of the minority housing scene as to appear virtually an inevitable process. A closer view, however, shows that racial transition is not an automatic consequence of nonwhite entry but the outcome of certain conditions that have existed in the past but may not exist in the future to the same extent.

The exodus of whites from an area entered by a minority group and the shrinkage of white demand appear to reflect a judgment that the minority group will become numerically dominant or that undesirable conditions will develop because of the presence of a lower-status group, or both. Evidence is plentiful that merely the entry of a few nonwhite families does not provoke white abandonment of a neighborhood unless it gives rise to one or both of these expectations. There are many whites, it can be said with confidence, who have little objection or none to the presence of a small number of nonwhites in their vicinity, but whites willing to live in a minority neighborhood are few indeed. The enforced concentration of nonwhite housing demand on a few areas, because of their exclusion from most neighborhoods, has provided a basis in experience for white expectations.

During the first decade after World War II, areas becoming open to Negroes sustained the impact of a huge volume of accumulated housing demand, resulting from population growth, higher and more stable incomes, and extreme shortage of housing available to Negroes during the war and early postwar years. House-hungry Negroes pressed urgently into areas newly open to them. At the same time, in many of these areas, the whites were looking eagerly toward the new housing developments arising in the suburbs. Under these circumstances, many areas, especially along the borders of existing minority communities, shifted rapidly from white to nonwhite occupancy. Negro demand was sustained by increasing availability of mortgage credit. Housing market institutions—the builders, mortgage lenders, real estate brokers—helped to channel the burgeoning Negro demand into particular areas. In some places, such as Atlanta, racial-occupancy transfers were expedited by deliberate planning between white and Negro leaders.

More recently, as the pent-up Negro housing demand has abated and as the supply of housing available to Negroes has increased, the speed of racial transition has slowed. If nonwhites continue to gain increasing freedom in the housing market, as seems likely, they will enter more areas than they can conceivably fill. As this prospect becomes realized, the grounds for anticipating a turnover of racial occupancy in many areas will be removed. In fact, this has apparently already occurred in respect to high-cost districts. Where nonwhites have gained entry to expensive neighborhoods, their presence, although often resisted, has not been regarded as the beginning of a racial change. An exception is the case of some high-rental apartment districts where some of the building owners decide their most profitable course is to subdivide existing dwellings into smaller units for rent to minority families who will accept the overcrowding.

The extent to which minority home seekers are gaining market freedom varies in different cities. In those cities where segregation remains tight in the face of increasing minority population and housing demand, the prospects for stable mixed areas are dim. Even where minorities have comparative freedom of choice, there will be some areas relatively more attractive to nonwhites than to whites. In these situations, a stable, racially mixed pattern would seem to be possible only through the imposition of quota controls.

Stable interracial neighborhoods are undoubtedly more likely to be realized in middle- to high-cost areas than in low-cost districts. For regardless of the level of racial discrimination, Negroes, Puerto Ricans, and Mexican-Americans will continue, for the foreseeable future, to be heavily concentrated in the cheapest housing. Therefore, unless the supply of low-cost housing should be greatly expanded, these groups must continue to be concentrated in the limited areas where they can afford to live.

Some Principles of Housing Desegregation

It is appropiate to conclude the present study with a brief summary of research findings that bear directly on methods for bringing about changes in the race relations of housing in the direction of equal opportunity. Knowledge of this kind is, of course, especially valuable to the numerous organizations dedicated to racial equality, and to legislative bodies and public officials responsible for public policy in the area. The findings summarized below are by no means the original contribution of the present study, although this research has affirmed them in various particulars. They are the product of many sociological and psychological investigations, not limited to the specific problems of housing or race relations. Some of the most significant contributions have come from basic research in human behavior without reference to practical application. Sources have been cited throughout the present work and will not be repeated here.

1. Action aiming to reduce discrimination is more promising if focused directly on controlling discriminatory conduct, rather than attempting to change attitudes of prejudice. Attitudes are important in discrimination, but they are not the cause either of discriminatory or nondiscriminatory behavior.

2. The most effective means of changing behavior as well as attitudes is through introducing a change in the situation in which decisions are made and attitudes formed. A change in the basis of expectations concerning the outcome of a racial situation (e.g., in an interracial neighborhood, the emergence of dynamic leadership or the inauguration of an urban-renewal program) will have more effect on behavior than any amount of exhortation or dissemination of information. It is doubtful whether attitudes can be significantly modified merely by educational means without changes in the surrounding conditions.

Another highly important type of situational change is the creation of counter pressures against the social forces which impel people to discriminatory action. In situations that are full of pressures to discriminate (within the real estate business, for example, or in an all-white suburban neighborhood) even the most tolerant individuals can scarcely follow their inclinations unless supported by counter pressures. It is unrealistic to treat discriminatory behavior as ignorant or irrational, requiring only a proper assessment of the facts for its correction. In many circumstances, discriminatory conduct may be entirely rational—certainly it is often the course of least resistance for an individual.

3. A social process can be changed by influencing the actions of those who make the critical decisions which the process calls for. In respect to housing segregation, this means affecting the decisions of those who immediately control access to housing—the builders, mortgage lenders, real estate brokers, and agencies of government.

4. Law can be an effective counterforce against pressures for segregation, especially when efficiently administered and supported by articulate citizen groups. An important function of laws for racial equality is not merely to compel or prohibit, but to give freedom of action to persons who would prefer not to discriminate. This function is particularly important in relation to individual real estate brokers and builders who are constrained to discriminate by the pressures of their business groups and some clients.

By changing the situation, law can influence the factors that shape attitudes and hence, indirectly, the attitudes themselves.

5. To influence private and public decision-makers, as well as legislation, effective organization and mobilization of power by citizens concerned with the problem are indispensable.

6. The majority of people, according to the evidence of attitude surveys, do not have firmly fixed opinions on racial equality. Hence, they may be influenced in their behavior and attitudes by those more concerned with the character of race relations, on one side or the other. This finding further underlines the critical importance of organization and leadership.

7. Association between members of majority and minority groups in the neighborhood or housing project leads such individuals to have better opinions of each other if contacts are on an equal-status basis, and if the participants are of similar social-class background. Mingling of lower-class minority individuals with middle-class whites is very likely to increase the racial antagonism of the whites.

8. Competition among racial groups (e.g., for dominance of housing areas) tends to increase racial hostility.

9. The most effective means of promoting interracial understanding and acceptance is by creating situations wherein members of different racial groups work together in solving common problems.

10. Efforts to achieve racial equality of access to housing will encounter less resistance and have greater chance of success if they are not confused with proposals to eliminate socioeconomic-group segregation. Some advocates of racial desegregation seem to think it desirable to mingle people not only of different races

but of differing economic and cultural levels in the same neighborhood, but this is an unfortunate confusion. It is one thing to ask people of the white middle class to share their neighborhoods with nonwhites of similar income, educational level, and social outlook. It is quite a different thing to ask them to associate as neighbors with people of lower income, education, and cultural standards. Socioeconomic segregation is in no way inconsistent with racial integration. Indeed, one of the benefits anticipated from reducing racial discrimination is an enhanced freedom of the minority groups to rise in the class structure of American society.

Appendices

NOTE ON RESEARCH METHOD

Because this study attempts to present a comprehensive analysis of a large and many-sided subject, data have been drawn, of necessity, from a variety of sources. There already exists an extensive research literature directly or indirectly pertinent to the subject. To canvass the existing studies and assess their findings was the logical first step in the present inquiry. This canvass endeavored to be exhaustive, covering not only published works but also masters' and doctoral dissertations on file in university libraries. Only a small proportion of the studies consulted are cited in the text.

In the analysis of population and housing characteristics and trends, extensive use was made of data of the U. S. Bureau of the Census, including not only the decennial censuses of 1950 and earlier years, but also the current census reports, special censuses, and the 1956 National Housing Inventory. Supplementing the published census reports, special tabulations of 1950 Housing Census data for selected metropolitan areas were obtained from the Census Bureau.

Published reports of the federal housing agencies were a third important source of data, supplemented by official but unpublished information made available by these agencies. Reports and hearings of congressional committees on housing and civil rights were searched for findings and testimony relevant to the concerns of the present study.

Primary sources for the analysis of the legal aspects of housing and race were court decisions, texts of legislation, and reports of state and municipal agencies responsible for administration of laws prohibiting racial discrimination, including transcripts of hearings and administrative rulings in disputed cases. As a guide to current legal materials, much use was made of the *Race Relations Law Reporter* (Vanderbilt University).

For original data, the present volume depends heavily on a series of special studies, elsewhere identified. Each of these developed methods and data sources corresponding to its particular objectives and the nature of the problem under investigation. Some were straightforward sampling surveys of defined populations, yielding quantitative distributions of responses to a questionnaire (Eagle, "The Puerto Ricans in New York City"; Kitano, "Housing of Japanese-Americans in the San Francisco Bay Area"; Helper, "The Role of the Real Estate Business in Minority Group Housing"). Others used sample survey techniques in combination with other procedures (Laurenti, *Property Values and Race,* and Rapkin and Grigsby, *Demand for Housing in Racially Mixed Areas*). Still others gathered their data mainly from records and interviews with selected key informants (Griers, *Privately Developed Interracial Housing,* and the Atlanta-Birmingham, Houston–San Antonio, New Orleans, Miami, and Detroit studies in the volume edited by Glazer and McEntire). Methods of the various special studies are described more fully in the published volumes.

Data on housing industry practices were obtained from the foregoing sources plus three others. One of the additional sources was an interview survey (not separately published) directed to builders, brokers, and mortgage lenders in six metropolitan areas. The latter were selected to include one area with extensive new construction for sale or rent to minority groups and one with comparatively little such building, both in the same region. Norfolk and Birmingham represented the South; Chicago and Detroit, the Midwest; and Los Angeles and San Francisco, the Pacific coast. Random sampling was not considered appropriate for the objectives of this survey. Instead, interviews were sought with (1) selected builders and lenders known for their experience in building or financing houses for sale or rent to minority groups, and

(2) others locally regarded as leading members of the housing industry and hence able to comment authoritatively on the local situation and practices. Interviews were conducted by persons of academic rank in universities. In all, 119 interviews were recorded.

Further information concerning the housing industry was sought through personal interviews and correspondence with about a hundred key informants throughout the country who, because of their experience and position, possessed expert knowledge of the subject. Informants included leading builders, brokers, and mortgage lenders, writers in housing industry trade journals, professional personnel of the Urban League and NAACP, racial relations officers in the federal housing agencies, representatives of state and municipal antidiscrimination commissions, authors of studies, and others.

The third source pertaining specifically to the housing industry was an exhaustive canvass of public statements by builders, mortgage lenders, real estate brokers, their organizations and spokesmen, over a period of twenty years, concerning housing and minority groups. An equally thorough canvass was made of similar statements by government housing agencies and officials.

Together, the various sources yielded extensive data pertinent to each major area under investigation. For each area, the factual picture was built up and conclusions arrived at by sifting through masses of information and checking the various bodies of facts against each other. This procedure obviously left a wide area of judgment in assessing the significance of particular facts and the adequacy of the factual picture as a whole. To this, however, there was no satisfactory alternative, since the purposes of the present study could not have been met by any single research procedure. My judgments were checked by my colleagues, members of the Commission on Race and Housing, the Commission's Research Advisory Committee, and other experts who read and criticized the manuscript at various stages in its preparation.

TABLE A-1

PERCENT DISTRIBUTION OF POPULATION BY COLOR, AND SELECTED HOUSING
CHARACTERISTICS IN URBAN AREAS OF VARYING NONWHITE
CONCENTRATION, FOR SELECTED CITIES, 1950

City	Census tracts with specified percent of tract population nonwhite in 1950						
	75+	50-74	25-49	10-24	1-9	Less than 1	All tracts
	DISTRIBUTION OF TOTAL NONWHITE POPULATION						
New York	53.4	14.8	12.7	9.4	7.8	1.9	100.0
Manhattan	69.0	10.0	6.4	8.3	5.4	0.9	100.0
Brooklyn	44.6	17.0	16.6	10.3	8.9	2.6	100.0
Bronx	28.2	22.9	25.2	11.5	9.2	3.0	100.0
Queens	22.5	29.2	20.8	8.4	13.9	5.2	100.0
Philadelphia and adjacent area	31.1	25.2	19.2	15.1	8.6	0.8	100.0
Washington and adjacent area	52.4	15.4	24.9	3.7	3.3	0.3	100.0
Chicago and adjacent area	71.6	9.4	8.0	6.2	3.8	1.0	100.0
Detroit and adjacent area	55.4	18.7	12.9	7.6	4.5	0.9	100.0
St. Louis and adjacent area	59.4	16.7	12.9	5.5	4.7	0.8	100.0
Atlanta and adjacent area	62.3	7.8	12.5	11.1	6.0	0.3	100.0
Birmingham	54.2	21.1	15.8	5.2	3.7	0.0	100.0
New Orleans	39.1	31.1	17.5	9.4	2.8	0.1	100.0
Houston and adjacent area	53.6	13.3	10.5	15.0	6.9	0.7	100.0
San Francisco							
Negro population	0.2	25.7	40.6	20.6	12.1	0.8	100.0
Other nonwhite population	26.8	15.8	27.2	11.7	16.1	2.4	100.0
Los Angeles and adjacent area							
Negro population	45.9	16.5	17.6	10.9	7.7	1.4	100.0
Other nonwhite population	4.1	10.4	15.5	23.1	36.6	10.3	100.0
	DISTRIBUTION OF TOTAL WHITE POPULATION						
New York	0.3	1.0	2.4	5.1	25.3	65.9	100.0
Manhattan	0.3	1.4	2.9	9.6	48.9	36.9	100.0
Brooklyn	0.5	1.0	2.3	4.7	18.4	73.1	100.0
Bronx	0.2	1.0	3.4	4.7	23.9	66.8	100.0
Queens	0.1	0.7	1.2	1.7	12.3	84.0	100.0
Philadelphia and adjacent area	0.7	2.0	5.2	12.3	29.2	50.6	100.0
Washington and adjacent area	4.8	4.5	18.9	9.1	35.0	27.7	100.0
Chicago and adjacent area	0.4	0.8	1.8	4.0	16.4	76.6	100.0
Detroit and adjacent area	0.8	1.6	3.4	5.8	17.2	71.2	100.0
St. Louis and adjacent area	0.9	1.8	3.5	4.5	22.9	66.4	100.0
Atlanta and adjacent area	1.3	1.5	9.0	18.4	48.9	20.9	100.0
Birmingham	3.8	7.8	16.8	20.1	41.0	10.5	100.0
New Orleans	2.2	8.5	15.6	20.5	33.8	19.4	100.0
Houston and adjacent area	1.1	1.8	4.8	17.4	38.4	36.5	100.0
San Francisco	0.2	1.4	7.9	8.7	44.7	37.1	100.0
Los Angeles and adjacent area	0.4	0.6	2.3	5.0	28.1	63.6	100.0

TABLE A-1—Continued

City	Census tracts with specified percent of tract population nonwhite in 1950						
	75+	50-74	25-49	10-24	1-9	Less than 1	All tracts
	PERCENT OF DWELLING UNITS IN STRUCTURES BUILT 1940 OR LATER						
New York	2.4	3.9	9.6	14.0	7.5	8.8	8.4
Manhattan	3.6	0.0	12.4	13.6	3.8	7.7	6.0
Brooklyn	0.0	11.2	16.9	13.5	5.0	4.7	5.6
Bronx	0.0	0.0	0.0	16.5	5.3	8.8	7.7
Queens	2.0	1.3	0.3	11.4	32.3	14.9	16.4
Philadelphia and adjacent area	3.6	4.7	4.7	8.9	13.2	17.9	13.4
Washington and adjacent area	25.5	16.9	17.3	11.0	31.2	47.6	28.3
Chicago and adjacent area	7.9	6.9	2.4	6.7	8.7	12.0	10.6
Detroit and adjacent area	8.4	12.0	7.1	1.2	9.4	34.9	25.3
St. Louis and adjacent area	5.6	1.2	4.9	8.5	14.2	15.2	12.9
Atlanta and adjacent area	12.6	14.2	34.6	35.6	30.6	24.0	27.2
Birmingham	11.0	17.9	21.0	21.7	19.0	33.7	18.8
New Orleans	12.6	20.5	27.3	12.3	9.8	29.5	17.6
Houston and adjacent area	28.8	49.9	29.6	42.7	41.3	50.6	42.7
San Francisco	0.2	3.2	25.6	13.7	6.8	21.9	14.1
Los Angeles and adjacent area	16.8	7.9	26.2	19.3	26.9	39.5	33.8
	PERCENT OF DWELLING UNITS IN STRUCTURES BUILT 1919 OR EARLIER						
New York	84.6	76.6	74.6	65.9	60.4	38.2	49.1
Manhattan	84.8	93.6	76.3	74.5	72.9	59.5	70.6
Brooklyn	93.7	76.7	76.5	71.3	60.6	48.0	54.8
Bronx	73.7	83.3	84.7	51.7	50.7	26.5	37.6
Queens	22.7	27.8	45.1	25.2	22.3	22.8	23.3
Philadelphia and adjacent area	89.5	88.2	84.1	71.2	63.2	47.6	60.9
Washington and adjacent area	54.3	51.2	52.9	55.3	18.3	6.3	33.9
Chicago and adjacent area	77.3	67.9	75.3	69.7	62.9	48.1	54.3
Detroit and adjacent area	64.5	50.5	52.9	66.3	49.8	13.8	28.6
St. Louis and adjacent area	76.5	87.6	67.5	65.5	55.8	46.4	54.1
Atlanta and adjacent area	50.8	55.1	23.9	30.3	28.0	25.7	32.2
Birmingham	48.8	45.0	38.7	34.0	37.3	18.1	39.2
New Orleans	56.6	55.0	46.8	67.8	61.0	28.9	54.1
Houston and adjacent area	19.0	16.5	33.2	13.0	12.1	6.5	12.6
San Francisco	62.8	74.7	50.8	63.0	59.8	31.8	50.0
Los Angeles and adjacent area	34.7	38.7	34.5	33.2	25.7	10.4	17.4

TABLE A-1—Continued

City	Census tracts with specified percent of tract population nonwhite in 1950						
	75+	50-74	25-49	10-24	1-9	Less than 1	All tracts
	PERCENT OF DWELLING UNITS SUBSTANDARD[a]						
New York	28.8	20.6	15.8	14.5	14.4	5.2	9.6
Manhattan	31.5	30.6	26.1	20.5	19.1	11.3	18.5
Brooklyn	27.9	21.8	13.8	13.2	12.2	5.3	8.4
Bronx	15.0	13.3	7.5	6.6	8.4	2.5	4.7
Queens	10.1	5.9	15.6	7.1	11.6	3.3	4.7
Philadelphia and adjacent area	40.1	28.0	22.7	17.0	12.4	6.2	12.9
Washington and adjacent area	23.4	19.3	16.3	14.4	3.1	1.9	10.9
Chicago and adjacent area	54.4	42.6	42.6	29.5	24.7	9.6	17.4
Detroit and adjacent area	24.3	25.2	13.6	13.4	12.3	5.2	9.0
St. Louis and adjacent area	65.3	50.0	37.2	47.9	25.5	16.4	25.8
Atlanta and adjacent area	57.7	60.5	44.6	36.6	18.4	15.6	30.8
Birmingham	68.1	61.4	42.8	28.6	16.7	10.2	38.5
New Orleans	52.2	38.3	36.2	21.5	12.5	4.1	25.7
Houston and adjacent area	34.4	49.0	42.0	30.5	12.8	11.0	20.3
San Francisco	67.1	42.3	15.8	16.6	9.1	2.6	10.2
Los Angeles and adjacent area	18.9	23.2	17.6	15.1	12.0	5.2	8.4
	PERCENT OF NONWHITE-OCCUPIED DWELLING UNITS SUBSTANDARD[b]						
New York	29.3	25.5	22.4	24.4	29.1	*	27.3
Manhattan	31.4	34.5	31.8	23.3	35.3	*	31.2
Brooklyn	30.0	31.2	23.9	29.4	31.2	*	29.1
Bronx	12.8	14.4	9.7	15.3	15.9	*	12.8
Queens	9.8	7.2	19.7	33.3	0.7	*	12.4
Philadelphia and adjacent area	42.3	34.8	37.4	38.9	38.7	*	38.7
Washington and adjacent area	27.2	24.3	27.9	36.2	16.1	*	27.0
Chicago and adjacent area	54.9	53.7	60.2	53.9	56.3	*	55.2
Detroit and adjacent area	25.6	31.2	20.3	18.8	23.9	*	25.4
St. Louis and adjacent area	66.3	57.9	57.0	75.8	54.7	*	63.9
Atlanta and adjacent area	58.7	78.2	76.2	81.8	84.7	*	65.6
Birmingham	71.9	78.9	79.6	84.6	75.5	*	75.3
New Orleans	55.7	53.0	68.4	64.4	59.3	*	58.0
Houston and adjacent area	35.0	57.2	63.5	65.8	47.6	*	46.3
San Francisco	70.3	45.2	19.5	19.3	20.0	*	34.6
Los Angeles and adjacent area	17.8	20.8	17.7	15.8	19.9	*	18.1

TABLE A-1—Continued

| City | Census tracts with specified percent of tract population nonwhite in 1950 | | | | | | |
	75+	50-74	25-49	10-24	1-9	Less than 1	All tracts
	PERCENT OF NONWHITE-OCCUPIED DWELLING UNITS WITH MORE THAN 1.01 PERSONS PER ROOM[b]						
New York	22.9	24.3	24.8	25.2	26.9	*	23.7
Manhattan	21.7	24.9	22.2	22.2	25.1	*	22.2
Brooklyn	26.8	28.0	28.3	30.1	29.1	*	27.8
Bronx	24.8	22.4	24.4	25.5	26.5	*	24.2
Queens	15.3	17.5	21.2	21.3	29.2	*	18.8
Philadelphia and adjacent area	23.3	21.4	21.2	20.1	22.4	*	21.9
Washington and adjacent area	29.0	24.7	28.0	31.8	29.3	*	28.1
Chicago and adjacent area	37.8	35.5	38.9	34.9	31.5	*	37.4
Detroit and adjacent area	24.5	29.8	24.1	21.9	23.6	*	25.2
St. Louis and adjacent area	35.6	35.1	30.8	33.8	28.5	*	34.6
Atlanta and adjacent area	37.7	42.8	40.6	42.7	42.7	*	39.1
Birmingham	39.0	41.7	37.6	34.6	30.8	*	38.8
New Orleans	38.7	38.4	38.5	37.3	36.4	*	38.4
Houston and adjacent area	24.2	26.7	27.3	30.4	26.5	*	25.9
San Francisco	33.7	26.9	30.5	29.0	25.3	*	29.7
Los Angeles and adjacent area	19.2	23.3	24.7	25.6	26.4	*	22.2
	PERCENT OF NONWHITE MARRIED COUPLES WITHOUT OWN HOUSEHOLD[b]						
New York	25.5	21.4	16.6	15.4	12.6	*	22.3
Manhattan	26.9	23.6	14.8	14.7	13.6	*	24.4
Brooklyn	21.7	20.6	14.3	13.2	13.1	*	18.9
Bronx	24.7	18.7	19.7	18.4	13.6	*	20.6
Queens	26.7	21.9	21.7	21.1	2.4	*	22.4
Philadelphia and adjacent area	13.9	14.0	13.8	17.1	18.7	*	14.6
Washington and adjacent area	26.5	26.3	28.7	27.2	17.8	*	26.9
Chicago and adjacent area	22.0	20.8	19.6	20.0	27.3	*	21.7
Detroit and adjacent area	29.4	25.7	27.2	25.4	21.4	*	27.8
St. Louis and adjacent area	15.6	14.7	15.8	14.2	15.1	*	15.4
Atlanta and adjacent area	18.1	14.8	15.6	13.7	16.7	*	17.0
Birmingham	14.0	12.7	12.5	15.0	9.0	*	13.4
New Orleans	14.5	13.6	15.4	17.7	15.2	*	14.7
Houston and adjacent area	12.8	11.5	8.2	9.8	13.3	*	11.7
San Francisco	5.5	21.9	13.4	14.7	14.4	*	15.0
Los Angeles and adjacent area	17.9	19.1	15.9	13.2	14.8	*	16.8

SOURCE: *U. S. Census of Population: 1950,* Vol. III, *Census Tract Statistics,* chapters for the respective cities.

[a] Units dilapidated or lacking private bath or toilet.

[b] Based on data for census tracts containing 250 or more nonwhites.

TABLE A-2

RESIDENTIAL CONCENTRATION OF NONWHITES IN SELECTED CITIES,
BY CENSUS TRACTS, 1940 AND 1950, AND CITY OF LOS ANGELES, 1956

City[a] and year	Census tracts with specified percent of tract population nonwhite[b]						
	75+	50-74	25-49	10-24	1-9	Less than 1	All tracts
	PERCENT DISTRIBUTION OF CITY NONWHITE POPULATION						
New York (all boroughs) 1940	49.2	12.3	14.3	10.9	9.8	3.5	100.0
1950	53.4	14.8	12.7	9.4	7.8	1.9	100.0
Number of tracts 1940-1950	(33-69)	(25-41)	(49-60)	(70-91)	(459-457)	(1652-1570)	(2288-2288)
Manhattan 1940	70.3	11.1	7.2	5.4	4.7	1.3	100.0
1950	69.0	10.0	6.4	8.3	5.4	0.9	100.0
Number of tracts 1940-1950	(27-35)	(11-9)	(10-9)	(11-22)	(88-105)	(126-93)	(273-273)
Brooklyn 1940	11.6	17.8	32.3	15.7	17.8	4.8	100.0
1950	44.6	17.0	16.6	10.3	8.9	2.6	100.0
Number of tracts 1940-1950	(4-21)	(7-13)	(27-21)	(25-31)	(175-148)	(593-597)	(831-831)
Bronx 1940	0.0	3.1	4.4	49.1	22.8	20.6	100.0
1950	28.1	22.9	25.2	11.5	9.2	3.1	100.0
Number of tracts 1940-1950	(0-4)	(3-5)	(2-13)	(14-14)	(58-84)	(320-277)	(397-397)
Queens 1940	10.6	13.2	31.1	21.2	16.5	7.4	100.0
1950	22.5	29.2	20.8	8.4	13.9	5.2	100.0
Number of tracts 1940-1950	(2-9)	(4-14)	(9-15)	(18-19)	(104-80)	(538-538)	(675-675)
Philadelphia 1940	18.7	35.6	20.6	16.1	8.4	0.6	100.0
1950	37.4	28.0	18.8	10.6	4.7	0.5	100.0
Number of tracts 1940-1950	(6-18)	(20-23)	(26-32)	(42-31)	(112-74)	(172-200)	(378-378)
Washington, D.C. 1940	37.3	22.7	21.8	14.1	3.9	0.2	100.0
1950	51.8	15.7	25.4	3.8	3.1	0.2	100.0
Number of tracts 1940-1950	(11-19)	(8-9)	(17-22)	(18-11)	(33-27)	(9-8)	(96-96)
Chicago 1940	85.6	3.2	4.2	2.7	2.9	1.4	100.0
1950	76.2	8.0	6.8	5.0	3.2	0.8	100.0
Number of tracts 1940-1950	(68-97)	(9-17)	(16-29)	(17-34)	(84-131)	(714-600)	(908-908)
Detroit area 1940	41.0	24.9	15.9	9.0	7.6	1.6	100.0
1950	55.7	18.8	12.9	7.3	4.5	0.8	100.0
Number of tracts 1940-1950	(17-43)	(18-19)	(18-27)	(19-35)	(86-86)	(326-274)	(484-484)
St. Louis area 1940	58.9	8.8	15.6	9.4	6.5	0.8	100.0
1950	59.4	16.7	12.9	5.5	4.7	0.8	100.0
Number of tracts 1940-1950	(11-14)	(2-8)	(11-12)	(26-11)	(67-59)	(130-143)	(247-247)
Atlanta area 1940	59.7	5.1	13.3	15.7	6.1	0.1	100.0
1950	62.3	7.8	12.5	11.1	6.0	0.3	100.0
Number of tracts 1940-1950	(17-18)	(2-4)	(7-7)	(34-18)	(41-43)	(10-21)	(111-111)
Birmingham 1940	58.6	21.6	8.4	7.3	4.1	0.0	100.0
1950	54.3	21.1	15.9	5.0	3.7	0.0	100.0
Number of tracts 1940-1950	(15-14)	(7-8)	(6-9)	(13-9)	(13-11)	(2-5)	(56-56)
New Orleans 1940	35.7	35.2	14.4	10.7	3.9	0.1	100.0
1950	39.1	31.1	17.5	9.4	2.8	0.1	100.0
Number of tracts 1940-1950	(15-16)	(19-17)	(25-22)	(30-31)	(39-35)	(14-21)	(142-142)
Houston 1940	57.4	19.5	2.6	11.0	9.3	0.2	100.0
1950	66.6	7.9	7.5	9.8	7.6	0.6	100.0
Number of tracts 1940-1950	(8-7)	(5-1)	(1-4)	(8-9)	(30-25)	(5-11)	(57-57)
San Francisco Negro population: 1940	1.2	0.0	35.5	22.1	34.3	7.9	100.0
1950	0.2	25.7	40.6	20.6	12.1	0.8	100.0

TABLE A-2—Continued

City[a] and year		Census tracts with specified percent of tract population nonwhite[b]						
		75+	50-74	25-49	10-24	1-9	Less than 1	All tracts
		PERCENT DISTRIBUTION OF CITY NONWHITE POPULATION						
Other nonwhites:	1940	47.4	0.0	24.8	9.4	14.3	4.1	100.0
	1950	26.8	15.8	27.2	11.7	16.1	2.4	100.0
Number of tracts 1940-1950		(3-3)	(0-5)	(5-9)	(5-11)	(37-55)	(66-33)	(116-116)
Los Angeles area								
Negro population:	1940	26.5	28.2	14.7	14.5	14.0	2.1	100.0
	1950	45.9	16.5	17.6	10.9	7.7	1.4	100.0
Other nonwhites:	1940	2.4	7.2	16.9	19.2	45.0	9.3	100.0
	1950	4.1	10.4	15.5	23.1	36.6	10.3	100.0
Number of tracts 1940-1950		(5-22)	(9-11)	(13-29)	(35-48)	(332-214)	(370-440)	(764-764)
Los Angeles City								
Negro population:	1950	51.2	16.2	16.5	10.4	4.8	0.9	100.0
	1956	38.7	34.4	16.6	6.8	3.0	0.5	100.0
Other nonwhites:	1950	5.3	13.0	17.8	28.7	29.4	5.8	100.0
	1956	10.5	15.5	24.4	20.2	24.8	4.6	100.0
Number of tracts 1950-1956		(20-26)	(9-33)	(21-30)	(34-35)	(120-111)	(159-128)	(363-363)

SOURCES: *U. S. Census of Population: 1950*, Vol. III, *Census Tract Statistics*, chapters for the respective cities. *Sixteenth Census of the U. S., 1940, Population and Housing Statistics for Census Tracts*, for the respective cities except New York. Welfare Council of New York City, *Census Tract Data on Population and Housing, New York City: 1940* (1942). U. S. Bureau of the Census, *Current Population Reports*, Series P-28, no. 927, "Special Census of Los Angeles, California: February 25, 1956."

[a] For Chicago, Philadelphia, San Francisco, Washington, D. C., New York City, and New Orleans, only census tracts within the cities proper are included. For Atlanta, St. Louis, and Detroit, data refer to census tracts both within the cities and in adjacent tracted areas. For Birmingham and Houston, only census tracts included within the 1940 city boundaries are compared. For Los Angeles, 1940-1950 data refer to the city and adjacent tracted area; 1950-1956 data are for the city only.

[b] The census tracts are those identified by the 1950 Census. The first figure within each set of parentheses is the number of tracts in 1940; the second figure is the number of tracts in 1950. Where census tract boundaries were changed between 1940 and 1950 or new tracts came into existence, the tracts were consolidated for the purpose of recording the 1940 data within the 1950 system of census tracts. Tracts containing an area newly tracted after 1940 were treated as if comparable with the 1940 tract unless the 1950 tract consisted entirely of newly tracted area, in which case it was eliminated from the table. Tracts with fewer than fifty persons in 1950 were not included in the table, except for Los Angeles, 1950-1956.

TABLE A-3

POPULATION CHANGES IN THE CITY OF LOS ANGELES, 1950-1956, BY RACE, IN CENSUS TRACTS CLASSIFIED BY PERCENT OF POPULATION NONWHITE IN 1950

Subject	Census tracts with specified percent of population nonwhite, 1950						
	75 and over	50-74	25-49	10-24	1-9	Less than 1	All tracts
Population increase, 1950-1956	−11,806	−8,414	−17,992	−18,008	102,334	227,429	273,543
Percent increase	−11.7	−16.4	−17.9	−9.7	16.4	25.0	13.9
Negro population increase	−6,089	−228	12,706	23,106	36,104	17,787	83,386
Percent increase	−6.9	−0.8	44.8	130.3	438.3	1,139.5	48.7
"Other nonwhite" population increase	−635	−556	348	1,931	9,881	5,456	16,425
Percent increase	−29.8	−10.6	4.8	16.6	83.2	233.2	40.7
Percent distribution of negro increase	−7.3	−0.3	15.3	27.7	43.3	21.3	100.0
Percent distribution of "other nonwhite" increase	−3.8	−3.3	2.1	11.7	60.1	33.2	100.0

SOURCE: U. S. Bureau of the Census, *Current Population Reports*, Series P-28, no. 927, "Special Census of Los Angeles, California: February 25, 1956."

TABLE A-4

COMPARATIVE OCCUPATIONAL DISTRIBUTIONS OF EMPLOYED WORKERS BY RACE (EXCEPT NEGRO) AND SEX: UNITED STATES, 1950

Occupation group and sex	Percent distributions by race[a]						
	Chinese	Japanese	Filipino	Indian	Spanish-name white[b]	Puerto Rican[c]	Total white
Male	100.0	100.0	100.0	100.0	100.0	100.0	100.0
Professional, technical	6.3	6.4	1.7	2.4	2.1	5.2	7.8
Proprietors, managers, officials[d]	22.2	8.6	1.6	1.8	4.4	5.3	11.6
Clerical and sales	11.2	9.1	3.2	3.0	6.4	9.5	13.7
Craftsmen, foremen	3.2	7.7	4.3	10.3	13.0	11.0	19.7
Operatives	16.4	9.7	9.7	12.3	18.8	32.5	20.0
Service workers	34.3	11.7	30.2	3.6	6.3	24.9	5.2
Nonfarm laborers	1.9	13.5	3.0	16.7	18.5	7.2	6.6
Farmers and farm workers	3.0	32.1	40.7	43.9	29.4	2.9	14.2
Female	100.0	100.0	100.0	100.0	100.0	100.0	100.0
Professional, technical	11.0	7.4	11.2	5.2	4.6	3.4	13.3
Proprietors, managers, officials[d]	7.9	3.7	4.3	1.4	3.9	1.2	4.7
Clerical and sales	38.8	27.3	24.5	8.9	24.0	10.9	39.9
Craftsmen, foremen	0.5	0.9	0.9	1.6	1.4	1.7	1.6
Operatives	20.7	19.8	20.6	25.6	28.1	71.7	19.8
Service workers	17.6	21.7	26.5	32.7	27.7	8.7	15.3
Nonfarm laborers	0.6	1.0	1.2	1.0	1.4	1.0	0.7
Farmers and farm workers	0.7	16.4	7.5	15.9	6.5	0.4	2.8

SOURCE: *U. S. Census of Population: 1950*, Vol. II, *Characteristics of the Population*, Part 1, "U. S. Summary;" Vol. IV, *Special Reports*, Part 3, chap. B, "Nonwhite Population by Race," chap. C, "Persons of Spanish Surname," chap. D, "Puerto Ricans in Continental United States."

[a] Percents do not add to 100 because of omission of the "occupation not reported" category.

[b] In the five states of Texas, Colorado, New Mexico, Arizona, California.

[c] Persons of Puerto Rican birth or parentage in the continental United States.

[d] Except farmers and farm managers.

TABLE A-5

Condition and Plumbing Facilities of Dwelling Units by Color and Tenure
of Occupants, for the United States, Urban and Rural, and
Selected Standard Metropolitan Areas, 1950
(percent distributions)

		Not dilapidated			
Area and color of occupants	Total dwelling units	With private toilet, bath, and hot running water	Lacking private toilet, bath, or hot water	No running water	Dilapidated
		OWNER-OCCUPIED DWELLING UNITS			
United States total					
White	100.0	71.3	12.9	10.8	4.9
Nonwhite	100.0	31.6	16.9	27.0	24.5
Urban					
White	100.0	87.6	8.4	1.4	2.7
Nonwhite	100.0	47.8	22.4	12.0	17.9
Rural nonfarm					
White	100.0	55.5	19.9	17.7	7.0
Nonwhite	100.0	7.5	10.6	48.0	34.0
Rural farm					
White	100.0	31.4	20.6	37.5	10.5
Nonwhite	100.0	3.7	4.9	54.7	36.8
Standard metropolitan areas					
New York					
White	100.0	95.4	3.1	0.2	1.3
Nonwhite	100.0	84.6	7.2	1.0	7.2
Philadelphia					
White	100.0	95.5	4.2	0.8	1.2
Nonwhite	100.0	81.1	10.2	2.3	6.4
Washington, D. C.					
White	100.0	93.1	3.7	2.0	1.2
Nonwhite	100.0	76.1	7.2	8.6	8.0
Detroit					
White	100.0	92.5	4.7	1.3	1.5
Nonwhite	100.0	84.2	7.1	1.2	7.5
St. Louis					
White	100.0	82.4	11.8	2.8	3.0
Nonwhite	100.0	41.4	30.0	8.2	20.5
Chicago					
White	100.0	89.8	7.0	1.3	1.9
Nonwhite	100.0	65.7	16.1	3.1	15.2
Birmingham[a]					
White	100.0	76.1	15.7	4.5	3.6
Nonwhite	100.0	20.9	40.1	20.8	18.3

TABLE A-5—Continued

| Area and color of occupants | Total dwelling units | Not dilapidated | | | Dilapi-dated |
		With private toilet, bath, and hot running water	Lacking private toilet, bath, or hot water	No running water	
New Orleans[a]					
White	100.0	82.6	12.1	1.1	4.2
Nonwhite	100.0	29.4	35.9	9.4	25.3
Houston[a]					
White	100.0	87.9	7.4	2.0	2.8
Nonwhite	100.0	39.0	26.8	19.2	15.0
San Francisco-Oakland					
White	100.0	96.6	1.9	0.1	1.5
Nonwhite	100.0	89.3	4.5	0.2	6.0
Los Angeles					
White	100.0	95.0	3.2	0.2	1.6
Nonwhite	100.0	92.6	2.1	0.2	5.1
		RENTER-OCCUPIED DWELLING UNITS			
United States total					
White	100.0	64.0	18.3	8.5	9.2
Nonwhite	100.0	24.2	19.1	18.6	38.1
Urban					
White	100.0	75.3	17.4	1.1	6.2
Nonwhite	100.0	34.4	25.7	7.7	32.1
Rural nonfarm					
White	100.0	39.0	22.4	22.1	16.5
Nonwhite	100.0	4.1	7.3	37.2	51.3
Rural farm					
White	100.0	17.4	18.0	44.3	20.2
Nonwhite	100.0	1.0	2.9	45.6	50.6
Standard metropolitan areas					
New York					
White	100.0	87.5	8.3	0.1	4.1
Nonwhite	100.0	63.6	14.5	0.2	21.6
Philadelphia					
White	100.0	82.5	12.7	1.2	3.6
Nonwhite	100.0	45.6	30.3	1.2	22.9
Washington, D. C.					
White	100.0	91.0	5.9	1.1	1.9
Nonwhite	100.0	61.2	17.6	4.1	17.1
Detroit					
White	100.0	84.5	10.1	1.0	4.3
Nonwhite	100.0	63.4	15.0	0.6	21.0

TABLE A-5—Continued

| Area and color of occupants | Total dwelling units | Not dilapidated | | | Dilapi- dated |
		With private toilet, bath, and hot running water	Lacking private toilet, bath, or hot water	No running water	
St. Louis					
White	100.0	59.1	30.4	1.9	8.6
Nonwhite	100.0	18.7	38.9	2.9	39.5
Chicago					
White	100.0	76.7	18.2	0.5	4.6
Nonwhite	100.0	38.0	37.4	0.7	23.9
Birmingham[a]					
White	100.0	57.1	27.4	5.4	10.2
Nonwhite	100.0	7.1	40.1	16.5	36.3
New Orleans[a]					
White	100.0	70.8	19.9	0.6	8.7
Nonwhite	100.0	13.3	38.3	7.6	40.8
Houston[a]					
White	100.0	76.9	14.1	1.7	7.3
Nonwhite	100.0	28.0	43.0	7.1	21.9
San Francisco-Oakland					
White	100.0	87.9	8.1	0.2	3.9
Nonwhite	100.0	69.4	20.6	0.3	9.7
Los Angeles					
White	100.0	88.3	6.9	0.4	4.5
Nonwhite	100.0	72.9	12.1	0.9	14.1

SOURCES: *U. S. Census of Housing: 1950*, Vol. I, *General Characteristics*, chap. 1, "U. S. Summary," table 7, and chap. 9, "District of Columbia," table 7; U. S. Bureau of the Census, "Selected Characteristics of Dwelling Units Occupied by Nonwhite Persons, for Selected Standard Metropolitan Areas: 1950" (unpublished table); unpublished special tabulations of 1950 Housing Census data supplied by the Bureau of the Census.

[a] Nonfarm dwelling units only, based on a 20 percent sample of dwelling units.

TABLE A-6

MEDIAN NUMBER OF ROOMS IN RENTER-OCCUPIED DWELLING UNITS BY INCOME
AND COLOR OF OCCUPANTS, FOR SELECTED METROPOLITAN AREAS, 1950

Standard metropolitan areas and color of occupants	Total report-ing	Income of primary families and individuals					
		Less than $2,000	$2,000-2,999	$3,000-3,999	$4,000-4,999	$5,000-6,999	$7,000 and more
New York							
White	3.8	3.5	3.7	3.8	3.8	3.9	4.2
Nonwhite	3.9	3.8	3.9	4.0	4.1	4.4	4.6
Detroit							
White	4.2	3.6	3.7	4.2	4.4	4.5	4.9
Nonwhite	4.2	4.0	4.1	4.2	4.5	4.8	5.0
Chicago							
White	4.0	3.4	3.7	4.0	4.1	4.2	4.7
Nonwhite	3.0	2.4	2.9	3.4	3.6	4.0	4.5
Los Angeles							
White	3.3	2.8	3.1	3.4	3.6	3.7	4.3
Nonwhite	3.3	3.1	3.3	3.5	3.6	3.9	4.4
St. Louis							
White	3.3	2.9	3.2	3.5	3.6	4.0	4.6
Nonwhite	2.9	2.7	3.0	3.1	3.4	3.4	3.7
New Orleans							
White	3.8	3.0	3.7	3.9	4.1	4.3	5.0
Nonwhite	2.8	2.7	3.1	3.4	3.8	4.1	4.3
Houston							
White	3.6	3.0	3.3	3.7	3.9	4.1	4.6
Nonwhite	3.3	3.2	3.5	3.6	3.8	4.1	3.6
Birmingham							
White	3.6	3.1	3.4	3.6	3.9	4.1	4.5
Nonwhite	2.9	2.8	3.0	3.1	3.2	3.0	3.1

SOURCE: *U. S. Census of Housing: 1950*, Vol. II, *Nonfarm Housing Characteristics*, chapters for the respective standard metropolitan areas, tables A-5, and unpublished special tabulations of the 1950 Housing Census supplied to the Commission on Race and Housing by the Bureau of the Census. Data are based on a 20 percent sample of dwelling units, hence are subject to sampling variability.

TABLE A-7

Median Number of Rooms in Owner-occupied Dwelling Units by Income
and Color of Occupants, for Selected Metropolitan Areas, 1950[a]

Standard metropolitan area and color of occupants	Total report-ing	Income of primary families and individuals					
		Less than $2,000	$2,000-2,999	$3,000-3,999	$4,000-4,999	$5,000-6,999	$7,000 and more
New York							
White	5.8	5.4	5.3	5.4	5.6	5.8	6.5
Nonwhite	5.6	5.4	5.4	5.6	5.8	6.0	6.4
Detroit							
White	5.3	5.3	5.1	5.1	5.2	5.4	6.0
Nonwhite	5.8	5.7	5.7	5.7	5.9	5.9	6.3
Chicago							
White	5.3	5.2	5.0	5.1	5.2	5.4	6.0
Nonwhite	5.2	5.1	5.1	5.2	5.3	5.4	5.7
Los Angeles							
White	5.1	4.7	4.8	4.9	5.0	5.3	6.0
Nonwhite	5.1	5.0	5.0	5.1	5.1	5.3	5.8
St. Louis							
White	4.8	4.4	4.4	4.6	4.8	5.0	5.9
Nonwhite	4.2	4.0	4.2	4.3	4.7	5.0	6.0
New Orleans							
White	4.9	4.4	4.4	4.7	4.9	5.2	6.2
Nonwhite	4.1	3.6	4.1	4.3	5.0	5.1	6.1
Houston							
White	5.0	4.6	4.6	4.8	4.9	5.2	6.0
Nonwhite	4.6	4.4	4.6	4.9	4.9	5.2	6.1
Birmingham							
White	5.3	4.8	4.9	5.1	5.4	5.7	6.3
Nonwhite	4.4	4.1	4.4	4.9	5.2	6.0	5.9

Source: *U. S. Census of Housing: 1950*, Vol. II, *Nonfarm Housing Characteristics*, chapters for the respective standard metropolitan areas, tables A-5, and unpublished special tabulations of the 1950 Housing Census supplied to the Commission on Race and Housing by the Bureau of the Census. Data are based on a 20 percent sample of dwelling units, hence are subject to sampling variability.

[a] Data refer to total owner-occupied dwelling units.

TABLE A-8

MEDIAN NUMBER OF PERSONS IN RENTER-OCCUPIED DWELLING UNITS BY INCOME
AND COLOR OF OCCUPANTS, FOR SELECTED METROPOLITAN AREAS, 1950

Standard metropolitan area and color of occupants	Total report-ing	Income of primary families and individuals					
		Less than $2,000	$2,000-2,999	$3,000-3,999	$4,000-4,999	$5,000-6,999	$7,000 and more
New York							
White	2.9	2.2	2.8	3.1	3.1	3.1	3.2
Nonwhite	3.1	2.7	3.3	3.4	3.4	3.7	4.0
Chicago							
White	2.7	2.0	2.5	3.0	3.0	2.9	3.1
Nonwhite	2.8	2.4	3.0	3.2	3.4	3.6	4.5
Detroit							
White	2.7	2.2	2.6	2.9	2.9	2.7	2.9
Nonwhite	3.4	3.1	3.5	3.5	3.4	4.0	4.4
Los Angeles							
White	2.2	1.8	2.3	2.5	2.6	2.4	2.4
Nonwhite	2.7	2.4	2.9	3.0	3.0	3.2	3.6
St. Louis							
White	2.7	2.1	2.8	3.0	2.9	2.8	3.0
Nonwhite	2.8	2.5	3.1	3.4	3.5	3.7	2.9
New Orleans							
White	2.8	2.2	3.0	3.1	3.1	3.2	3.2
Nonwhite	2.8	2.5	3.4	3.6	4.6	4.4	4.5
Houston							
White	2.7	2.3	2.8	2.9	2.9	2.6	2.6
Nonwhite	2.9	2.5	3.2	3.2	3.7	3.8	3.3
Birmingham							
White	2.9	2.5	3.1	3.1	3.0	3.0	2.7
Nonwhite	3.2	2.8	3.6	4.5	4.7	4.2	4.5

SOURCE: *U. S. Census of Housing: 1950*, Vol. II, *Nonfarm Housing Characteristics*, chapters for the respective standard metropolitan areas, tables A-4, and unpublished special tabulations of the 1950 Housing Census supplied to the Commission on Race and Housing by the Bureau of the Census. Data are based on a 20 percent sample of dwelling units, hence are subject to sampling variability.

TABLE A-9

MEDIAN NUMBER OF PERSONS IN OWNER-OCCUPIED DWELLING UNITS BY INCOME
AND COLOR, FOR SELECTED METROPOLITAN AREAS, 1950[a]

Standard metropolitan area and color of owner	Total report- ing	Income of primary families and individuals					
		Less than $2,000	$2,000- 2,999	$3,000- 3,999	$4,000- 4,999	$5,000- 6,999	$7,000 and more
New York							
White	3.5	2.4	3.1	3.5	3.6	3.7	4.0
Nonwhite	3.7	3.2	3.7	3.9	4.2	4.1	4.7
Chicago							
White	3.4	2.3	2.8	3.4	3.5	3.6	4.0
Nonwhite	3.7	3.1	3.7	3.9	3.9	4.1	4.3
Detroit							
White	3.5	2.4	3.1	3.4	3.6	3.6	4.1
Nonwhite	4.0	3.6	4.0	4.1	4.1	4.3	4.9
Los Angeles							
White	3.0	2.1	2.8	3.2	3.3	3.3	3.4
Nonwhite	3.4	2.9	3.3	3.6	3.7	3.8	4.7
St. Louis							
White	3.2	2.2	2.9	3.3	3.4	3.4	3.8
Nonwhite	3.3	2.9	3.6	3.6	4.2	3.8	4.4
New Orleans							
White	3.2	2.4	3.1	3.4	3.4	3.7	3.7
Nonwhite	3.4	2.9	4.0	3.8	4.3	4.7	4.4
Houston							
White	3.2	2.4	3.2	3.4	3.4	3.3	3.4
Nonwhite	3.3	2.7	3.2	3.3	3.7	3.6	3.3
Birmingham							
White	3.3	2.5	3.3	3.4	3.5	3.5	3.6
Nonwhite	3.4	2.9	3.8	4.2	4.5	4.2	5.7

SOURCE: *U. S. Census of Housing: 1950,* Vol. II, *Nonfarm Housing Characteristics,*
chapters for the respective standard metropolitan areas, tables A-7, and unpublished
special tabulations of the 1950 Housing Census supplied to the Commission on Race and
Housing by the Bureau of the Census. Data are based on a 20 percent sample of dwelling
units, hence are subject to sampling variability.

[a] Data refer to total owner-occupied dwelling units.

TABLE A-10

MEDIAN GROSS RENT OF RENTER-OCCUPIED DWELLING UNITS BY INCOME AND
COLOR OF OCCUPANTS, FOR SELECTED METROPOLITAN AREAS, 1950
(Medians rounded to nearest dollar)

Standard metropolitan area and color of occupants	Total report-ing	Income of primary families and individuals					
		Less than $2,000	$2,000- 2,999	$3,000- 3,999	$4,000- 4,999	$5,000- 6,999	$7,000 and more
New York							
White	$49	$42	$45	$48	$52	$57	$74
Nonwhite	42	39	42	44	46	48	54
Chicago							
White	50	42	44	47	50	54	67
Nonwhite	43	38	44	47	50	53	56
Detroit							
White	50	45	46	49	52	54	64
Nonwhite	46	44	45	47	49	52	55
Los Angeles							
White	45	37	42	46	49	55	71
Nonwhite	39	36	39	43	44	48	46
St. Louis							
White	40	32	36	41	44	48	67
Nonwhite	29	27	31	33	38	39	42
New Orleans							
White	34	27	32	34	38	46	60
Nonwhite	21	20	23	25	27	28	31
Houston							
White	47	37	43	47	52	57	74
Nonwhite	39	37	41	42	46	45	53
Birmingham							
White	38	27	33	40	45	51	64
Nonwhite	19	18	19	21	22	25	22

SOURCE: *U. S. Census of Housing: 1950*, Vol. II, *Nonfarm Housing Characteristics*, chapters for the respective standard metropolitan areas, tables A-3, and unpublished special tabulations of the 1950 Housing Census supplied to the Commission on Race and Housing by the Bureau of the Census. Data are based on a 20 percent sample of dwelling units, hence are subject to sampling variability.

TABLE A-11

Median Market Value of Owner-occupied, Single-unit Properties[a] by Income
and Color of Owner, for Selected Metropolitan Areas, 1950
(Medians rounded to nearest multiple of $50)

Standard metropolitan area and color of owner	Total reporting	Income of primary families and individuals					
		Less than $2,000	$2,000- 2,999	$3,000- 3,999	$4,000- 4,999	$5,000- 6,999	$7,000 and more
New York							
White	$12,250	$10,400	$10,000	$10,700	$11,450	$12,600	$16,400
Nonwhite	8,200	7,200	7,550	8,500	8,600	9,200	12,600
Chicago							
White	11,950	9,950	9,450	10,400	11,350	12,400	15,800
Nonwhite	7,050	5,850	6,650	7,000	7,600	8,800	10,950
Detroit							
White	9,000	7,600	7,450	8,000	8,950	9,650	12,350
Nonwhite	7,000	6,450	6,750	7,100	7,400	7,500	7,850
Los Angeles							
White	9,950	8,600	8,800	9,150	9,800	11,250	15,450
Nonwhite	8,150	7,250	8,000	8,300	8,850	9,050	10,900
St. Louis							
White	9,000	6,850	7,000	8,200	9,200	10,800	14,900
Nonwhite	3,400	2,650	3,550	3,950	4,750	5,750	8,100
New Orleans							
White	10,100	6,650	7,050	8,950	10,200	12,100	18,100
Nonwhite	3,700	3,100	3,950	4,550	6,600	5,850	9,000
Houston							
White	8,000	6,200	6,100	7,000	7,850	9,100	13,950
Nonwhite	3,800	3,350	3,850	4,650	4,950	6,100	7,500
Birmingham							
White	6,900	5,000	5,450	6,600	7,250	8,250	11,600
Nonwhite	2,800	2,450	2,900	3,500	3,900	4,650	5,800

Source: *U. S. Census of Housing: 1950*, Vol. II, *Nonfarm Housing Characteristics*, chapters for the respective standard metropolitan areas, tables A-7, and unpublished special tabulations of the 1950 Housing Census supplied to the Commission on Race and Housing by the Bureau of the Census. Data are based on a 20 percent sample of dwelling units, hence are subject to sampling variability.

[a] Value data available only for properties containing only one dwelling unit and are, therefore, not strictly comparable with data in preceding tables which refer to total owner-occupied dwellings. Single-unit properties occupied by nonwhite owners tend to be of somewhat poorer quality than the two- to four-unit properties of nonwhite owner occupants.

TABLE A-12

MEDIAN NUMBER OF ROOMS IN RENTER-OCCUPIED DWELLING UNITS,
BY GROSS MONTHLY RENT AND COLOR OF OCCUPANTS,
FOR SELECTED METROPOLITAN AREAS, 1950

Standard metropolitan area and color of occupants	Total report-ing	Gross monthly rent								
		Less than $15	$15-19	$20-24	$25-29	$30-34	$35-39	$40-49	$50-59	$60 or more
New York										
White	3.7	2.0	2.6	3.0	3.3	3.6	3.8	3.7	3.8	4.0
Nonwhite	4.0	1.5	2.5	2.7	3.2	3.6	3.9	4.1	4.5	5.0
Chicago										
White	4.0	1.3	1.9	2.5	3.5	3.7	3.8	3.8	4.0	4.6
Nonwhite	3.0	1.4	1.2	1.4	1.7	2.1	2.8	3.0	3.8	4.4
Detroit										
White	4.2	2.0	2.2	2.3	2.8	3.1	3.6	3.7	4.6	5.0
Nonwhite	4.2	2.0	1.9	2.4	3.0	3.2	3.9	4.1	4.7	5.2
Los Angeles										
White	3.3	1.5	2.0	2.2	2.6	2.8	3.1	3.3	3.5	4.1
Nonwhite	3.3	1.8	2.0	2.4	2.9	3.1	3.3	3.4	3.6	4.2
St. Louis										
White	3.3	1.7	2.4	2.8	3.0	3.1	3.3	3.6	4.0	4.4
Nonwhite	2.9	1.8	2.3	2.7	2.9	3.0	3.1	3.3	3.8	4.0
New Orleans										
White	3.8	2.2	3.0	3.5	3.8	3.9	4.0	3.9	3.9	4.6
Nonwhite	2.9	1.9	2.7	3.1	3.5	3.6	3.6	3.7	3.4	4.1
Houston										
White	3.6	2.5	2.3	2.3	2.7	2.8	3.2	3.4	3.8	4.4
Nonwhite	3.4	2.3	2.8	2.9	3.1	3.2	3.4	3.6	3.7	4.1
Birmingham										
White	3.6	3.1	3.5	3.5	3.2	3.2	3.3	3.6	3.9	4.3
Nonwhite	2.9	2.4	2.8	3.0	3.2	3.6	3.7	3.4	4.1	4.0

SOURCE: *U. S. Census of Housing: 1950*, Vol. II, *Nonfarm Housing Characteristics*, chapters for the respective standard metropolitan areas, tables A-3, and unpublished special tabulations of the 1950 Housing Census supplied to the Commission on Race and Housing by the Bureau of the Census. Data are based on a 20 percent sample of dwelling units, hence are subject to sampling variability.

TABLE A-13

Median Number of Rooms in Owner-occupied, Single-unit
Properties by Market Value and Color of Owner,
for Selected Metropolitan Areas, 1950

Standard metropolitan area and color	Total reporting	Market value							
		Less than $2,000	$2,000-2,999	$3,000-3,999	$4,000-4,999	$5,000-5,999	$6,000-7,499	$7,500-9,999	$10,000 or more
New York									
White	6.1	5.5	4.6	4.9	5.1	5.3	5.7	5.8	6.3
Nonwhite	6.3	4.4	5.3	5.7	5.9	6.0	6.1	6.3	6.8
Chicago									
White	5.5	3.9	4.0	4.3	4.5	4.8	5.1	5.2	5.7
Nonwhite	5.3	4.0	4.7	4.7	4.8	5.1	5.3	5.3	6.0
Detroit									
White	5.4	4.2	4.1	4.4	4.7	5.1	5.3	5.2	5.8
Nonwhite	6.1	4.9	5.1	5.7	5.6	5.9	6.0	6.2	7.0
Los Angeles									
White	5.2	3.8	3.7	3.8	4.1	4.3	4.5	4.9	5.7
Nonwhite	5.2	3.6	4.2	4.5	4.7	4.9	5.0	5.2	5.8
St. Louis									
White	5.0	3.4	3.7	3.9	4.1	4.4	4.6	4.9	5.4
Nonwhite	4.3	3.6	4.0	4.3	4.5	5.0	5.3	5.8	6.3
New Orleans									
White	5.1	3.1	3.4	3.9	4.1	4.5	4.5	4.8	5.9
Nonwhite	4.2	3.2	3.7	4.1	4.2	4.9	5.1	5.4	5.6
Houston									
White	5.0	3.0	3.4	4.0	4.3	4.6	4.8	5.0	5.9
Nonwhite	4.5	3.5	4.1	4.4	4.7	4.9	5.1	5.4	5.7
Birmingham									
White	5.5	3.7	4.2	4.7	5.0	5.2	5.4	5.6	6.3
Nonwhite	4.5	3.6	4.3	4.8	5.3	5.5	5.3	5.6	6.5

Source: *U. S. Census of Housing: 1950*, Vol. II, *Nonfarm Housing Characteristics*, chapters for the respective standard metropolitan areas, tables A-5, and unpublished special tabulations of the 1950 Housing Census supplied to the Commission on Race and Housing by the Bureau of the Census. Data are based on a 20 percent sample of dwelling units, hence are subject to sampling variability.

A Selected Bibliography

of Housing and Race

This selection, aside from listing the studies prepared for the Commission on Race and Housing, is limited to works of general significance and important source materials. Texts of legislation, court decisions, and administrative orders are not included, these being adequately cited in the text.

STUDIES AND RESEARCH MEMORANDA PREPARED FOR THE COMMISSION ON RACE AND HOUSING, 1956-1958

The unpublished studies prepared for the Commission on Race and Housing are deposited in the library of the University of California, Berkeley.

Amerman, Helen E. "Studies of Attitudes toward Housing and Race." Unpublished.
    Analysis of research literature on attitudes toward racial residential segregation and related questions.
Case, Fred E., R. Clay Sprowls, and S. Lynn Clark. "The Housing Status of Mexican-American Families in Central Los Angeles." Unpublished.
    A sample survey of approximately 750 Mexican-American households in Los Angeles. Data are presented on household characteristics, housing conditions, and house-financing arrangements.
Case, Fred E., James H. Kirk, and S. Lynn Clark. "The Housing Status of Minority Families in Los Angeles." Prepared in coöperation with the Los Angeles Urban League. Unpublished.
    A sample survey of approximately 700 minority families, predominantly Negro, in Los Angeles. Data include household characteristics, financial status, housing conditions and preferences.

Clarkson, Diana. "Sunnyhills: A Privately Developed Interracial Housing Project." Unpublished.

A case history of an interracial housing development in Santa Clara County, California.

Connecticut Commission on Civil Rights. *Racial Integration in Private Residential Neighborhoods in Connecticut* by Henry G. Stetler. Hartford: The Commission, 1957.

A study of selected, stable neighborhoods occupied by both white and Negro families in Connecticut cities.

Demerath, Nicholas J., and Associates. "Private Enterprise Housing for Negroes in Seven Metropolitan Areas." Unpublished.

House building and financing practices concerning new housing for sale or rent to Negroes in the Birmingham, Chicago, Detroit, Los Angeles, Norfolk, St. Louis, and San Francisco metropolitan areas.

Dodson, Jack E. "Minority Group Housing in Two Texas Cities," in Glazer and McEntire, eds. *Studies in Housing and Minority Groups.*

A comparative study of factors affecting the availability of housing to Negroes and Latin-Americans in Houston and San Antonio, Texas.

Eagle, Morris. "The Puerto Ricans in New York City," in Glazer and McEntire. *Ibid.*

A sample survey of housing conditions, preferences, and demographic characteristics of approximately eight hundred Puerto Rican households in the Boroughs of Manhattan, Brooklyn, and the Bronx, New York City.

Edwards, E. Franklin, and Harry J. Walker. "The Impact of Urban Renewal on Minority Group Housing Opportunities in Six Cities." Unpublished.

A field study of urban renewal programs in relation to housing of minority groups in Birmingham, Chicago, New York, Norfolk, Philadelphia, and Washington, D. C.

Glazer, Nathan, and Davis McEntire, eds. *Studies in Housing and Minority Groups.* Special Research Report to the Commission on Race and Housing. Berkeley and Los Angeles: University of California Press, 1960.

A collection of local studies (individually described under their authors' names) on housing conditions and problems involving racial or ethnic minority groups in nine large cities, with an introduction by Nathan Glazer. Groups and cities studied include Negroes in Atlanta, Birmingham, Detroit, Miami, and New Orleans; Mexican-Americans in Houston and San Antonio; Japanese-Americans in San Francisco; and Puerto Ricans in New York.

Goldner, William. *New Housing for Negroes: Recent Experience.* Research Report No. 12, Real Estate Research Program, University of California, Berkeley, 1958.

An analysis of data gathered by the Mortgage Bankers Association of America on more than eighty new private housing developments for Negro occupancy in the United States.

Grier, Eunice and George. *Privately Developed Interracial Housing: An Analysis of Experience.* Special Research Report to the Commission on Race and Housing. Berkeley and Los Angeles: University of California Press, 1960.

A study of the experience of some fifty private housing developments open on initial occupancy to members of all races.

Helper, Rose. "The Role of the Real Estate Business in Minority Group Housing: A Chicago Study." Unpublished.

Policies and practices of real estate boards and data of interviews with ninety real estate brokers in three racial transition areas in Chicago. A longer report by the same author is "The Racial Practices of Real Estate Institutions in Selected Areas of Chicago." Unpublished Ph.D dissertation, Department of Sociology, University of Chicago, 1958.

Kitano, Harry H. L. "Housing of Japanese-Americans in the San Francisco Bay Area," in Glazer and McEntire, eds. *Studies in Housing and Minority Groups.*

A field sample survey of housing conditions, preferences, experiences, and related social and financial characteristics of over five hundred Nisei households in the San Francisco Bay Area.

Laurenti, Luigi. *Property Values and Race: Studies in Seven Cities.* Special Research Report to the Commission on Race and Housing. Berkeley and Los Angeles: University of California Press, 1960.

The effects on property values of nonwhite entry into formerly all-white neighborhoods. Analysis of some ten thousand property transfers in selected areas of San Francisco, Oakland, and Philadelphia is supplemented by data from other studies in Chicago, Detroit, Kansas City, and Portland, Oregon.

LaViolette, Forrest E. "The Negro in New Orleans," in Glazer and McEntire, eds. *Studies in Housing and Minority Groups.*

A study of social, economic, and political factors affecting the availability of housing to Negroes in New Orleans.

Masuoka, Jitsuichi, and Preston Valien. "A Memorandum on Social Consequences of Racial Residential Segregation." Department of Social Sciences, Fisk University, Nashville, Tennessee. Unpublished.

An analytical review and summary of research literature pertaining to the social consequences of racial residential segregation.

Mayer, Albert J. "Russel Woods: Change without Conflict. A Case Study of Neighborhood Racial Transition in Detroit," in Glazer and McEntire, eds. *Studies in Housing and Minority Groups.*

A case history of orderly racial transition in an upper middle-class Detroit residential neighborhood.

Nason, Milton. "Comparative Analysis of White and Nonwhite Home Mortgage Experience Based on Data from the Census of Housing, 1950." Unpublished.

A statistical study of racial differentials in home mortgage financing.

National Association of Intergroup Relations Officials. "The Professional Intergroup Relations Worker and Minority Housing Problems," *Journal of Intergroup Relations*, Vol. 1, no. 2 (July, 1958).

A questionnaire survey of approximately 450 intergroup relations agencies concerning activities in the housing field.

Population Research and Training Center, University of Chicago. "Illustrative Projections of United States Population by Color, Urban-Rural Residence, and Broad Region to 1975." Prepared under the direction of Philip M. Hauser. Unpublished.

Population projections under alternative assumptions of fertility and level and patterns of migration, with analytical text.

Rapkin, Chester, and William G. Grigsby. *The Demand for Housing in Racially Mixed Areas: A Study of the Nature of Neighborhood Change.* Special Research Report to the Commission on Race and Housing and the Philadelphia Redevelopment Authority, prepared in the Institute for Urban Studies, University of Pennsylvania. Berkeley and Los Angeles: University of California Press, 1960.

An analysis of factors affecting the demand for housing by whites and nonwhites in four racially mixed residential areas of Philadelphia.

Reid, Margaret G. "Housing in Relation to Income." Unpublished.

A statistical analysis of white-nonwhite differentials in the relationships of housing and family income, based on unpublished tabulations of 1950 Housing Census data.

Selltiz, Claire, and Stuart W. Cook. "Studies in the Social Psychology of Race and Housing." Unpublished.

Three papers prepared in the Research Center for Human Relations, New York University: "How People Feel and Act about Interracial Housing"; "Factors Influencing Actions Regarding Interracial Housing"; and "An Evaluation of the Probable Impact of Various Types of Action to Encourage Interracial Housing." Beliefs, attitudes, actions, and motivations of white Americans concerning racially mixed neighborhoods, and evaluation of possible methods for encouraging racial integration in housing.

Sollen, Robert H. "Real Estate Board Policies toward Minority Groups in a Southern California Urban Community." Unpublished.

A case study of the publicized disciplining of two brokers by their real estate board, allegedly for having sold properties in "Anglo" neighborhoods to minority families.

Thompson, Robert A., Hylan Lewis, and Davis McEntire. "Atlanta and Birmingham: A Comparative Study in Negro Housing," in Glazer and McEntire, eds. *Studies in Housing and Minority Groups.*
  A comparative study of housing conditions and opportunities for Negroes in Atlanta, Georgia, and Birmingham, Alabama.
Virrick, Elizabeth L. "New Housing for Negroes in Dade County," in Glazer and McEntire. *Ibid.*
  A study of Negro housing in Miami, Florida, with emphasis on new housing construction and civic efforts for improvement of housing conditions for Negroes.

BOOKS AND PAMPHLETS

Abrahamson, Julia. *A Neighborhood Finds Itself.* New York: Harper & Brothers, 1959.
Abrams, Charles. *Forbidden Neighbors: A Study of Prejudice in Housing.* New York: Harper & Brothers, 1955.
――――. *Race Bias in Housing.* Statement sponsored jointly by the American Civil Liberties Union, National Association for the Advancement of Colored People, and American Council on Race Relations. New York, July, 1947.
Allport, Gordon W. *The Nature of Prejudice.* Cambridge: Addison-Wesley Publishing Co., Inc., 1954.
American Council To Improve Our Neighborhoods, Inc. *Fight-Blight Fund, Inc.: Baltimore.* Report from ACTION No. 3. New York, rev. September, 1956.
――――. *Housing Court: Baltimore.* Report from ACTION No. 2. New York, rev. September, 1956.
American Jewish Committee. *The People Take the Lead, A Record of Progress in Civil Rights, 1948 to 1958.* New York: The Committee, 1958.
American Jewish Congress and National Association for the Advancement of Colored People. *Civil Rights in the United States, 1952: A Balance Sheet of Group Relations.* New York, 1952.
American Public Health Association, Committee on the Hygiene of Housing. *Basic Principles of Healthful Housing.* New York, 1939, reprinted, 1954.
Bauer, Catherine. "Redevelopment—A Misfit in the 'Fifties," in Coleman Woodbury, ed. *The Future of Cities and Urban Redevelopment.* Chicago: University of Chicago Press, 1953.
Berger, Morroe. *Equality by Statute.* New York: Columbia University Press, 1952.
Beyer, Glenn H. *Housing, A Factual Analysis.* New York: Macmillan, 1958.
Beyer, Glenn H., Thomas W. Mackesey and James E. Montgomery.

Houses Are for People: A Study of Home Buyer Motivations. Research Publication No. 3, Housing Research Center, Cornell University, 1955.

Bloom, L., and R. Riemer. *Removal and Return: The Socioeconomic Effects of the War on Japanese Americans.* Berkeley and Los Angeles: University of California Press, 1949.

Bogue, Donald J. *Components of Population Change, 1940-50: Estimates of Net Migration and Natural Increase for Each Standard Metropolitan Area and State Economic Area.* Studies in Population Distribution Number 12, Scripps Foundation for Research in Population Problems. Oxford, Ohio: Scripps Foundation, Miami University, 1957.

————. *The Population of the United States.* Glencoe: The Free Press, 1959.

Burma, John H. *Spanish-Speaking Groups in the United States.* Durham: Duke University Press, 1954.

Carter, Deane G., and H. Keith Hinchcliffe. *Family Housing.* New York: John Wiley & Sons, Inc., 1949.

Chicago Community Inventory, University of Chicago. *Population Growth in the Chicago Standard Metropolitan Area, 1950-1957.* February, 1958.

Clark, Tom, and Philip Perlman. *Prejudice and Property.* Washington, D. C.: Public Affairs Press, 1947.

Colean, Miles L. *American Housing: Problems and Prospects.* New York: The Twentieth Century Fund, 1944.

————. *The Impact of Government on Real Estate Finance in the United States.* New York: National Bureau of Economic Research, Inc., 1950.

Coolidge, Mary R. *Chinese Immigration.* New York: Henry Holt and Co., 1909.

Davis, William W. "The Federal Enforcement Acts," in *Studies in Southern History and Politics.* New York: Columbia University Press, 1914.

Dean, John P., and Alex Rosen. *A Manual of Intergroup Relations.* Chicago: University of Chicago Press, 1955.

Deutsch, Morton, and Mary Evans Collins. *Interracial Housing, A Psychological Evaluation of a Social Experiment.* Minneapolis: University of Minnesota Press, 1951.

Drake, St. Clair, and Horace R. Cayton. *Black Metropolis: A Study of Negro Life in a Northern City.* New York: Harcourt, Brace and Co., 1945.

Duncan, Otis Dudley and Beverly. *The Negro Population of Chicago: A Study of Residential Succession.* Chicago: The University of Chicago Press, 1957.

Fisher, Ernest M., and Robert M. Fisher. *Urban Real Estate*. New York: Henry Holt and Co., 1954.

Ford, James. *Slums and Housing*. Cambridge: Harvard University Press, 1936.

Frazier, E. Franklin. *Black Bourgeoisie*. Glencoe. The Free Press, 1957.

———. *The Negro in the United States*. Rev. ed.; New York: Macmillan, 1957.

———. *Negro Youth at the Crossways: Their Personality Development in the Middle States*. Washington, D. C.: American Council on Education, 1940.

Garner, James W. "Southern Politics Since the Civil War," in *Studies in Southern History and Politics*. New York: Columbia University Press, 1914.

Ginzberg, Eli. *The Negro Potential*. New York: Columbia University Press, 1956.

Gittler, Joseph B., ed. *Understanding Minority Groups*. New York: John Wiley & Sons, Inc., 1956.

Grebler, Leo. *Housing Market Behavior in a Declining Area: Long-term Changes in Inventory and Utilization of Housing on New York's Lower East Side*. New York: Columbia University Press, 1952.

———. *The Role of Federal Credit Aids in Residential Construction*. Occasional Paper 39, National Bureau of Economic Research, Inc. New York, 1953.

Grebler, Leo, David M. Blank, and Louis Winnick. *Capital Formation in Residential Real Estate, Trends and Prospects*. Princeton: Princeton University Press, 1956.

Grodzins, Morton. *The Metropolitan Area as a Racial Problem*. Pittsburgh: University of Pittsburgh Press, 1958.

Grodzins, Morton, and Edward C. Banfield. *Government and Housing in Metropolitan Areas*. New York: McGraw-Hill Book Co., 1958.

Hamilton, J. D. de Roulhac. "Southern Legislation in Respect to Freedmen, 1865-66," in *Studies in Southern History and Politics*. New York: Columbia University Press, 1914.

Handlin, Oscar. *Race and Nationality in American Life*. Boston: Little, Brown and Company, 1948.

Horowitz, Eugene L. " 'Race' Attitudes," in Otto Klineberg, ed. *Characteristics of the American Negro*. New York: Harper & Brothers, 1944.

Hoyt, Homer. *One Hundred Years of Land Values in Chicago*. Chicago: University of Chicago Press, 1933.

Johnson, Charles S. *Patterns of Negro Segregation*. New York: Harper & Brothers, 1943.

———, et al. *Into the Main Stream: A Survey of the Best Practices in*

Race Relations in the South. Chapel Hill: University of North Carolina Press, 1947.

Johnson, Franklin. *The Development of State Legislation Concerning the Free Negro*. New York: The Arbor Press, Inc., 1919.

Key, Jr., V. O. *Southern Politics in State and Nation*. New York: Alfred A. Knopf, 1949.

Kibbe, Pauline R. *Latin Americans in Texas*. Albuquerque: University of New Mexico Press, 1946.

Krech, David, and Richard S. Crutchfield. *Theory and Problems of Social Psychology*. New York: McGraw-Hill Book Co., 1948.

Lewis, Hylan. *Blackways of Kent*. Chapel Hill: University of North Carolina Press, 1955.

Long, Herman H., and Charles S. Johnson. *People* vs. *Property, Race Restrictive Covenants in Housing*. Nashville: Fisk University Press, 1947.

MacIver, R. M., ed. *Discrimination and the National Welfare*. New York: Institute for Religious and Social Studies, 1949.

Mackintosh, J. M. *Housing and Family Life*. London: Cassell and Co., 1952.

May, Arthur A. *The Valuation of Residential Real Estate*. New York: Prentice-Hall, Inc., 1942.

McMichael, Stanley L. *McMichael's Appraising Manual*. 4th ed.; New York: Prentice-Hall, Inc., 1951.

Mears, Eliot G. *Resident Orientals on the American Pacific Coast: Their Legal and Economic Status*. Chicago: University of Chicago Press, 1928.

Merton, Robert K. "Discrimination and the American Creed," in R. M. MacIver, ed. *Discrimination and the National Welfare*. New York: Institute for Religious and Social Studies, 1949.

————. "The Social Psychology of Housing," in Wayne Dennis, ed. *Current Trends in Social Psychology*. Pittsburgh: University of Pittsburgh Press, 1948.

————. *Social Theory and Social Structure*. Glencoe: The Free Press, 1949.

Meyerson, Martin, and Edward C. Banfield. *Politics, Planning, and the Public Interest: The Case of Public Housing in Chicago*. Glencoe: The Free Press, 1955.

Millspaugh, Martin, and Gurney Breckenfeld. *The Human Side of Urban Renewal*. Baltimore: Fight-Blight Fund, Inc., 1958.

Mortgage Bankers Association of America, Committee on Financing Minority Housing. *Report to the Board of Directors*. Chicago, October 29, 1955.

Murray, Pauli. *States' Laws on Race and Color*. Cincinnati: Woman's Division of Christian Service of the Board of Missions of the Methodist Church, 1950. And *Supplement*, 1955.

Myrdal, Gunnar. *An American Dilemma: The Negro Problem and Modern Democracy.* New York: Harper & Brothers, 1944.

National Community Relations Advisory Council. *Equality of Opportunity in Housing: A Handbook of Facts.* New York, June, 1952.

——. *A Guide to Changing Neighborhoods.* New York, 1956.

National Urban League. *Mortgage Financing for Properties Available to Negro Occupancy.* New York, 1954.

Park, Robert E. *Race and Culture.* Glencoe: The Free Press, 1950.

Pierce, Joseph A. *Negro Business and Business Education: Their Present and Prospective Development.* New York: Harper & Brothers, 1947.

Price, William L. *Factors Influencing and Restraining the Housing Mobility of Negroes in Metropolitan Detroit.* Detroit: Detroit Urban League, 1955.

Puerto Rican Population of New York City. A series of papers by A. J. Jaffe, Louis Weiner, Sophia M. Robison, and Carl Raushenbush delivered before the New York area chapter of the American Statistical Association, October 21, 1953. New York: Bureau of Applied Social Research, Columbia University, 1954.

Rose, Arnold, ed. *Race Prejudice and Discrimination.* Readings in Intergroup Relations in the United States. New York: Alfred A. Knopf, 1951.

Rose, Arnold and Caroline. *America Divided.* New York: Alfred A. Knopf, 1948.

Ruchames, Louis. *Race, Jobs, and Politics: The Story of FEPC.* New York: Columbia University Press, 1953.

Senior, Clarence. *Strangers and Neighbors: The Story of Our Puerto Rican Citizens.* New York: Anti-Defamation League of B'nai B'rith, 1952.

Sterner, Richard. *The Negro's Share.* New York: Harper & Brothers, 1943.

Taeuber, Conrad and Irene B. *The Changing Population of the United States.* Prepared for the Social Science Research Council in coöperation with the U. S. Department of Commerce, Bureau of the Census. New York: John Wiley & Sons, Inc., 1958.

Talbert, Robert H. *Spanish-Name People in the Southwest and West.* Fort Worth: Leo Potishman Foundation, Texas Christian University, 1955.

Thomas, Dorothy W., and Richard S. Nishimoto. *The Spoilage: Japanese-American Evacuation and Resettlement.* Berkeley and Los Angeles: University of California Press, 1946.

Vance, Rupert, and Nicholas Demerath, eds. *The Urban South.* Chapel Hill: University of North Carolina Press, 1954.

Vose, Clement E. *Caucasians Only: The Supreme Court, the NAACP, and the Restrictive Covenant Cases.* Berkeley and Los Angeles: University of California Press, 1959.

Weaver, Robert C. *The Negro Ghetto.* New York: Harcourt, Brace and Co., 1948.

Welfare Council of New York City. *Census Tract Data on Population and Housing, New York City: 1940.* Prepared under the supervision of Leon E. Truesdell. New York: Welfare Council Committee on 1940 Census Tract Tabulations for New York City, 1942.

Wendt, Paul F. *The Role of the Federal Government in Housing.* Washington, D. C.: American Enterprise Association, Inc., 1956.

Williams, Jr., Robin M. *The Reduction of Intergroup Tensions: A Survey of Research on Problems of Ethnic, Racial, and Religious Group Relations.* New York: Social Science Research Council, 1947, Bulletin 57.

Wilner, Daniel M., Rosabelle Price Walkley, and Stuart W. Cook. *Human Relations in Interracial Housing: A Study of the Contact Hypothesis.* Minneapolis: University of Minnesota Press, 1955.

Winnick, Louis. *American Housing and Its Use: The Demand for Shelter Space.* New York: John Wiley & Sons, Inc., 1957.

Wirth, Louis. *Community Life and Social Policy.* Chicago: University of Chicago Press, 1956.

———. "The Problem of Minority Groups," in Ralph Linton, ed. *The Science of Man in the World Crisis.* New York: Columbia University Press, 1945.

Wood, Elizabeth. *Public Housing and Mrs. McGee.* New York: Citizens Housing and Planning Council, 1956.

Woodbury, Coleman, ed. *The Future of Cities and Urban Redevelopment.* Chicago: University of Chicago Press, 1953.

Woodward, C. Vann. *The Strange Career of Jim Crow.* New York: Oxford University Press, 1955.

GOVERNMENT DOCUMENTS

Baltimore Housing Authority. *Problem Families in Public Housing, Baltimore, Maryland.* 1956.

Bogue, Donald J. *Population Growth in Standard Metropolitan Areas, 1900-1950, with an Explanatory Analysis of Urbanized Areas.* Housing and Home Finance Agency. *Housing Research.* Washington, D. C.: USGPO, 1953.

Chicago Commission on Human Relations. *The Trumbull Park Homes Disturbances, A Chronological Report, August 4, 1953, to June 30, 1955.* 1956, mimeographed.

Hoyt, Homer. *The Structure and Growth of Residential Neighborhoods in American Cities.* Washington, D. C.: Federal Housing Administration, 1939.

Johnson, Charles S. *Negro Housing*. Report of the Committee on Negro Housing of The President's Conference on Home Building and Home Ownership. Washington, D. C.: The Conference, 1932.

New York City Department of Health. "Selected Vital Statistics for White, Nonwhite, and Puerto Rican Populations." Annual, 1950-1956. Unpublished.

New York City Housing Authority. "Racial Distribution in Operating Projects at Initial Occupancy and on June 30, 1955, All Programs." Dittoed table.

New York City Planning Commission. Estimates of number of dwelling units created by conversion, 1940-1950. Unpublished tabulations supplied by James Felt, Chairman, Planning Commission, to the Commission on Race and Housing.

———. *Tenant Relocation Report*. January, 1954.

New York State Commission Against Discrimination. *Legislation on Discrimination in Housing*. New York, 1956.

———. *Progress Report on Integration in Publicly Assisted Housing*. March 1, 1957, mimeographed.

———. *Summary Progress Report on Housing for the Year of 1956*. Mimeographed.

New York Temporary State Housing Rent Commission. *Incomes and Ability to Pay for Housing of Nonwhite Families in New York State*. New York, August, 1955, mimeographed.

———. *People, Housing and Rent Control in Buffalo*, by Frank S. Kristof. New York, 1956.

Philadelphia Housing Association. "Philadelphia's Negro Population, Facts on Housing." Prepared for the Commission on Human Relations. Philadelphia: Commission on Human Relations, October, 1953, hectographed.

Puerto Rico, Commonwealth of, Migration Division, Department of Labor. *A Summary in Facts and Figures*. Revised periodically. New York, mimeographed.

Rapkin, Chester, Louis Winnick, and David M. Blank. *Housing Market Analysis: A Study of Theories and Methods*. Housing and Home Finance Agency. *Housing Research*. Washington, D. C.: USGPO, 1953.

Rose, Arnold M. *The Roots of Prejudice*. Paris: United Nations Educational, Scientific, and Cultural Organization, 1951.

United Nations, Commission on Human Rights. *Main Types and Causes of Discrimination*. Memorandum submitted by the Secretary General. Lake Success, New York, 1949.

United States, Commission on Civil Rights. *Hearings before the United States Commission on Civil Rights, Housing. Hearings Held in New York, Atlanta, and Chicago*. Washington, D. C.: USGPO, 1959.

United States, Commission on Civil Rights. *Hearings before the United States Commission on Civil Rights, Housing.* Vol. 2. *Conference with Federal Housing Officials.* Washington, D. C.: USGPO, 1959.

————. *Report of the United States Commission on Civil Rights, 1959.* Washington, D. C.: USGPO, 1959.

United States, Congress, Joint Committee on the Economic Report. *A Program for the Low-Income Population at Substandard Levels of Living.* Washington, D. C.: USGPO, 1956.

————, Subcommittee on Low-Income Families. *Characteristics of the Low-Income Population and Related Federal Programs.* Washington, D. C.: USGPO, 1955.

United States, Congress, House. *Your Congress and American Housing: The Actions of Congress on Housing from 1892 to 1951* by Jack Levin. House Document No. 532. 82d Cong., 2d Sess. 1952.

————. *Hearings: Housing Act of 1949.* 81st Cong., 1st Sess., April-May, 1949.

————. *Hearings: Housing Act of 1954.* 83d Cong., 2d Sess., March, 1954.

————, Committee on Banking and Currency. *Hearings: Housing Act of 1956.* 84th Cong., 2d Sess., 1956.

————, Subcommittee on Housing. *Hearings: Housing Act of 1957.* 85th Cong., 1st Sess., March, 1957.

————. *Investigation of FHA and VA Housing Programs.* Final report, December 8, 1952. Washington, D. C.: USGPO, 1952.

————. *Slum Clearance and Urban Renewal.* Report No. 1. 84th Cong., 2d Sess. Washington, D. C.: USGPO, 1956.

United States Congress, House, Committee on Veterans' Affairs, Subcommittee on Housing. *Hearings: Operations of Loan Guaranty Program and Placing Farm Home Loans on Parity with City Loans.* 84th Cong., 1st Sess., March, 1955.

U. S. Congress, Senate, Committee on Banking and Currency. *Hearings: Housing Act of 1954.* 83d Cong., 2d Sess., March-April, 1954.

————, Subcommittee. *Hearings: Housing Amendments of 1957.* 85th Cong., 1st Sess., March-April, 1957.

————. *Hearings: General Housing Legislation.* 81st Cong., 1st Sess., February, 1949.

————. *Hearings: Urban Renewal in Selected Cities.* 85th Cong., 1st Sess., November-December, 1957.

United States, Department of Commerce. *Construction Review,* vol. 2, no. 3 (March, 1956).

————, Bureau of the Census. *Fifteenth Census of the U. S., 1930, Census of Agriculture.* "The Negro Farmer in the U. S."

————. *Fifteenth Census of the U. S., 1930, Census of Population.* Vol. II. *General Report.* "Statistics by Subjects."

————. *Sixteenth Census of the U. S., 1940, Population and Housing Statistics for Census Tracts.*

————. *Sixteenth Census of the U. S., 1940, Housing.* Vol. II. *General Characteristics.* Vol. III. *Characteristics by Monthly Rent or Value.* Vol. IV. *Mortgages on Owner-Occupied Nonfarm Homes.*

————. *Sixteenth Census of the U. S., 1940, Population.* Vol. II. *Characteristics of the Population.* Vol. III. *The Labor Force.*

————. ————. "Characteristics of the Nonwhite Population by Race."

————. ————. "Nativity and Parentage of the White Population: Mother Tongue."

————. ————. Series P-10, no. 1 *Racial Composition of the Population, for the United States, by States: 1940.* No. 20. *Racial Composition of the Urban and Rural Population of the United States, by Regions, Divisions, and States: 1940.*

————. *U. S. Census of Housing: 1950.* Vol. I. *General Characteristics.* Vol. II. *Nonfarm Housing Characteristics.* Vol. IV. *Residential Financing.* Vol. V. *Block Statistics.*

————. Special tabulations of 1950 Housing Census data for selected standard metropolitan areas. Tabulated for the Commission on Race and Housing. Unpublished.

————. *U. S. Census of Population: 1950.* Vol. II. *Characteristics of the Population.* Vol. III. *Census Tract Statistics.* Vol. IV. *Special Reports.*

————. *Current Population Reports.* Series P-20. *Population Characteristics.* Series P-25. *Population Estimates.* Series P-28. *Special Censuses.* Series P-50 and P-57. *Labor Force.* Series P-60. *Consumer Income.*

————. *1956 National Housing Inventory.* Vol. I. *Components of Change, 1950 to 1956.* Vol. II. *Financing of Owner-Occupied Residential Properties.* Vol. III. *Characteristics of the 1956 Inventory.*

————. *Construction Reports.* Series C-40. "New Dwelling Units Authorized by Local Building Permits." Before July, 1959, published by Department of Commerce, Business and Defense Services Administration and Department of Labor, Bureau of Labor Statistics.

————. *Negroes in the U. S., 1920-1932.* Washington, D. C., 1935.

————. *Negro Population, 1790-1915.* Washington D. C., 1918.

————. "Selected Characteristics of Dwelling Units Occupied by Nonwhite Persons, for Selected Standard Metropolitan Areas: 1950." Unpublished table.

United States, Department of the Interior. *People in Motion. The Postwar Adjustment of the Evacuated Japanese Americans.* Washington, D. C.: USGPO, 1947.

United States, Department of Justice. "Brief for the United States as *amicus curiae*." Submitted to the U. S. Supreme Court by Attorney

General Tom C. Clark and Solicitor General Philip Perlman, and relating to the four cases concerning racial restrictive covenants appealed to the Supreme Court, October term, 1947. Washington, D. C.: USGPO, 1947.

———. Immigration and Naturalization Service. *Annual Report, 1947* to date.

United States, Department of Labor, Bureau of Labor Statistics. *Negroes in the United States: Their Employment and Economic Status.* Bulletin No. 1119. Washington, D. C.: USGPO, 1953.

United States, Department of Labor and Department of Commerce. *Construction Volume and Costs, 1915-1954.* December, 1954.

United States, Housing and Home Finance Agency, Office of the Administrator. *Annual Report.* 1947 to date. Washington, D. C.: USGPO.

———. *Housing of the Nonwhite Population, 1940 to 1950.* Washington, D. C.: USGPO, 1952.

———. *Housing Statistics.* Monthly report.

———. "Joint Statement on Relationship of Slum Clearance and Low Rent Housing Programs." June 29, 1950.

———. *Living Space Available to Racial Minority Families.* Local Public Agency Letter No. 16. February 2, 1953.

———. *Nondiscrimination Statutes, Ordinances, and Resolutions Relating to Public and Private Housing and Urban Renewal Operations.* Prepared by the Racial Relations Service and Office of the General Counsel. Washington, D. C., rev. October, 1958.

United States, HHFA, Office of the General Counsel. *Federal Laws Authorizing Assistance to Slum Clearance and Urban Renewal.* Revised periodically.

United States, HHFA, Federal Housing Administration. *Insured Mortgage Portfolio.* Quarterly. Occasional articles on minorities and housing.

———. Housing market reports, various areas. Issued irregularly.

———. *Underwriting Manual.* Revised periodically.

———, Division of Research and Statistics. *Nonwhite Population Trends in Standard Metropolitan Areas, in Central Cities, and Outside Central Cities, 1930-1950.* Table. Washington, D. C., August, 1953.

———. "Trends in Occupied Dwelling Units and Components of Nonwhite Housing Change." Mimeographed table, March 11, 1959.

United States, HHFA, Public Housing Administratinon. *Low-Rent Housing Manual.* Revised periodically.

———. *Open Occupancy in Public Housing.* Washington, D. C., 1953.

———. *Trends Toward Open Occupancy.* Periodic report.

United States, HHFA, Urban Renewal Administration. "Racial Minority Aspects of Urban Renewal." Technical Memorandum No. 19. Washington, D. C., December, 1958.

——. *Relocation from Urban Renewal Project Areas.* Periodic report.

United States, HHFA, Voluntary Home Mortgage Credit Program. *Annual Report.* 1955 to date.

United States, President's Advisory Committee on Government Housing Policies and Programs. *Government Housing Policies and Programs: A Report to the President of the United States.* Washington, D. C., 1953.

United States, President's Commission on Migratory Labor. *Migratory Labor in American Agriculture.* Report of the Commission. Washington, D. C.: The White House, 1951.

United States, President's Committee on Civil Rights. *To Secure These Rights.* Report of the Committee. Washington, D. C., 1947.

United States, President's Committee on Government Contracts. *Equal Job Opportunity Program.* Washington, D. C., 1956.

Wendt, Paul F., and Daniel B. Rathbun. *The San Francisco Bay Area Residential Mortgage Market.* Housing Research Paper 20. Prepared by the Bureau of Business and Economic Research, University of California, Berkeley, for the Housing and Home Finance Agency. Washington, D. C.: Housing and Home Finance Agency, May, 1952.

Woodruff, A. M. *Conversion of One-Family Houses to Multifamily Use.* Housing and Home Finance Agency Housing Research Paper 7. Washington, D. C., April, 1954.

ARTICLES AND PERIODICALS

Abrams, Charles. "The New 'Gresham's Law of Neighborhoods'—Fact or Fiction," *The Appraisal Journal*, XIX, no. 3 (July, 1951).

"A Northern City 'Sitting on Lid' of Racial Trouble," *U. S. News & World Report*, May 11, 1956.

Anti-Defamation League of B'nai B'rith. "Housing Discrimination Against Jews," *Rights*, vol. 2, no. 5 (January-February, 1959).

——. "Housing: The Role of the Real Estate Agent," *Rights*, vol. 2, no. 2 (April-May, 1958).

The Appraisal Journal. Quarterly. Occasional articles on minority occupancy and property values.

Architectural Forum. Monthly. Frequent articles on housing policies and problems.

Bacote, Clarence A. "The Negro in Atlanta Politics," *Phylon*, Fourth Quarter, 1955.

Bauer, Catherine. "The Dreary Deadlock of Public Housing," *Architectural Forum*, May, 1957.

Bauer, Catherine. "Housing Policy and the Educational System," *The Annals of the American Academy of Political and Social Science*, November, 1955.

———. "What City Pattern?" *Architectural Forum*, September, 1956.

Blumer, Herbert. "Attitudes and the Social Act," *Social Problems*, vol. 3, no. 3 (October, 1955).

———. "Social Science and the Desegregation Process," *The Annals of the American Academy of Political and Social Science*, vol. 304 (March, 1956).

Brookover, W. B., and J. B. Holland. "An Inquiry into the Meaning of Minority Group Attitude Expressions," *American Sociological Review*, vol. 17 (April, 1952).

"Builder Opportunities in Minority Group Housing," *PF—The Magazine of Prefabrication*, Reprint of series, May to September, 1954.

Chapin, F. Stuart. "The Psychology of Housing," *Social Forces*, vol. 30 (October, 1951).

———. "Some Housing Factors Related to Mental Hygiene," *American Journal Public Health*, vol. 41 (July, 1951).

Coe, Paul F. "Nonwhite Population Increases in Metropolitan Areas," *Journal of the American Statistical Association*, vol. 50, no. 270 (June, 1955).

Cowgill, Donald O. "Trends in Residential Segregation of Nonwhites in American Cities, 1940-1950," *American Sociological Review*, vol. 21, no. 1 (February, 1956).

"The Dreary Deadlock of Public Housing—How to Break It," *Architectural Forum*, June, 1957.

Fauman, S. Joseph. "Housing Discrimination, Changing Neighborhoods, and Public Schools," *Journal of Social Issues*, XIII, no. 4 (1957).

Fisher, Ernest M., and Louis Winnick. "A Reformulation of the 'Filtering' Concept," *The Journal of Social Issues*, VII, nos. 1 and 2 (1951).

Frazier, E. Franklin. "Race Contacts and the Social Structure," *American Sociological Review*, XIV, no. 1 (February, 1949).

Ben Gaffin and Associates, Inc. "How to Solve Our Race Problem: Opinions of White and Negro, North and South," *Catholic Digest*, June through December, 1956.

Glazer, Nathan. "Social Characteristics of American Jews, 1654-1954," *American Jewish Year Book*, vol. 56 (1956).

Greater New York Taxpayers Association. *Real Estate News*. Monthly. Occasional articles on minority aspects of housing.

Guandolo, Joseph. "Housing Codes in Urban Renewal," *George Washington Law Review*, vol. 25 (October, 1956).

Hallman, Howard W. "Public Housing Site Opposition: Experience

Reviewed in Light of Today's Culture," *Journal of Housing*, vol. 14, no. 2 (February, 1957).

Horowitz, Eugene L. "Development of Attitudes towards Negroes," *Archives of Psychology*, no. 194, 1936.

House and Home, Monthly. Frequent articles on racial problems in housing.

Housing Yearbook. Washington, D. C.: National Housing Conference, 1954 to date. Annual.

Hyman, Herbert H., and Paul B. Sheatsley. "Attitudes Toward Desegregation," *Scientific American*, vol. 195, no. 6 (December, 1956).

Jahoda, Marie, and Patricia West. "Race Relations in Public Housing," *Journal of Social Issues*, VII, nos. 1 and 2 (1951).

Johnson, Corwin W. "Constitutional Law and Community Planning," *Law and Contemporary Problems*, XX, no. 2 (Spring, 1955).

Journal of Social Issues, XIII, no. 4 (1957). Special issue on housing and race.

Kenealy, William J. "The Legal Profession and Segregation," *Social Order*, December, 1956.

Kennedy, Tolbert Hall. "Racial Survey of the Intermountain Northwest," *Research Studies of the State College of Washington*, XIV, no. 3 (1946).

Law and Contemporary Problems. Housing. Symposium. XII, no. 1 (Winter, 1947).

———. *Low-Cost Housing and Slum Clearance*. Symposium. I, no. 2 (March, 1934).

Lee, Rose Hum. "The Recent Immigrant Chinese Families of the San Francisco–Oakland Area," *Marriage and Family Living*, XVIII, no. 1 (February, 1956).

Lohman, Joseph D. and Dietrich C. Reitzes. "Note on Race Relations in Mass Society," *American Journal of Sociology*, LVIII, no. 3 (November, 1952).

Long, Herman H. "Race Prejudice and Social Change," *American Journal of Sociology*, LVII (July, 1951).

Loring, William C. "Housing Characteristics and Social Disorganization," *Social Problems*, vol. 3 (January, 1956).

Maisel, Sherman J. "Policy Problems in Expanding the Private Housing Market," *Papers and Proceedings, American Economic Review*, XLI, no. 2 (May, 1951).

Maslow, Will. "The Uses of Law in the Struggle for Equality," *Social Research*, vol. 22 (1955), 297.

Merton, Robert K. "The Self-fulfilling Prophecy," *The Antioch Review*, VIII, no. 2 (Summer, 1948).

———, *et al*. "Social Policy and Social Research in Housing," *Journal of Social Issues*, VII, nos. 1 and 2 (1951).

Morgan, Belden. "Values in Transition Areas: Some New Concepts," *The Review of the Society of Residential Appraisers*, XVIII no. 3 (March, 1952).

National Association of Home Builders. *Housing Almanac, 1955*. Washington, D. C.: The Educational Committee, NAHB, 1955.

———. *NAHB Correlator*. Periodical. Occasional articles on housing for minority groups.

National Association of Intergroup Relations Officials, Commission on Housing and Family Life. "Forwarding Intergroup Justice and Harmony in Housing—A Review of Some of the Major Issues and Problems in 1958," *Journal of Intergroup Relations*, I, no. 2 (July, 1958).

National Association of Real Estate Boards. "Protecting Neighborhoods," by Eugene P. Conser. *Realtor's Headlines*, XXV, no. 43 (October 27, 1958).

Nelson, Herbert U. "The Real Estate Code of Ethics," *Journal of Land and Public Utility Economics*, I, no. 3 (July, 1925).

Race Relations Law Reporter. Bimonthly. Vanderbilt University. The only journal specialized in the law of race relations.

"Redevelopment Today," *Architectural Forum*, April, 1958.

The Residential Appraiser. Monthly. Formerly issued as *The Review of the Society of Residential Appraisers*. Occasional articles on minority occupancy and property values.

Riemer, Svend. "Sociological Theory of Home Adjustment," *American Sociological Review*, VIII, no. 3 (June, 1943), 272-278.

Robinson, Corienne. "Relationship between Condition of Dwellings and Rentals, by Race," *Journal of Land and Public Utility Economics*, August, 1946.

Rose, Arnold M. "Intergroup Relations vs. Prejudice," *Social Problems*, vol. 4, no. 2 (October, 1956).

Rose, Arnold, Frank Atelsek, and Lawrence McDonald. "Neighborhood Reactions to Isolated Negro Residents: An Alternative to Invasion and Succession," *American Sociological Review*, vol. 18, no. 5 (October, 1953).

Ross, Thurston H. "Market Significance of Declining Neighborhoods," *The Appraisal Journal*, XXIII, no. 2 (April, 1955).

Schietinger, E. F. "Race and Residential Market Values in Chicago," *Land Economics*, XXX, no. 4 (November, 1954).

———. "Racial Succession and the Value of Small Residential Properties," *American Sociological Review*, XVI, no. 6 (December, 1951).

Slayton, William L. "Conservation of Existing Housing" in *Urban Housing and Planning*. Symposium in *Law and Contemporary Problems*, XX, no. 3 (Summer, 1955).

Stern, Oscar. "The End of the Restrictive Covenant," *The Appraisal Journal*, XVI, no. 4 (October, 1948).

————. "Long Range Effect of Colored Occupancy," *The Review of the Society of Residential Appraisers*, XII, no. 1 (January, 1946).

Trends in Housing. New York: National Committee Against Discrimination in Housing. August, 1956, to date. Bimonthly. The only journal devoted to discrimination in housing.

Weaver, Robert C. "The Effect of Anti-Discrimination Legislation upon the FHA- and VA-Insured Housing Market in New York State," *Land Economics*, XXXI, no. 4 (November, 1955).

————. "Integration in Public and Private Housing," *The Annals of the American Academy of Political and Social Science*, vol. 304 (March, 1956).

————. "Race Restrictive Housing Covenants," *Journal of Land and Public Utility Economics*, August, 1944.

————. "Racial Policy in Public Housing," *Phylon*, Second Quarter, 1940.

————. "Recent Developments in Urban Housing and Their Implications for Minorities," *Phylon*, Third Quarter, 1955.

Williams, Jr., Norman. "Planning Law and Democratic Living" in *Land Planning in a Democracy*. Symposium in *Law and Contemporary Problems*, XX, no. 2 (Spring, 1955).

UNPUBLISHED STUDIES

Committee on Civil Rights in Manhattan, Inc. "Summary of Survey on Countrywide Instances of Open Occupancy Housing," by Sophia M. Robison *et al.* New York, 1957, mimeographed.

Council for Civic Unity of San Francisco. "Civil Rights Inventory: Real Estate Brokers and Lending Institutions." San Francisco, 1956, dittoed.

Deutsch, Morton, Rose Helper, and Claire Selltiz. "New Housing which Is Available to All Groups without Discrimination," in *Studies of Interracial Housing*. Research Center for Human Relations, New York University, 1952, dittoed.

Hughes, Everett C. "A Study of a Secular Institution: The Chicago Real Estate Board." Ph.D. dissertation, Department of Sociology and Anthropology, University of Chicago, 1928.

Hyde Park–Kenwood Community Conference. "A Report to the Community." Preliminary review of area problems and possibilities. Chicago, 1951, mimeographed.

Institute for Urban Studies, University of Pennsylvania, in coöperation with Institute for Urban Land Use and Housing Studies, Columbia University. "Program for Eastwick Housing Market Development Analysis." Philadelphia: Institute for Urban Studies, University of Pennsylvania, December, 1954, mimeographed.

Merton, Robert K., Patricia S. West, and Marie Jahoda. *Social Facts*

and Social Fictions: The Dynamics of Race Relations in Hilltown.
New York: Bureau of Applied Social Research, Columbia University,
1949, hectographed. Part of a larger work by the same authors to
be published under the title, *Patterns of Social Life: Explorations
in the Social Psychology and Sociology of Housing.*
Rapkin, Chester. "Market Experience and Occupancy Patterns in Inter-
racial Housing Developments: Case Studies of Privately Financed
Projects in Philadelphia and New York City." Institute for Urban
Studies, University of Pennsylvania, July, 1957, mimeographed.
Roper, Elmo. "A Study of Anti-Minority Sentiment in the United
States." Prepared for the Anti-Defamation League of B'nai B'rith,
New York, 1948.
Rose, Arnold M. "Studies in the Reduction of Prejudice." Chicago:
American Council on Race Relations, 1947, mimeographed.
Schietinger, E. F. "Racial Succession and Changing Property Values
in Residential Chicago." Ph.D. thesis, Department of Sociology,
University of Chicago, 1953.
Senn, Milton A. "Memorandum Report on Efforts in the Los Angeles
Area to Circumvent the United States Supreme Court Decisions on
Restrictive Covenants." Los Angeles: Anti-Defamation League of
B'nai B'rith, December 31, 1948, mimeographed.

MISCELLANEOUS

Cole, Albert M., Administrator, Housing and Home Finance Agency.
Address to the National Urban League, Pittsburgh, Pennsylvania,
September 8, 1954.
————. "What Is the Federal Government's Role in Housing?" Address
to the Economic Club of Detroit, February 8, 1954.
Council for Civic Unity of San Francisco. "Housing a Giant: Memoran-
dum on the Willie Mays Incident," by Edward Howden. November,
1957, mimeographed.
National Association for the Advancement of Colored People. "Mem-
orandum to the President of the United States Concerning Racial
Discrimination by the Federal Housing Administration," by Thur-
good Marshall. February 1, 1949, typewritten.
National Association of Home Builders. "Housing for Minority Groups,
'Package Program.'" Washington, D. C., June, 1954, mimeographed.
National Association of Intergroup Relations Officials, Commission on
Housing. "Non-discrimination Firsts in Housing." 10th Annual Con-
ference, Philadelphia, November 29, 1956, mimeographed.
Schwulst, Earl B., Chairman, Commission on Race and Housing. *Race
and Housing: The Basic American Dilemma.* Address before the
National Urban League of Greater New York, April 14, 1959.

Index